SHIPS, SEAFARING AND SOCIETY

ESSAYS IN MARITIME HISTORY

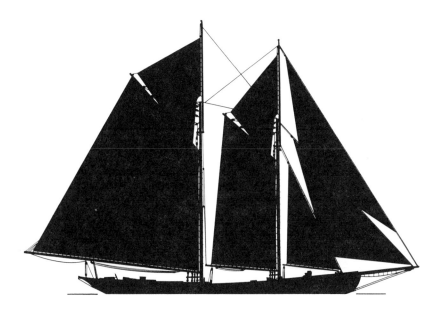

Edited by
TIMOTHY J. RUNYAN

Published for the Great Lakes Historical Society by
WAYNE STATE UNIVERSITY PRESS

387.509 S557

C.2 JUN 2 '88

Library of Congress Cataloging-in-Publication Data

Ships, seafaring, and society.

    Includes bibliographies and index.
      1. Navigation—History.   2. Naval history.
I. Runyan, Timothy J.   II. Great Lakes Historical
Society.
VK15.S55   1987   387.5'09   87-14226
ISBN 0-8143-1990-4
ISBN 0-8143-1991-2 (pbk.)

The editor and authors wish to acknowledge the previous publiction of all or
part of the following articles: J. Richard Steffy, *The International Journal of National Archaeology and Underwater Exploration* 11.1 (1982) by permission of the
editor, Dr. James Kirkman; Tyrone G. Martin, *The American Neptune* XLVI
(Summer, 1986) and Fred Hopkins *ibid* XL (January, 1980); Edwin Doran Jr.,
The National Fisherman 62.11 (1981).

SE

In memory of John Lyman, William Baker and Richard Wright

CONTENTS

Illustrations and Maps

PREFACE

Ships, Seafaring and Society presents to the reader a selection of essays touching on the fragile yet enduring relationship between man and the sea. The seas are presented as frontiers, barriers, and avenues providing the means to discovery, conquest, and control. But here the reader will discover how ships and seafaring shaped the lives of mariners, merchants, women, and entire communities. Whether the essays' concerns are a medieval ship found off Turkey, American prisoners of war in 1812, or diplomatic activities involving ships in Russia or the Mediterranean, we find a symbiotic relationship between society ashore and the community of mariners abroad. Often these links are political, but these essays demonstrate other relationships as well. Mariners and their doxies were abused ashore or by the laws and customs of nations. Black seamen certainly felt the constraints at sea of societies which held color as a principal factor in determining status or advancement in service. The all too familiar tales of the lash aboard ship are found to be extensions of the practice ashore.

Ships are technological products of the highest order. Often this technological achievement is presumed without careful examination before we move on to measure affairs at sea. In these essays the technology is not overlooked, but presents itself in the shipbuilding skills employed in the Mediterranean in the eleventh century, the sailing ships employed by medieval English kings to carry troops and supplies to France in order to fight, or in the nineteenth century sea mines utilized in the same waters plied by those medieval vessels. The ship was the mechanism by which the world was encompassed and the age of colonial empires began. The essays in this volume are brought together as contributions to this complex and international story. The reader will find no lengthy port-of-call in these pages, as the authors quickly transport us to such distant places as Turkey, England, Italy, Russia, the Baltic, Mexico, Asia, the Americas, Africa, and other fascinating ports. It is the ship which permits men and women to travel the globe.

The genesis of this volume can be found in the creation of the North American Society for Oceanic History. The Society was created by the common agreement of a number of prominent maritime scholars who met in 1971 at the University of Maine. They recognized that in North America there was no forum for maritime history or a society devoted to the study and promotion of maritime history. Successive meetings were held in Maine and Annapolis, Maryland. Encouraged by a little money and a lot of enthusiasm, Clark

Reynolds, John Lyman, Philip Lundeberg, Jeffrey Safford, Cy Hamlin, Eric Allaby, William Baker and others launched NASOH officially by incorporating it in Maine in 1974. An organizing committee was formed, a constitution drawn up, and in 1976 officers were selected. Over one-hundred members, principally Canadians and Americans, constituted the membership. Under the leadership of William A. Baker, a distinguished naval architect and curator of the Hart Nautical Museum at the Massachusetts Institute of Technology, and vice-presidents W.A.B. (Alec) Douglas (Directorate of History, Canadian Forces), Jack Kemble (Pomona College), John H. Parry (Harvard University), and Secretary- Treasurer Clark Reynolds (University of Maine; U.S. Merchant Marine Academy), the Society began its annual meetings. Sites for these meetings are always important for their maritime and historical significance. A meeting was held during a howling March blizzard at the Peabody Museum in Salem. The U.S. Naval Academy was host for the meeting at Annapolis in 1978, and in succession each spring (under calmer skies!) came meetings at the Mariner's Museum at Newport News; Halifax, Nova Scotia; Cleveland, Ohio, hosted by the Great Lakes Historical Society; Charleston, South Carolina at Patriots Point Naval and Maritime Museum aboard the USS *Yorktown*; Mystic Seaport; the U.S. Merchant Marine Academy at Kings Point, New York; Salem, Massachusetts at the Peabody Museum and at the Rosenberg Library in Galveston, Texas in 1986.

Such a recitation has significance to those familiar with the Society because the locations of the meetings reflect to some extent the growth and the diversity of the membership. The Spring 1987 meeting will again be in Canada at the Marine Museum of the Great Lakes at Kingston, Ontario, followed by a meeting at Woods Hole, Massachusetts.

The aim of the organizers was to create a diverse organization based initially on Canadian and American membership which would gain the interest of others. Now there are members in England, France, Australia, and elsewhere. The purpose of the Society is to promote the exchange of information among its membership and among others interested in the history of the seas and the inland waterways; to publish and make known articles, notes, and documents concerning the history of the seas and waterways; and to work with local, regional, national, and international organizations interested in the history of these seas and waterways. The Society works to foster a more general awareness of historical matters pertaining to the open waterways and their relationship to North America. NASOH houses the U.S. Commission on Maritime History which is a constituent member of the International Commission on Maritime History.

In order to encourage quality in the field of maritime history, the John Lyman Book Awards are given annually by the Society after the careful review of a selection committee. The Lyman Awards are prized by their recipients because they represent the highest standard of achievement in the maritime field. They are named for the late Professor John Lyman, University of North Carolina. The Society publishes its *Newsletter* three times each year and for a few years published proceedings of papers read at the annual conference. However, members voiced a concern that a better way to distribute the research presented by members was in a volume of essays. The present volume was compiled from papers presented at meetings and revised by the authors. Not all papers presented could be included because of the restrictions of space and the necessity to create a coherent body of essays. The essays were selected and edited to make a contribution to the corpus of scholary literature on maritime history and to demonstrate to the public the range of interests of the Society, although this volume is *not* to be viewed as fully comprehensive of those interests. Membership in NASOH includes teachers, engineers, geological scientists, museum curators, archaeologists, naval architects, and interested persons from various non-maritime fields. In fact, it is this great diversity of membership which is such a strength as well as a unique aspect of the Society.

Debts are always accumulated in projects of this nature and I wish to thank several persons for their assistance. The shaping of the volume owes much to the suggestions of Professors Jack Bauer and William Still. I am unable to acknowledge the anonymous referees for this volume, but their suggestions have been incorporated in many instances, including choice of essays. The typing and word processing work was ably provided by Connee Choi, Ruth Ponikvar, and especially Kathleen Bowden. Marian Sachs, aided by her staff members Patricia Gifford and Thomas Engel, did an excellent job of typesetting the volume. Susann Bowers provided the guidance for the production of the final printed copy. J. Michael Ludwig did drawing and design work for the cover and Nathan Eatman the photography. All are colleagues or students at Cleveland State University, which has been very supportive of this project. Recognition is due to a very helpful library staff which was always ready to locate an elusive source. A special thanks is due to the College of Graduate Studies and the College of Arts and Sciences for their support.

Contributors

Dean C. Allard is a senior historian with the U.S. Naval Historical Center in Washington, D.C., and adjunct professor at George Washington University. He has written *Spencer Fullerton Baird and the U.S. Fish Commission: A Study in the History of American Science* (1984), and co-authored *The United States Navy and the Vietnam Conflict* (1976); *U.S. Naval History Sources in the United States* (1979); and articles on naval and maritime history.

Lawrence C. Allin teaches history at the Univeristy of Maine and at Bangor Theological Seminary. He is author of *Maine Maritime Miscellany* (1984), *The Federal Engineers: From Dam Sites to Missile Sites* (1984), and articles in *Naval War College Review*, *The American Neptune* and other journals.

Alan A. Arnold teaches history at the U.S. Merchant Marine Academy at Kings Point, N.Y. His research interests focus on mariners in the age of sail and he has published his findings in *The American Neptune*, a chapter in *Literature and Lore of the Sea* (1986) and elsewhere.

Hugh F. Bell, Professor of History at the University of Massachusetts-Amherst, earned degrees at Princeton (International Affairs), Michigan (Law) and Cornell (History). He authored *Points of Power in Early America* (1975) and articles in *Essex Institute Historical Collections*, *The American Neptune*, *The American Journal of Legal History* among others.

James C. Bradford taught at the U.S. Naval Academy before moving to Texas A&M University. He published a microfilm edition ot the *Papers of John Paul Jones* (1986) and the letterpress edition of his correspondence is in press. He is the editor of the multi-volume 'Makers of the American Naval Tradition' series and contributed an essay on John Paul Jones to *Command Under Sail*, its first volume.

Paolo E. Coletta is Emeritus Professor at the U.S. Naval Academy. His publications include: *William Jennings Bryan* (1969), *The Presidency of William Howard Taft* (1973), *Admiral Bradley A. Fiske* (1979), *A Bibliography of American Naval History* (1981). *The American Naval Heritage in Brief* is in its third edition.

Edwin Doran, Jr. is Professor Emeritus of Geography at Texas A&M University. His interest in the culture history of primitive watercraft has led to a number of books and papers on Caribbean boats and Pacific rafts and canoes, including *The Tortola Boat: Characteristics, Origin, Demise* (1970), *Nao, Junk and Vaka: Boats and Culture History* (1973), and *Wangka, Austronesian Canoe Origins* (1981).

Ira Dye, Senior Research Fellow in Civil Engineering, University of Virginia, rose to the rank of Captain in the U.S. Navy. He served as Chief of the Office of Program Planning, U.S. Maritime Administration 1962-67, as well as an officer in the Department of Transportation where he was awarded three medals for superior achievement. He has authored over a dozen articles on American naval history.

Barry M. Gough is Professor of History at Wilfrid Laurier University, Waterloo, Ontario. He is author of several books including *Distant Dominion* (1980) and *Gunboat Frontier* (1984) which won the John Lyman Prize of the North American Society for Oceanic History.

Fred Hopkins holds degrees in Classics and English, did Chinese translations for the Army and is Associate Provost at the University of Baltimore. He has authored *Thomas Boyle, Master Privateer* (1976), *War on the Patuxent* (1981) with Donald Shomette, and numerous articles on the Chesapeake Bay. An active diver, he continues to conduct underwater surveys of ships wrecked in the Bay.

Philip K. Lundeberg is Curator Emeritus of Naval History of the Smithsonian Institution. He has directed several major exhibitions and his publications include *Samuel Colt's Submarine Battery: The Secret and the Enigma* (1974) and *The Continental Gondola* Philadelphia (revised, 1985). He was awarded the Bronze Medal of the International Commission of Military History.

Linda M. Maloney is currently studying at the University of Tübingen after teaching posts which included the University of South Carolina. A National Merit, Woodrow Wilson and NDEA Fellow, she has authored many articles on naval history and a book, *The Captain from Connecticut: The Life and Naval Times of Isaac Hull, 1773-1843* (1986).

Tyrone G. Martin is a retired U.S. Navy commander. He was captain of the historic U.S.S. *Constitution* during her restoration for the American bicentennial celebration. He has written the award-winning *A Most Fortunate Ship* (1980). His articles have appeared in U.S. Naval Institute *Proceedings, The American Neptune* and other journals.

Mary Emily Miller is Professor of History at Salem State College, the author of *A Tricentennial View of Frederica, Delaware* (1984) and is currently working on a study of British warships in the Caribbean in the eighteenth century.

Walter E. Minchinton is Professor of Economic History at the University of Exeter. He is author or co-author of numerous books and articles including *The Trade of Bristol in the Eighteenth Century* (1957), *The Growth of English Overseas Trade in the Seventeenth and Eighteenth Centuries* (1969) and *Virginia Slave Trade Statistics 1698-1775* (1984).

Eric J. Ruff was born in England, emigrated to Canada, graduated from the Royal Military College and served in the Royal Canadian Navy. His interests are in sailing vessels, 1800-1950. He is curator of the Yarmouth County Museum and Historical Research Library in Nova Scotia.

Timothy J. Runyan teaches in the Department of History at Cleveland State University. A member of the editorial board of *The American Neptune*, he is co-author with A.R. Lewis of *European Naval and Maritime History, 300-1500* (1985) and has published extensively on medieval maritime history.

Gaddis Smith is Larned Professor of History at Yale University where he teaches diplomatic and maritime history. He is author of several books and articles, including *Britain's Clandestine Submarines, 1914-1915* (1964), *American Diplomacy During the Second World War,* (2nd ed., 1985) and *Morality, Reason, and Power: American Diplomacy in the Carter Years* (1986).

David J. Starkey received his Ph.D. at the University of Exeter where he is now a research assistant in the Department of Economic History. His area of special interest is British privateering in the eighteenth century.

J. Richard Steffy is an associate professor of nautical archaeology at Texas A&M University and a ship reconstructor for the Institute of Nautical Archaeology. A MacArthur Fellow, he has served as reconstructor or consultant to numerous shipwreck projects on four continents, and has lectured and published widely on wooden ship construction.

Virginia Steele Wood is the author of *Live Oaking: Southern Timber for Tall Ships* (1981), and recipient of the 1981 John Lyman Book Award in the History of Marine Science and Technology given by the North American Society for Oceanic History. She is a Reference Specialist and the Recommending Officer for Naval and Maritime History at the Library of Congress.

Part I

Ships and Fleets

The Reconstruction of the Eleventh Century Serçe Liman Vessel

A Preliminary Report

J. Richard Steffy

Introduction

Twenty per cent of the 11th century Serçe Liman hull survived, much of it in fragmentary condition. Yet so little is known of 11th century Mediterranean ship-building and ship handling that any quantity of hull survival must be regarded as important. To make a comprehensive study of this ship, its timbers were preserved and new research methods developed in order to interpret their characteristics more thoroughly. We wanted to learn as much as possible about the ship and its builder, but the primary target of our investigation was to determine what contributions this generation of builders made toward the transition from shell-first to frame-first forms of hull construction. The results of the first phase of our study are disclosed in this report.

The Hull Remains

Hull survival was primarily limited to the bottom of the vessel and a small area of the upper port stern. A few dozen small, widely-scattered fragments represented various portions of the hull sides up to deck level. Most of the timbers were fragmentary, frequently concreted, and in poor surface condition.

The hull had settled on its port bottom, perpendicular to a gentle slope. Since its bottom was broad and flat, the port list was not great; its sides simply flattened out in port and starboard directions, while the sternpost and some of the starboard stern planking fragments settled to port. The after end of the keel had apparently nestled on or against an outcropping of rock, causing a large part of the lower stern to disappear. Cargo, artefacts, and ballast covered most of the bottom from the rock to about 1 m forward of amidships, thereby preserving that area (Bass & van Doorninck, 1978). The forward part of the lower hull was also preserved, although it was damaged by anchors, ballast, and amphoras. A few fragments from the upper hull sides, especially around the bower anchors, were preserved due to iron permeation. The keelson and some transverse ceiling planking, situated under ballast and glass cargo in the after part of the hold, were the only internal members to survive (Fig. 1).

Hull Recording

Hull remains were recorded by using standard naval architectural designations, a procedure which we hoped would simplify later cataloguing and research. As soon as enough cargo and overburden had been removed from the wreck to see structure details, the area of greatest hull width was located from a series of photographs. The frame suspected of coinciding with the widest part of the hull was designated the midship frame, shown in the illustrations as frame ⌀ ; frames aft of this station were numbered successively while forward of it they were assigned capital letters. Planking was numbered in succession from the keel outward, with P and S prefixes denoting port

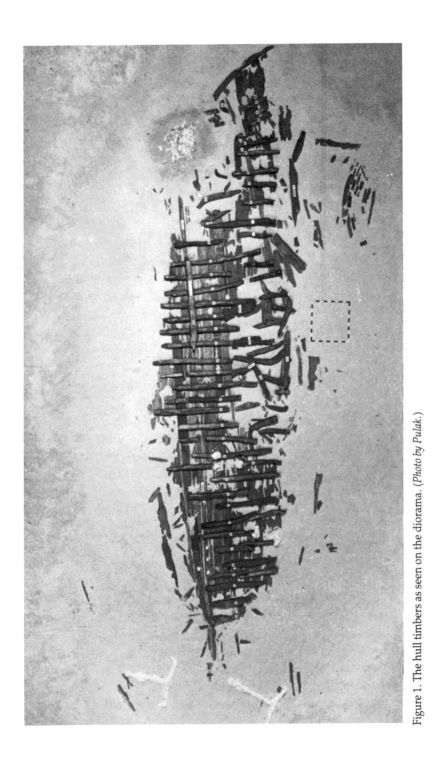

Figure 1. The hull timbers as seen on the diorama. (*Photo by Pulak.*)

and starboard strakes. Ceiling planking was similarly prefixed with a C, except for the transverse ceiling which was designated TC. The labelling method can be studied in further detail by consulting the revised wreck plan (Fig. 2).

Disposition of the wood, recording methods and conservation have been described elsewhere (van Doorninck, 1982).

Diorama

Our original site maps included a gradual slope and some uneven seabed. Several fragments rested atop a rock outcropping while others lay askew or in tilted positions. It was necessary to revise this site map into a drawing which would indicate minute details and precise measurements without angular distortion. Although there are numerous ways to accomplish such results, I chose to turn immediately to three-dimensional forms of interpretation.

In order to acquire a better perspective of our sparsely preserved wreck, I first built a diorama of the entire site to a scale of 1:10 (Fig. 1). It is an exact miniature of what the archaeologists saw on the seabed. There are seabed contours, anchor and nail concretions, unexcavated perimeters, and even teredo worm holes in the wood. It can be fitted with grid frames, ballast, cargo, artefacts or anything else which might assist specialists in their study of site distribution. Such a diorama has distinct advantages over a site map and, in a sense, even permits study that was not practical underwater. It presents a three-dimensional perspective not available even to those who excavated the wreck, since the entire hull could not be uncovered at one time. Most importantly, wood fragments can be shifted or extra ones placed in other locations to study dispersal of hull timbers and objects.

Dioramas such as this can be quickly and cheaply made, the investment being directly proportional to the requirements. In this case, materials cost under $20 and it was built in less time than it took to draw the site map. It was made on a hardboard base nailed to a wooden frame. The seabed composed of various shades of sawdust; hull timbers were made from pine scraps which had to be accurately reproduced only on upper surfaces and which were drilled and tooled to indicate erosion and teredo damage. Concretions and rock outcrop-

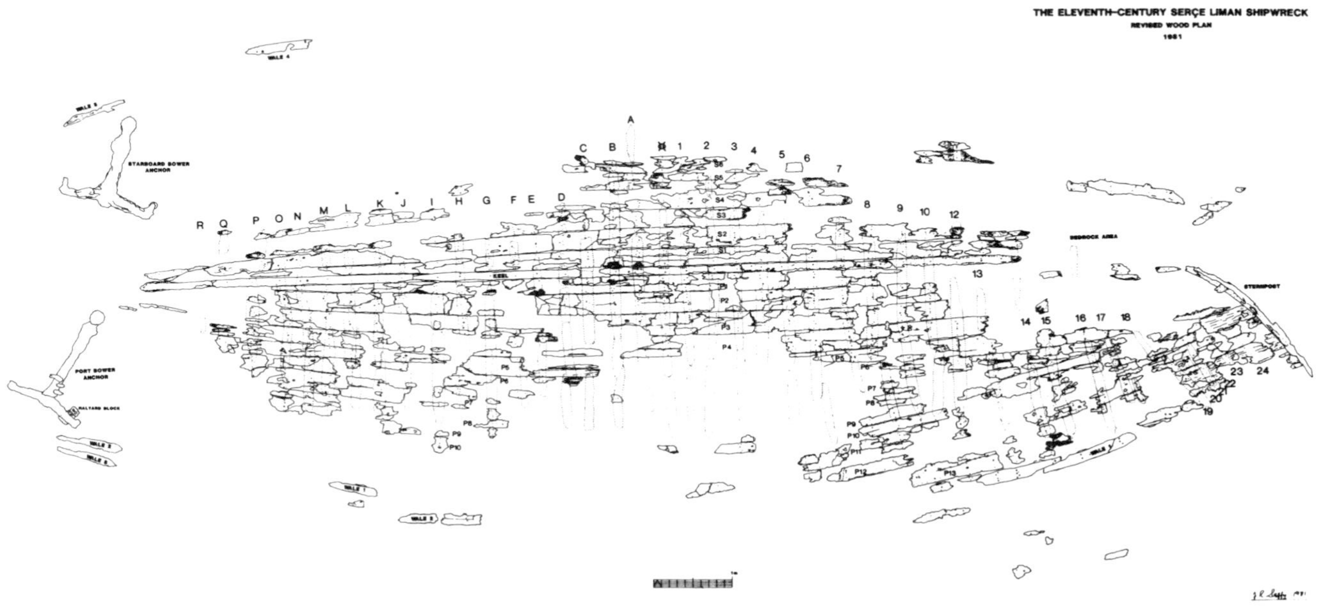

Figure 2. The revised wreck plan. (*Drawn by the author.*)

pings were formed from tinted plaster, while ballast and cargo might be represented by a variety of materials.

The diorama was originally intended as a first step in the hull reconstruction, but it has become so popular in briefings, lectures, interdisciplinary studies and even as a photographic subject that I predict it will be repeated for future INA excavations.

Revised Wreck Plan

The diorama made it possible to revise the original site plan of the hull remains into something which more accurately described the relationship of one fragment to another. I consider the proper execution of this plan to be the most important single step in any ship reconstruction. Regardless of period, hull type, extent of survival, or the intended disposition of fragments, it is necessary to acquire some sort of arrangement of basic hull information before attempting to convert that information back into its original form. The Serçe Liman wreck represented an undocumented ship type from a period and area in which comparatively little is known about maritime matters. It was therefore necessary to devise as accurate and elaborate a plan as possible.

The revised wreck plan shown in Fig. 2 assumes a horizontal seabed with each surviving hull member placed in close and relative proximity to its original neighbours. At first glance, it appears as if some giant hand had picked up the pieces, smoothed and levelled the seabed, and then replaced the fragments as close to their original positions as could possibly be achieved on a flat surface. Long pieces seem to flare away from adjacent edges, frames tend to distort where they turn the bilge, and grid perimeters expand or contract in proportion to the change in seabed elevations, but after one has experience at using such drawings it is possible to visualize hull forms by mentally shaping the structure so that edges align and frames become straight.

To devise this wreck plan, individual fragments drawings were first precisely reproduced in 1:10 scale. Hundreds of bottom photographs, wood photographs, field notes, sketches and catalogue entries were assembled. Using the full scale wood drawings first, planking seams were located on outer frame faces and frame limits were indicated on inner planking surface drawings by aligning nail locations, pressure marks, wood discolourations and other features. This information was then transferred to the scale drawings.

Using the foregoing data, both full and scale drawings were fitted together to represent large sections of the hull, using floors and walls as lofting areas for the full scale fitting. During this process, fragment replicas were moved around on the diorama to determine their original locations. Photographs and field notes were used to compare grain and knot patterns, pertinent dimensions and other information which might help to determine to which line of strakes a displaced fragment originally belonged. The diorama was also helpful in removing the distortion in the original site map due to uneven and sloping bottom conditions, camera lens distortion, and to establish breakage patterns caused by cargo and anchor stress. As each fragment location was confirmed, additions and revisions were made to the catalogue and the fragment was indicated in its final form on the wreck plan.

This plan is essentially a giant data sheet, indicating internal timber and planking dimensions, fastening patterns, scarphs, butts, seams and most of the other information needed to proceed with the reconstruction. It also doubled as an inventory of hull remains and thus will serve as a fragment located for the physical reassembly to follow.

The Fragment Model

Having now armed ourselves with all the raw data available, it was next possible to convert that information into the original hull form it represented. Reconstructions can evolve from catalogues and wreck plans into graphic or three-dimensional forms. I prefer to reconstruct in three dimensions for all but the most elementary projects because that is the medium to be described and it is by far the most accurate method of expressing such a complex object. For the Serçe Liman project, a new form of reconstruction model was devised which was intended to serve many functions beyond the mere determination of hull shape. It goes by the dubious name of "fragment model" and is essentially a three-dimensional expression of the revised wreck plan (Fig. 3). To build it, each surviving hull fragment was reproduced at

1:10 scale in white pine by the use of drawings, catalogue information and photographs as guides. Broken edges, important tool marks, surface blemishes and even iron concretions had to be accurately reproduced. Fragment blanks were first cut on a bandsaw, then dressed to precision with small files, chisels, dental grinders, and knives.[1] Holes were drilled at nail and treenail locations, frame face angles precisely reproduced, and even distorted curvatures were duplicated.

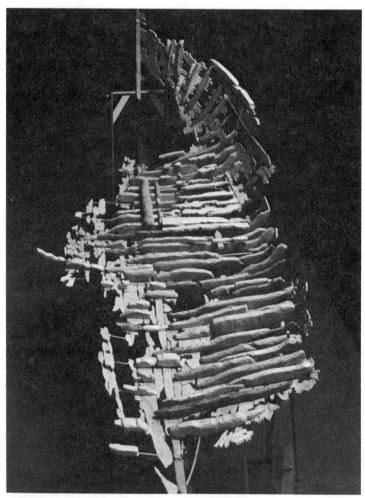

Figure 3. The fragment model. (*Photo by Cemal Pulak.*)

Although the model was devised as a more accurate method of determining hull shape than the graphic methods now in use, it was also intended to provide us with an assembly sequence to be used for the planned physical reconstruction at the Bodrum Museum in Turkey and to supply the advance information needed to design a fragment fastening system, temporary scaffolding, and the final ghosting and stanchioning required for the museum environment. Therefore, the model was assembled, fastened and supported only by methods which could be duplicated later in the full scale reassembly.

Construction began by laying the keel piece located beneath the midship frame. Fabrication fanned out in all directions from this central piece, the assembly of the contiguous portion of the hull ending with the installation of the transverse ceiling planking (Figs 4, 5 and 6). When all adjacent and nearly adjacent fragments were on the hull, tables of offsets were taken off the structure as one would measure any wooden hull and converted into a basic lines drawing. Final hull shapes could now be calculated or projected, resulting in the lines drawing shown in Fig. 13.

Figure 4. Starting the reconstruction of the hull remains. (*Photo by Jay Rosloff.*)

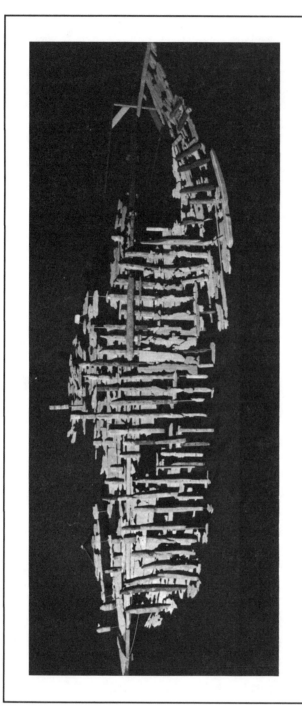

Figure 5. View of the completed model. (*Photo by Cemal Pulak.*)

Figure 6. View of the completed model. (*Photo by Cemal Pulak.*)

Keel and Keelson

The keel survived over a total length of 11-23 m but is now in eight pieces. It was originally sided 11 cm and moulded 16 cm throughout, but had been eroded so that its bottom surface was almost entirely gone. Tool marks indicated that its sides were sawn and its upper surface both sawn and hewn. A curvature was visible along the upper surfaces of all but the aftermost piece, indicating either distortion or a rocker design.

Keelson bolts and frame nails traversed the keel at the locations indicated in Fig. 2. They are described later in this section. A flat scarph with a table length of 50.2 cm and nibs of 6.7 cm was located 2.65 m aft of the midship bend. It was fastened with at least six iron nails having shanks 7 mm square and heads of 2.2 cm diameter. There were no other scarphs present in this member, the forwardmost piece beginning its curvature into the stempost without the familiar keel/stem scarph.

There was no evidence for a shoe or false keel, nor were there rabbets for the garboards. Not a single fastening was found in the keel sides, confirming that the garboards were in no way attached to that member. Traces of pitch were evident along the garboard line, however, indicating the caulking of that seam. In one case, a pitch covered material suspected of being used for caulking seams was identified as a type of grass.[2]

The keelson was sided 18 cm and moulded 20 cm, having more than twice the cross-sectional area of the keel. Although it survived for a length of only 2.17 m, we know that it extended to the ends of the ship because of discolouration and pressure marks on frame tops and keelson bolts running through the keel from bow to stern. The keelson was bolted between, never through, the floor timbers with iron forelock bolts having minimum lengths of 50 cm, shank diameters of 2.1 cm, head diameters of at least 3 cm, and washers under the forelock keys whose outer diameter was 3.5 cm. Keys were apparently bent and held in place by two nails. Although the keys and upper washers did not survive, their impressions atop the keelson did and were easy to interpret. They were reminiscent of similar bolts found on the 7th century Yassi Ada ship (van Doorninck, 1982).

One of the keelson bolts survived in the bottom of the keel at the scarph. It was recessed nearly 3 cm into the keel, although no wood remained close enough to the bolt to determine how the recess was made or what sort of caulking was inserted below the bolt. The keelson was bolted at intervals of 1.52, 1.48, 1.08, 1.43, 1.77, and 1.55 m between a point 7 cm aft of frame N and the aftermost keel extremity. A possible bolt concretion was located between frames R and Q.

Sternpost

The sternpost was our most fortunate hull discovery, for its location and fabrication told us so much about the work of the shipwright. It was a naturally curved timber with half of a flat scarph at its upper end and 7 cm of a similar scarph at its broken lower tip. It was sided 10.4 cm at its forward face and moulded 12.7 cm. A rabbet was cut into its sides for the termination of planking ends. Dozens of small nail shafts (but no treenails) within this rabbet had shanks between 4 and 6 mm square. Although the post's after surface had almost entirely disappeared, the portions still extant around nail heads and the partially preserved sides indicated that the post narrowed toward its after end.

Nothing survived of an inner post, although the existence of one can be confirmed. Rows of nails in the stern planking just forward of the extant post and 1 cm square nails or small bolts which ran through it and were broken off at or just beyond its inner surface, established the fact that there was a substantial timber here.

Frames

While few of the starboard frames were preserved, most of the port frames remained and half of them were in good condition (Fig. 7). Only one frame timber remained unbroken from keel to turn of bilge. All were made from grown shapes; tool marks indicated that they were sawn on the sides and hewn on their faces with axes and adzes. Outer faces revealed the working of small dubbing adzes, although the flats dubbed into frame faces for better seating of strakes on latter day hulls were not evident here.

Within the hold area, floor timbers with long arms to port alternated with those having long arms to starboard (Fig. 8). Long arms

Figure 7. Port side frames and ballast stones. (*Photo by Robin Riercy*)

rounded the turn of the bilge and all were rotted away short of their original upper terminus. Short arms ended inboard of the turn of the bilge. The few floor to futtock joints which did contain fastenings were attached with only one or two iron nails having 5 mm square shafts.

Limber holes, averaging 2.5 cm in depth and 4.5 cm in width, were cut into the plank faces of the frames about 10 cm on either side of the keel (Fig. 9). Planking nails were found within the limber holes in several cases. The frames were not cut for notching over either keel or keelson, although a few of the larger ones had recesses gouged out of their upper surfaces to permit a level seating of the keelson.

The frames were nailed into the keel with iron nails having 0.9 to 1.2 cm square shanks and heads of 4 cm diameter. Heads were frequently set into triangular recesses to permit better seating of the keelson. Most of these nails penetrated at least two-thirds of the keel

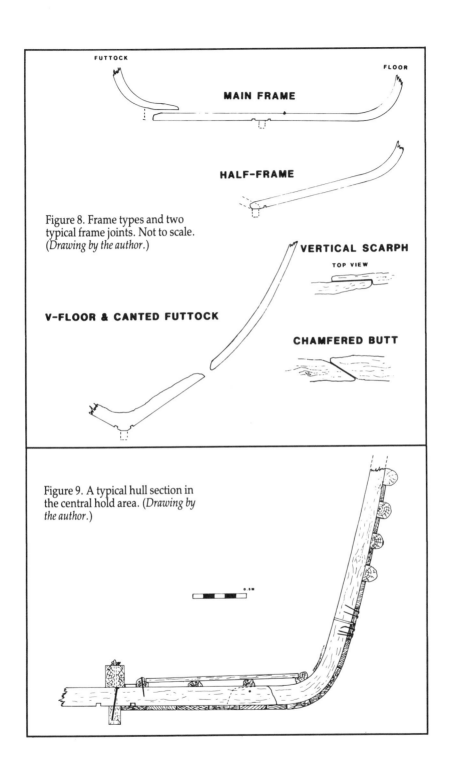

FUTTOCK

MAIN FRAME

FLOOR

HALF-FRAME

Figure 8. Frame types and two typical frame joints. Not to scale. (*Drawing by the author.*)

VERTICAL SCARPH

TOP VIEW

V-FLOOR & CANTED FUTTOCK

CHAMFERED BUTT

Figure 9. A typical hull section in the central hold area. (*Drawing by the author.*)

0.5M

depth; those for frames A, 2 and 4 are known to have gone completely through the keel. These through-nails appeared to have been cut off; there was no evidence for piening or clenching any of the fastenings. All through-nails were 8 mm square at their points of exit.

There were short floors, cant frames and half-frames in the bow and stern. The framing plan for this vessel is important in understanding early skeletal construction, and its catalogue already consists of hundreds of data sheets, photographs and drawings. In a preliminary report such as this it is impossible to provide even a condensation of that catalogue. Nor can I offer a complete framing plan for the ship at this stage, since more research will be necessary after the timbers are removed from treatment. Figures 5, 8, 9 and Table 1 should shed some lights on this strange pattern.

Planking

None of the planking strakes survived in a continuity from bow to stern. Most of the planking fragments were less than 20 cm in length; the longest, nearly 1.76 m, had surface cracks that threatened further breakage. Many of the fragments did not have any original surfaces left, some were marred by iron concretion, and all were teredo riddled. At frame locations, however, iron permeation and frame contact usually preserved both sides of the plank, providing good dimensioning for nearly all of the fragments which contained fastenings.

Planking thickness averaged 3.5 cm, although proud spots and the shipwright's adze frequently created variations of a half centimetre or so. All of the planking was sawn, but more investigation is necessary to determine the manner in which the logs were sectioned. While there were no flats on the frame faces at the very sharp turn of the bilge, there also were no cracks on the planking surfaces at that location which could be attributed to drawing planks against sharply curved frames. In at least two cases, however, port strake 8 had the appearance of having been hollowed toward its centre as much as a centimetre in the areas of frames. Perhaps the medieval shipbuilder solved his curvature problems in this manner.

Table 1

Frame no.	Long arm to	Sided at keel (cm)	Moulded at keel (cm)	Centreline spacing (cm)	Futtock attachment
Q		– insufficient data –		25	–
R		– insufficient data –		38	–
P	½-frame	17	17	35	overlap
O	½-frame	12	10	18	overlap
N	stbd	11·6	13	35	nailed scarph
M	port	15	15	27	?
L	stbd	– no wood at keel –			nailed vertical scarph
K	port	13	?	38	?
J	stbd	– no wood at keel –		26	vertical overlap
I	port	15	?	45	?
H	stbd	16·2	?	29	overlap
G	port	13	?	38	?
F	stbd	?	?	33	overlap
E	port	?	?	27	?
D	stbd	?	?	33	nailed lap
C	port	14·2	15	27	?
B	stbd	?	?	36	diagonal scarph
A	port	13·2	14·5	28	?
⋈	stbd	8·3	17	33	overlap
1	port	9	15·2	27	?
2	stbd	12	15	36	diagonal scarph
3	port	13	17	28	?
4	stbd	12	17	34	champher
5	port	12	17·5	29	?
6	stbd	14	17	35	nailed scarph
7	port	13·5	16·8	36	?
8	stbd	16	15	37	overlap
9	port	14	19	40	?
10	stbd	10·7	18	35	overlap
12	½-frame	?	?	32	–
13	V-floor	8·0 rem.	c. 19	32	–
14		– no information at keel –		25	
15		– no information at keel –			
16		– no information at keel –			
17	V-floor	9·5 rem.	11 rem.		–

Notes: 1. There are canted futtocks aft of frame 17. 2. There is double framing at futtocks 5, 15, 17, 19, and 20. 3. There are intermediate frames between 1 and 2, 5 and 6, 8 and 9, and 12 and 13. 4. Sided dimensions were given for the planking faces only.

Planking was fastened to the frames with iron nails having shanks 4 to 6 mm square and heads of 1.2 cm diameter (some impressions and concretions measured up to 2.5 cm), and also with wooden treenails whose diameter varied from 1 to 1.2 cm (Fig. 9). All fastenings were probed and it was found that the shipwright used a scatter pattern of angles in driving both nails and treenails. Probing was not very successful in determining nail lengths, but where nails could be seen at frame breaks, they penetrated the frame for a depth of about 10 cm. I suspect that most, if not all, the planking nails were about 13.5 cm in length. Treenails were driven completely through the frames. Less than half of them seemed to be wedged, and only three wedges were found on the inside of the treenails. Wedges came in a variety of shapes but were most frequently square to pentagonal. A few treenails were wedged with small nails, and in one tiny scatter fragment, a treenail was wedged with a thorn.

Though the average fastening pattern consisted of five nails and one or two treenails per frame in each strake, the patterns were essentially random and varied. Garboards contained relatively few treenails but usually were double-nailed near their keel edges. Strakes at the turn of the bilge were fastened much more frequently than strakes elsewhere, while the few pieces of wale which survived indicated that more treenails than nails secured those timbers. There were more disciplined patterns noted for the placement of treenails than there were for nails. They were often found centrally located in planks or exactly halfway between two nails, whereas nails did not seem to be so carefully distributed. In analysing these clusters of fastenings, I have come to the conclusion that the strakes were first lightly nailed, then additionally nailed after planking was completed, and finally treenailed.

Planks were joined into strakes in a variety of scarphs and butts. This joinery can be seen in Figs. 2 and 10 and will be discussed in the analysis of construction. Except for the fact that a couple of scarph tips were nailed to prevent their separation, there were no edge fastenings in the planking of the Serçe Liman hull.

Figure 10. Schematic diagram of the portside planking. Not to scale. (*Drawing by the author.*)

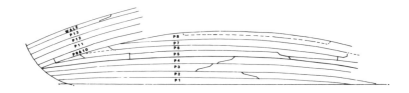

Wales

Nine pieces of timber representing four wales were catalogued. Two more eroded fragments possibly were also wales. They were formed by cutting logs in half and flattening their edges so that a fitted seam could be made with adjoining planking (Fig. 9). Although dimensions were difficult to determine because of the poor condition of the wales, the three best preserved pieces averaged 15 cm in thickness and 14.8 cm in width. At least one of them was joined with a flat scarph having a table length of 40 cm. Here the outer faces were flattened, perhaps to facilitate a more accurate joint, so that this portion of port main wale was nearly 15 cm square. A piece of the same wale located at frame H had a rounded surface. There were planking spacers between the wales whose original thickness is unknown, but a flat on the main wale edge at frame H suggests that their thickness was about 3.5 cm. Their widths apparently varied from 10 to at least 20 cm and were probably dependent on the size and sweep of the wales they segregated.

Pitch was found on many of the outer planking surfaces, between seams and scarphs, and on the sides of the keel. But the wales seemed to be much more heavily coated with the material, and the corners formed by the seam of wales and planking contained thick layers of it. The heaviest layers of pitch bore marks that it was troweled rather than brushed onto the surfaces. It has not yet been analysed.

Ceiling

Ceiling was found only beneath the glass cargo and large ballast stones. It consisted of three types — stringers, transverse boards and standard longitudinal planks (Fig. 11). The stringers, half round in section, were undoubtedly longitudinal stiffening members although they served to support the transverse planks as well. They were nailed into the frame tops at infrequent intervals. Nail shafts found in the tops of frames N and O indicated that these members continued into the bow area. The inner stringer, or limber shelf, had a groove cut into its upper surfaces to receive the transverse planks as did the outer (bilge) stringer (Fig. 9). The two inner stringers doubled as footwales and their upper surfaces were flattened to support the transverse

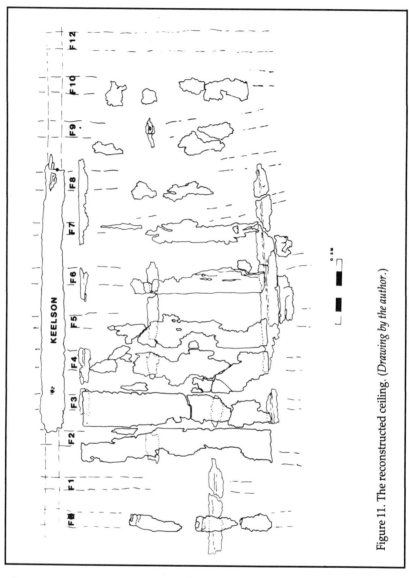

Figure 11. The reconstructed ceiling. (*Drawing by the author.*)

planks. A 13 cm space between the limber shelf and the keelson probably once contained a limber board, since it was directly over the limber
holes in the frames.

There were no fastenings in the transverse planks; they were merely wide, 4.5 cm thick boards which rested in the grooves of the outer stringers. Their outer ends were curved to fit the contour of the hull. Edges were planed, giving the appearance that these planks were carefully fitted.

Two fragments of longitudinal ceiling, one of them 2.6 cm thick, were found just above the turn of the bilge. No fastenings or other pertinent information could be determined.

There were no clues for decks, beams, or knees although it seems unlikely that a vessel with such a midship configuration and structural plan could have been serviceable without strong upper support. Steering must have been accomplished by quarter rudders; the stern-post was too light and angular to have supported a rudder. Eight anchors, a few rigging remains, and "artefactual" evidence for living accommodations were also found. These matters are being investigated by others.

Wood Identification

Wood samples taken from the various hull members were identified as follows:[3]

Keel — ring-porous hardwood belonging to the Ulmaceae, possibly a species of elm (*Ulmus*).

Keelson, frames, planking, transverse ceiling, stringers and wales — all are softwoods, very probably all pine (*Pinus*) species, although the degraded condition of some of the samples prevented positive identification.

Treenails — a species of the Leguminosae family, possibly one of the "broom" plants such as *Genista*, but this cannot be determined definitely.

Beside the fact that these treenails were the smallest I have ever studied, it is interesting to note that they were produced by different methods. Some were multi-sided, though the sides were uneven and were cut with a knife or small drawknife. Others were too perfectly round and uncompressed to have been made that way; the lack of turning marks on these treenails causes me to believe that they were cut from some conveniently sized stalk or branch.

Thus our vessel was built entirely of soft-woods except for the keel, not a surprising revelation for a Mediterranean hull. They were building them that way at least as early as the 4th century BC and are still using similar woods only a few miles from Serçe Liman.

Transitions on Construction

Ship design has constantly been subjected to a state of transition. Changes in design were affected by many factors such as available materials, trade routes, economics, and politics, frequently occurring so slowly and obscurely that they could hardly be detected within generations of builders. The Mediterranean is an excellent area in which to study such transition because it provides well-preserved examples of a great variety of hull designs and periods. Three of our projects convey precisely such a study.

On the 4th century BC Kyrenia hull, [4] it was obvious that the builder did not work to baselines and centrelines in the modern sense; each piece fabricated was based on the one he had just completed (Steffy, 1975). Hull planking was carefully edge-joined with tightly fitted mortise-and-tenon joints which were locked on either side of the seam with pegs. The planking shell was the primary structure and was so self-supporting that the shipwright could have planked the entire hull before inserting any internal members. The framework was secondary to the planking here, and was in no way attached to the keel. Indeed, the keel was not a proper backbone at all but merely the keystone of the arch formed by the planking shell. Because frames were attached to planking only, the Kyrenia builder was required to shape the planks before erection. Some of the more complex shapes must have required that an entire log be used to make one twisted plank. I estimate that 70% of all the timber felled for the Kyrenia hull was cut away as waste. Thus the Kyrenia shipwright was as much a wood carver as he was a fabricator, and the paucity of internal stiffening severely limited the practical size and design variations of the vessels he built. That is not to say he was primitive or indifferent, however; ship technology at the time dictated such a vessel. I am certain that he did a masterful job for that time and place.

The 4th century AD Yassi Ada ship[5] revealed an enormous change in technology (van Doorninck, 1976). Mortise-and-tenon joints were now smaller and more widely spaced, the planking shell was noticeably weaker, but internal structure was considerably stronger. Although planks were still erected before frames, the hull depended on its skeleton and internal planking for much of its strength. The keel had now become a proper backbone and many of the frames were fastened to the keel. Iron and wood replaced copper as fastenings. Long and frequent planking scarphs suggested that perhaps this shipwright was bending many of his planks rather than shaping them. Although only a sampling of the 4th century wood was raised for study, more saw marks were noticed on the few pieces I was able to examine than were recorded for the entire Kyrenia hull. Obviously, this builder was more a fabricator than a carver and his hull designs were, therefore, stronger and more flexible. Furthermore, such hulls could be built faster with less wastage of materials.

The 7th century Yassi Ada wreck yielded the first clues that pure shell forms of construction were soon to disappear from the Mediterranean (Steffy, 1982). Although this Byzantine merchantman still had mortises cut into its lower planking edges, they were small, loosely fitted, and widely spaced. No longer did pegs lock the joints on either side of the seam, and we suspected these joints were merely intended to keep planking edges aligned until frames could be inserted. This, and other evidence, caused us to suggest that the builder erected no more than five strakes at a time before inserting more frames to secure the standing planks. The essential method of planking attachment was now iron nails to frames, not edge joints. After the shell had been planked up to the flat sides, no more mortise-and-tenon joints were made. Here, from about the waterline upward, the builder already had the necessary expertise to erect frames first and then simply nail the planking and wales to them. The 7th century Yassi Ada hull had little shell strength, but it did have a strong internal structure in the form of a substantial framing pattern, footwales, clamps, keelson and heavy ceiling. It obviously could be built quickly with relatively little waste of timber.

Years of investigation of these and other wrecks leads to two important conclusions. Within practical limits, ships built by

Mediterranean forms of shell-first construction were far more restricted in size and design variations than were ships built by later frame-first methods. The ability to determine hull shape by cutting frames to that desired shape and then simply bending a watertight skin to it permitted such innovations as tumble-home, hard bilges, deep draft, roomy ends and hull symmetry. The Kyrenia builder did not have such latitude.

Secondly, it was quite apparent that the major structural problems confronting all these early builders was the turn of the bilge. One can see it in the way they erected their planking. This area of ever-changing curvatures and elevations was a geometric puzzle on all but hard-chined vessels. Even in modern drafting rooms, many of us who frequently draw hull lines find this to be the area of greatest effort. But we have ship curves, splines and battens, geometric knowledge, and even computers to assist our efforts. The Kyrenia builder overcame this area with a combination of careful shaping and ingenious strake configurations. Both Yassi Ada builders solved the problem more expeditiously by using shorter and narrower planks. And so I assumed that when shipbuilders learned to pre-determine bilge shapes, frames could be erected before planks. That was not totally correct. The Serçe Liman shipwright did set frames before planks but he had as much trouble with the turn of the bilge as did his predecessors, and he could determine little more than the midship shape in advance.

11th Century Construction

The method of hull assembly described below is a generalization. Much of it has not been proved beyond a shadow of doubt — at least not yet. But the wood is now undergoing treatment and it may be another two years before study can resume in an attempt to answer the questions which the initial research raised. Additional details will undoubtedly be forthcoming, but I doubt they will appreciably alter or expand what we already know. Hundreds of hours have been spent experimenting with research models, making drawings of details, compiling lists of evidence to confirm or deny a process, or just pondering the reasons for assembling things the way we found them. Always the results were the same; only one construction sequence satisfied all the evidence at hand.

Primary Structure

Keel and posts were set up in the conventional manner, although their design was far from familiar. The keel consisted of two timbers which were scarphed together aft of amidships and whose ends curved upward to scarph into the posts. The keel was rockered in an imperfect arc which had a concavity of about 1 cm for every metre of length. Nothing is known about the stem or its scarph, but the keel was already curving upward at its forward limit of survival. Part of the lower scarph of the sternpost was preserved, however, and there was little room and no reason for an extra piece of keel to be scarphed between the sternpost and the existing after end of the keel, especially since there was already a keel scarph situated rather far aft. As a result, I have drawn both ends of the keel as a curving upward.

The shipwright next selected 10 similar logs from which he sawed and hewed nearly identical floor timbers with sharply curved ends. The longitudinal centre of the keel was located next and a floor timber was set athwart the keel 10 cm afore and abaft that centre point, one (floor) with its curved end to starboard and the other (floor A) with its curved end to port. When they were properly levelled and braced, these floor timbers were drilled and nailed into the keel. In the 11th century, this shipwright had determined the midship shape before erecting a single plank. It was a simple one — flat floor, hard bilge and at least the start of a flat side. Note that he used two floor timbers to accomplish it.

Four more timbers were set on either side of this midship bend in alternate centreline spacings of approximately 27 cm and 35 cm. Long arms were alternated to part and starboard so that there were five on each side and their curvatures were equidistant from the keel centreline.

I contend that these were the only frame timbers erected before the first planks were installed. Frames O, N, 7 and 9 were too poorly configured for pre-erection. Frames P and 12, and probably a few frames fore and aft of them, were paired half-frames with only one side nailed to the keel and possessing comparatively difficult face angles. Frames N, M, G, 5, 10 and 12, and possibly H and 6, were eliminated because there were nail head impressions beneath these frames on the inside surfaces of port strakes 2, 3 and 4. Surrounding some of these impressions were circular scrapings, appearing as if something had been rotated around them. The same circular impressions were duplicated in our laboratory with a bow drill (which came from a Kuwaiti shipyard) and occurred when pressure applied to the stock caused the ferruled chuck to slam against the wood as the bit cleared its hole. Apparently pilot holes were drilled, as they were for all plank fastenings on this vessel, for nails which were intended to attach something to the outside of the hull. The nails were later removed and new ones driven through the same holes in the opposite direction when frames were finally set at these locations. There was an exception in strake 3 under frame 6 where a possible nail head concretion remained. Here the shaft may have been cut off on the outer planking surface. It is unfortunate that I did not realize the full significance of these impressions before the wood entered treatment. More of them will undoubtedly be discovered when we can scrutinize the planking fragments more carefully under strong lights and lenses after conservation is completed.

Similar impressions were recorded for the two lower side strakes at frames 8 and 12, but the circular scrapings were not evident here. None was found beneath frames E through 4. There was not enough remaining of the rest of the frames, or their adjacent planking, to establish evidence for or against pre-erection.

Fitting the Strakes

Surviving port and starboard planking patterns were nearly identical with two exceptions. Strake 2 scarph locations spanned different sets of frames, and the starboard garboard contained a scarph but none was evident for the port garboard. The following information refers to port side planking; starboard results would have been the same except for the above variations.

It is unlikely that the garboard was installed first. It was not rabbeted or fastened to the keel at all, and its configuration seemed to suggest that it was fitted to a standing strakes rather than being deliberately so shaped. I can recall boatbuilders who planked the garboard last to facilitate the removal of sawdust and shavings from inside the hull, but this builder's reasons were different. On the models and drawings, I could only make mechanical sense out of these planking shapes and still satisfy excavated evidence if strake 4 were the first to be attached. It was a straight, sawn strake which reached and maintained a maximum width of 28 cm along the standing floor timbers. It was joined amidships with a flat scarph having angled nibs (Z-scarph) and was set parallel to the keel and lightly nailed to the standing timbers. To reach its location at the sternpost in a fair curve, it required only to be twisted in against the post. The same was probably true for the bow. On the models, the ends of the strake could not be rabbeted permanently at this stage, so they were simply clamped or bound to the sides of the posts until final adjustments were made. The models used for these experiments were simple hardboard moulds fastened to wooden spines around which scale versions of the planking strakes were bent.

Strakes 3 and 2 were installed in the same fashion as strake 4. The three strakes were then braced together with formers or cleats attached to the outside of the planks by nails driven from within. These formers could have been simple straight timbers, since the excavated hull had no curvature athwartships between strakes 2 and 4; the assembly formed a flat belt of planking which merely changed plane as it went fore and aft.

Having now described the bottom shape, our shipwright began planking the side. It could not be determined how far the curved ends of the standing floor timbers extended since all of them had rotted away short of their upper terminus, but enough of Frames A and C survived to determine that at least one side strake could have been erected before any more framing became necessary. I suggest that was strake 9, the lower side strake. This was unfortunately labelled as two separate planks between frames 7 and 10 during excavation, but there were no finished edges between the two pieces and they appeared to be parts of a single piece that split. The 70 cm long section of strake 9 at the sternpost must represent a repair. There was little curvature this close to the rabbet to require such a short piece, nor could the frame on which it was butted have been standing before planking was completed. Strake 9 was also a straight plank which curved smoothly into the stern when drawn inward. Its sweep was quite different from that of the bottom strakes since it traversed a wider arc and remained nearly vertical throughout. Consequently, there was a separation of almost 1.3 m between strakes 4 and 9 amidships, but they nearly touched where they entered the stern rabbet (Fig. 12).

Figure 12. The bottom and side strakes meeting in the stern, as seen during the excavation. (*Photo by Robin Piercy.*)

Perhaps two or more side strakes were fitted but, even if only strake 9 were standing, the shipwright could have determined the rest of the frame shapes. Face angles and curvatures could have been derived from the lay of that single strake and the three on the bottom. Even the 7th century Yassi Ada builder could have handled it from this point. Probably only a few key frames and futtocks were added to the hull next, the planking completed, and the intermediate framing inserted.

There remained at some stage that curious gap between the sequence in which these planks were installed. What is important here is the ingenious combination of scarphs, butts and strake configurations which were used to close this difficult area (Fig. 10). I suspect that the entire arrangement was devised to make the best use of whatever planking scraps remained around the yard.

Analysis

There are departures from traditional methods of representing hull lines in the drawings shown in Fig. 13. Most of these variations were made to better illustrate the interpretation of excavated material. The bow is drawn to the left of the page because the port side yielded most of the information. The rabbets of the posts are not drawn in the conventional manner since it was not known where they began or exactly how deep they were. Forwardmost and aftermost preserved timbers are shown, and a heavy dashed line wandering through the sheer plan indicates the extent of contiguous hull survival. A 60 cm high bulwark, or weatherboard, is suggested by dashed lines; stem and upper sternpost are similarly represented, although we known nothing of these features.

I have located waterlines, buttock lines, and a 45 degree diagonal in positions where they would prove most interesting to ship scholars. The station lines indicate general coverage of the frames they represent rather than the centrelines of frames. Most of the frames were so crooked that their true centreline representation would be confusing. The waterline indicated as TWL is a test line for laboratory study and has nothing to do with indicated tonnage.

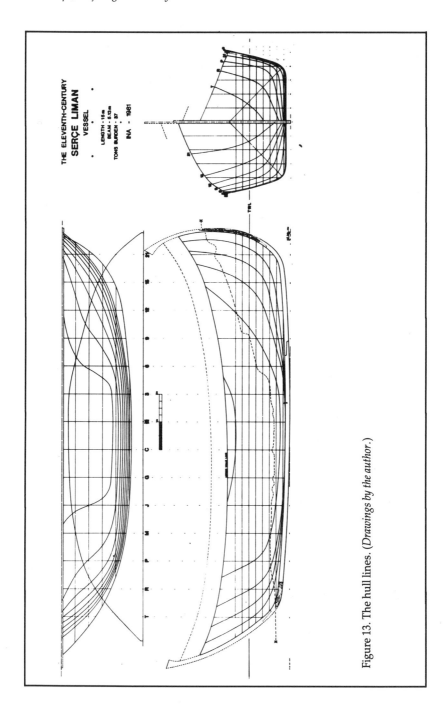

Figure 13. The hull lines. (*Drawings by the author.*)

There was plenty of evidence with which to project the after two-thirds of the hull. I am quite confident of the accuracy of this part of the line drawings except for the size and extent of the upper sternpost. The bow is a different story. There was no direct evidence for the fore-peak; wales and anchor dispersion in this area contributed little dimensional support. Additionally, the frames forward of station J were difficult to evaluate, especially with respect to their plane of seating across the keel. There is a possibility that some of these flat floors came off the keel at a higher (but never lower) angle than the body sections indicate. Thus the bow may not be as full as it indicated.

The Serçe Liman hull was 15 m long on deck, about 14.5 m at the waterline, and its moulded beam was 5.13 m. The lines show a deep, full-ended vessel with no deadrise amidships, a sharp turn of the bilge, and a steep sheer. Its length to beam ratio slightly exceeded 3:1; it was a stable craft but probably not a comfortable one.

The lack of deadrise and the sharp turn of the bilge amidships was at first a surprise. It is a radical departure from the softer shell-built hulls of only a few centuries before. The Kyrenia builder could not have made such a hull at all; mortise depths of 7 to 10 cm and the problems of shaping and setting planks around such a bilge would have rendered the design impractical, if not impossible. It is interesting that even early in the frame-first era, when only a few frames could be erected at the start, a hull form was employed that was not even practical for the pure forms of shell-first construction.

Spaciousness and simplicity are the best words with which to describe the hull lines, and the first was a result of the second. But I doubt that simplicity was as much an intention as it was a result of the building process. If one contends that the shell-first builder could not have assembled this hull, then it is equally true that our shipwright might not have been able to construct many of the shell-first types by his skeletal method. During the reconstruction process, it became increasingly obvious that the flat bottom and sides were a necessity rather than an intention. They were required to satisfy the flat belts of planking and even the slightest compounding of frame curvatures might have created insoluble problems. In short, the study suggested that we are probably looking at the limits of this shipbuilder's technological ability.

Nevertheless, there were so many advantages to even this simple form of skeletal construction as opposed to edge-joined fabrication, especially in the saving of time and timber, that it represents an enormous advance over the Yassi Ada ships. Another bonus, intentional or not, was the extra hold volume. Although this ship had nearly the same length and beam as did the Kyrenia ship, its hold could accommodate nearly 10 volume tons of extra cargo.

The tonnage rating of 37 metric tonnes is based on displacement and is really a reference tonnage; all the ships studied in our laboratories are rated for maximum displacement. It is based on the supposition that there were strong cross-beams, clamps and decks binding the upper hull. At that rated tonnage, allowing for a 15 tonne hull and gear weight, the vessel's draft would be just below waterline 8, or about 1.9 m. Even though Mediterranean and Black Sea boats can still be seen floating with scuppers awash, it is uncertain whether this construction would have supported 37 tonnes safely. Custom house tonnage formulas do not apply to ancient hulls, but a volume tonnage based on 100 ft^3/tonne for a hold extending between frames Q and 12 would yield a more practical figure of about 27 tonnes.

In further studies to determine a rig and hydrostatic properties, waterline 6 (WTL) will be used. Here the vessel displaced 43.2 tonnes of saltwater, and tonnes burden is below 30. The ship was lightly stowed when excavated; cargo and ballast weight tabulated to date indicate that she floated even higher.

Conclusions

Frames were erected before planks and there were no edge joints, and so I have called the Serçe Liman ship a skeletal-built vessel. But this construction was no more a pure skeletal process than that of the 7th century Yassi Ada ship was a pure shell process. Our shipwright was still essentially using planks to determine frame shapes in all but the middle of the ship. He still had apparent problems with the bilge and there were many weaknesses in his framing plan. Nevertheless, he was able to determine a midship shape, and that was a start. It seems obvious that not too many generations would evolve before shipwrights learned to predetermine a few more shapes fore

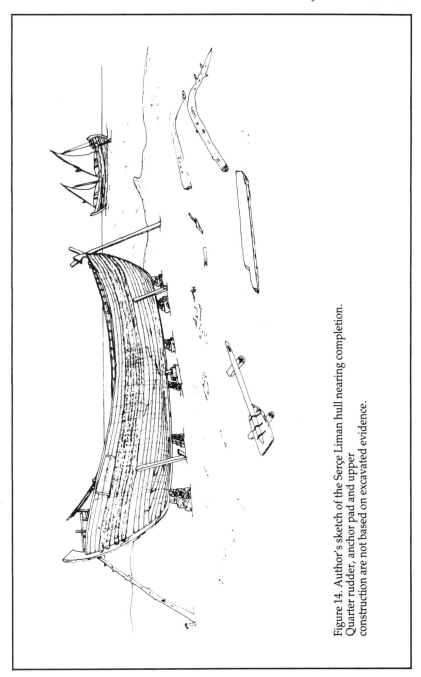

Figure 14. Author's sketch of the Serçe Liman hull nearing completion. Quarter rudder, anchor pad and upper construction are not based on excavated evidence.

and aft, to soften the bilges, and to add complexity to frame curvatures, all of which would lead to carracks and beyond.

If I had to list a second most important contribution from this wreck, it would be the symmetry of the hull. There were far too many dimensions complementing centrelines and baselines to be coincidental. This was the earliest vessel in which I could detect such a mensuration discipline. Perhaps the measurements refer only to notches on a stick but no matter how crude, it is important to the history of naval architecture. Before the first elementary hull shapes and rising lines could be drawn on wood and parchment, there had to be a system of controlled measurement in the shipyard.

There have been no references to outside factors affecting design, comparisons to contemporary paintings and sketches, or even a relationship to cargo and artefacts. This is a preliminary report, however, and these things will be disclosed eventually. I have ignored medievalists, too, but will leave them to meditate this parting volley. I am certain the Serçe Liman vessel represents a round ship design. Although the starkness of the lines drawing belies the fact, the appearance of the fragment model is one of extreme roundness from any angle. So much so, in fact, that lay visitors who have never heard of round ships apply that term. Such a hull would appear even more round if one were to view it afloat, with its broad beam, steep sheer, full ends, and incurving stern.

Round ships bring to mind the horse transports, which suggest spacious holds, and that brings us back to our own spacious hold and its mysterious transverse ceiling. Only one medieval cargo comes to mind which might require such a strong, flat floor in the hold. I suggest that the Serçe Liman medieval ship was fitted out for the occasional transport of animals.

Addendum

Since the above information was compiled, the hull remains have been conserved and are being reassembled in the ship museum at Bodrum, Turkey. Final research is providing much additional information, as well as correcting and expanding the above preliminary reconstruction. Of note is new evidence suggesting that part or all of the keel rocker resulted from seabed distortion and probably was not an original construction feature. A new report will be published upon completion of this phase of research.

Acknowledgements

This work was made possible through the assistance of a research grant from the National Endowment for the Humanities. The findings and conclusions presented here do not necessarily represent the views of the Endowment.

Additional support was provided by the Institute of Nautical Archaeology and Texas A&M University.

I am indebted to George F. Bass and Frederick H. van Doorninck, Jr. for advice and assistance. Photographic, recording, and laboratory assistance was provided by Texas A&M graduate students Paul Hundley, Sheila Matthews, Thomas Oertling, Cemal Pulak and Jay Rosloff.

Notes

[1] Along with classifying and reducing the fragment drawings, cutting the blanks was a thankless and tedious task which was done almost entirely by Thomas Oertling, a graduate student in nautical archaeology at Texas A&M University.

[2] The identification was made by Vaughn M. Bryant, Jr., an ethnobotanist at Texas A&M. Further classification is anticipated.

[3] Wood identification was made by Donna J. Christensen of the Center for Wood Anatomy Research, US Forest Products Laboratory at Madison, Wisconsin.

[4] The Kyrenia ship excavation, directed by Michael L. Katzev, yielded a well-preserved hull which was physically reconstructed in Kyrenia, Cyprus.

[5] I paid only a brief visit to the Yassi Ada site. Credit for the investigation of this hull must go to F.H. van Doorninck, Jr., who provided me with the information upon which my interpretations were based.

References

Bass, G.F. & van Doorninck, F.H., Jr., 1978, An 11th century shipwreck at Serçe Liman, Turkey. *International Journal of Nautical Archaeology and Underwater Exploration*, 7.2;119-32.

Steffy, J.R., 1975, Construction techniques of ancient ships: evidence from nautical archaeology. *Naval Engineers J.*, 87.5:85-91.

Steffy, J.R., 1982, In G.F. Bass, F.H. van Doorninck, Jr., et al., (Eds), *Yassi Ada, volume 1. A seventh-century Byzantine ship-wreck:* chapter 5. Texas.

van Doorninck, F.H., 1976, The 4th century wreck at Yassi Ada: an interim report on the hull. *IJNA*, 5.2:115-31.

van Doorninck, F.H., 1982, In G.F. Bass, F.H. van Doorninck, Jr., et al., (Eds), *Yassi Ada, volume 1. A seventh-century Byzantine shipwreck:* chapter 5. Texas.

van Doorninck, F.H., 1976, The 4th century wreck at Yassi Ada: an interim report on the hull. *IJNA*, 5.2:115-31.

van Doorninck, F.H., 1982, In G.F. Bass, F.H. van Doorninck, Jr., et al. (Eds), *Yassi Ada, volume 1. A seventh-century Byzantine shipwreck:* chapter 5. Texas.

van Doorninck, F.H., 1982, Report No. 8: an 11th century shipwreck at Serçe Liman, Turkey: 1978-81. *IJNA*, 11.2: 7-11.

The Organization of Royal Fleets in Medieval England

Timothy J. Runyan

England from the Norman Conquest through the Hundred Years' War was brimming with naval activity, both commercial and military. We are aware of the scope of the commercial activity because of the extensive studies of the wine and wool trade, as well as those of other major commodities.[1] Port cities and towns have also received a good deal of attention by scholars, and the resultant combination of these efforts is a fairly comprehensive portrait of the commercial life of England during this period.[2] On the more strictly military or naval side of this issue we have less impressive studies and information. In part this is quite understandable since the Royal Navy proper did not exist in its modern form with a fleet independent of the merchant marine or with an extensive administrative organization necessary to generate a uniform and comprehensive body of records on the activities of the ships and men of the navy. For the Middle Ages the historian must dredge up information where he or she might and the result is often fragmented and inconclusive, reflecting the nature of the sources which must be utilized. The object of this essay is to bring together some of the fragments touching on the subject of naval organization in England between the eleventh and fifteenth centuries.

It can be argued that the core of the medieval navy was always the privately owned fleet of vessels which constituted England's merchant marine. When the Conqueror found a need for a fleet, he recruited those ships he could from Norman merchants and fishermen, the remainder were recruited from a variety of western ports. Once the expedition was completed, these vessels with their masters and crews returned to their previous employment. William maintained little in the way of a ducal fleet and it is not until the establishment of the *Clos des Galées* at Rouen in 1298 that Normandy rates as a major naval center.[3] However, Norman merchants (who often behaved more like pirates), remained a force to contend with throughout the medieval period. William and his successors made frequent crossings of the North Sea and Channel but not in what we would identify as ships of the king's navy. Most of the ships were privately owned merchantmen which were arrested or hired by the king.

The Norman kings were able to take advantage of a unique naval resource in England — the Cinque Ports. This ancient confederation originally consisted of Romney, Hastings, Hythe, Dover and Sandwich, but over thirty other maritime communities were associated with them. The ports actually served as the early royal navy since they pledged 57 ships, each manned by twenty-one men, for fifteen days service each year in exchange for tax exemptions and other special privileges. The king could depend upon the fleets of the ports since he was, in effect, hiring them. Since few expeditions lasted less than fifteen days, the crown normally paid the portsmen for their additional service. The ports proved reliable under these conditions and certainly less expensive to the king than the maintenance of a standing royal navy. The terms of this arrangement were not renegotiated, but with the construction of larger ships in the fourteenth century the number recruited could be far fewer and yield a more effective fighting force carrying even greater manpower.[4]

It is important to note the technological changes in ship construction during this period since these factors have such an obvious impact on the raising of a fleet. In addition to ship size, the types of ships and their rigging are also important considerations. We know that the Viking *knarr*, a cargo vessel used for trade to Ireland, Greenland and the Mediterranean (suggested by illustration in the Bayeux Tapestry), or the longship, so clearly represented by the Oseberg or Gokstad ships, in Oslo, were not the same ships recruited and utilized by the French or English in their wars from the thirteenth century onwards. In fact, even the twelfth century saw some of the changes which produced these large fully-rigged sailing ships which did not depend upon oarsmen.[5] The tonnage and carrying capacity increased accordingly as the oared galley or single-masted sailing ship gave way to more advanced models in the fourteenth century. While the *knarr* used in trade or perhaps the Norman invasion of 1066 had a limited carrying capacity commensurate with its length of about fifty feet, it is not uncommon to find a ship list for a campaign in the Hundred Years' War that includes vessels of over 200 tons burthen.[6]

Not only was there an increase in the size of vessels but there were modifications in type and rigging as well. The earlier single-masted craft carried less cargo and were less seaworthy than their successors. The development of barges and balingers which were usually powered by both oar and sail came into widespread use.[7] But the true sailing ship of the late medieval period and mainstay of the Northern forces was the cog. High-sided and with a large carrying capacity of several hundred tons, the cog served well as a merchantman, victualling ship or ship-of-the-line. Superior height enabled all manner of objects to be hurled down from her gunnels, castles and topcastles onto smaller vessels. Another utilitarian aspect of the cog was her large troop carrying capacity, enabling more soldiers or marines, to be maintained aboard and used in the sea battles which were generally waged hand-to-hand after grappling and boarding. Cogs were easily converted from mercantile to military use. If not used as fighting ships they could be taken as outfitted and employed for service as carriers of troops, horses or supplies. If converted, castles were constructed fore,

A medieval fleet with soldiers at sea, the expedition of the Duc de Bourbon to Barbary, Froissart's *Chronicle*, late 15th c. Harley MS. 4379, f.60b. *(By permission of the British Library, London.)*

aft and atop the mainmast. These were to shield archers and soldiers during battle and provide the additional height advantage so useful in combat at sea.[8]

The technological developments relating to ship design and construction obviously had a significant impact on naval organization. As armaments changed and cannon began to become a part of naval armament, further strictures were imposed upon the crown's ability to convert mercantile vessels to men-of-war. Special requirements of impressed ships involved the reinforcements needed to withstand bombardment, the speed to escape and the structural shell necessary to allow conversion to military use by the addition of cannons and the construction of castles.[9]

An important exception to the above were galleys. Long the mainstay of Mediterranean seafaring, galleys were important in northern warfare but are seldom found in mercantile use there. Northern shipping depended upon the sailing ship and very little upon the oared galley. However, for military use, galleys were thought superior to the often cumbersome sailing vessels as late as the fourteenth century and were in general use from the Mediterrarean to the Caribbean in the seventeenth century. Galleys and sometimes barges or balingers were purpose-built by the crown for military use. They were not efficient cargo carriers since carrying capacity was limited and large crews were needed to man the oars.[10]

Moving from the subject of the ship itself we can turn to the process of recruitment and assembly of men and supplies for a naval expedition. Again the Cinque Ports became an important part of this process. They provided the core of most naval forces from the eleventh century onwards. The king called upon the portsmen for their services and supplemented this with his own ships and those arrested by his order. Foreign vessels might be hired and in some cases municipalities or individuals provided or hired their ships to the crown by special arrangements.

Two key elements of interest in the process of creating a fleet are the number and type of vessels enlisted and their origin or ownership. Throughout most of the eleventh and twelfth centuries ships were recruited from the Cinque Ports and ships from other ports were arrested as needed. Little existed in the way of a royal fleet. The Norman and Angevin kings frequently travelled to the Continent, but possessed only a few ships. No royal navy proper existed with an established administrative structure until at least the reign of John. His "keeper of the king's ships" was William de Wrotham whose office was continued until the creation of the Navy Board in 1546 and the Secretary of the Admiralty.[11] The importance of this office is that these clerks kept accounts which were rendered to the exchequer and provide a record of the ships in the king's navy. Unfortunately, the office was not held continuously and the available records only provide us with good information from the fourteenth century.[12]

Many of the king's ships were not constructed at the monarch's expense or order. Some were captured foreign vessels and others were privately-owned ships given to or taken by the crown. The arguments against the crown building and maintaining its own standing fleet were many and persuasive. Construction cost was a key factor and in addition there were the maintenance, docking and manning charges which went with royal ownership. It was far simpler and cheaper to depend upon the Cinque Ports and the long-established practice of impressment of both ships and mariners than to invest in a large standing navy. What the king maintained was a small naval force which mainly served military purposes and as a royal transport and escort fleet. The nature, number and effectiveness of this fleet is very difficult to ascertain. The royal interest in the navy changed with and often within each reign. As the private possession of the crown under the administration of the Council, the king's fleet might flourish or rot at its dockyard at the Tower or Ratcliffe. The accounts of the clerk of the king's ships chronicle the good and bad times of the royal fleets, the worst of times accounted for by an absence of any record and the disappearance of the clerk's office.

The importance of the royal fleet was primarily strategic. If the king needed to move at sea on short notice, a standing fleet was important. If a naval force was required to repel an invader or clear the sea of pirates, a ready fleet was necessary. There was no time for conversion of mercantile vessels or the regular process of the arrest of ships, the impressment of mariners and the necessary victualling. Although the advantages of maintaining a standing royal fleet seem apparent, they were not always persuasive. While King John clearly owned ships, it is unclear that his predecessors built or maintained their own fleets. Henry III inherited the legacy of John's naval interest and maintained the office of clerk of the king's ships and crown vessels. When not used in royal service it appears the royal ships were hired out to merchants, a common practice.[13] Edward I was a builder of royal shipping and ordered the construction of galleys to be used in his various military expeditions. The fleet never grew to large numbers, but under Edward II there were still ten or eleven ships of the crown. The reign of Edward III marks a dividing point. He was energetic in all aspects of military affairs and paid a good deal of attention to the navy. As the victor of Sluys in 1340 and L'Espagnols sur Mer in 1350, Edward was an experienced seaman and one who appreciated the advantages of a superior naval force. We must not, however, forget that the navy was only a secondary element in the waging of war. The army remained the principal force and ships were mere carriers necessary for the transport and victualling of armies. Although Edward maintained a larger royal fleet, ranging upwards of twenty-five ships, it was not maintained or enlarged to provide a truly powerful navy.[14] The usual method of raising fleets was employed and some lengthy arrests of shipping in advance of expeditions prompted parliamentary complaints.[15] Not only were merchants denied the opportunity for personal gain because of the lengthy arrests of their ships, but the port towns were chaotic with large armies quartered in them awaiting embarkation. Purveyors, that hated and grasping element in every royal campaign, fleeced the coastal areas in search of provisions for the army and navy. All of England must have prayed for a quick departure of the armies and praised the Lord for the favorable tide and wind that took them to sea.[16]

The navy at the end of Edward III's reign was in sad shape and Richard II did little to improve it. The payment of ton-tight, a sum given to shipowners for use of their vessels, was instituted in 1380 at the rate of 3s 4d per quarter per ton of carrying capacity and reduced to 2s five years later. In this same year, 1385, there were no more than twenty-five royal ships remaining — most in need of refitting. While there were temporary reversals, the fourteenth century ended with the king's navy in sorry condition.

The revival of the French war by Henry V temporarily changed matters for the better. The royal navy was expanded and larger ships were constructed, ranging in size up to 800 tons, multi-masted and highly decorated with ornamentation and painted sails. Well enough administered by William Catton and William Soper, Henry V's royal navy was the greatest a monarch had produced.[17] Its life was brief. After his death in 1422, the navy was sold as part of the settlement of the king's estate. When the *Libelle of Englyshe Polycye* was penned in 1436, it praised the power of a strong navy and its role in providing security and glory to the state, but it was a reminisence on things past, not the contemporary situation. Ships were used in the civil wars of the fifteenth century to the advantage of the crown, but it was not a period of expanded royal shipbuilding. Mercantile construction continued, however, making this a growth period in overseas trade and coastal shipping. The crown continued to rely upon impressment to secure ships for its needs, until advances in cannonry made mandatory the purpose built man-of-war. The conversion of merchantmen for use in war was no longer a crown option. The Tudors responded to this fact by building and organizing a royal fleet of fighting ships.[18]

The medieval English navy suffered from being the monarch's personal possession in more ways than it benefited. Subject to disbandment or sale, neglect or attention as the king chose, the navy was personal property. The king's ships were not those of the nation, but the crown, and their administration by the king's council should not obscure this fact. For much of the fourteenth century the royal navy was accounted for in the records of the king's chamber and repaired and manned from those funds. After 1356 the fleet appears under exchequer scrutiny and audit, but it remained a part of the king's personal property.[19]

This review of the use and state of the royal fleets should not distort the overall shape of the English maritime forces. While the crown may have done little with its own vessels, merchants were constructing them at a steady pace. Trade and commercial activity increased during this period and one might even suggest that the crown's neglect of its own ships was due partly to the ready impressment of privately-owned ships. In most instances the ships were arrested with no compensation to the owners. As long as the royal prerogative to arrest ships was maintained, a fleet could always be assembled. While military expeditions cost a great deal, most of the expenses were for soldiers and victualling. Frequently, vessels were impressed for service and the owners not only lost the use of their ships and the potential gains by trade, but also they risked the loss of their ships without compensation. One instance was in 1372 when the crews of 24 ships were held 105 days before their wages began.[20] The resistance of seamen to royal impressment is well enough known, but perhaps expressed itself more candidly when a band of fugitive mariners turned on their pursuers and locked them in a barn.[21] Complaints from merchants made little headway against the royal practice which was both cheap and expedient.

Shipowners frequently complained about the length of time that their vessels were arrested. The king often arrested ships for months before they were needed or used. Sometimes the forces of Nature prevented a sailing. Edward III spent the period from 27 August to 14 October 1372 attempting to get a large fleet with over 6000 archers and soldiers to France. He paid out mariners' wages of over £10,000 besides what he paid the army.[22] One might argue that the masters and mariners did not lose by such government financed expeditions and could tolerate them comfortably. But the real loss was to the merchant and ultimately the king since ships lost to mercantile activity paid no duties on wine, wool or other items carried. Also, the crown's reluctance to build its own fleet led to the passage of restrictive legislation concerning shipping. From 1340 the sale of English ships was forbidden and wood suitable for shipbuilding was forbidden to be exported. The Navigation Acts of 1381 and 1382 made it illegal to charter foreign ships for trading purposes, unless no English ships were available.

The routine of impressment continued to operate. Letters were issued stating that seaworthy ships over a certain tonnage along a stated segment of coast line (*e.g.* west of the Thames, etc.) be arrested and assembled at a certain port on a given date. The arrests were done by a variety of persons, but normally by the king's sergeants-at-arms. These men also were commissioned to impress mariners and reported to the clerk of the king's ships who dispensed monies for their wages. The clerks were the key figures in this process since they received money from the Exchequer, supervised the sergeants and had overall responsibility for seeing that the king's orders were carried out and that a fleet was assembled. Sometimes they failed, generally they did not. During the fourteenth century, sergeants like Walter de Harewell and Richard Larch appear to be in continous motion, arresting ships, gathering victuals and impressing mariners. Sergeants were also ordered abroad on occasion. Larch, for example, was sent to Gascony with a fleet he organized to deliver victuals there. He went first class, I might note, as his wages included the services of a valet.[23]

The concluding segment to this essay will focus on some of the economic consequences of naval organization as practiced during this period. The king's ships and the merchant marine of the realm were important factors in the amount of tax revenues generated and in their reallocation. The crown clearly depended upon the income from the wine and wool trade to run the kingdom. These staples were the mainstay of annual income. When England was unable to maintain a high level of trading activity with the Low Countries and Gascony, revenues tapered off rapidly. Dubious as we may be of the figures measuring sacks of wool or tons of wine, a significant drop in their numbers had significant consequence for crown revenues.

As an example, customs accounts for 1337-1343 show wild variations in wool exports. These range from a low of 4,326 sacks in 1337 to a high of 41,293 sacks in 1339. In part the fluctuations can be explained by the course of the war, *e.g.* Bristol, Ipswich, Lynn and Sandwich had no exports in 1337-38, but substantial exports when the French stopped raiding along these coastal areas.[24] The wine trade reflects a similar pattern with alien imports reduced to 2,146 tons in 1336-37, up the next year to 3,487 and then down again the following year to 2,022 tons. The imports for 1340-41 saw the volume double to 4,259 tons. Convoys were used on the sea lanes to Gascony and clearly helped to increase the volume of exchange.[25]

But not only was trade slowed because of enemy fleets during the "off" years noted above, but also because large numbers of merchant ships were impressed into royal service. There were fewer carriers available to transport wool or bring wine from Gascony. In 1337 the merchants pleaded that they be allowed freedom from arrest in order to transport the Gascon vintage to England. Edward III agreed only on condition that the released ships be back in royal service at a

Account of William de Clewar, clerk of the king's ships, 20 January 1355. He records payment to the master and crew of the cog *Thomas*. (*By permission of the Public Record Office, London.*)

specificed date.[26] The convoy system was effective for all parties since we note an increase in the number of denizen ladings which reached England in 1339-40.[27] Accompanying the increased supply of wine was a drop in wine prices at the local pub, an event that doubtless inspired cheer among English men and women.[28]

A quick glance at the estimated annual revenues of the crown shows that there were dramatic variations annually. These fluctuations are particularly noticeable during periods of increased naval activity during the Hundred Years' War.[29] What these figures mean to the naval historian, if one can assume income other than that derived from maritime commerce is stable, is that the king's sergeants have been very effective at arresting ships and mariners. The removal of these vessels from the carrying trade doubtless reduced crown revenue. Their return to commercial activity and the royal efforts to protect the shipping routes was equally reflected in the royal revenues, particularly in the bulk trade of wine and wool or cloth. Coupled with the previously mentioned fluctuations in customs' revenue, the annual figures reinforce the argument that the health of the merchant marine is reflected in the revenues of the crown. Fluctuations in the wine and wool trade occurred for political, military or other reasons also, but rarely with such apparent consequence.

As we have noted, a dramatic transformation was taking place concerning the nature and size of medieval ships. With the physical transformation of the navy, royal and private, to larger more seaworthy vessels, the nature of both war and trade was transformed. Ships were larger, but now fewer were needed for commercial use to transport the vintage, the wool or other commodities involved in English commerce. The volume index of exports of cloth and wool combined show a steady decline between 1360 and 1480, but it seems clear that precipitous drops, such as those in the 1370's and 1380's, were due to the lively raiding of English commercial routes by French, or pro-French forces.[30] It has become clear from recent research that as many men were employed in the naval as in the military aspects of the war. Professor Postan suggested such a conclusion and some few scholars have worked to bear this out.[31] The difficulties of organizing and maintaining fleets in the face of pressing military demands, technological change, manpower and financial problems make the organizing of medieval navies a subject of far ranging interest. It was the press of such demands that helped push kings to impose harsh *maltoltes*, demand extraordinary taxes and send their purveyors to beat the bounds of both town and countryside. Naval organization was clearly an important concern of all medieval kings — even if maintaining their own navies was not.

Notes

I would like to thank Professor James Brundage of the University of Wisconsin-Milwaukee for his helpful criticisms of an earlier version of this paper.

[1] Examples include E. Power, *The Wool Trade* (Oxford, 1941); T.H. Lloyd, *The English Wool Trade in the Middle Ages* (Cambridge, 1977); E.M. Carus Wilson, *Medieval Merchant Venturers* (2nd ed., London, 1967); M.K. James, *Studies in the Medieval Wine Trade* (Oxford, 1971), A.R. Bridbury, *England and the Salt Trade in the Later Middle Ages* (Oxford, 1955), E. Power and M.M. Postan, *Studies in English Trade in the Fifteenth Century* (London, 1933); J. Munro, *Wool, Cloth and Gold: The Struggle for Bullion in the Anglo-Burgundian Trade, 1340-1476* (Toronto, 1974). On seafaring during this period, see Timothy J. Runyan, "Ships and Mariners in Later Medieval England," *Journal of British Studies*, XVI (Spring, 1977), pp. 1-17.

[2] Note especially the work of M. Oppenheim in essaying the ports throughout the appropriate volumes of the *Victoria History of the Counties of England* (London, 1906, ff.).

[3] On the Clos des Galées see C. Bréard, "Le compte du Clos des Galées de Rouen pour 1382-1384," *Melanges Société de l'Histoire de Normandie*, 2nd. ser. (Rouen, 1893), pp. 53-154. A. Merlin-Chezelas, ed., *Documents Relatifs au Clos des Galées de Rouen*. Collection des documents inédits sur l'histoire de France. Section philologie et d'histoire jusqu'a 1610. Vols. 11 and 12 (Paris: Bibliothèque nationale, 1977-78); and for the development of the French navy, C. de la Roncière, *Histoire de la marine française*, 5 vols. (3rd ed., Paris, 1909-32).

[4] See K. M. E. Murray, *The Constitutional History of the Cinque Ports* (London, 1935); F.W. Brooks, "The Cinque Ports," *Mariner's Mirror*, XV (April, 1929), pp. 142-81 and the chapter on the ports in his *The English Naval Forces 1199-1272* (London, 1932).

[5] For the evolution of the ship see: R. and R.C. Anderson, *The Sailing Ship* (London, 1947); George Bass, ed., *A History of Seafaring based on Underwater Archaeology* (London, 1972), especially chapters 7-10. For Viking ships, A.W. Brogger and H. Shetelig, *The Viking Ships* (2nd ed., Oslo, 1971).

[6] Public Record Office, London. Exchequer Accounts E. 101/30/30; E. 101/32/9 are examples. This later record for 1372 includes the *Christofre* of 260 tons, *Trinite* of 200 tons. For comparison of the size of English and foreign ships in the mid-fifteenth century, see D. Burwash, *English Merchant Shipping, 1460-1540* (Toronto, 1947; reprinted London, 1969), Chapter III and Appendix II.

[7] On this see J. W. Sherborne, "English Barges and Balingers of the Late Fourteenth Century," *Mariner's Mirror*, 63 (May, 1977), pp. 109-14.

[8] See T.J. Runyan, "Merchantmen to Men-of-War in Medieval England," in C.L. Symonds, ed., *New Aspects of Naval History* (Annapolis: Naval Institute Press, 1981), pp. 33-40. Examples of appropriate illustrations and artistic reconstructions can be seen in B. Landstrom, *The Ship* (New York, 1961). A study of the ship based on illustrative and documentary sources is R.W. Unger, *The Ship in the Medieval Economy, 600-1600* (London, 1980). The cog of ca. 1350-1400 recovered from the waters of the Weser River is the best surviving example of a ship of this era. For information on this vessel see: S. Fliedner, *The Cog of Bremen* (Bremen, 1972); D. Elmers, "The Cog of Bremen and Related Boats," in S. McGrail, ed., *Medieval Ships and Harbours in Northern Europe* (Oxford, 1979), pp. 1-16.

[9] Cannons were in use during the second quarter of the fourteenth century and are noted in the clerical accounts and inventories of arms at the Tower. However, they were not yet a major factor in naval warfare.

[10] J.T. Tinniswood, "English Galleys, 1272-1377," *Mariner's Mirror*, XXXV (October, 1949), pp. 276-315. Edward I was the last great builder of galleys. He ordered 30 to be built, but they were not all completed. At least two of these were constructed to carry 120 oars apiece.

[11] F.W. Brooks, "William de Wrotham and the Office of the Keeper of the King's Ports and Galleys," *English Historical Review*, XL (October, 1925), pp. 570-79; M. Oppenheim, *A History of the Administration of the Royal Navy and of Merchant Shipping in Relation to the Navy, 1509-1660* (London, 1896), Introduction.

[12] The accounts of the clerks are continuous from 1358. Enrollment was made on the Pipe Rolls (Public Record Office, E. 372) until 1371 when changed to the Rolls of Foreign Accounts (E. 364).

[13] M. Oppenheim, *The Administration of the Royal Navy*, p. 4, states that "There is hardly a reign, down to and including that of Elizabeth, in which men-of-war were not hired by merchants. . . ." I have found this difficult to document for the fourteenth century. Due to war and a scarcity of ships this practice was probably curtailed. The repetition of ship names also makes it difficult to trace a ship — there are dozens of vessels named *St. Mary, Godale, John*, etc.

[14] J. W. Sherborne, "The English Navy: Shipping and Manpower, 1369-1389," *Past and Present*, 37 (July, 1967), pp. 163-75, notes over 40 royal vessels between 1369 and 1375, while I have identified 50 for the period 1344 to 1352. (P.R.O., E 101/20/14; E. 101/24/1 m.5; E. 101/24/7 mm 5-6; E. 101/24/14). However, because ship names are often repeated the number is probably less. On this problem, see T.J. Runyan, "Ships and Fleets in Anglo-French Warfare, 1337-1360," *American Neptune*, XLVI, 2 (Spring, 1986), p. 92, n.10.

[15] *Rotuli Parliamentorum*, ed. J. Strachey, *et al* (6 vols.; London, 1832), II, 311.

[16] Some attention is given to purveyance in H.J. Hewitt, *The Organization of War under Edward III* (Manchester, 1966), chapters 3 and 7.

[17] The records of these clerks are found in the National Maritime Museum in Greenwich. Soper's account has been edited by Susan Rose, *The Navy of the Lancastrian Kings: Accounts and Inventories of William Soper, Keeper of the King's Ships, 1422-27* (London, 1982).

[18] C.F. Richmond has written two valuable pieces on the fifteenth century: "The Keeping of the Seas during the Hundred Years War: 1422-1440," *History* XLIX (1964), pp. 283-98, and "English Naval Power in the Fifteenth Century," *History*, LII (1967), pp. 1-15, See also his chapter "The War at Sea" in K. Fowler, ed., *The Hundred Years War* (London, 1971), pp. 96-121. For the innovations by the Tudors: E.B. Fowler, *English Sea Power in the Early Tudor Period, 1485-1588* (Ithaca, 1965); G.V. Scammel, "War at Sea Under the Early Tudors: Some East Coast Evidence," *Economic History Review*, 2nd ser. XIII (April, 1961), pp. 327-41; "Shipowning in the Economy and Politics of Early Modern England," *Historical Journal* XV (1972), pp. 385-407. M. Oppenheim, ed., *Naval Accounts and Inventories of the Reign of Henry VII* (London, 1896); for navigational capabilities, D.W. Waters, *The Art of Navigation in England in Elizabethan and Early Stuart Times* (London, 1958).

[19] Earlier payments for ships and mariners will be found scattered throughout household account books. One example is the Wardrobe Account for 1338-40 (P.R.O., E.36/203). The "Vadia Nautarum" section lists the ships, masters, constables and number of mariners and boys employed with dates of

service and wages owed. I am grateful to Professor Bryce Lyon and Mary Lyon for providing me a copy of this section of the account book.

[20] Sherborne, "English Navy," *Past and Present* (1967), p. 165.

[21] Two sergeants-at-arms were treated thus at Wells, Norfolk in 1380. *Calendar of Patent Rolls* (1377-81), p. 475.

[22] P.R.O., Foreign Accounts, E.364/8 mm. I, K; Issue Rolls, E. 403/446 m. 37.

[23] For Harewell, P.R.O., E. 403/344 m.3; E.403/353 m.10; E.403/347 m. 27; For Larch, E.403/341 m. 24; E. 403/347 mm. 12, 15, 18; E. 403/355 m.9.

[24] R. L. Baker, *The English Customs Service, 1307-43: A Study of Medieval Administration*, Transactions of the American Philosophical Society, N.S. 51, part 6 (Philadelphia, 1961), Appendix I.

[25] M. K. James, "Fluctuations in the Ango-Gascon Wine Trade during the Fourteenth Century," *Economic History Review*, 2nd ser., IV (1951), and reprinted in *Essays in Economic History*, ed. E. Carus Wilson (London, 1962), II, p. 148 Appendix II. The pagination cited here is from the *Essays.*

[26] P R.O., Chancery, Gascon Rolls, C. 61/49 mm. 5, 7.

[27] James, "Fluctuations in Wine Trade," Appendix III. The number reached 235 ships.

[28] *Ibid*, Appendix IV, a graph of prices paid for the king's wines.

[29] J.H. Ramsay, *A History of the Revenues of the Kings of England, 1066-1399* (Oxford, 1925). Ramsay's figures are not completely satisfactory, but remain a useful guide. He shows revenues (rounded) of: £79,642 for 1336-37; a rise to £272,833 the following year; a drop the next two years to £167,039 and £157,562. In 1340 the yield was a disastrous £35,641. A dramatic recovery followed in 1341 with revenues of £193,342. This base was maintained over the next decade.

[30] See E.M. Carus-Wilson, *England's Export Trade* (Oxford, 1963) and the convenient graph in A.R. Bridbury, *Economic Growth, England in the Later Middle Ages* (London, 1962) pp.31-32.

[31] See M.M. Postan, "The Costs of the Hundred Years' War " *Past and Present*, 27, (April, 1964), pp. 34-53. Also James W. Sherborne, "The English Navy: Shipping and Manpower,1369-1389," *ibid.*, 37 (July, 1967) pp. 163-75.

The Laguna Madre Scow Sloop

Edwin Doran Jr.

Toward the end of his book *American Small Sailing Craft* Howard Chapelle[1] describes a formerly "very numerous" scow sloop, used near Brownsville, Texas "until quite recently," which he named the Port Isabel Scow Sloop. In the early 1950's, I was living only 300 miles from Port Isabel and wondered if any of the craft were still in existence, either in South Texas or perhaps on the Mexican Laguna Madre in Tamaulipas. No effort was made to check the idea, and after a move it was filed away.

Upon returning to the state I vacationed near Corpus Christi in the early 1960's and in Port Aransas saw a scow sloop sitting in the front yard of a small home. It was unmistakably the boat that Chapelle had described, but a brief conversation with the lady of the house revealed only that the boat had belonged to her father who had won many races with his "skimmity scow" years before. Five years later a trip was made to measure the boat, and it had disappeared.

Finally, in January of 1976, on a trip to Northeast Mexico, I drove ten miles off the main highway, not far south of Brownsville, and found a full dozen of Chapelle's scows in use. Fishermen informed me that a hundred more were at work on the Laguna Madre. The boat type reported extinct more than a quarter of a century ago is thus alive and thriving and is one of the largest fleets of commercial sail remaining in the Western Hemisphere.

Two conclusions may be drawn from this introductory personal history. One, that I sometimes take a quarter-century to follow through on an idea, is painfully obvious. Much more important is a reemphasis of the value to geographers and historians of going into the field and observing what is there. Literary research is fundamental in both disciplines, but we can never be sure of exact meanings and what has been missed until we go out and look for ourselves.

Description

In basic form and rig the scow sloop is exactly as Chapelle described it, a gaff-rigged sloop with transom ends, a bit of V-bottom fore and aft, and two trunk cabins (Fig. 1). The length is about 30 feet, the beam about 12, and the draft, with long centerboard up, about a foot.

A more precise description is provided by Chapelle's lines drawing and sail plan.[2] The above points may be noted as well as much more detail, presented in his inimitable style.

Lines taken off a beached and abandoned hull in August, 1976 are in general very similar to those given by Chapelle (Fig. 2). There can be little doubt that the boat type is the same, but several minor differences may he noted. The bow transom of the more recent boat is appreciably smaller than the stern transom and is not raked forward very much. The forward V-bottom is not so pronounced as in Chapelle's drawing, the after part has very little dead rise, and the boat has less sheer and rocker (perhaps because of hogging after being abandoned). A partly-finished new boat shows considerably more rocker than the one measured. Wales just below the sheer and above the

Figure 1. Pair of scow sloops on Laguna Madre.
(*Photo by author.*)

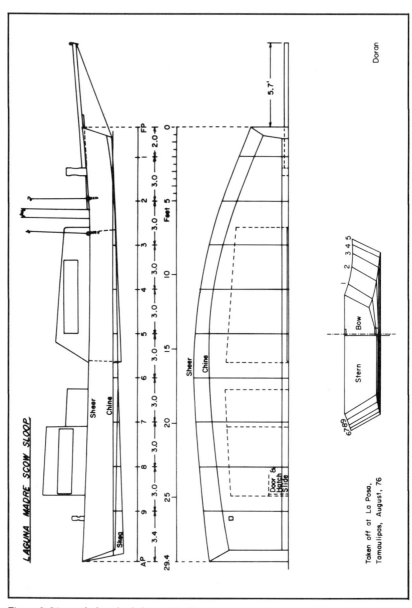

Figure 2. Lines of a beached sloop at La Posa.

chine evidently add appreciably more to the longitudinal strength of the boat than does the plank keel.

Construction materials are still much the same as those described by Chapelle. Frames are made of pine, oak, or *fresno* (ash?). Yellow pine is used for planking of topsides and transoms; the latter with a few frames, outline the shape of the boat as it is built. Bottom planking in a fore and aft direction goes on last and is strengthened by 1x6 inch floors. Masts are made of pine, or in one case of six-inch diameter iron pipe.

Although most of the boats are built in Matamoros and hauled to the Laguna Madre on large trailers for launching they also are constructed in several other towns in Tamaulipas. Victoria and Monterrey (outside the state) were mentioned by an informant as were Soto la Marina and La Pesca, closer to the water. No signs of sailboat building were noted in either of the latter towns, and it seems likely that the main location is Matamoros. Boatbuilding in this city is still an active business as witnessed by names and addresses of six different builders which were collected. At least one young man in his 20's is active, so the art is not dying with old artisans. The standard method of purchasing a boat is by part payments at each of several stages. A partially completed boat seen in Matamoros in January was still sitting untouched in August because the prospective owner had failed to meet his installment. The cost of a completed boat in 1976 was about 4,000 American dollars.

When boat bottoms become fouled with marine growth the usual practice on the Laguna Madre is to haul the scows on inclined skidways in shallow water called *astilleros* (Fig. 3). A heavy, multi-part tackle is made fast to a post ashore and men (or a truck) haul the boat up sideways for scraping and painting.

A fairly standard color scheme is followed in painting the sloops. Decks, transoms, and topsides are usually a greenish blue, perhaps most accurately described as aquamarine, then the sheer is accented by white paint on the upper wale and often by another stripe just above the chine. Trunk cabins most often are aquamarine on top and white on sides, but occasional artistic dashes of green occur on the latter. Rarely the entire boat is painted white. For the most part sails are white, but a blue one was seen. Another sail had two red stripes paral-

Figure 3. Sloop hauled on *astillero*.
(*Photo by author.*)

lel to the leach and two others each had four blue stripes alternating with white and parallel to the leach. One may guess that multi-colored sails are a recent change influenced by color television display of some of the more gaudy modern catamarans.

A number of proper names of boats were collected and are mentioned here to convey some notion of boatmen's attitudes. Most common are names of women, but almost equally so are such names as *Solitario* (solitary), *Vago* (vagrant), *Malviviente* (tough life), *Andariego* (restless traveller), *Pisafuerte* (press on strongly), and *Quitate Que Te Piso* (don't go aground). The fishermen's perception of their lives aboard is clear from their choice of names.

Performance

A few bits of information gained by sailing on a scow sloop at La Posa may be added to Chapelle's comment that the boats ". . . very often were smart sailers . . . ." Only an hour elapsed between getting under way and having to let the fishermen get at their business, but it was possible to make a few measurements with simple pitot type wind and boat speed meters and a wind direction vane. On the wind the boat (*Solitario*) did not hold on well because the water was too shallow to use more than half the board, but on a reach and downwind she sailed 4.5 to 4.0 knots in a true wind of about 12 knots. Considering the fact that the jib was not set and the boat had a very strong weather helm, with obvious bad effects on speed, she sailed very well, although not in the same category with a modern racing yacht of the same size.

Numbers and Distribution

In August, 1976 I chartered a plane at Brownsville and flew about one hundred miles south above the Laguna Madre, noting all boats under sail and those with masts which were tied up or anchored. The count was 120 sailboats. A number of low altitude, oblique photographs were made, and later careful inspection indicates that about ten boats are derelict, some sunk and others in suspicious attitudes ashore. Of the 63 boats photographed two definitely had pointed bows, 42 clearly were scow sloops, and 18 were indeterminate. The statistical sample of 44 boats out of 120, with 95% of the sample being scows, would seem strong grounds for estimating that more than a hundred scow sloops are active in fishing the Mexican Laguna Madre.

Taken as a whole the Caribbean probably has a greater number of working sail, and a recent photograph of *jangadas* off Recife, Brazil shows 56 sailing rafts racing. Although these may represent larger clusters it is probable that the Laguna Madre scow sloops form one of the three largest fleets of working sail in the Western Hemisphere. The 30 skipjacks remaining on Chesapeake Bay rank no higher than fourth.

The distribution of scow sloops in Northeastern Mexico is shown in Figure 4. Most of the boats work toward the north end of the lagoon, where circulation with the ocean was restored after hurricane Beulah reopened a pass through the barrier island in 1967. Prior to that time all fishing had stopped for ten years or more. A smaller number of boats fish farther to the south where the Boca Jesús María has remained open for a long time. The pilot of the plane stated that few or no boats are to be found yet farther south, and no boats can work in the very shoal area which has been filled by sedimentation from the Rio Conchos (Rio San Fernando on the Mexican 1:500,000 map).

Because of its distribution, past and present, over the entire Laguna Madre of the United States and of Mexico there appears to be sufficient basis, with due respect to Mr. Chapelle, to change the name of the Port Isabel Scow Sloop and retitle it the Laguna Madre Scow Sloop.

Fishing Technique

In addition to sailing scows there are several hundred boats on the Laguna Madre, mostly skiffs with pointed bows, ranging from 12 to perhaps 30 feet in length, which also are engaged in fishing. Many of the boats tend zigzag shrimp weirs which are concentrated in shallower water south of the main sailboat fishing area. But the principal business of seining is done with the scows.

The sailing scows work in pairs, *a campo* with two trunk cabins almost always pairing off with a *mercadero* carrying only the after cabin. One or two large skiffs are used as tenders for storing and laying

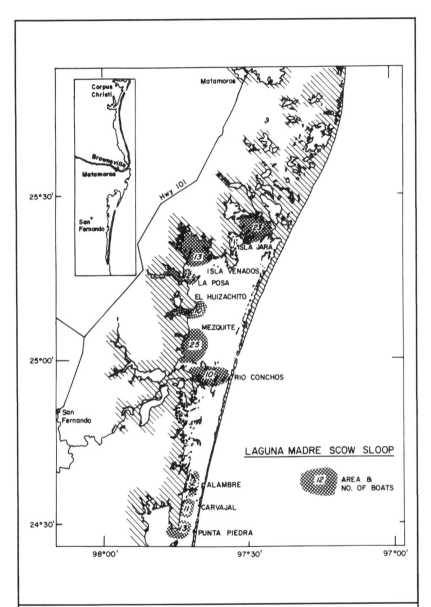

Figure 4. Distribution of scow sloops in Northeastern Mexico.

out the nets, six to eight feet wide and 60 fathoms long, which are the principal means of catching fish. Occasionally one sloop will anchor with an end of the net while the other sails around to encircle a school of fish, but more commonly the two boats will head on opposite beam reaches, thus stretching the net between their transoms. Jibs are not set and main sheets are slacked until the sails are drawing just enough to keep the net taut. Under these conditions the two boats drift off to leeward, gradually sweeping the net down wind until a catch has been made. One or two sets can be made each day, depending on the wind, and a lucky catch may amount to as much as two tons of fish.

A *patrón* owns the boats, pays for all gear and food, and collects the fish ashore for sale in a nearby town. He pays the six-man crew a set price per kilogram, a slightly larger amount going to cook and captain. The latter also receives a premium for every 100 kilograms caught. "No fish — no pay" insures energetic work on the part of the fishermen. The crew was cautious in making estimates of the *patrón's* earnings, but it is quite clear that theirs is only a small fraction of the owner's. Despite low wages the skipper's liking for boats and for the quiet life away from the distractions of Matamoros was explicit. Then he echoed a skipjack oysterman of a dozen years ago, "When I'm on the bay I'm a free man."

Origins

The discovery that the Laguna Madre Scow Sloop is still "alive and well," as described above, hopefully justifies this paper. Only a cursory examination of the literature, attempting to learn something of the boat's history and origin, has been possible and that with minimal results.

Chapelle's comments are still basic to what we know. There is a long history of flat-bottomed, transom-bowed boats in Europe and in America that has been given little attention. We have some awareness of scows, radeaus, gundalows and the like along the east coast of the United States from Maine to the Carolinas during colonial times and later, but there seem to have been no such craft on the Gulf of Mexico east of Texas.[3] The scows in Texas have some general similarities to those of Chesapeake Bay, as exemplified by hull form, and certain more specific similarities such as a complicated web of lazy jacks and a sprit rather than club on the jib which suggest a relationship, but this has not been documented.

Several histories of the Rio Grande area[4] do not mention scow sloops but do emphasize the Mexican War and Civil War when many ships from the East Coast visited the Brownsville area and were usually unloaded with lighters. These are logical periods in which to expect the introduction of the scow sloop idea, but this is only inference.

The report of the Commissioner for Fish and Fisheries for 1880[5] describes Texas fishing boats as sloop-rigged and flat-bottomed, using smaller boats to lay out seines, and mentions a number of men fishing at Brazos Santiago (near the mouth of the Rio Grande) for the Brownsville and Matamoros market. Unfortunately, there is no evidence that these boats were scows. Again, the report for 1889-91[6] comments that most Texas fishermen were from Southern Europe, Austria (Trieste?), and Mexico. The boats were of sloop, cat, and schooner rig, and of the "same style as New England and the Mid-Atlantic states" but "built very shallow." No mention is made of scows, and Plate 12 of the report, taken at Galveston, shows about eight sharp-bowed boats. One gaff-rigged sloop in the photo has a very wide transom and is probably a scow, but the bow is invisible. A Galveston photograph of about the same time shows a 40-foot scow schooner, evidence that scows did exist that far north.[7] As of this date, just before the construction in 1904 of a railroad from Corpus Christi to Brownsville opened up a market, there were only two seines being operated in the vicinity of Port Isabel.[8] No other information on the problem is to be found in the several reports for the years 1885 to 1901.

One further bit of evidence comes from a small glossary of boat vocabulary collected in the field. Of 24 terms some 17 were found to be proper nautical Spanish words and only one could he considered a Hispanicization of the English word. It is obvious that at some time or other sailors from a Spanish nautical background taught the local people the correct names for the parts of their boats.

In summary, the area of origin of the Laguna Madre Scow Sloop probably is the Chesapeake Bay or elsewhere on the United States east coast. But the fact that scow sailors always have been Mexicans using a good Spanish nautical vocabulary is a caution that a Hispanic origin, in Mexico or in Spain, must not be excluded as a possibility.

Notes

[1] Howard I. Chapelle, *American Small Sailing Craft* (New York: W.W. Norton, 1951), pp. 334-336.

[2] *Ibid.*, p. 335.

[3] Capt. J.W. Collins, "Report on . . . Fishing Grounds . . . Along the Atlantic Coast and in the Gulf of Mexico," in U.S. Commission of Fish and Fisheries, *Report of the Commissioner for 1885*, App. B., pp. 217-305. 48th Cong., 2nd Sess., Senate Misc. Doc. 70, (Washington: Government Printing Office, 1887), pp. 251-305.

[4] Paul Horgan, *Great River, The Rio Grande in North American History* (New York: Holt, Rinehart and Winston, 1964); Arthur Ikin, *Texas* (London: Sherwood, Gilbert and Piper, 1841 and reprinted Austin: University of Texas Press, 1964); Frank C. Pierce, *A Brief History of the Lower Rio Grande Valley* (Menosha, Wisconsin: G. Banta, 1917).

[5] Silas Stearns, "Fisheries of the Gulf of Mexico," in G.B. Goode, *The Fisheries and Fishery Industries of the United States*, Sec. II. A Geographical Review . . . 1880, pp. 533-87. U.S. Commission of Fish and Fisheries (Washington: Government Printing Office, 1887), pp. 583, 586.

[6] Charles H. Stevenson, "Report on the Coast Fisheries of Texas" in U.S. Commission of Fish and Fisheries, *Report of the Commissioner for 1889 to 1891*, Part XVII, pp. 373-420. 52d Cong. 2d Sess. House of Rep. Misc. Doc. 113 (Washington: Government Printing Office, 1893), pp. 375-76.

[7] John L. Colp, "Commercial Sailing Scows in the United States," Manuscript Seminar Report. (College Station, Texas: Texas A&M University, 1970), p. 25. The reference is to a newspaper photograph in Rosenberg Library, Galveston, Texas.

[8] Stevenson, *op. cit.*, p. 415.

Specifications of a Barque

Eric J. Ruff

The Book of Genesis, Chapter 6, verses 14 to 16, gives us the specifications of an ark. I would like to share with you some details of a book entitled *Specifications of a Barque . . . .* I found the book in the library of the Yarmouth County Museum some years ago. In my fascination for the contents I resolved to research the book and, at some future date, complete a study on the book.

The book, whose full title is *Specification of a Barque to be built by Archd M'Millan & Son, Steel and Iron Steam and Sailing Ship Builders, Dock Yard, Dumbarton, N.B.* outlines in detail the specifications of the iron barque *Bowman B. Law.* It was some time, however, before I linked the book with the vessel it described for the book gave no name, owner or date. In fact the book initially posed a number of questions — most notably "Why is it in our collection?" Yarmouth's fleet had been al-most entirely constructed of wood in local shipyards. Something else that did not seem to make sense was the yard's location: Dumbarton, N.B. I was not aware of a Dumbarton in New Brunswick, furthermore, I did not think that New Brunswick had a yard capable of building iron and steel square-riggers. Upon investigation "N.B." proved to be North Britain[1] — that made sense!

On coming across a decorative half model in our museum of the iron barque *Bowman B. Law*, built by Archibald MacMillan & Son, things fell into place. A check in *Lloyd's Register* confirmed that the specifications indeed applied to this vessel.

Frederick William Wallace also helped. In *Wooden Ships and Iron Men* he said:

> The year 1885 saw the first break in the ranks of Yarmouth shipping, which for 100 years had developed a mighty fleet of merchantmen of wooden hulls. William Law & Co. — leading Yarmouth shipowners — added the British-built iron barque *Bowman B. Law*, 1359 tons, to their fleet. She was the first iron sailing vessel to be owned in the port.[2]

She was, I believe, the first iron sailing vessel in Nova Scotia and only the second in Canada. The Troop Line of Saint John, New Brunswick, Yarmouth's rival port across the Bay of Fundy, had had built only the previous year the iron ship *Troop* of 1526 tons by the same builders, Archibald MacMillan & Son. Was William Law & Co. trying to "keep up with the Joneses" or had they seen "the writing on wall" on the future of wooden ships? Yarmouth's fleet had peaked in 1878 and had been in decline since then — bowing out to steamers and iron and steel square-riggers.

This movement into iron vessels was a daring one for, although Britain had been building in iron and steel for years, it was only two years earlier in 1883 that the first iron sailing vessel was launched in North America.[3] William Law must have been convinced of the valid-ity of his decision to turn to iron when, in 1886 (one year after building the *Bowman B. Law*), he had built the wooden ship *Louisa M. Fuller* (of 1680 tons) at Tusket, Nova Scotia. Wallace indicates that:

she was a Jonah from the time of her launch, when she stuck
on the ways for about a fortnight. Before the year was out, in
December, while bound from New York to Liverpool with oil,
she met heavy weather, sprung a leak, and had to be
abandoned.[4]

However, in 1890 Law built the small 890 ton wooden ship *Mary A.
Law,* named after his wife. But when, in 1892, he replaced the ship
named for himself, the new *William Law* (of 1631 tons) was of steel.

The *Bowman B. Law* had been named for William Law's eldest
son. Mr. Bowman Brown Law was a well-known man in Yarmouth,
having worked in his father's company which, along with being auc-
tioneers and commission merchants, was the Yarmouth agent for the
Boston Marine Insurance Company, as well as managing, at one time,
a fleet of fourteen or fifteen sailing vessels. Bowman Law was a member of Yarmouth's first town council. He continued in politics and was
elected to the House of Commons in 1902. He held this seat until, in
1916, he died tragically in the conflagration which destroyed the federal Parliament Buildings. He was the only Member of Parliament who
died in the fire.

The vessel, like her namesake, was successful. The fact that she
was still on the Yarmouth registry in 1900 would at least seem to indicate this. A partial list of voyages, provided by the Maritime History
Group at Memorial University, Newfoundland, indicates that the
Bowman B. Law traded to every continent except Africa, but she did
round the Cape of Good Hope at least a dozen times on Far Eastern
voyages. These voyage lists show that she was not necessarily a fast
sailer — one voyage, from Manila to Philadelphia, took 196 days. Also,
like her namesake, the vessel came to an abrupt end; she was cut in
two by a Panamanian freighter.

We must now turn to the specifications of this vessel. Page one of
Specifications of a Barque . . . indicates that the vessel to be built had the
following dimensions: length 232', breadth 37', depth 21.9' "or
thereby." The Nett Tonnage was to be 1325 tons and the "Deadweight
Carrying Capacity with a Freeboard of 2-1/2 inches to each foot of
Hold, 2100 tons."

The iron barque *Bowman B. Low*. (Courtesy of the Yarmouth, Nova Scotia, County Historical Society.)

Once these basic details are covered the book concerns itself with descriptions of the vessel's varous structural elements and equipment. The second part gives an "Inventory of Outfit." For the student of marine history both parts of the book form a valuable insight into the building and outfitting of an iron sailing vessel.

The book starts of off with a section entitled "Class and description" in which the builders indicate that the vessel is:

> To be built to Class 100A1 at Lloyd's under special survey . . . . The vessel is to be barque rigged, and to have a full East India Outfit of the highest class as aftermentioned . . . The plating, frames, beams, etc., etc., are to be of the best quality, and all material and workmanship on the vessel to be of the very best and strongest description, as required by the Society and passed by the Surveyors of Lloyd's Register of Shipping and accepted by the Owners.

The reference to "a full East India Outfit" indicates the quality of the vessel to be built, as the East Indiamen were long regarded as the *ne plus ultra* of the shipping world.[5]

There follows a reference to the deck plan which is "to be submitted for Owner's approval." Unfortunately this is missing. Then follow descriptions of varying lengths, usually short, on Collision Bulkhead, Fittings Before Collision Bulkhead, Sailroom, Etc., Cementing, Scuppers, Bulwarks, Hatches, and Decks. The section dealing with the Main Deck is interesting and representative of the book's detailed descriptions:

> Main Deck of thoroughly well seasoned yellow or pitch pine, reasonably free from knots, efficiently fastened to beams with galvanized screw bolts and nuts, covered with dools set in white lead. One strake of hardwood, 8-in wide next each main deck waterway, and one strake of hardwood, fore and aft, from poop to forecastle, each side of hatches for ringbolts, 8-in wide. Decks to be planed on underside as well as on top, and to be thoroughly caulked, payed and properly finished.

The 'Tween Decks, Poop, Forecastle and Deckhouse Decks are covered, as is the Ceiling:

The bottom to be ceiled with 2/1-2" red pine, well seasoned, and above that to be sparred with pine 8-in, berth and space.

De Kerchove's *International Maritime Dictionary* indicates that this "berth and space" method of ceiling a vessel, also called "spar ceiling", "sparring", "hold sparring", "open sparring" or "open ceiling" simply means that the ceiling above the turn of the bilge was spaced about 9 inches apart. The sparring simply kept the cargo away from the frames and plating which, being iron, was subject to sweating and could cause damage to the cargo. De Kerchove also tells us that this method of sparring was used in ships other than colliers, tankers, and timber and ore carriers. William Law must have been quite optimistic to think that his vessel would not carry coal or timber when these cargoes were becoming "bread and butter" cargoes for sailing ships of the period.

The book continues on to describe the Fiferails, Ladders and Carving, which included "Handsom figure-head and trailboards, with name on bow in brass letters, tastefully painted and gilded."

When the Windlass is described the builder reserved the right to choose between several makes — Harfields, Emerson & Walker's, M'Onie's, Paul's, Napier's or Muir & Caldwell's. Whichever was chosen it was to be fitted on the main deck and was "to be wrought by capstan on forecastle." There were to be two capstans, the one just mentioned, and another, this one a "large double-powered capstan on main deck . . . to be brass-mounted with builder's name engraved." The Pumps, Mooring Bits, Hawsepipes and Steering Gear are enumerated and/or described.

When we come to the description of the tanks we find penciled corrections to the book. I presume that these were made by the owner. They generally indicate reductions in the inventory by crossing out various items. In this instance the "six galvanized bread tanks to contain 10 cwt each" are reduced to two in number. The two galvanized flour tanks and two galvanized pea tanks are crossed out entirely. Presumably his wooden vessels had not required these, why should this vessel! The section on tanks also tells about two 2000 gallon water tanks and four 30 or 40 gallon tanks for oils.

The book indicates that a Portable Fire Engine along with 80 feet of leather hose was to be provided.

The Forecastle, Deckhouse, Poop and Saloon are described. These descriptions are interesting in that they show, by their length alone, the emphasis and lack of emphasis placed on the accommodations provided for the officers and for the crew respectively. These are, I feel, worth quoting:

> *Forecastle* — To plan approved by owners, to accommodate crew. To be fitted up complete with berths, pegs, lockers, tables, stove, etc. Front of forecastle to be of iron. W.C. and boatswain's locker outside of forecastle.

It is interesting to note that the crew was to benefit from the provision of the stove.

The accommodation for the apprentices and petty officers, in the Deckhouse, was a little more luxurious — they were "fitted up with all necessary berths, seats, pegs, lockers, shelves, drawers, dressers, etc."

The captain's and officer's quarters were of a different class entirely. But before quoting the description of the Saloon reflect back for a brief moment on that of the forecastle — "To be fitted up complete with berths, pegs, lockers, table, stove, etc." Here is the corresponding account of the Saloon:

> *Saloon* — sides neatly finished with pannelling of polished maple, teak, or other woods. Polished pilaster, cornice, and gilt trusses. Moulding of beams to be gilded. Rudder stock to be neatly cased.
>
> Sideboard with marble top and brass guard. Large mirror with neat lever clock set in gilt frame. Polished hardwood table, with guards, Six swinging chairs alongside saloon table, and armchair at end of table, stuffed with hair and covered with crimson or other shade of velvet, secured to deck with brass screws. Brass rods in skylight, with large lamp and racks for bottles and glasses. Candle or oil lamp in each room. Six camp stools. Neat stove with iron funnel cased in brass. Neat scuttle for coals and set fire-irons. Saloon staterooms and cap-

tain's room to have Brussels carpet, with runners. Officers'
rooms, pantry, passage, and bath-rooms laid with best wax
cloth or coir matting, or linoleum as required.

All staterooms and officers' rooms to be neatly finished,
with berths, sofas, pegs, wash-basins, soapboxes, jugs, and
receivers, mirrors, bottle, and brush and comb racks; and
brass, oil, or candle gimble lamps. Captain's room to have
berth to draw out with drawers underneath, rack and book-
case, and chronometer stand, in polished hardward. First
officer's room to have polished hardwood drawers underneath berth, also desk. Waxcloth cover and cloth cover for
saloon table. All sofas, settees, chairs and seats in saloon and
staterooms to be stuffed with hair, and covered with velvet.

Following this, the book reverts to the external features of the
vessel. There is a section indicating what painting will be done, the
types of paints used as well as the number of coats to be applied:

All iron work to have one coat oxide of iron and two coats oil
paint. Bottom outside to have an extra finishing coat of colour
as wished. Masts and spars and all wood work to have three
coats of oil paint. Sparring in 'tween decks, underside of main
deck-house, and forecastle decks, to have two coats oil paint.
Buckets, boats, and buoys, to have ship's name painted on
them. All bright work to have a preparatory coat of goal size
and two coats of copal varnish.

The Masts and Spars are described. The fore and main lower
masts and topmasts were to be of one length. These and the mizzen
masts were to be of iron or steel and so fitted as to ventilate the hold.
The bowsprit and jibboom were to be one. This and the lower yards
and lower topsail yards were also to be of iron or steel. Other masts,
yards, booms and gaffs were to be of pitch pine.

The standing rigging was to be of best charcoal or steel wire,
galvanized, served and parcelled to the height of the top. Running
gear was to be of best Russian boltrope.

There were to be four boats:

Size according to Board of Trade requirements, copper fastened, keel and stem plates of iron. Each boat to have six oars, boat-hook, rudder, bailer, axe, galvanized thole-pins and plates, and brass plug. Two boats to have a 40 gal. water breaker. Captain's gig to have brass rowlocks and plates, and fitted with gratings, backboard, and yoke. Two boats with spars and sails.

The final description, in this section of the book, describes the Winches: "a double powered hand winch at fore and main hatch and a portable stevedore's winch." The unknown hand has here pencilled in "none."

The second half of the book is made up of the "Inventory of Outfit." This section is fascinating since it provides such a vast amount of detail. It lists, for example, everything from the bower anchors to the cook's mincing knife, from the house flag to 3 cwt of oakum and from 16 rolls of lamp wicks to one storm spanker.

The following is a list of general headings included in the book and some comments on unusual, at least to me, items in the inventory. The headings for the inventory are:

Anchors & Cables	Sails
Lamps	Upholstery
Ventilators	Small Stores
Sundry Chandlery	Smith's Stores
Cooking Range	Rigger's Stores
Armoury	Napery
Brushes	Glass & crockery ware
Flags	Electroplate & cutlery
Compasses	Hawsers
Paint & Oils	Spare rope
Cooperage	Bells, and
Cook's Stores	Sundries

One of the most interesting observations about the inventory is what is missing. Some items are obvious, for example, "Polished medicine chest with ship's name — but no medicines." Other items are not so obvious. The carpenter's tools and equipment were of particular interest, but were scattered throughout the inventory. Such items as 4 cold chisels, 1 brace and set of drills, 1 grindstone and iron trough, 2 hand hammers and 6 slices are provided, along with 12 dozen screws, 200 each of 3*d*, 4*d*, 6*d*, 8*d*, 10*d* and 1*s* nails and 56 lbs spikes, but basic tools such as saws, planes and screwdrivers are missing. Was a carpenter supposed to bring along his own set of tools, or a partial set, or any?

Similarly, the sailmaker's gear includes 6 sail hooks, 6 palms, 6 seaming and 2 roping palms, 4 dozen sail needles. Six steel marlin-spikes are provided, although the necessary prickers, awls and seam rubbers are not. However, a seam rubber could be easily fashioned on the spot and, in desperation, so could prickers and awls.

Likewise in the navigation department, items such as deep sea lead and line, hand leads and lines, logs, both the patent logline and the old fashioned log roll, along with 2 each of 28 second and 14 second glasses are provided. The basics such as sextants/octants, parallel rules, divider books and charts are not provided (but 12 assorted pencils are!). Most of this is understandable. For example, the builders could not be expected to provide a world-wide outfit of charts. But then, most owners did not provide charts either, that was the master's responsibility, as was the sextant. This too is readily understandable since if a master left one employer who provided a sextant to work for another who did not provide one, the first employer may have found himself short one sextant. The matter of parallel rules might also be explained away by a master's preference for a certain type of rule, although judging from those in the Yarmouth Museum's collection only the conventional type of "parallel rules" was used. What I really do not understand, however, is the crossing out in the inventory, by the unknown hand, of "1 best night binocular glass" and "1 26″ telescope." It seems to me almost criminally negligent to take away such safety items. To pay approximately £12,500 and to scrimp on, at the most, £10 for binoculars, is incredible to me. A brass "Barometer and Sympiesometer combined" was, however, provided.

Another pencil correction eliminates the armory of 6 Enfield muskets and bayonets, 2 revolvers, and the associated cartridges, as well as 2 pairs of handcuffs.

The unkown hand made the comment "Reduction to be made here" in the Electroplate and cutlery section which provided, in the cutlery part, for 12 each of electroplated dinner forks, dinner spoons, dessert spoons, dessert forks, tea spoons, egg spoons, and 12 ivory table knives and dessert knives. Much to Mr. Law's credit, although being a supporter of prohibition and temperance, he did not indicate reduction or omission of 2 cut quart decanters, 2 cut pint decanters, 2 dozen wine glasses, 1 dozen champagne glasses, and 1 dozen claret glasses. I doubt, however, that his Nova Scotian built vessels, or anyone else's Nova Scotian built vessels for that matter, were so well provisioned in this area.

While the saloon was provided with napery, glass, and crockery ware, electroplate and cutlery to do justice to a naval mess dinner, the tableware provided for use by the before-the-mast crew was almost nonexistent. Only 12 mess kits were listed, all in the Cooperage section. The crew's health was safeguarded, however, by the provision of 2 lime-juice measurers.

It is of interest to note that while the carpenter's and sailmaker's tools were restricted, the equipment provided for the cook and steward required two pages to enumerate.

Likewise, the boatswain's stores were well stocked. Included was a large selection of paints and oils provided in built-in tanks and in drums. Some idea of the size of the vessel may be gained from a look at the amount of paint provided: 14 lb packages each of common green, Venetian green, Italian yellow, 2 lbs of vermilion, and 1 lb each of Emerald green and ultra marine. But these were limited quantities when compared with 4 cwt black paint, 4 cwt red lead, 4 cwt white zinc, 4 cwt oxide paint, and 3 cwt mast colour paint, all provided in 1 cwt round iron drums for a total of 19 cwt of paint. Also listed was 3 cwt oakum, 1 barrel pitch, 1 barrel resin, and 2 barrels of Archangel tar.

Spare rope provided for the barque ranged from 450 fathoms of variously sized rope (90 fathoms each of 4-1/2", 4", 3-1/2", 3", and 2-1/2" boltrope) to quantities of small stuff. This did not include two 90 fathom rope hawsers and a steel wire hawser; the latter as per Lloyd's requirement.

As to be expected, all the sails are listed by name, number of each, and type of canvas used for each. But again the unknown hand has made reductions. He has opted for only 1 mainsail and 1 main topmast staysail instead of the 2 each listed and has crossed out the main royal staysail, the mizen topgallant staysail, and mizen royal staysail. The choice of canvas to be used was open. To his credit, and probably his pocketbook as well, the unknown hand has written in "Yarmouth Duck Co." I am assuming that the unknown hand was William Law's, and I expect that he, like most of the influential Yarmouthians of his time, had shares in the Yarmouth Duck and Yarn Company.

Finally, the *Specifications of a Barque . . .* concludes with the following general statement and written-in comment:

> The vessel to be built to the satisfaction of owners, or their superintendent, in accordance with the requirements of Lloyds for the highest mark under special survey. To be completely and efficiently equipped in all respects . . . the vessel is to be delivered to owners all complete, with a suit of sails, bent sheeted home, and stowed . . . all running gear rove, boats, water casks, spars, etc., lashed and everything ready for use . . .

Then, the pencilled comment, undoubtedly the most important of the book: "9 pounds-10(s) per register ton nett."

This then is the specification book for an iron barque. Although rare on this side of the Atlantic, such books were, at one time, quite common in Britain. They were used by many of the larger shipyards and were issued not only to the owner, *Lloyd's Register* and others, but also to foremen and managers working on vessels.[6]

Interestingly enough, the quality of workmanship referred to throughout the book was indeed carried out — a fact proven by the Lloyd's survey report on the *Bowman B. Law* which states under the "General Remarks" section, "Workmanship good." This report also indicates that following her survey she was to begin her working life under Capt. Bryon Abbott of Yarmouth on a voyage to Rio de Janeiro.

Notes

Quotations, items of gear, etc., referred to in the text of this paper were spelled, capitalized, and abbreviated as they appeared in *Specifications of a Barque* . . . .

[1] Richard Dell, Principal Archivist, Strathclyde Regional Archives advised me that "N.B." standing for "North Britain" "was standard usage in the United Kingdom after the Union (evidently to play down Scottish separation)."

[2] F.W. Wallace, *Wooden Ships and Iron Men* (London, n.d.), p. 297.

[3] J.M. Lawson, *Yarmouth Reminiscences* (Yarmouth, 1902), p. 633 indicates: "First iron sailing vessel built in U.S. or on American continent, was launched in May, 1883, by John Roach, at Chester, Pa. She was 250' Keel, 42-1/2' beam, 23-1/2' deep, 220 tons burden and carried 3300 tons deadweight with a draught of 21-1/2'."

[4] F.W. Wallace, *op. cit.*, p. 300.

[5] Peter Kemp, ed., *The Oxford Companion to Ships and the Sea* (London, 1976), p. 281.

[6] A.S.E. Browning, Deputy Director, Glasgow Museums and Art Galleries.

Live oak (*Quercus virginiana*) along the Ashley River, South Carolina. (*Courtesy, Library of Congress.*)

Live Oaking for Ships Timber

Virginia Steele Wood

A hundred and fifty years ago when a shipwright said he was going live oaking, friends and neighbors all knew he was headed south for a winter of cutting trees and hewing out ships' timber. For over a century thousands of skilled craftsmen worked in the live-oak hummocks and the ultimate results of their labor — naval vessels, whaleships, packets, and clipper ships — were found in seaports around the world.

A member of the beech family, live oak (*Quercus virginiana*), is found only along the Atlantic seaboard from southeastern Virginia to the Texas border and on the west coast of Cuba. Its height is usually 40 to 70 feet but the crowns of single trees can span 150 feet or more, easily shading half an acre. The trunks are often 20-odd feet in circumference dividing 5 to 18 feet from the ground to form several

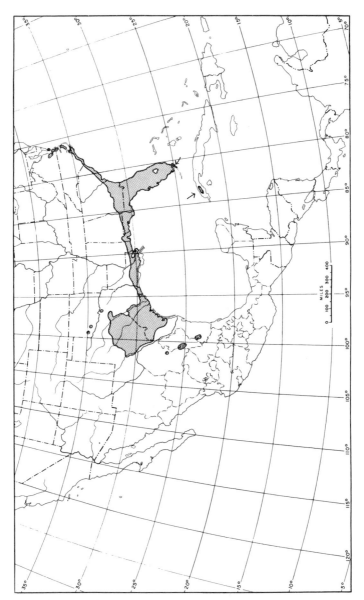

Natural range for live oak (*Quercus virginiana*).
(*Courtesy of the U.S. Department of Agriculture.*)

immense, curved, horizontal limbs. The weight of a single branch stretching 60 to 75 feet is measured in tons and attests to the toughness and durability of the wood. From Colonial times, shipwrights were attracted to these naturally curved branches that demonstrated great tensile strength and resistance to rot; such qualities provided the ideal combination for shipbuilding.

Because the foliage sheds only once a year after new growth appears, the trees are known as semi-evergreens. For this reason we call them live oaks; during the Colonial period they were often referred to as "evergreen oaks." Live oak is the heaviest oak we have; its denseness is accounted for in part because the wood contains less air than most trees. As the heartwood forms, the vascular system fills with a waxy gum, blocking the air passages. The tree's tolerance to salt spray permits it to dominate rival hardwoods along river bluffs, the edge of salt marshes, creeks, and swamps.[1] Some varieties of live oak are found in California and other regions of the southwest, but they should not be confused with *Quercus virginiana.*

Contrary to a misconception based on a statement published in the last century, live oak *was* used in shipbuilding well before 1740.[2] The early American colonists were too dependent on sailing vessels to survive without building their own, and they were quick to appreciate the excellent timber at hand for construction. Although finding southern live oak extremely difficult to work, they used it nevertheless, proclaimed its value in descriptions of the New World's resources, and even named their ships for it. In 1709, for example, John Lawson wrote that the curved limbs made excellent knees for ships but "the firmness and great Weight thereof frightens our Sawyers from the Fatigue that attends the cutting of this Timber. A Nail once driven therein 'tis next to an Impossibility to draw it out."[3]

Prior to the Revolutionary War shipbuilders at least as far north as Philadelphia found live oak worth the expense of freighting to their yards, and it was used there in building ships during the war.[4] Following the Revolution, domestic needs for the timber were limited to merchant vessels, and efforts of southern planters to export it for naval use in Britain and France met with little success although it was much favored in commercial shipyards abroad.

A major change occurred in 1794 when the United States was forced into building a navy to protect her commercial interests from the scourge of the Barbary pirates, and Georgia live oak was required by the War Department as an "indispensable" component in the first six frigates. Futtocks, knight heads, hawsepieces, bow timbers, stanchions, knees, transoms, and breasthooks were to be made of live oak. It was expected to last five times as long as white oak, and given the life expectancy of ten years for a wooden warship, this meant the ships would last fifty years barring shipwreck and other disasters.[5] (One of the six frigates, USS *Constitution*, launched in 1797, was nicknamed "Old Ironsides" because of her live oak frames).

Since local labor along the southern coast was primarily agricultural, skilled shipwrights had to be recruited in the North because the War Department decided that unless moulds were transported to the site, expensive mistakes would be made. The saving on shipping space and freight charges would also be advantageous. During the summer of 1794, eighty skilled shipwrights from New London, Connecticut and the New Bedford, Massachusetts area were hired to go south, live in camps of their own making, fell and hew the timber to mould.[6] This ushered in a practice that resulted in large-scale live oaking operations that continued for nearly a hundred years.

Demands for naval and commercial ships timber were particularly high between the American Revolution and Civil War , both here and in Europe. Such demands precipitated the federal government's attempt to protect its timber needs by designating more than a quarter million acres of land as public domain exclusively for the live oak and red cedar.[7] The problem of protecting so vast a semitropical wilderness from illegal cutting, however, was never satisfactorily solved; neither legislative action nor limited patrols of the area could effectively stop indiscriminate pillage that was carried on for decades. The one attempt at conservation — cultivating live oak in a government-sponsored nursery — soon ended because of bitter animosity between political factions and the nation's tenaciously held myth of inexhaustible resources. Meanwhile, the finest whaleships, clippers, and packets were those whose builders and owners could boast were "live-oak built."

Throughout most of the nineteenth century along the Atlantic and Gulf coasts from Maine to Louisiana, the terms *live oaking* and *live oaker* were in common use from high government official to shipyard worker. As Congress authorized construction of naval vessels and the Navy Department advertised for live oak in quantities of thousands of cubic feet "cut to mould," bids were eagerly submitted by northern shipbuilders who could hire the skilled labor necessary to supply it. Their undertaking — locating available timber and obtaining cutting rights; recruiting, organizing, and transporting large groups of men and equipment, oxen, timber carts, and provisions for five- to six-month periods; overseeing the operation; and chartering and scheduling vessels to ship the timber north — seems formidable. Setting up camps; overcoming the physical hazards in cutting roads for hauling through a veritable jungle; felling immense trees; hewing and hauling the timber to landings; loading it onto scows; then reloading onto schooners for twelve, fourteen, or more hours a day while living under primitive conditions is a testimony to remarkable endurance and skill. Untold thousands of men were involved in the work, until it tapered off as the age of sail gave way to transport by steel ships and rail, powered by steam engines. Live oaking then became a thing of the past; it faded from memory and is now all but forgotten.

Since the maritime requirements for live-oak timber called for cutting it in winter while the sap was down, the labor force was recruited through newspaper advertisements each fall in northeastern shipbuilding communities. The contracts were non-negotiable; signing on meant agreeing to abide by all terms. Employers carried on, blissfully free of such notions as social security, minimum wages, fair-employment practices, health insurance, and withholding tax. There was no portal-to-portal pay and no workmen's compensation to cover injury or illness; a day's pay for a day's labor was the practice. Wages commenced after the men reached their destination and unloaded the schooners; they were paid at the season's end. Each man supplied his own tools and bedding, each was guaranteed passage south and "wholesome provisions" from the time of sailing until discharge.[8]

Among a group of nearly one hundred men who signed on with Swift Brothers in New Bedford for the 1855-56 season, wages for ordinary choppers were $15 to $18 a month; for hewers it was $23 to $28;

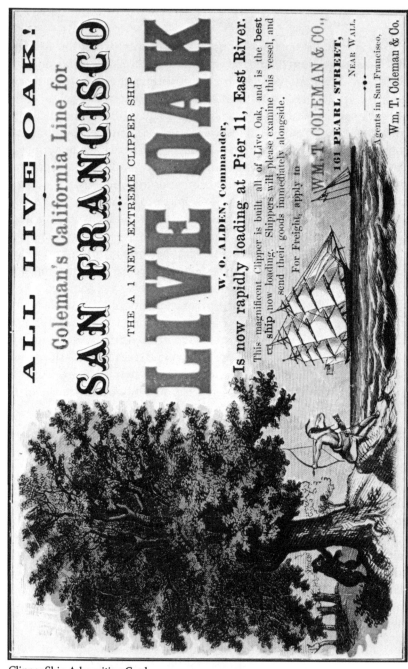

Clipper Ship Adversiting Card
(*Photography by M.W. Sexton, courtesy of the Peabody Museum of Salem.*)

narrow axemen, $15 to $18. The two cooks received $21 and $25; two teamsters each received $20; two blacksmiths $20 and $23; seven flat-boatmen were paid $18 and $19, but the captain got $40. There was a liner at $26 and a road cutter at $19. Nine young boys went along to do odd jobs and start learning how to use an axe — they each received $10. Pay of the foreman was $100 a month — twice as much as a general in the United States Army.[9]

The group was sent south on schooners with all their equipment and supplies including food, oxen, and timber carts. There was something of a holiday spirit aboard since the live oakers were passengers and the crew did all the work — unless there was a bad storm and all hands were called out to help.

On arrival they unloaded everything from schooner onto scows then took it ashore. There they got busy cutting poles for the frame-work of huts. Great palmetto leaves were bound together and used for the roof and sides as protection against rain.[10] Then the real work began.

Since green live oak weighs about 75 pounds a cubic foot it could not be floated downstream. So from the spot where it fell and was hewn, all of it had to be hauled to a landing by oxen and timber carts. For this reason, the first job of choppers was to cut oaks nearest the landing. As available timber was cleared, the men began working back into the woods, eventually walking several miles away from camp to find suitable trees.

Whether the men were clearing roads, felling trees, removing branches, or hewing great timbers, their only tool was a simple axe. The felling or narrow axe they used was single-bitted, the sides slightly concave, smooth or beveled. The helve was straight. Its weight depended on the type work to be done and on individual pref-erence, but three to four pounds was average. Its main purposes were for felling trees, swamping underbrush, and making logs.

All the work on hand-hewing timber was done with broadaxes. Because their poles are heavy and square, they generally have a re-versible bit — that is, they can be used by either a right-handed or left-handed hewer, depending on which way the helve is wedged into the eye. The head's inner face is flat and the outer side slightly concave, with a cutting bevel of half to three-quarters of an inch. Heads generally weigh six to nine pounds; helves vary in length and shape, but all are curved so the user can hew at the proper angle and avoid scraping his knuckles.

From each camp the superintendent sent in periodic reports to shipyard offices or Navy Board Commissioners indicating the quantity of inspected, moulded timber on hand and the number of "sticks rolled up" ready for shipment. "Sticks" are felled trees with branches removed. They can measure over a hundred feet in length and weigh more than a ton. The hauling was done with a vehicle variously called a timber cart, logging cart, big wheels, logging wheels, balance wheels or merely "a set of wheels." These were taken south each fall by the live oakers and when dismantled they were relatively easy to transport on schooners.

Made of wood, the carts were a simple device for lifting and moving heavy objects over bad roads. The huge wooden wheels had a diameter of seven to twelve feet; they were bound with iron tires six to eight inches wide, and the pair connected with a single axle. It required less labor and time to raise objects under this high axle than it did to load onto the top of conventional wagons. The principle involved in loading is simple. Attached to the wooden bed over the axle were a pole and a tongue, to which chains were fastened. The teamster had his cart pulled alongside the stick at an angle and "jumped it" with one wheel, to straddle the stick. Then he positioned the cart a few inches behind the balance point. This was a little tricky. The cart was then tilted backward and the teamster passed a strong, heavy chain under the stick and hooked it to the pole. As the tongue was pulled forward and down by the oxen, it acted as a lever, hoisting the stick under the axle and swinging it off the ground. A second chain secured it to the tongue. With the heavy butt end of the stick forward, the pull on the animals was uniform. If a cart fell on its side while "jumping" a stick the driver simply used his oxen to right the cart; and then began all over again. The principle involved in releasing a load was even more straightforward: As one experienced in such matters put it, "Just unhook the chain and git outta th' way." It all sounds simple, but it required patience as well as skill, and good temper helped.[11]

These two-wheeled carts pulled by teams of oxen were used for hauling timber
in the shipyards and in the "live oak fields" down South. The wheels measured
up to 12 feet in diameter.
(*Courtesy Library of Congress. Photo by Barry Donahue.*)

Driving one of those carts was a hazardous occupation. They were unwieldy vehicles, and they could be killers. As a Florida logging man explained, "Sometimes the tongue gets away when lifted upright and falls over backward. At that time the driver is in double danger. If the tongue doesn't get him, when the axle turns upside [down] the linchpins come out letting the wheels fall off."[12] No one could expect to escape serious injury or death if one of these huge wheels crushed him, but when accidents happened on the job they were usually considered the victim's own fault for being careless.

"Skidding" timber meant raising the long stick butt end first under the axle and dragging it behind the cart. Up to fourteen oxen would be used in skidding, the number depending on the weight of the stick, the distance to be covered, and conditions of the road or trail.

"Snaking" was the method employed to drag timber out of the forest using oxen but no timber cart. It was recommended only for short distances — a few hundred feet through thick undergrowth, or over crude trails where only large obstacles had been removed — until a better road was reached where the timber could be hauled or skidded. Oxen continued to be used long after horses and mules became popular. Horses were too nervous for the job and mules panic when their feet are mired in the swamps, but cloven feet of oxen prevent this. In addition, oxen could endure pulling heavy loads day after day for longer periods.

Blacksmiths were as necessary to the live-oaking operation as they were to the shipyard, the town, and country village. Any smith who joined a live-oak gang was responsible for keeping the group's equipment in good working order. He made iron dogs for hewing; mended chains for snaking and hauling timber; repaired the trace chains on ox harnesses, the pole rings and bowpins on ox yokes, and all the bolts, screws, washers, and pins that held the yokes and wheels together. Iron tires for timber carts were too big and heavy to be made outside a full-equipped blacksmith shop where a crane was necessary to lift them from forge to anvil, but the smith could patch and mend the tires in camp.

Since there were too few draft animals in a live-oak camp to warrant hiring farriers, the smith took on that task as well. Southern oxen were rarely shod, but New England cattle needed protection from rocky ground and the clutter of shipyards; therefore, they were accustomed to it. Shoeing an ox was more complicated than shoeing a horse, because the animal's cloven hoof required a pair of shoes for each foot, and since the animals were unable to stand on three small feet, their tremendous weight had to be supported in a sling. It is impressive to watch three strong men pushing and cajoling, pulling and goading an obstinate ox into position while staying clear of his great horns as he lunges suddenly and tried to turn or back away. Once inside the ox frame, his head is placed in a stanchion, then tied to supports on either side with a rope. A canvas sling fitted under his belly and raised by means of a winch, supports rather than suspends, his weight. Kicking is prevented by securing each leg to the frame with a rope, and the tail is anchored. One at a time, each foot requiring a shoe is pulled back with a hook or rope and tied down on a small wooden shelf for the smith's convenience. All this is accompanied by great moaning, bellowing, straining and thrashing about — the shoeing is not painful, only frightening to the ox.[13]

The tenor of life in a live-oak camp and morale of the men was contingent upon the extent of their daily labor; the weather; the rules and regulations; the competence and fairness of their superintendent; and, most of all, their food. From the time of embarkation until discharge, employers were usually obliged to feed the gang; however, there is a dramatic contrast between our notions of good food and what they called "wholesome provisions." Dried salt fish, salt pork and beef; dried beans; flour; cornmeal; salt; pepper; tea; coffee; and molasses were the provisions best suited to survive a journey south. Hardtack was a staple familiar to all. Baked beans, johnny cake, and hasty pudding were frequently served.[14] Doughnuts, those irregular, deep-fried lumps dubbed the cook's own langrage-shot, became the familiar "pellets of indigestion."

Meals were informal, and the men sat around on logs or simple split-log benches, the latter known in New England as "deacon seats." Pieces of salt pork were "tried out" in three-legged frying pans (called "spiders") set directly over the coals. These in turn became common platters, each man taking turns sopping up the melted hog lard with his bread, salt, fish, or meat. This, it was claimed, served to lubricate the joints; molasses gave tenacity to the muscles. Later on, individual tin plates and cups were considered necessities.

Occasional surprises necessitated altering the predictible daily menu. A newly opened barrel of pork was found spoiled and unfit to eat, the hardtack got wet or became infested with maggots that "wouldn't budge," or they discovered the meal and flour alive with weevils. In a pinch there was always the reliable old shipboard special called "souse" or "lobscouse" — a combination of finely pounded hardtack, bits of salt beef, and potatoes boiled together in water and presumably made palatable with salt and pepper. The sweet served up was usually "duff," the dough pudding well known ashore and rated such a luxury among American seamen. Tea or coffee helped aid digestion.

Considering the hard labor, poor food, and casual standards of hygiene, it is not surprising that illness was common among the live oakers. Stomach ailments, bowel disorders, colds, and the chills and fever of malarial attacks were common. It was, of course, the era of "heroic" medicine when rigorous treatments of blood-letting, sweating, blistering, purging the system, and inducing sleep were commonly prescribed. A physician's treatment often seemed worse than the cure, so it is little wonder that good tasting patent medicines with a high alcoholic content were popular. In camp, when live oakers sustained serious injury from the cut of a sharp axe or a falling branch, they were dependent on their superintendent to tend them unless help could be obtained from some doctor in a nearby community.[15]

When the weather was inclement, idleness bred a dangerous discontent in camp and before the temperance movement successfully eliminated the grog ration, a good deal of drunkenness and fighting took place. One group of live oakers was supplied with nearly a gallon of whiskey a week, per man in 1816.[16] During the fall of 1820 Isaac Thomas of Bath, Maine purchased his own rum at twenty-five cents a quart and during the winter live-oaking season he bought as much as half a gallon of rum a day. The following March notice of his demise was entered simply as one more item against his account: "Funeral expenses, $2.00."[17] In all fairness, it must be noted that many refused the rum ration either out of personal preference or on religious grounds.

As spring advanced and available timber was cleared, employers began closing down their operations. In camps where live oakers numbered a hundred men or more, dismissal took place gradually over a period of weeks. Each man packed his belongings, checked over his account in the ledger, signed it before a witness, was paid off (minus what he owed his employer), and made his way back North. The superintendents and teamsters were the last to leave.

Most of the men returned home as they had arrived, by ship. It was the least expensive way, and they had to pay their own passage. In the mid-nineteenth century a ship passage from Louisiana to Massachusetts cost about $50, over half the total wages for some. Therefore, the expense of transportation home made live oaking no more profitable than whaling to an ordinary seaman.[18]

After a season in camp there was nothing ambiguous about the meaning of *toil*, and many bid the job goodbye forever. Each gang's experience was unique; together they endured common dangers and hardships, together they shared camaraderie and humor. Whether a man returned to camp or not, he took home memories enough to last a lifetime.

Appendix

The following letter provides one New Englander's reaction to life in a Louisiana live-oak camp during the 1850s:

Attakapas [Louisiana] Sunday March 11th [18]58

Brother Jonathan i have just received your letter and it was as good as a feast To get a few words from poisett [Mattapoisett] once in a while This is what i call a hard old country and most eny thing new goes well after being shut up in The woods for four months it is now twelve oclock and The horn is blowing for dinner so i will go and see what They have got so nice well i have got my dinner down. They had what They call duff a passel of flour boiled up in a rag one pound of it is as heavy as Two pounds of lead Taking our group on an everage i Think wee have lived very well for a Live oak gang wee have had plenty of sweet potatoes and dough nuts evry night wee have Two Cooks They cook a flour barrel full of Them evry day Thair is Thirty seven men all told in our gang Twenty hewers wee have now Twenty five thousand feet of Timber and one hundred and Twenty five sticks rowled up for morning The other two gangs i suppose have about The same wee begin to have the weather pretty warm now The Trees are leafed out The black bury vines have been in bloom about a month and begin to fall of i suppose will be ripe The last of next month i rather Think wee shall get away for home by The 2nd of April i dont Think our Timber will hold out eny longer Then That wee will not moove agane at eny rate wee have had it very muddy The most of The Time but it is now getting quite dry wee havnt had eny rain of eny account for a month The snakes and Aligators begin to crawl out quite smart one of our boys killed a morgason yesterday mesureing six feet and eight inches and another fellow a rattle snake with nign rattles i have not got the paper you sent me yet i suppose likely some one will read it before i get it it generaly Takes a paper one week longer To come Then it does a letter i expect you Fellows will make your whack on building That ship Tell Dan not to work To hard on Them plank i wish i was Thair To help him Tell him That i Think he missed it awfully by not comeing out hear for the privalidge of leaving hear for home will be worth a few hundred Tell him not to curse old Deacon quite so bad Tell Bill darkey it pears like its going to rain Tell Studly to keep that steam box not for i calculate to be Thair To put Them bottom plank on The boys plague Burbank all most to death he sez ile be damed if i would go live oaking agane if They would give mee all of Louiseanna for thair is nothing goes but a pack of god damed hogs he sayed when wee first get hear if eny one got to fighting they should be discharged so evry once in a while after dark about a dozen of Them will mat in and pretend to be fighting untill they get The old fellow to rairing They keep him in a fret about all the Time They dont like him atal and i rather Think when They get payed of he will get knocked if he dont keep scarse give my how de do to all hands and tell them i hope to bee among them soon

Ben

Notes

[1] H.A. Fowells, comp., *Silvics of Forest Trees of the United States*. Agriculture Handbook No. 271. (Washington: Division of Timber Management Research, Forest Service, U.S. Department of Agriculture, 1965), pp. 584-87.

[2] J. Leander Bishop, *A History of American Manufactures from 1608 to 1860* . . . (Philadelphia: Edward Young & Co., 1868), I, p. 85.

[3] John Lawson, *A New Voyage to Carolina: Containing the Exact Description and Natural History, of That Country* . . . (London: J. Knapton, 1708-1710), p. 92.

[4] Wharton and Humphreys Ship Yard Accounts, 1773-1795. Joshua Humphreys Papers, Historical Society of Pennsylvania; *Naval Documents of the American Revolution*, ed. William Bell Clark (vols. 1-4), William James Morgan (vols. 5-8) (Washington, D.C.: U.S. Government Printing Office, 1968-81), 3, pp. 1039-40; 5, p. 1046.

[5] *American State Papers, Naval Affairs* (Washington: Gales and Seaton, 1834), I, pp. 6-8.

[6] Tench Coxe to John T. Morgan, 12 June 1794; Coxe to Jedediah Huntington, 15 June 1794; Letters of Tench Coxe, Commissioner of the Revenue, Relating to the Procurement of Military, Naval, and Indian Supplies, 1794-1796, RG75, Microcopy M-74, Naval Records Collection of the Office of Naval Records and Library. Correspondence on Naval Affairs when Navy was under the War Department 1790-1798, RG45, Entry 374, National Archives; *Connecticut Gazette* (New London), 26 June, 25 September 1794.

[7] Franklin B. Hough, *Report Upon Forestry* (Washington: U.S. Government Printing Office, 1878), p. 11; H. Ex. Doc 116, 40th Cong., 2 d. sess. (1869).

[8] Theodate Geoffrey (Dorothy Wayman), *Suckanesset: Wherein May Be Read a History of Falmouth, Massachusetts* (Falmouth: Privately printed, 1930), p. 89; Swift Brothers of New Bedford, collection of live oaking contracts, 1855 and 1857, in possession of Obed N. Swift.

[9] *Ibid*.

[10] "Live-oaking in Southern Forests. Jacob W. Chase, One of the Few Surviving Woodmen Who Worked for Swift Brothers in 1855," *Sunday Standard* (New Bedford), 13 February 1910.

[11] "Log Carts, with Enormous Wheels, Carried 100-Foot Pines to Sawmill," *Tribune* (Tampa), 13 January 1957; " 'Frog' Smith discusses the Old Log Cart — Team of Mules and No Brakes," *Tribune* (Tampa), 27 January 1957; J. Brewer Owens, personal interview, Brunswick, Ga., 18 March 1973. See also:

Ralph Clement Bryant, *Logging. The Principles and General Methods of Operation in the United States* (New York: John Wiley and Sons, 1914).

[12] *Tribune*, 27 January 1957.

[13] Dawes Markwell, "Handy Oxen," *The Chronicle of the Early American Industries Association, Inc.* 35 (June 1972):18; See also: Lewis F. Allen, *American Cattle: Their History, Breeding and Management* (New York: Taintor Brothers & Co., 1868), pp. 293-96.

[14] Henry Adams, *History of the United States of America During The First Administration of Thomas Jefferson, 1801-1805* (New York: Charles Scribner's Sons, 1889), I, pp. 44-45: Swift Brothers Account Book, 1858-1859, Whaling Museum, Old Dartmouth Historical Society.

[15] Virginia Steele Wood, ed., "James Keen's Journal of a Passage from Philadelphia to Blackbeard Island, Georgia, for Live Oak Timber, 1817-1818," *The American Neptune* 35 (1975), pp. 227-47.

[16] J.H. Easterby, "Shipbuilding on St. Helena Island in 1816," *South Carolina Historical and Genealogical Magazine* 47 (1946), pp. 218-19.

[17] Green & Emerson Account Ledger, 1819-1821, Maine Maritime Museum.

[18] *Sunday Standard* (New Bedford), 13 February 1910.

[19] Ben (surname not given) to Jonathan Hiller, 11 March 1858, in possession of Mrs. Howard Hiller, Rochester, Mass.

Underway Replenishment, 1799-1800

Tyrone G. Martin

It is a popular view that the technique of underway replenishment — the mobile logistic support of naval forces at sea — was developed and brought to a high level of efficiency by the United States Navy in the course of World War II. Samuel Eliot Morison, in his voluminous naval history of that era, took a somewhat longer view and traced the origins of the procedure to the world cruise of Teddy Roosevelt's Great White Fleet. A still longer view has uncovered evidence that the United States Navy first intentionally practiced underway replenishment during the Quasi-War with France.

The Quasi-War may be said to have begun with President John Adams' signing of the act authorizing maritime defense measures against French transgressors on 28 May 1798, four weeks after the creation of the Navy Department and three before the first Navy

Secretary, Benjamin Stoddert, took office. The conflict with France basically was caused by the infringement on neutral American commerce by a France embroiled in a war with England. The act signed by President Adams provided for the defense of that commerce, nothing more.

During the summer of 1798, the new United States Navy was created from vessels purchased for the purpose and a pitiful few built for it. As the number of units increased and stronger measures were authorized, the defensive operations shifted outward from sparse patrols along our coast to the stationing of units in the West Indies, which then was the scene of the bulk of American trade. The first squadron ordered in December 1798 was under Commodore John Barry, senior officer of the young Navy, in *United States* (44 guns), to be based on Prince Rupert's Bay, Dominica. From this friendly anchorage, protective patrols were sent out to cover American shipping and suppress French naval and privateering activity coming principally from nearby Guadeloupe. Barry's theater of operations encompassed the area from St. Kitts southward through the Windward Islands to the continent and westward to include Curaçao. A second squadron was established under Commodore Thomas Truxtun in *Constellation* (38) to patrol between St. Kitts and Puerto Rico, the former being his rendezvous. Two smaller squadrons (generally two or three ships) were organized to protect American shipping in the Windward Passage and the waters north of Cuba. All of these squadrons were sustained through supplies delivered to, or purchases made in, their places of rendezvous.

To regress for a moment: in August 1791, Saint Domingue, the French western end of Hispaniola Island, erupted in revolution, black slaves against white masters. In the intervening years, General Pierre François Domingue Toussaint L'Ouverture, a former slave, had emerged as the strongest and most responsible among several rebels vying for power. As a part of the action taken by Congress and the President during May-July 1798 to protect American shipping, an embargo was placed on all trade with the French colony which, until then, had derived the bulk of its needed supplies from the United States. Driven by the increasing plight of his people, in November of that year L'Ouverture wrote to Adams urgently requesting resumption of trade. In March 1799, the President responded that all privateering originating in Haiti would have to be suppressed as a prerequisite condition. The island leader initiated the action in April, and Adams issued a decree late in June which would lift the trade embargo with Haiti effective 1 August. On 27 July, Secretary Stoddert issued orders to Captain Silas Talbot of *Constitution* (44) to proceed to Santo Domingo by a circuitous route and once there "assume command of all American vessels on that station . . . ."[1]

Talbot sailed from Norfolk, Virginia, on 25 August. After passing east and southward of the Windward Islands and reconnoitering the South American coast between Cayenne and Surinam, he turned northward along the islands, looked in at Basseterre Roads, Guadeloupe, and arrived off Monte Cristi, Haiti, on 15 October. There, he rendezvoused with frigate *Boston* (28). In the offing were frigate *General Greene* (28) and brig *Norfolk* (18). The three subordinate Captains soon were on board the flagship, briefing Talbot on the situation as they had found it. None had been in the area very long. One matter they almost certainly apprised Talbot of was the concern of Consul Edward Stevens about having the American units appear in Haitian ports, particularly once their protective activities began to have an effect on local "enterprise." So volatile were conditions ashore that it was impossible to predict what might result if, say, *Constitution* came in for some time in order to make routine repairs. And so strong were Dr. Stevens' concerns in this regard that he already had written to Benjamin Stoddert requesting the Secretary to make every effort to sustain the squadron with minimum use of these ports. The matter was not of immediate import, however, as all units were recently from home or friendly ports. Following dinner and receipt of the Commodore's orders, the captains returned to their ships and made for their several stations. Until the squadron was increased in size, little more could be done than patrol the likeliest areas of danger and hope for the best. *Constitution's* area kept her generally within thirty miles of Cap François (Cap Haitien today)[2]. Ship *Herald* (20) joined the squadron on 16 November. She was first assigned a patrol area closer inshore of *Constitution*.

As the days passed, and his correspondence with Dr. Stevens flourished (via ship's boat or itinerant trader), the Commodore gained a deeper understanding of conditions in the strife-torn land. In line with the Consul's wishes, Talbot wrote to Naval Agent Nathan Levy at the Cap on 24 November requesting that he seek to charter a "watering vessel" with which to supply his units that most necessary commodity on-station. He also ordered quantities of limes, oranges, onions, yams, plantains, beeves, goats, sheep, and Indian meal or oat meal. Clearly, the intent was to keep all American warships clear of the local citizenry. Unfortunately, Levy reported three days later that no ship was available. In consequence, Talbot evolved, in the weeks which followed, a practice of using the smaller units of the squadron and amenable passing merchantmen calling at Cap François to bring out supplies to the others, and especially to his immediate command, *Constitution*.

By this time, *Constitution* had been literally scraping the bottom of the barrel, so long had she been underway. Twice in recent days she had received small amounts from *General Greene*, but not enough to sustain so large a crew (about 400). Talbot thus was forced to leave his station and proceed westward to Saint Nicholas Mole, a port removed from the Americans' principal scene of activity, where water could be had and the presence of another Naval Agent offered the prospect of additional logistic support. The big frigate arrived on 2 December, coming to anchor in twenty-four fathoms just as eight bells struck in the dog watches. Noted the log:

> From our last anchorage to this is one hundred days which time we have been at Sea three men we lost overboard and 6 died, Sent a Commissioned officer and three midshipmen on watering service . . . .

Watering the ship and overhauling her rigging proceeded smoothly. The ground tier of ninety leaguers, forty-six butts, and thirty gang casks was filled before noon on 5 December. The whole watering operation ended on the afternoon of the 6th, with 191 tons of water stowed below — 45,840 gallons. She was on her way back to patrol station 6 AM on Sunday, 8 December.[3]

The routine known in October and November 1799 was reestablished with one change: fresh water was strictly controlled. Schooner *Experiment* (12) and brig *Augusta* (14) joined the squadron, and *General Greene* was permitted to enter port for a badly needed overhaul. On 14 December, Talbot began experiencing some of the top hamper problems that had plagued the ship during her earlier operations with Commodore Barry's squadron. The foremast tressletrees were found to be sprung and had to be replaced, and it was necessary to redo the gammoning on the bowsprit, which had somehow loosened. On the 17th, a more serious problem became apparent: "Observed the Mainmast to labour very much about 10 or 12 feet below the Treeltrees (sic)." Further observation revealed severe checking in the mast. For the next month, the Carpenter strove to insure that the mast would not be lost completely, ultimately fitting it with two 32-foot-long oaken fishes wolded in place with 120 fathoms of 6-inch hawser.[4] In this case, the range of talent and extent of supplies inherent in the big frigate made is possible to effect these repairs within her own resources while at sea. The smaller ships were much less capable.

The Navy Department-chartered schooner *Elizabeth*, twenty-six days from Philadelphia, rendezvoused with *Constitution* at 10 AM on 30 December, laden with stores for the Santo Domingo Squadron. She was the first in a series arranged for by Benjamin Stoddert in response to Consul Stevens' urging. In the first underway replenishment in the United States Navy, Commodore Talbot took the merchantman in tow and commenced the transfer of stores by ships' boats. In twelve hours, the frigate took aboard 260 barrels of bread, seventy-five each of beef and pork, fifteen of Indian meal, ten of flour, thirty of potatoes, and eight of cheese, as well as four tierces of rice and one of pease, another "small cask" of pease, and six kegs of butter. A heavy swell from the northward brought a halt to the operation until daylight. Another ten hours of heavy labor completed the task, and at eight bells of the afternoon watch *Elizabeth* was ordered to proceed and replenish *Boston*.[5]

There exists a tale about *Constitution* wherein she conducts a highly successful six month cruise, regularly capturing enemy ships and just as regularly relieving them of their stocks of spiritous liquors. The story concludes with the frigate returning to Boston with the same thousands of gallons of water with which she sailed, but totally bereft of the strong stuff. There is the smallest grain of truth in the story, witness this log entry for the afternoon watch on 8 January 1800:

> Served half allowance of Spirits to Ships company the Rum being Totally expended.

Fortunately for all hands, *Boston* soon rendezvoused with the flagship and early the next afternoon transferred "thirty gallons of Rum for ships use, served out full allowance of Spirits to Ships company." On 13 January, *General Greene*, newly cut from Cap François following overhaul, improved the situation markedly by delivering sixteen kegs and four pipes of brandy, two puncheons of rum, and fifteen small kegs of gin to *Constitution*, together with at least nine hogsheads of molasses, four casks of vinegar, one of oil, two casks of stonelime, one cask of fruit limes, and a box of candles.[6]

Late in January, Talbot chased and brought to an "American polacky" (polacre: a three-masted vessel with lateen rig). He received 120 gallons of rum from it to insure against running dry again. *Constitution's* log for this period bears witness to the continuing good health and generally high morale of her crew. Discipline was exercised for only the second time in the new year on 10 February.

On the afternoon of 20 February, a chartered supply sloop out of New York appeared. She was taken in tow for two days as, through intermittent heavy weather, another big load of stores was transferred. As the operation was concluding, Talbot discovered to his dismay that the heel of the foretopmast had sprung: another wolding job for the carpenters. Carrying two damaged masts, the Commodore must have been most thankful that the hurricane season was not yet upon him.

Experiment appeared on the morning of the 27th, escorting two prize schooners (one was *Amphitheatre*) laden with stores for the flagship. Through the day, the boats plied back and forth, restocking the frigate's hold and storerooms with many of the things required for a large crew: 110 barrels of bread, twenty-eight bags and two barrels of potatoes, seventeen of beans, twenty-six casks of brandy, forty-two firkins of butter, fifty-eight boxes of candles, and twenty dozen shirts.[7] *Amphitheatre*, subsequent to her unloading, was armed and outfitted for inshore patrol duty and young Lieutenant David Porter placed in command.

On 13 March, Talbot once again was faced with the imminent end of his water supply and put in at Saint Nicholas Mole at noon the next day. *Constitution* had been at sea for 195 of the previous 201 days, no mean record for any ship. Watering was completed in rapid order; the frigate was underway for her post at 9 AM on the 17th. A welcome last-minute acquisition undoubtedly looked upon with delight by the crew was a precious supply of coffee and sugar.

For more than three weeks, the humdrum patrolling went on. *Constitution* received stores from *Enterprize* on 6 April and from a chartered stores ship on the 13th (both Sundays — how familiar in today's Navy), from *Amphitheatre* on the 24th (6 cords of wood), and *Herald* on 28 April. During this same period, the Commodore sent sixteen invalided seamen and marines from his ship's company to the homeward-bound *General Greene* in exchange for twenty-five seamen — another form of replenishment.[8]

Operationally, May was the busiest month of Talbot's tour as Commodore. On the 8th, *Constitution* and *Amphitheatre* captured the French privateer *Esther* (3) and retook her prize, the American brig *Nymph*. On 9 May, one of the frigate's boats managed to cut out the American trafficker sloop *Sally* from the tiny port of St. Iago. Talbot, a day later, used *Sally* as a "Trojan horse" in which an assault party from *Constitution* entered the port of Puerto Plata and captured the privateer schooner *Sandwich*. The brilliant attack was led by Lieutenant Isaac Hull, later *Constitution*'s Captain in her victory over HMS *Guerrière* in 1812, but had to be repudiated by the government because the port was technically neutral Spanish territory.

Buoyed by the success and activity of these events, Talbot next took his ship and her attendant *Amphitheatre* on a sweep to the eastern tip of Hispaniola, seeking other opportunities to cut out and cut up privateering efforts on the coast and in adjacent waters. The earlier successes were not repeated. Faced once more with a shortage of water, he returned westward, arriving at Saint Nicholas Mole on the afternoon of 11 June. The watering party was dispatched immediately.

Watering was completed at 3 AM on Saturday, the 14th, and after again taking on a supply of coffee and sugar, *Constitution* headed to sea at 6. Patrolling once more off Cap François, it soon was apparent that ship and crew alike were coming to the end of their endurance. Since the preceding August, they had been in port just twelve days — and those all too brief periods had been given over to the backbreaking labor of watering and supplying the ship. The log for 16 June noted thirty sick with fever, and scurvy was becoming prevalent despite Talbot's best efforts to afford them antiscorbutics. Many a man's term of enlistment was about done.

The crew resumed measuring their patrol time in weeks. Heavy squalls on 29 June must have reminded the Commodore that this was the start of the hurricane season in these waters — another worry for a commander with a tired ship and a weary crew. Two days later, a log entry read:

> Our principle [sic] sails except a foresail has [sic] from actual service become worn out so much as to be totally unserviceable, on a lee shore, or pursuing an enemy under a press of sail. We have repeatedly split the fore and main topsails when every effort would have been useless to bend others. Notwithstanding, forty bolts of canvas has [sic] been [illegible] on them.[9]

Talbot did his duty relentlessly. *Constitution* held her station although others came and went. *Augusta* was ordered into Cap François on 5 July for overhaul. The following day Chaplain William Austin took advantage of the Commodore's stoppage of a homeward-bound American sloop to end his term of service on board. Ironically, it was a Sunday. *Augusta* came back out a week later and supplied the frigate with thirty barrels of beef, two tierces of rice, and five pipes of brandy (one of which was sixty gallons short). Serious trouble came for the Commodore on the afternoon of the 13th:

> . . . at 5 Observed the Main Mast to Incline forward Although various ways has [sic] been used in order to Regain its Perpen-

dicular which is not Obtain'd the sprung part of the Mast which I have Mentioned near the Cat Harpin legs [sic] Increases and runs downwards and runs In a winding Direction nearly four feet on first Observing a small curve in the Main Mast was the 17th December 1799 — After Chasing to windward under a press of sail . . . the bolts which rivet through and secure the cheeks of the mast is [sic] of little use as they bent and became loose.[10]

A port call was mandatory. They arrived safely in Cap François on the morning of the 15th. Repairs began immediately; by midafternoon, both main and maintopsail yards had been sent down. A stores party brought aboard thirty barrels of pork and five of flour. (An armed French ship was in the port, but was not inclined to start anything, even with *Constitution* at sixes and sevens.) The maintopmast was gotten down the following morning, double runners were rigged fore and aft of the injured mast, and "by Degrees" it was hove straight once more. While the carpenters began fitting fishes to the mast, others took advantage of the opportunity to overhaul the rigging that had been taken down. In three days " . . . we compleated the Mainmast by Carrying a fish of 51 feet from the Heel of the Topmast down the main Mast — Which was made from a Sprung Topmast Leaving the full round on the fore part for a Wolding surface . . . . " By midnight of 21 July, the upper masts had been swayed up once more, the rigging rerigged, and the sails bent on. Talbot put to sea the next morning.

Commodore Alexander Murray in *Constellation* arrived just as Talbot was clearing the channel out of port, and succeeded Talbot as squadron commander on the afternoon of the 24th. Talbot sailed north a few hours later, escorting a dozen merchantmen away from those dangerous waters. The group arrived off the Virginia Capes on 13 August, where the merchants went their separate ways and Talbot thankfully bent on additional sail to get his exhausted command home to Boston. It could be none too soon:

> . . . our State of Provisions being as follows Viz. Beef none Pork 14 barrels Rum 60 gallons put the Ships Company on half Allowance of Spirits . . . .

At long last, Boston Light was raised on 24 August. *Constitution* anchored in President Roads at 2 PM. It had been an epic voyage that had commanded the utmost of the leadership talents of Silas Talbot. Using a crude, somewhat haphazard form of underway replenishment, he had maintained his command active on her assigned mission for 347 of the preceding 366 days — a record that few ships could claim, even in World War II.

Notes

[1] Letter, SecNav Benjamin Stoddert to Capt Silas Talbot, 27 July 1799. Record Group 45, National Archives, Washington, D.C. The Silas Talbot Papers are in the Mystic Seaport Library.

[2] Log of USS *Constitution*, 1 December 1798-15 February 1800 (entries for 15-31 October, 1799), USS *Constitution* Museum, Boston, MA.

[3] *Ibid.* (entries for 24 and 26 November, and 2 and 6 December, 1799).

[4] Tyrone G. Martin, *A Most Fortunate Ship* (Chester, CT: Globe Pequot Press, 1980), p. 11.

[5] *Ibid.*, p. 12.

[6] Log of USS *Constitution*, 6 December 1798-20 October 1800 (entry for 13 January 1800). Record Group 45, National Archives, Washington, D.C.

[7] *Ibid.* (entry for 27 February 1800).

[8] *Ibid.* (entries for 6, 13, 14, and 28 April 1800).

[9] *Ibid.* (entry for 1 July 1800).

[10] *Ibid.* (entry for 14 July 1800).

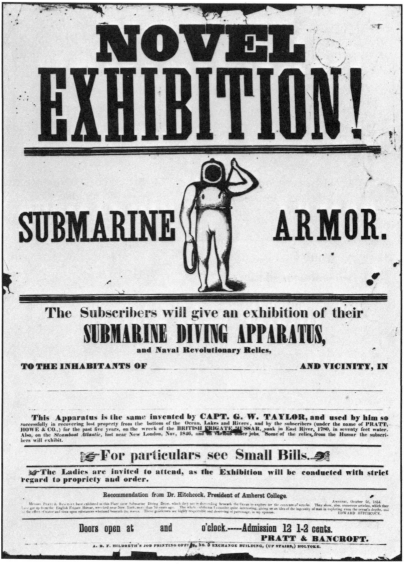

Ultimate Recognition of Taylor's Submarine Armor. This illustrated broadside, published during demonstrations of George W. Taylor's later diving dress in New England in 1854, includes a recommendation by the early American anatomist, President Edward Hitchcock of Amherst College. (*Reproduced by courtesy of the Edward Hitchcock Papers, Amherst College Library.*)

Marine Salvage and Sea Mine Technology in the 1840's: The Taylor Connection

Philip K. Lundeberg

Late in the spring of 1837, the New York mercantile community found diversion from the nation's deepening financial crisis in the appearance of a romantic promotional tract, unabashedly entitled *New and Alluring Sources of Enterprise in the Treasures of the Sea*, an anonymous brochure clearly inspired by an obscure Carolinian, Captain William H. Taylor, described therein as one "most particularly familiar with the Colombian Coast, where both pearls and rich wrecks abound . . . ." Such prose was to launch more than a decade of underwater ventures that brought Taylor's name repeatedly to the attention of Federal officials, not only in the emergent realm of submarine enterprise but, ultimately, of galvanic sea mine development. Like a handful of Yankee rivals, as well as Britain's noted John and Charles

Anthony Deane, Captain Taylor sought his fortune through the development and employment of a range of underwater devices. These included, in his own sadly truncated experience, an air-supplied diving apparatus, India-rubber airlift bags, life buoys and schemes for underwater demolitions, the latter for both warlike and commercial purpose.

An experienced metalworker residing in Manhattan, Taylor designed in 1837 a ponderous "Sub Marine Armor" that was intended to provide a diver maximum physical protection while working the old pearl fisheries of the Spanish Main, located in shark-infested waters between the Isle of Margareta and the Colombian mainland. To dramatize the venture, Taylor undertook an initial demonstration of his Armor on the Hudson River bottom on August 3, as reported by the *New York Express*:

> Captain Taylor first put on the dress, composed of India-rubber and tin plate, and remained in the water 36 minutes. He could have staid down for hours . . . . Afterwards, Mr. J.W. Hale, of the News Room, put on the dress and was in the water for over a quarter of an hour. There is no doubt that the novel apparatus of Captain Taylor will prove highly useful in recovering property from the bed of the ocean.[2]

Taylor's tactic of involving a reporter in his first New York trial was repeated in later demonstrations, reflecting the Captain's instinct for full exploitation of the press. Taylor registered his "Apparatus for Diving" at New York on December 23, 1837, an event witnessed by a fellow Carolinian, George W. Taylor, currently a purveyor of India-rubber goods, who appears already to have been intimately involved with development of the Sub Marine Armor. Captain Taylor's patent petition, finally approved in June 1838, revealed an inventor not only familiar with contemporary innovations in diving dress but who, as later observed by Sir Robert H. Davis in his classic work, *Deep Diving and Submarine Operations*, had achieved "the first design for a completely armored and articulated diving dress intended to safeguard its wearer against deepwater pressure . . . . "[3] While water pressure may have figured less in Taylor's armored design than the prospect of shark attack, his employment of articulated joints in this cumbersome apparatus provided a motive for his reliance on Manhattan's India-rubber community, initially in the person of George W. Taylor. Armed with his preliminary patent registration, Captain Taylor had begun salvage operations in February 1838 on the wreck of the merchantman *Bristol*, recently sunk off Rockaway Beach. To legitimize that frigid venture, the Captain and four associates secured a charter for the "Sub Marine Armor Company" at Albany in April, and books were subsequently opened in hopes of securing a capitalization of $200,000. Accounts of the *Bristol* salvage operation, which recovered quantities of railroad iron and other metal goods, offered no indication that Taylor had employed demolition charges to free portions of that vessel's cargo. [4] The idea was not long in presenting itself, however, for on June 23, 1838, the *New York Commercial Advertiser* reported in some detail on current operations of the British Army's Corps of Royal Sappers and Miners, directed by Colonel Charles William Pasley, in which large cylinders of blasting powder had been detonated with galvanic batteries during salvage activities on the Thames. [5]

The publicity possibilities of such underwater demolitions were not lost on Captain Taylor, who barely six weeks later was to include several spectacular underwater explosions during demonstrations of his Sub Marine Armor at New York in September 1838 at the popular Annual Fair of the Mechanics' Institute. The military significance of Taylor's underwater explosions, observed the *New York Commercial Advertiser*, "is too manifest to need explanation." For New Yorkers, including a young arms exhibitor by the name of Colt, who recalled the underwater ventures of David Bushnell and Robert Fulton on the Hudson, Taylor's demonstrations, staged at a time when Anglo-American relations had been severely strained by incidents on the Canadian border, proved more than casually significant. For his demonstrations, witnessed by Mayor Aaron Clark and several thousand spectators, Captain Taylor was awarded a gold medal by the Fair Committee of the Mechanics' Institute, whose Chairman, Oliver Whittlesey, later cited that Committee's opinion "as to the originality and real merit of your inventions and submarine experiments." [6]

Ironically, Whittlesey's testimony, offered in 1845, was ultimately submitted on behalf not of William H. Taylor but of "Captain George W. Taylor", who subsequently emerged under obscure if not sinister circumstances as principal proprietor of the Taylor system of submarine engineering. As the winter of 1838-39 approached, the harsh prospect of further operations in Northern waters led the Armor's proprietors to a fateful decision to head southward in search of profitable salvage operations that might sustain their hazardous enterprise. Departing New York early in December on the Schooner *Princess*, the Taylors headed for the east coast of Florida, a territory still tormented by the protracted Seminole War. The two Carolinians (who may conceivably have been related) arrived at St. Augustine on December 13, accompanied by Robert and Henry Bateman Goodyear, younger brothers of that tragic inventor, Charles Goodyear, who was, within the year, to make his epochal discovery of vulcanization. As was his custom, Captain William H. Taylor visited the editor of the *Florida Herald and Southern Democrat*, James M. Gould, who obligingly published an account of the recent New York demonstrations and announced a similar trial of the Sub Marine Armor early in the New Year at Fort Marion, the venerable Castello San Marco. While displaying his Armor at the Florida House on Christmas Eve, Taylor also disclosed an operating model of an "electro-magnetic machine," doubtless earlier procured at New York during the Mechanics' Institute Fair. Gould's subsequent account of Taylor's St. Augustine demonstration, held on January 5, 1839, offered no reference to this galvanic attraction or, indeed, to a promised underwater explosion. Difficulties appear to have developed during the Captain's diving exercise, for although Taylor reportedly traversed some 150 feet submerged, Gould observed that "He did not remain a very long while under water." A flaw in the Armor's air supply system, later described by Davis as providing for "a single air-pipe and a short outlet pipe exhausting into the water," may have made itself apparent, particularly if the diver's attendants topside slackened their pumping, permitting water to enter via the outlet pipe. Ostensibly, Taylor remained confident of future success, advising Gould of his group's imminent departure for the mouth of the St. Johns River in hopes of recovering the boiler of the steamer *Dolphin*, which had blown up off the bar in December 1836.[7]

Mystery still surrounds the Sub Marine Armor Company's ensuing operations on the lower St. Johns, a region ravaged earlier in the Seminole conflict and currently frequented by highwaymen. Contemporary records and newspapers offer no clue as to whether these hardy adventurers were waylaid en route to Jacksonville or, indeed, whether they actually attempted the hazardous *Dolphin* salvage, which would have been undertaken in waters remote from emergency support. Judging by limited contemporary evidence, Captain William H. Taylor did not survive the ensuing six weeks, though his obscure demise became apparent only in 1840, with the publication of his widow's address in *Longworth's New York Directory.*[8] Whether the victim of some unrecorded ambush, ill health, the imperfections of his ponderous Armor or, indeed, foul play, this ill-starred pioneer of American submarine engineering was missing and unaccounted for when his erstwhile partners finally reappeared on February 26, 1839 at Charleston, S.C., having reportedly arrived on board the Schooner *Motion* from Jacksonville.[9]

The time was propitious for a major demonstration of the Sub Marine Armor, for reports from Washington brought news of Congressional debates on the issue of war over the Canadian boundary dispute. Such was the setting in which George W. Taylor now took center stage, introducing himself to the Charleston press as "Captain Taylor" and adding that he was a native of North Carolina. As his fellow "proprietors" of the Armor now discovered, George W. Taylor proved an exceptionally apt pupil of his now unheralded mentor, promptly exhibiting the novel diving equipment to local editors and civic officials and offering to "scientific gentlemen" a display of the electromagnetic machine. Taylor bracketed his initial diving demonstrations on March 14 with thunderous barrages of underwater detonations, a procedure repeated during his trials on March 26, in which Lieutenant Richard S. Pinckney, USN, was persuaded to undertake an underwater perambulation in the Armor. A climactic "Great Explosion" was staged off the Battery on April 3, the central action being the destruction of an aged target hulk, beneath which Taylor affixed a barrel, charged with 75 pounds of powder and fired with a fuse that consisted "of rope, prepared with a composition which burns under water." The ensuing watery catastrophe literally transfixed the multitude assembled on White Point:

> The convulsed waters lifted up her burden, and held it
> for a moment as in a bowl, until with tremendous force it burst

into innumerable fragments, shooting high into the air, and falling with impetuous plunge within a wide circumference. This spectacle was one of interest and grandeur, and illustrated very strikingly the effect of the torpedo, with which Brother Jonathan was wont to scare John Bull out of his seven senses, when he paddled his canoe too near our coast.[10]

This graphic account by the *Charleston Courier*, reprinted in numerous East Coast journals, firmly fixed the name of Captain George W. Taylor in the public mind. Though press accounts obscured the practical employment of Taylor's Armor in the preparations for such grim watery spectacles, its significance was stated with classic brevity by a venerable Charleston diarist, Jacob Frederic Schirmer, who noted simply on April 3, 1839: "Submarine man this afternoon blew up a vessel." For the considerable military community in this Carolina entrepot, who recalled its vulnerability six decades earlier to British seaborne assault, the evident potential of undersea warfare for strengthening their harbor's fortifications had been strongly suggested and, within a quarter century, was to prove grimly prophetic.

Taylor's Charleston demonstrations of 1839 virtually concluded the brief history of the Sub Marine Armor Company, for while the Goodyear brothers were soon drawn north by the India rubber trade, Captain Taylor embarked on a series of demonstrations of his system in New England, where he introduced his designs for an India-rubber ship camel, an underwater lantern and what he described as "Submarine Rockets". The latter devices, which Taylor demonstrated in Boston harbor on Thanksgiving Day 1839, were graphically described by Joseph Bennett, a local engineer, as consisting of:

> . . . simply an India rubber bag, filled with powder (in this case 10 lbs) into which was inserted a flexible fuse, and all was made water-tight around it; this fuse burns freely under water; in this case there was 3 feet projecting from the bag, which being lit and thrown over in a depth of probably about 35 feet, exploded in half a minute, throwing up a body of water and foam 13 feet. . . .[12]

Bennett's extensive descriptions, which reveal Taylor as a remarkably candid, indeed ingenuous inventor, proved the prelude to the Captain's most bizarre underwater venture, a "Sub Marine Descent" undertaken on January 4, 1840, into the pit of Boston's National Theater, flooded for the occasion to display Taylor's subaqueous technique. Undeterred by the rigors of Massachusetts winter, the venturesome Carolinian turned the very elements to advantage, journeying to nearby Lowell where he demonstrated his Rockets' utility for clearing ice jams in rivers and canals.[13] Later in the winter Taylor was called on to locate the wreck of the Long Island Sound steamer *Lexington*, an operation off Bridgeport in which he reportedly worked at depths exceeding one hundred feet.[14]

These debilitating operations appear to have cost Taylor the opportunity to participate in significant underwater blasting operations conducted at the Portsmouth Navy Yard in the summer of 1840. It is apparent, however, that the Captain meanwhile profited by published accounts of the galvanic demolition system employed at Portsmouth by the eminent engineer, Alexander Parris, as well as the widely publicized galvanic system developed by Colonel Pasley during the extended salvage of the *Royal George*.[15] Such was the conceptual prelude to Taylor's arrival in Washington early in 1841, shortly after the inauguration of President William Henry Harrison. History intervened in the form of that Chief Executive's unexpected demise, but on April 10 and 21, Taylor was able to conduct demonstrations of his "Sub Marine Armor" and "Submarine Rockets" at the Navy Yard before the Board of Navy Commissioners and, on the second occasion, President John Tyler and members of his Cabinet. Taylor exhibited plans for galvanic detonation of his Rockets, but prime official interest focused on his Sub Marine Armor, six sets of which the Navy Commissioners subsequently ordered.[16]

While Taylor was preoccupied with delivery and further demonstration of his diving apparatus, he was suddenly overtaken in the realm of galvanic sea mine development by that inventive Yankee, Samuel Colt, who arrived in Washington two months after Taylor's Navy Yard demonstrations and succeeded in securing Navy Department support for development of his own "Submarine Battery" proposal. Thanks to interested assistance from Professors John William Draper and Samuel F.B. Morse of the University of the City of New York, Colt subsequently succeeded in perfecting his unique system for galvanic control of riverine minefields and demonstrated it twice at New York and Washington, on the final occasion demolishing a target vessel *under sail* off the Washington Navy Yard in April 1844.[17] These were hard years for George W. Taylor, who late in 1841 had been obliged, as he later recalled, "To abandon, for the time, the execution of his aforesaid plans; and he commenced operations on the lakes at the north, where he was busily employed in raising sunken vessels, laying foundations in deep water, and other submarine operations. . .."[18] One may readily sense the physical toll exacted by those sustained cold-water operations, including a nightmare venture salvaging the steamboat *Erie* in Lake St. Clair north of Detroit, early in 1843. During this period Taylor developed two systems of diving bells, which he included in a collection of submarine devices that he determined to present to the Federal Government early in 1845.[19]

Ironically, Samuel Colt's claims for his "Submarine Battery" were under final critical review by the Navy Department when, midway in January 1845, Captain Taylor approached the War Department with what were described as "diagrams and descriptions of various inventions for sub-marine, coast and harbor defence . . . . " Gratified by the Carolinian's ingenuous manner, Secretary William Wilkins promptly constituted a Board of Examination which proceeded to evaluate Taylor's successive proposals for diving bells, a submarine boat, submarine armor and, most particularly, his "Submarine Rockets." Notwithstanding Taylor's forthcoming manner, which contrasted sharply with the determined secrecy of Samuel Colt, the Carolinian received no satisfaction from the Board, which neglected the opportunity to subject his Rockets to trials on the proving ground.[20]

The foregoing constitutes a curious prologue to Professor K. Jack Bauer's fascinating account of Captain Taylor's subaqueous ventures during the Mexican War, notably his remarkable success as a critical element in Commodore Matthew C. Perry's Tabasco River expedition of June 1847. On that occasion Taylor directed the demolition of massive underwater obstructions by means of galvanically-fired charges, an undertaking that marked the climax of his long quest to master the galvanic art and indeed fairly identifies George W. Taylor as the U.S. Navy's pioneer underwater demolitions specialist.[21] That long-obscured accomplishment came late in Taylor's career, for the badly crippled Captain died at Washington in 1850, not long after undertaking a survey of the wreck of the ill-fated steam frigate *Missouri*, earlier sunk off Gibraltar.[22] Thus ended the tragic saga of the Taylors, an account clouded with yet obscure passages, arduous adventure and crushing disappointments, yet one worthy of remembrance, combining in unique if complex fashion the early development of submarine engineering, modern salvage operations and the evolution of sea mine warfare technology.

Notes

[1] Anon., *New and Alluring Sources of Enterprise in the Treasures of the Sea, and the Means of Gathering Them* (New York: J. Narine, 1837), pp. 25-26; House of Representatives, 28th Congress, 2nd Session, *House Report No. 192: George W. Taylor. Washington, 3 March 1845*, pp. 2-3.

[2] *Ibid.; New York Express*, August 4, 1837.

[3] Robert H. Davis, *Deep Diving and Submarine Operations* (London: St. Catherine's Press, 1951), p. 586; U.S. Patent and Trade Mark Office, Specification of Letters Patent N. 578, dated January 20, 1838: Apparatus for Diving Submitted by William H. Taylor of New York, N.Y., Record Group 241, U.S. National Archives.

[4] *Longworth's New York Directory, 1836-1837* (New York: Thomas Longworth, 1836), p. 617; and *idem., 1837-38*, p. 600; "An act to Incorporate the Sub Marine Armor Company," dated April 2, 1838, in Manuscript Collection, New York State Archives; *Albany Evening Journal*, March 21, 30 and 31, 1838; *New York Commercial Advertiser*, May 30 and June 1, 1838.

[5] *Ibid.*, June 23, 1838; Philip K. Lundeberg, "The Emergence of Galvanic Sea Mine Warfare: Patterns of Interprofessional Collaboration," in *International Commission of Military History Acta, Bucharest 1980*, (Bucharest, 1981), pp. 352-354.

[6] *House Report No. 192: George W. Taylor*, 15-16; *New York Commercial Advertiser*, September 11, 12 and 15, 1838.

[7] Davis, *Deep Diving*, p. 586; St Augustine *Florida Herald and Southern Democrat*, December 13, 27, 1838, and January 10, 1839.

[8] *Ibid.* January 7-March 1, 1839; *Longworth's New York Directory, 1839-1840*, p. 637; and *idem., 1840-41*, p. 616.

[9] *Charleston* (South Carolina) *Mercury*, February 27, 1839.

[10] *Charleston Courier*, March 8, 9, 11, 15, 27 and 29, April 3-5, 1839; *The* (Charleston) *Southern Patriot*, March 7, 1839.

[11] See "The Schirmer Diary," in *The South Carolina Historical Magazine*, LXIX (1968), p. 263; *Alexandria* (Virginia) *Gazette*, April 11, 1839; *The* (Baltimore) *Sun*, April 11, 1839.

[12] *Boston Daily Advertiser*, December 4, 1839; *Boston Post*, November 23, 28, 30 and December 4 and 14, 1839; Grace Kirkman Goodyear, *Genealogy of the Goodyear Family* (San Francisco: Cubery, 1899), pp. 5, 130; Ralph F. Wolf, *India Rubber Man: The Story of Charles Goodyear* (Caldwell, Idaho: Caxton, 1940), pp. 28-29, 123-129, 275.

[13] *Army and Navy Chronicle*, IX:26 (December 26, 1839), p. 411, and X:6 (February 6, 1840), p. 93; *Boston Morning Post*, January 4, 1840.

[14] *New York Herald*, January 15 and March 9, 1840; Robert G. Albion, *The Rise of New York Port 1815-1860* (New York: C. Scribner's, 1939), p. 160.

[15] *Army and Navy Chronicle*, XI: 24 (December 10, 1840), pp. 380-382.

[16] *House Report No. 192: George W. Taylor*, pp. 14, 16; *The National Intelligencer*, May 10, 1841.

[17] Philip K. Lundeberg, *Samuel Colt's Submarine Battery: The Secret and the Enigma* (Washington: Smithsonian Press, 1974), pp. 16-46.

[18] *House Report No. 192: George W. Taylor*, pp. 2-3.

[19] *Detroit Gazette* as quoted in the *Brandon* (Vermont) *Telegraph*, February 15, 1843; Erik Heyl, *Early American Steamers* (6 vols., Buffalo: Erik Heyl, 1965), IV pp. 91-92.

[20] *House Report No. 192: George W. Taylor*, pp. 4-9; Lundeberg, *Colt's Submarine Battery*, pp. 47-57, 67-68.

[21] K. Jack Bauer, *Surfboats and Horse Marines: U.S. Naval Operations in the Mexican War* (Annapolis: U.S. Naval Institute, 1969), pp. 113, 118.

[22] *The National Intelligencer*, April 29, 1850; *Gleason's Pictorial Drawing-Room Companion*, VI: 25 (June 24, 1854), p. 400.

Part II

Fishing and Trading

Science, Diplomacy, and Rum:
The Halifax Fisheries Commission
of 1877

Dean C. Allard

Students of the tangled controversy between the United States, Great Britain, and Canada over the fisheries of the Northwest Atlantic may recall the weary comment of James Russell Lowell, Washington's minister to London in the early 1880's, upon once again approaching the British Foreign Minister on this prolonged dispute. Lowell commented: "I fear I shall always present myself to your fancy like the young Tobit in the picture, trailing a fish which certainly is not growing fresher in the process."[1] Yet, the specific subject of this paper, the arbitration at Halifax, Nova Scotia in 1877, presents a story of diplomatic acumen and blunder, the pursuit of nationalistic goals, and the application of marine science that may be of interest to modern maritime historians. This story also is topical since the relative rights of Canadian and U.S. fishermen in their exclusive economic zones, that now extend 200 miles from the American coastline, is once again a troublesome issue in the relationships between our two countries.

The commission at Halifax grew out of the comprehensive Anglo-American treaty signed at Washington in 1871 that, among many other features, authorized U.S. fishermen to use all of the inshore fisheries of the Dominion of Canada and the then separate Crown Colony of Newfoundland for a period of at least twelve years. Previously, under a convention reached in 1818, only designated areas within Canada's three-mile limit, which then defined the territorial seas, had been opened. In return for the complete grant of 1871, the Treaty of Washington required the United States to allow the free importation of Canadian fish and fish oil and authorized Canadians to use inshore fisheries as far south as the Delaware Bay. The United States felt that the value of these reciprocal concessions essentially balanced each other. But, Canadian leaders, who resented continuing English control of their foreign affairs and who had attempted in vain to exclude the fisheries clauses from a general Anglo-American accord, vigorously argued that additional compensation was due for the unrestricted use of their inshore fisheries. It was largely because of this Canadian position that the Washington Treaty established an arbitral commission to determine what payment, if any, the United States owed its northern neighbors for fishing rights.[2]

When this Commission met at Halifax between June and November 1877, it was composed of three members. The British appointee was the exceptionally able Sir Alexander T. Galt, who previously had served as Canada's Minister of Finance. In unfortunate contrast, the United States designated Ensign H. Kellogg. An obscure New England politician, Kellogg had been the speaker of the Massachusetts House of Representatives and was said to be interested in sports fishing. But, his chief claim to membership on the Commission appears to have been his close friendship with the influential Senator George S. Boutwell. When the United States and Great Britain failed to agree on the crucial third member, who almost certainly would hold the balance of power, this Commissioner was named by a neutral third nation, as provided for in the Washington Treaty. He was Maurice Delfosse, who in 1877 served as the Belgian Minister to the United States.[3]

Both parties also designated legal counsel and enlisted scientific talent to support their national cases. An Englishman, Francis Clare Ford, was the chief agent of the Crown, but it was evident from the outset that the Canadians who served as Ford's primary assistants were determined to dominate the presentation of a case that was of chief concern to their Dominion. This outlook was represented very well by Alexander Mackenzie, the Canadian Prime Minister, who noted in 1875 that "we were all but ruined from first to last by English diplomacy and treaty making, and we would have no more of it at any price."[4] On the U.S. side Dwight Foster was the principal lawyer, but one of his assistant counsel, Richard Henry Dana, Jr., author of *Two Years Before the Mast*, is much better known. Scientific personnel included William F. Whitcher and A.J. Smith, who were senior Canadian fisheries officials, and their counterpart, Spencer Fullerton Baird, the U.S. Commissioner of Fish and Fisheries. Despite his impressive title, however, Baird primarily was concerned with the operations of the Smithsonian Institution, where he was a senior official. The Fish Commission, established six years earlier at his initiative, received Baird's primary attention mainly during the summer months.[5]

By far the most important substantive issue before the Halifax Commission was the actual value of Canada's inshore waters to U.S. fishermen. Both sides agreed that the principal species at issue was the mackerel and that the chief mackerel fishery was in the Gulf of St. Lawrence. In describing the richness of these resources, Canadian witnesses at times waxed almost poetic. But, they also could back up their claims with statistical tables issued annually by their government since the early 1870's. These data showed that at least a thousand U.S. boats visited Canada each year, taking mackerel with an annual value of about $4,200,000. Fishery scientists also supported this position by testifying that virtually the entire mackerel stock in the Northwest Atlantic was within Canada's three-mile limit during the spring and summer spawning season. But, in addition to the actual mackerel harvested, the Canadians asserted that the free use of their territorial seas offered other benefits to the United States. One of these was the right to purchase bait in Canadian ports that could be used to support fishing activities outside the three-mile limit. Further, the opening of the entire coast freed the United States from the ambiguous stipulations in the 1818 treaty that attempted to define fishing rights in Canada's coastal waters. Previous differences between the two countries in interpreting these provisions had led to the harassment or seizure by Canadian authorities of many U.S. boats.[6]

In attempting to rebut these arguments, the United States depended to a large extent upon its part-time Commissioner of Fish and Fisheries. Spencer Fullerton Baird was a distinguished zoologist and noted leader of scientific institutions in the United States. During the previous six summers, his organization had undertaken pioneering studies of the marine biology of New England and also was operating hatcheries that aimed to replenish American fisheries. But, it soon became evident that Baird's agency had a limited knowledge of the U.S. commercial fishing industry and fell far short of full, scientific understanding of the mackerel.

As was true for the Canadians, the United States paraded before the Commission a number of witnesses from the fishing industry, many of whom had been enlisted by Spencer Baird. These apparent experts were unanimous in stating that virtually all of the mackerel caught above the U.S. border came from outside the three-mile limit. The claim also was made that, in any event, the mackerel were steadily deserting northern waters for more hospitable areas off the United States. The witnesses concluded that no more than a hundred boats per year operated to any extent in the Canadian waters. But, overall statistics from the U.S. government in support of this somewhat impressionistic evidence were not available until after the Halifax award was granted. At that time, Washington claimed the annual value of Canadian inshore fisheries for its boats to be no more than $25,000 per year. Since the Halifax arbitration had been authorized for six years, Washington's tardiness in compiling the basic data needed to support its case is a sad commentary on the foresight of U.S. diplomacy.[7]

Spencer Baird took a more direct role in challenging Canadian scientific testimony. The Fish Commissioner probably would have agreed with the comment of one of his assistants that "all recent treatises on ichthyology by Canadian writers have appeared in the form of campaign documents, apparently intended to influence the decisions of Diplomatic Commissions."[8] But Baird, who later admitted to an incomplete knowledge of the Atlantic mackerel, also may have been influenced by patriotism in presenting data on this elusive species. For example, Baird claimed that there was no evidence whatsoever that the principal spawning grounds of these fish were in the Gulf of St. Lawrence or, for that matter, in any inshore region. In addition, his research indicated that two of the three major mackerel stocks in the northwest Atlantic were to be found off the U.S. coast. Nevertheless, this testimony was far from compelling, especially when skilled Canadian cross examination revealed that Baird previously had published differing conclusions on the location and spawning habits of the mackerel. As intended, the opposing lawyers cast considerable doubt on the validity of Baird's testimony.[9]

Finally, the United States sought to address the Canadian claim that the grant of all of its coastal regions provided the U.S. industry with an important base of operations for fishing outside the three-mile limit. In this regard, Washington's representatives acknowledged, at least privately, that there was some benefit in avoiding Canadian interference with U.S. boats accused of ignoring the murky rights and restrictions in the treaty of 1818. But, Baird and other witnesses presented apparently persuasive evidence that minimized the value of Canadian bait sources, especially by demonstrating that U.S. fishermen were making increased use of preserved bait brought from their home ports.[10]

The other major questions at Halifax included the value of Canada's duty-free importation of fish products into the United States and the benefit that the Dominion's fishermen enjoyed in harvesting U.S. maritime resources. The Canadian position on the first issue reflected a traditional free trade point of view by suggesting that the true beneficiary was the U.S. consumer who, because of a lack of tariffs, could buy a desired commodity at a bargain price. In response, the United States noted that in this instance reliable, official statistics demonstrated that the Canadians avoided paying about $400,000 a year in duties. Without this direct subsidy, it was argued, the Canadian export market would be greatly diminished.[11]

As for the value of U.S. inshore fisheries, both sides agreed that Canada made little use of these waters. But, whether employed or not, the United States claimed that the intrinsic value of its resources needed to be thrown into the balance. If it could be shown that these fisheries were thriving, that fact also could lend credence to the more general contention that there was little need for U.S. fishermen to take the long voyage to the Gulf of St. Lawrence. Again, however, the lack of reliable statistics became a problem in supporting U.S. contentions. To be sure, late in the summer of 1877, Spencer Baird mailed stocks of questionnaires to postal authorities in every coastal settlement between Eastport, Maine and Cape May, New Jersey. These were distributed within the fishing industry and, in little more than a month, the returns were tabulated and presented at Halifax. But, as the U.S. Fish Commissioner later admitted, these data were "imperfect" and "hastily gathered."[12] That situation, together with alarming statements made by Baird in earlier reports regarding the decline of U.S. fish resources, were not ignored by the opposition's lawyers in their cross examination.

Looking at all of the case's elements, Canadian and British authorities argued that the United States owed a total of $14,880,000 for the net benefits it received. In contrast, Washington formally claimed that the advantages to each side offset each other, with the result that no payment was due. Privately, however, Washington's delegation admitted that a reasonable outcome might be a judgement against the United States of about $1,200,000, or $100,000 per year for the minimum duration of the fishery clauses.[13]

On 23 November 1877, however, and to the horror of the United States, the Commission ruled that an award of $5,500,000 was due to its northern neighbor. Since the U.S. representative, Ensign Kellogg, dissented from this judgement, it was signed only by the Canadian and Belgian members. This led the United States to advance the belated claim that any reasonable interpretation of the Treaty of Washington required that a valid award receive the unanimous concurrence of all three commissioners. The force of this argument was gravely weakened since Washington had made the legal error of failing to take a formal stand on the critical issue of voting mechanics at the outset of the Halifax proceedings. As one U.S. senator later noted, the absence of unanimity might have been used to avoid paying an unfair award "at first — but not at last."[14] In addition to the legal sufficiency of the decision, the U.S. delegation was convinced that there was no substantive basis for a judgement of more than five million dollars. Spencer Baird, for example, suggested that it was nothing less than a "monstrous travesty of the facts,"[15] while Richard Henry Dana commented in a private letter to an associate that "You may use as strong language, respecting my opinion on the injustice and baselessness of the award, as you see fit."[16] Such protests regarding the reasonableness and legal sufficiency of the award later were addressed in diplomatic correspondence between Washington and London. But, when the British firmly supported the equity of the judgement, the United States had no choice but to meet its obligation. In November 1878, a U.S. draft for $5,500,000 grudgingly was sent to the British Foreign Office.[17]

In attempting to explain the outcome at Halifax, there is little doubt, as Spencer Baird later observed, that the "absence of proper, methodical, and digested information" on the fisheries placed his country at "very great disadvantages."[18] Maritime historians will be interested to know that this conclusion and the anticipation of further diplomatic negotiations on the apparently never-ending fishing controversy led the Fish Commission to undertake an exhaustive investigation of the U.S. industry and the species upon which it depended. An outstanding example of this work was a seven-volume study entitled *The Fisheries and Fishery Industries of the United States (1884-1887)* that remains a classic study of its subject. The new program also featured Baird's success in the early 1880's in obtaining appropriations for the famed research vessel *Albatross*. One of the most important justifications used by the Fish Commissioner in securing Congressional approval for this ship, which served the cause of marine science for more than four decades, was her intended use in studying the life history of the North Atlantic mackerel and in discovering new fishing grounds. The latter presumably would be as far removed from Canada as possible.[19]

Aside from the absence of reliable data, which Baird attempted to correct after 1877, it is evident that another major factor at Halifax was the energy, intelligence, and character of Alexander T. Galt. Although the Canadian Commissioner was willing to reduce the initial British claim of almost fifteen million dollars by more than half, he argued vigorously that a major award was due to his country for the U.S. use of Canada's inshore fisheries. Galt also stressed the indirect value of these territorial waters in supporting the general U.S. fishing industry in northern latitudes. Galt held firmly to the position that the duty-free shipment of Canadian fish to U.S. markets was of mutual benefit to both nations. Further, he entirely dismissed the value of U.S. inshore fisheries, which admittedly were not used by his countrymen. Although Galt's position on all these matters differed from Washington's interpretations, they were entirely logical. More to the point, in the hands of a skilled advocate, such as Galt, they could be made to appear reasonable and just to Maurice Delfosse who, in the last analysis, was to cast the deciding vote.[20]

In contrast to Galt, the U.S. commissioner, Ensign H. Kellogg, proved to be entirely inept in supporting his national case. Dwight Foster, the chief U.S. agent, summarized his attributes in a private letter to Secretary of State William M. Evarts indicating that "Kellogg's behavior was not always very creditable or dignified. He got drunk sometimes, and did ridiculous things."[21] Spencer Baird observed more slyly that Kellogg has been "usually attentive, when not asleep."[22] But perhaps the most compelling evidence is the statement of Maurice Delfosse. The third and pivotal commissioner wrote in a private letter to Galt shortly after the award was announced: "You know how indignant I was for the position in which the passivity of the U.S. Commissioner placed me, by not discussing your arguments nor giving any of his own. If it was a policy, . . . I fail to perceive the wisdom or expediency of it."[23]

In its failure to collect reliable information on the Atlantic fisheries, as well as Washington's technical blunder on the issue of unanimous voting, not to mention the appointment of Ensign Kellogg, the United States was "scandalously outwitted" at Halifax, to use the phrase of a later official of the Department of State.[24] On the other hand, the Canadians, who played a leading role in the arbitration, won a signal victory over their southern neighbors. For the assertive Dominion of Canada, established only ten years earlier, this outcome had special significance since, as Prime Minister Mackenzie stated, it would represent the "first Canadian diplomatic triumph, and will justify me in insisting that we know our neighbors and our own business better than any Englishman."[25]

In the longer run, however the significance of the proceedings at Halifax is not that it was an American defeat or a Canadian success, but rather that it cast a long shadow over Canadian — U.S. amity. By the time Washington reluctantly paid the Halifax award, it was evident that the United States would refuse to renew the Washington Treaty's fishing clauses when they expired in 1885. At that point, the United States once again reverted to the partial and confusing privileges granted by the 1818 treaty. An attempt was made after 1885 to reach a more general accord, but the rankling conviction of U.S. leaders that an injustice had been done at Halifax assured the defeat of a new agreement.[26]

As a result, although the Treaty of Washington settled most of the outstanding disputes within the Anglo-American community, the Halifax award assured the continuation of a festering animosity regarding U.S. rights within Canada's three-mile limit. A resolution of this dispute would not come until 1912 when both sides, apparently exhausted by a conflict that began when the United States won its independence in 1783, formally endorsed a decision of the International Court at The Hague. After almost 130 years, that judgement finally resolved the conflicting claims of the two countries regarding the exact privileges of the United States in the inshore fisheries of Canada.[27]

Notes

[1] Quoted in David Saville Muzzey, *James G. Blaine* (New York: Dodd, Mead, 1934), p. 148.

[2] Recent discussions of the diplomatic background of the Halifax Commission include Dean C. Allard, *Spencer Fullerton Baird and the U.S. Fish Commission* (New York: Arno Press, 1978), pp. 180-195; and Charles S. Campbell, *From Revolution to Rapprochement: The United States and Great Britain,*

1783-1900 (New York: John Wiley and Sons, 1974), pp. 137-142. References in this paper to Canada or to Canadian waters and fisheries apply to the Dominion of Canada, as well as the Crown Colony of Newfoundland which in 1877 was not part of the Dominion.

[3] See Allard, *Spencer Fullerton Baird*, pp. 189-192; Campbell, *Revolution to Rapprochement*, pp. 137-141.

[4] Mackenzie to Galt, 15 July 1875, quoted in Oscar Douglas Skelton, *The Life and Times of Sir Alexander Tilloch Galt* (Toronto: Oxford University Press, 1920), pp. 502-503. See also Allard, *Spencer Fullerton Baird*, pp. 228-229.

[5] Allard, *Spencer Fullerton Baird*, pp. 193-194.

[6] For the proceedings of the Halifax Commission, see U.S., Congress, House, *Documents and Proceedings of the Halifax Commission, 1877* (45th Cong., 2d sess., House, Executive Doc.89) (3 vols.; Washington: Government Printing Office, 1878). See also Allard, *Spencer Fullerton Baird*, pp. 204-205, 207-208, 215.

[7] Allard, *Spencer Fullerton Baird*, pp. 205-208.

[8] George Brown Goode, "The Migration of Fishes," *Transactions of the American Fish Cultural Association* (1878),pp. 46-47.

[9] Allard, *Spencer Fullerton Baird*, pp. 208-209.

[10] *Ibid.*, pp. 215,218.

[11] *Ibid.*, pp. 210-211.

[12] *Ibid.*, pp. 211-214.

[13] *Ibid.*, pp. 204, 218-219.

[14] George Franklin Edmunds, "The Fishery Award," *North American Review*, CXXVIII (Jan. 1879), p. 7. For recent discussions of the unanimity issue, see Campbell, *Revolution to Rapprochement*, pp. 142-143 and Allard, *Spencer Fullerton Baird*, pp. 198-203.

[15] Baird to Francis Clare Ford, 5 Dec.1877, Letters Sent, Records of the U.S. Fish Commission, National Archives.

[16] Dana to Dwight Foster, 28 Dec.1877, Records of the North Atlantic Fisheries Dispute, Halifax Arbitration, envelope 4, Department of State, National Archives.

[17] For the post-award diplomacy, see Campbell, *Revolution to Rapprochement*, pp. 143-144.

[18] Baird to William M. Evarts, 15 Dec.1877, Letters Sent, Records of the U.S. Fish Commission, National Archives.

[19] See Allard, *Spencer Fullerton Baird*, pp. 296-316; Joel W. Hedgpeth, "The United States Fish Commission Steamer *Albatross*," *The American Neptune*, V (Jan. 1945),pp. 5-26.

[20] Allard, *Spencer Fullerton Baird*, pp. 225-228.

[21] Quoted in William M. Evarts MS Journal, 12 Dec.1877, Evarts Papers, Library of Congress.

[22] Quoted in *Ibid.*, 7 Nov.1877.

[23] Delfosse to Galt, undated (March 1878?), quoted in Skelton, *Galt*, p. 512.

[24] Francis Wharton, quoted in Charles C. Tansill, *Canadian American Relations, 1875-1911* (New Haven: Yale, 1943), p. 20.

[25] Mackenzie to Galt, 2 Oct.1877, quoted in Skelton, *Galt*, p. 514.

[26] Allard, *Spencer Fullerton Baird*, pp. 299-302.

[27] See Samuel Flagg Bemis, *A Diplomatic History of the United States*, 4th ed. (New York: Henry Holt and Co., 1955), pp. 429-430.

Canada and China:
Early Trading Links by Sea

Barry Gough

The myth of the China market dates from the age of Marco Polo and spurred many European and later American adventurers to search for short seaborne links to China, Japan, Korea, and the exotic spice islands of Southeast Asia. Magellan's voyage revealed a southwest passage to the Spiceries; but it was long and hazardous and uneconomic for venture capital. Spanish, Portuguese and Dutch predominance in Southeast Asia did not allow Englishmen even in the age of Drake to sail with impunity in those southern latitudes.

For four centuries beginning with the sixteenth, English navigators had sought northwest and northeast passages which would put English merchants directly in touch with East Asia by a short and thus commercially advantageous route. Attempts by Tudor navigators had been hardly more successful in prosecuting the northeast than the northwest passage, for problems of distance and of sea travel in northern, icy latitudes mitigated against any easily won success. France, too, attempted to outflank Spanish trade in the Americas and the Pacific by finding a northern route, through Canada; and the history of the early exploration of Canada is tied inseparably to the search for channels, rivers or seas leading to Asia.

Canada's interest in Asian trade thus stems directly out of the objectives of her two founding European mother nations, and much of her earliest trade to China is related to the seaborne success of Great Britain, who by 1763 had ousted France from predominant position in Canada. By the late eighteenth century Britain possessed the military capability, the capital, and the techniques for distant voyaging — the material means that brought forth what Professor Vincent Harlow called "swing to the East" that laid the foundations of the second British Empire.[1]

The predominance of what John Bartlett Brebner called the North Atlantic Triangle has been so prevalent in Canadian history that scant attention is given to Pacific affairs in the shaping of the Canadian experience. The following essay attempts to explain how Canada shared in a wider historical phenomenon, the maritime fur trade in the distant Pacific. The oceans linked rather than divided the countinents of Europe, the Americas and Asia — once, of course, man possessed the deep-water technology and skills to cross distant seas in safety. Canada's links with China came from both her Atlantic and Pacific shores, and at almost the very same time that the transcontinental fur trade had been established Canada's sea links with Asia were instituted. This was the origin of a trade which now approaches billions of dollars annually, though minerals, wheat and industrial products have replaced furs as the principal export from Canadian ports.

The following essay will focus, in turn, on (1) the dimensions of the Pacific, (2) Captain James Cook's third voyage and the beginnings of the maritime fur trade, and (3) the North West Company of Montreal and its role in the early growth of general Canadian trade with Canton. In this way we will see how distance shaped the early trading links; how the fur resources of the Northwest Coast (as distinct from those of the Rocky Mountain cordillera, Athabaska and the continental interior) became the first staple of trans-Pacific trade; and how the continental fur trade succeeded the maritime fur trade in penetrating the China market. It will also show that at the same time that maritime fur traders were pioneering direct commerce by sea, continental fur traders' interests were opening the trade in their own way through an extended and intricate commercial network that involved British, Russian and American business contracts.

1. Dimensions of the Pacific.

For the British the Northwest Coast was from Tudor times until the Panama Canal was completed the "ocean's farthest shore." Approachable only by a sea route of 18,000 nautical miles via troublesome Cape Horn or an even more lengthy passage via the Cape of Good Hope, that remote shore nevertheless continued to be of compelling interest to explorers, merchant traders, geographers and the governments of several nations, most notably Spain, Russia, Britain and the United States.[2] The Northwest Coast was indeed a "distant dominion," as Edmund Burke said;[3] and distance at once shaped its development and deterred its growth in European hands until the mid-19th century. Distance kept it secret from the wider world until the late 18th century. The Chinese had known of "Fousang," the land of shining mountains, the country of the extreme east. But the Chinese chose not to pursue trade beyond their own shores; their discoveries on the Northwest Coast, dating from the first few centuries A.D. might have led to a profitable trade but the Chinese chose, instead, to engage in an active maritime commerce in their own seas. Nonetheless, the role of China in our story is not unimportant, for until San Francisco's rise to prominence as a port, Canton was the premier city of the Pacific rim, the focal point of commerce and European maritime activity.

Canton lay 8,000 nautical miles from Nootka Sound, Vancouver Island, along a relatively easy track for ships outward bound from the Northwest Coast. Captains would sail with their fur cargoes in September and aided by northeast trades and north equatorial currents could confidently expect that they would reach Canton by late November. The return passage from Canton took longer, for winds and currents along what is now called the Great Circle route were less dependable, and the track along the northern route, especially through the China Seas, was fraught with problems so well described by Joseph Conrad. Ships would sail between monsoons, make their way between the numerous islets and reefs that flank the east coast of Asia, and sail along the still unsurveyed shores of Japan, Korea and Sakhalin. Beyond the Kurile Islands lay Kamchatka and farther north still the intricate Aleutian chain. If a ship were bound from Canton to Cook's Inlet or Prince William Sound, Unalaska or Kodiak could provide a secure haven. If a ship were to sail in more southerly latitudes, her track across the Pacific would be reasonably safe north of the Hawaiian Islands, though delays could be painfully long if currents and winds proved obstinant. In the late eighteenth century, when scientific sailing directions were unheard of, every ship's captain was an oceanic pathfinder in the Pacific.

Before the age of steam the passages to the Northwest Coast from California and Panama were among the most difficult of all approaches to the coast. The northeast trades which assisted mariners on southerly tracks proved the archenemy for northward bound sailing vessels. From a northern California port, for instance, a ship would have to sail far outwards from the land before reaching winds suitable for a reasonable reverse track to Nootka. In these circumstances the shortest sea route in terms of time from Monterey to Vancouver Island or Alaska actually lay by the Hawaiian Islands.[4] While the northeast trades defied ships and crews bound north, they could be their ally on the way south. For instead of beating into the wind between storms ships could make their way leisurely south along the shore investigating river mouths, straits and inlets. Consequently almost all of the great maritime discoveries on the Northwest Coast occurred on southward bound tracks.

The length of passages in the Pacific meant that ships required able commanders who had the health of their seamen at heart.[5] They also meant that certain Pacific foodstuffs acquired importance, the Galapagos turtle being noteworthy. These long voyages meant that places of refreshment and repair were needed within the Pacific rim, such as Monterey, Nootka Sound, Hawaii, and Petropavlovsk on the Kamchatka Peninsula. It meant, too, that emporiums were needed on the Northwest Coast, in particular Sitka, Nootka Sound and Astoria (Fort George under North West and Hudson's Bay Company control). And long distance voyaging required strong ships with adequate storage, ships that could be efficiently manned and manoeuverable in inshore waters. The snow, a two-masted, square-rigged vessel usually measuring 100 to 200 tons, was the preferred choice of the English maritime fur traders. The intricacies of the Northwest Coast as well as the type of coasting trade made it necessary that the traders bring schooners, shallops and other small vessels to the coast in frame, and to complete them in quarters on shore. In this way distance gave birth to the European shipbuilding industry on the same coast.

In the late 18th century the vastness of the Pacific still defied description. It was a desert of waters, a trackless expanse, a vast empty space that provided not only physical but psychological difficulties. Only by sailing over the profoundly deep, blue waters of the Pacific for weeks together, Charles Darwin said, could a person comprehend the immensity of the world's largest ocean.[6] The passage from Canton to the Northwest Coast might take seven to ten weeks by sail. A voyage from London round Cape Horn would consume nearly half a year (witness the passages of the *Columbia* and *Lady Washington* or of the *Isaac Todd*); Montreal or Boston were not much closer to Nootka than London. Via the Cape of Good Hope the passage to the Northwest Coast was even longer, and avoiding the notorious Cape Horn was hardly a compensation given the tricky track through the straits of Southeast Asia and Polynesia. The southern route eastwards from the Cape of Good Hope along the "roaring forties" was not then frequently used; but some ships, George Vancouver's command, H.M.S. *Discovery*, among them, found this a fast, safe route to the Northwest Coast.

2. Origins of the Maritime Fur Trade

The first America-to-Asia trade in the latitude of the British Columbia coast began as an incidental feature of Cook's third voyage to the Pacific. That great navigation of the North Pacific rim — from Oregon to Macao via Nootka, Cook's Inlet, Unalaska, Kamchatka, and Japan — opened a new branch of European commerce. This trade did not predate the Russian trade from Alaska nor the Spanish commerce via the Manila galleon; it did not predate any aboriginal seaborne traffic with the Orient — if ever such existed. But Cook's voyage inaugurated the great sea link between the Northwest Coast and China. This trade grew from small beginnings, and what seems particularly curious about it is that it began not by any great design of merchants in the City of London or even by some trade mission of government agents. It began by accident, and its repercussions were greater than Cook's men could have imagined.

At Nootka, Cook's ships had been met in March 1778 by eager Nootka natives shouting "Macook" — will you trade? And for almost a month officers and men sold trinkets, nails, knives, clothes, indeed anything they could lay their hands on for the lustrous sea-otter pelts that the Nootka offered in quantity.[7] Farther north, on the Alaska Coast, the British again traded with the natives for skins. An early indication of the wealth of the British cargo came at Unalaska where a canny Russian trader attempted, unsuccessfully in part, to convince the British to sell their peltry at the Russian port of Kamchatka rather then waiting for Canton.[8]

But when the *Resolution* and *Discovery* anchored at the Chinese port they quickly realized that small fortunes could be made in the trade. Many are the stories of the huge profits realized.[9] One sea-otter pelt was worth approximately two years salary of an able seaman. In these circumstances, Captain John Gore, in command, feared a near mutiny on his hands because his men wanted to return to the Northwest Coast. Indeed two seamen stole a navy cutter and sailed for Nootka, never to be heard of again.

When the official account of Cook's voyage appeared in 1784 it contained a blueprint for a new branch of commerce. Lieutenant James King, R.N., who prepared the published account, described a scheme for a surveying-fur trading voyage to open the trade.[10] Two ships, one of 200 and the other of 150 tons, he said, should with the knowledge and help of the East India Company, sail with the southwesterly monsoon in early April. They should shape a course for Cook's Inlet, coast eastwards and southwards, trade on the Northwest Coast for three months, and then return to China in early October.

King's scheme contained an appreciation of several elements subsequently necessary for the successful prosecution of such a venture: the nature of winds and currents in the Pacific; the consent or even involvement of the East India Company, which possessed the rights by charter of British trade in China; the demands of the Northwest Coast Indians as consumers; the necessity to send two ships to make cruising in hazardous waters safe for the expedition as a whole; and the obligation for maritime fur traders to conduct further surveys. King's plan was read by a number of entrepreneurs, some of whom immediately grasped the project and took steps to outfit ships. There was at least one false start: the project of William Bolts and the Imperial Asiatic Company to send a ship under an Austrian flag of convenience did not reach fruition. But in April, 1785, the snow *Harmon*, James Hanna master, sailed from Macao for Nootka and was back in Macao in December with a rich cargo that realized over 20,000 Spanish dollars on the China market. The voyage showed that a small, economical vessel could realize a handsome profit for her investors.

Subsequently several expeditions from China, India, and London ventured forth to the distant coast.[11] James Strange sailed from Madras; John Meares sailed from Bombay and later Macao; Portlock and Dixon sailed from London. By 1789 the British had almost the sole control of the trade, though Yankee traders had by now appeared and the Spanish were selling California pelts on the China market through agents in Manila. At just the time that James Colnett, another English trader, was about to establish a permanent, armed base at Nootka the British government had decided to back the claims of the traders against foreign enroachment by sending an armed expedition to build a similar military base-emporium. Both these projects were stopped by the famous Nootka crisis, when a Spanish captain, Martinez, seized or interferred with several British merchant ships as interlopers in a claimed Spanish preserve and in doing so sparked off a crisis that almost led to war. Ultimately the British gained rights of restitution to their shore establishment as claimed by John Meares. More importantly, they won from Spain by convention the recognition of British rights of trade in most areas of the Pacific. Now one ancient obstacle to

British commerce had been overcome; it now remained for the British to compete with the Yankee merchantmen who were engaging in the maritime fur trade. With the British at war with France, Spain and the United States during much of 1792-1815, distant merchant venturing from English and colonial ports was confined. And after the French wars and the War of 1812, though British maritime fur traders continued to go from Nootka to Canton, they nonetheless found the restrictive practices of the East India Company detrimental. It was not until the third decade of the nineteenth century that the monopolistic hindrance was removed for all time, by which time the sea otter had been all but exterminated on the Northwest Coast. For these reasons Americans ultimately acquired an ascendancy in the trade.

3. North West Company trade to Canton.

The Nor'westers built on the foundations of the British maritime fur trade. They used the connections established by the Americans in Canton to good use. By the early years of the nineteenth century competition with the Hudson's Bay Company on the north and John Jacob Astor's American Fur Company on the south had drawn the Nor'westers west to the Pacific cordillera. Despite a lack of a government-granted monopoly as enjoyed by their Bay rivals, the Nor'westers had successfully established an east-west commerce from the St. Lawrence River to the mouth of the Columbia River that foreshadowed, Harold Innis rightly tells us, the Canadian confederation.[12] North West Company interests penetrated south of the present Canadian-United States border and north into the Athabaska and Mackenzie River water-sheds. But the push to the Pacific constituted their greatest achievement, for it provided them with new markets for Athabaska and cordillera furs to China. But more, it afforded a link with the western sea, for Hudson Bay was denied to them and Montreal lay too distant from Athabaska for economical transport of supplies imported and furs exported.

About the same time that the Nootka Convention recognized British rights of trade in the Pacific and rights to claim territory on the Northwest Coast hitherto unoccupied land by European nations, the

Nor'westers had begun their efforts to penetrate the China market.[13]
Ships from Montreal took furs to London for transshipment to Moscow, Irkutsk and ultimately Peking. In the early 1790's one quarter of
all Company furs were destined for Russia with the majority subsequently going to China. The route was long and transshipment was
both difficult and expensive. Thus Company directors reasoned direct
access to Canton by sea — either from Montreal or Nootka (or elsewhere on the Northwest Coast) — would provide for an expansion of
this trade and for cost benefits. In 1792 the North West Company appealed to the British government to request that Lord Macartney, then
undertaking an embassy to Peking to open Chinese gates to British
Empire trade, should press for direct admission of Canadian furs to
China. Macartney was unsuccessful, and the Nor'westers were forced
to undertake new initiatives to penetrate the Chinese market.

In 1792 the Nor'westers began using American business connections to trade in Canton. After the New York ship *Empress of China* had
arrived in Macao in August 1784, several ships had sailed for China
from New York, Boston and elsewhere on the eastern American seaboard. In 1788 the ships *Columbia* and *Lady Washington* solved the
riddle of the China trade by exchanging their cargoes of peltry for tea
and returning to Boston round the world.[14] In Canton recently arrived
American agents were prepared to receive any furs, Canadian or otherwise, they could sell to the mandarins. This induced the Nor'wester
partnership in Montreal of McTavish, Frobisher and Alexander Henry
to smuggle large quantities of furs across the border to American ports
and to charter, possibly in conjunction with John Jacob Astor of New
York, the ships *Washington* and *America* to convey pelts to China via
Cape Horn. The return cargo of yard goods, tea and porcelain purchased in Canton was sold to Astor. This was followed by a second,
more ambitious North West Company undertaking, the outlay for
which was £279,894, a princely sum indeed. On this occasion the
Company sent 4,000 beaver pelts to China in an 800-ton vessel chartered in New York. Some indication of the volume of trade to the
Orient is given by the fact that in the years 1792 to 1795 the
Nor'westers sent annually to China furs worth 40,000 Spanish dollars
on the China market. In 1798 the Nor'westers, on Alexander Henry's
initiative, bought an American ship, the *Northern Liberties*, induced

Messrs. Seton, Maitland & Company of New York to invest heavily in the project, and sent a cargo of Canadian furs expected to realize 40,000 Spanish dollars in Canton. The *Northern Liberties* was to sail to Canton and thence to any European port, with leave to call at Falmouth, England, for "orders warranted American property."[15]

This sort of trade contravened British regulations, of course, and it circumvented existing charter rights of the East India Company. But for the Canadians it was a skillful, necessary subterfuge (not unlike British trader John Meares trading in Nootka sea-otter skins under a Portuguese flag of convenience, or Charles Barkley masquerading under Austrian colors, or John Henry Cox sailing under the Swedish flag), for American ships could not enter British ports in North America or the West Indies. Moreover, American ships were neutrals during the war then raging between Britain and France, and the Canadian-American fur link to China was partly born out of necessity.

Meanwhile, Alexander Mackenzie, after his famous 1793 continental crossing to the Pacific, became the promoter of what the Nor'westers came to call the "Columbia enterprise." He believed that in order to outrival the Hudson's Bay Company the Nor'westers had to control the Canadian northwest, get access to the Pacific, and absorb the Hudson's Bay Company. He did not believe that the Nor'westers' salvation lay in collaboration with the Americans. Rather, he envisioned founding a new company, the Fishery and Fur Company, that would send ships to the Northwest Coast, where an entrepôt would be built at Nootka. A commerce in sea-otter skins would be conducted on the coast and the furs sent to China. Concurrently the whale fishery of the North Pacific could be developed. Furs from Athabaska would be sent via Hudson Bay to Europe. The success of this scheme was predicated on removing two legal obstacles — getting rights of fishing and navigation from both the East India Company and the South Sea Company and obtaining a license of transit for trade goods through Hudson's Bay and Rupert's Land. Mackenzie's scheme proved impossible: his North West Company partners, seeking a balance between the Company's European and China interests, could not give approval to the project. Moreover, the Colonial Office could not be persuaded to supply the necessary military support. And, not least, the Hudson's Bay and East India

Companies could not be persuaded to yield their precious charter rights.[16]

For these several reasons the Nor'westers could not press their advantage in trade with China until such time as the secrets of the Pacific corderilla, as discovered by David Thompson and Simon Fraser, revealed the great fur wealth of the farthest west. The Nor'westers planned to establish a depot at the mouth of the Columbia, to send supplies and trade goods annually to the Northwest Coast, and to ship furs from the coast and the interior directly to China. This was the "golden round" from Europe, eastern North America, the Northwest Coast, China and the Atlantic again. The Nor'westers found themselves forstalled by the Astorians at the mouth of the Columbia, but it was not long before they had purchased Astoria from the Pacific Fur Company and sent their first trans-Pacific shipment directly to China. Their purchase of Astoria in 1813 had been effected because their American rivals knew of North West Company plans to send a heavily-armed merchantman, the *Isaac Todd*, from Portsmouth to the Columbia, and that His Majesty's Ships *Phoebe*, *Racoon* and *Cherub* were providing armed protection for the ship round the Horn to secure her from American privateers then known to be preying on British whalers in the southern oceans.

In any event, by 1813 the Nor'westers were relatively secure at the Columbia River mouth, and for a decade they exported furs directly or indirectly to China. Furs sent in the *Isaac Todd*, for instance, sold in Canton for $101,115.40, not "a flattering price," one Company servant mused,[17] but evidently sufficiently attractive to encourage subsequent voyages. At Canton her supercargo, Angus Bethune, secured a lading of tea which the *Isaac Todd* carried to London for the East India Company; this brought only freight charges and no profits to the Nor'westers. The East India Company monopoly allowed other British ships only to be common carriers on this distant leg.

The next ship, the schooner *Columbia*, twice conveyed peltry to Canton and also pioneered Nor'wester trade with the Spanish in Alta California, the Hawaiians at Kailua, and the Russians at Bodega Bay and at Sitka.[18] The "golden round" was not now dependent merely on British manufactures, Northwest Coast furs, and Chinese tea. Such items as sandalwood, rum, powder, ball, bar-iron, livestock, tallow, seal skins, provisions, naval stores, and tobacco were conveyed by the *Columbia* within the broad confines of the Pacific. A third Nor'wester ship, the *Colonel Allen,* took not only furs from the Northwest Coast as was customary but specie from Spanish America to Canton in 1816, adding yet another dimension to North West Company trade.

Thereafter, however, the sea links between Canada and China languished until the mid-nineteenth century. The Nor'westers found it more economical to revert to the system of having American houses facilitate their business in Canton. Between 1815 and 1821 five or six ships sailed for the Nor'westers under arrangement with Perkins & Co. of Boston and J. & J.N. Perkins of Canton. In order to make this trade appear legal the North West Company even considered Old Oregon a United States possession in order to circumvent the East India Company monopoly. Canadian trade was thus aided in a somewhat peculiar way by American independence, and apparently the Company was willing to sacrifice claims to sovereignty in the far west in order to earn profits. Dividends bulked larger in importance than dominion.

After 1821, when the Hudson's Bay Company replaced the North West Company on the Pacific slope, the China trade continued, though (as in the 1790s) through London rather than directly to Canton. The East India Company's restrictive licence did not allow the Bay traders to penetrate the China market except under burdensome charges. Politicians such as George Canning continued to bemoan the octopus-like control that the East India Company enjoyed. The trans-Pacific trade, Canning said, was the most promising trade of the future.[19] But it was not until 1833 that Parliament suspended the Company's exclusive privileges in the China trade.

James Cook had thought the trade in furs in the North Pacific trade too distant from England to be profitable;[20] but in fact this became a paying proposition in luxuries for the China market. As in some other trades of this sort it brought forth smuggling and flags of convenience, subterfuges and surreptitious arrangements. The British pioneered the maritime fur trade; the Americas later acquired ascendancy in the same trade; and the North West Company had began their Columbia enterprise and "adventure to China". Canadian traders employed direct and indirect trading links with China; frequently they found it best to deal through London and New York rather than sending their peltry directly to Canton. In this way the North Atlantic Triangle played its own peculiar and distant role in the opening of Canadian-Chinese trade and in the emerging commerce beyond the great southern capes.

Notes

[1] Vincent T. Harlow, *The Founding of the Second British Empire, 1763-1793. Vol. I. Discovery and Revolution; Vol. II. New Continents and Changing Values* (London, 1952-64); see also, David Mackay, "British Interests in the Southern Oceans, 1782-1794," *New Zealand Journal of History*, III (Oct. 1969), pp. 124-42.

[2] For a survey of British interests, see Barry M. Gough, "The Northwest Coast in late 18th Century British Expansion," in Thomas Vaughan, ed., *The Western Shore: Oregon Country Essays Honoring the American Revolution* (Portland, 1976), pp. 47-80.

[3] *Parliamentary Debates*, XXVIII, 1790, p. 781.

[4] See Matthew F. Maury, *Explanations and Sailing Directions to Accompany the Wind and Current Charts* (8th ed.; 2 vols., Washington, D.C., 1859), pp. 64-67, and, by the same, *Physical Geography of the Sea* (new ed., London, 1869), plate VIII.

[5] Nathaniel Portlock and George Dixon were appointed to the command of the King George's Sound Company maritime fur trading expedition in 1785 because, as William Beresford put it, they were "not only . . . able navigators, but (having been on this voyage with Captain Cook) they well knew what parts of the Continent were likely to afford us the best trade; and also form a tolerable idea of the temper and disposition of the natives; add to this, they are men of feeling and humanity, and pay the most strict attention to the health of their ship's companies, a circumstance of the utmost consequence in a voyage of such length." William Beresford, George Dixon, *A Voyage Round the World* (London, 1789), .p. 3.

[6] Alan Moorehead, *Darwin and the Beagle*, (London, 1969), p. 218; also Harry Morton, *The Wind Commands: Sailors and Sailing Ships in the Pacific* (Vancouver, 1975), p. 166.

[7] J.C. Beaglehole, ed. *The Journals of Captain James Cook on his Voyages of Discovery: The Voyage of the* Resolution *and* Discovery, *1776-1780* (2 parts; Cambridge: Hakluyt Society, 1967), part 1, pp. 296-7.

[8] *Ibid.*, p. 452.

[9] One example may suffice. At Tahiti William Bligh purchased 30 large green Spanish beads from the natives for a hatchet worth one shilling. At Prince William Sound he bought six sea-otter skins with twelve of the beads, skins which sold in China for £15 each. "Here," Midshipman Trevenen mused, "we find a quick return of 90 pounds for one shilling!" Christopher Lloyd and R. C. Anderson, eds., *A Memoir of James Trevenen* (London: Navy Records Society, 1959), pp. 21-2.

[10] James Cook and James King, *Voyage to the Pacific Ocean* (3 vols.; London, 1784), III, pp. 437-440.

[11] See Harlow, *Founding of the Second British Empire*, II, ch. VII.

[12] H. A. Innis, *The Fur Trade in Canada* (Toronto, 1956), p. 262.

[13] The following is based on Barry M. Gough, "The North West Company's 'Adventure to China'," *Oregon Historical Quarterly* (Dec. 1975), pp. 305-311, where full documentation can be found.

[14] S. E. Morison, *The Maritime History of Massachusetts, 1783-1860* (Boston, 192), chs. IV-VI.

[15] Alexander Mackenzie to McTavish, Fraser & Co., London, March 10, 1798, in W.K. Lamb, ed., *Journals and Letters of Sir Alexander Mackenzie* (Cambridge; Hakluyt Society, 1970), p. 470.

[16] Gough, "North West Company's 'Adventure to China'," p. 322.

[17] *Ibid.*, p. 327.

[18] Marion O'Neil, "The Maritime Activities of the North West Company, 1813 to 1821," *Washington Historical Quarterly*, XXI (October 1930), pp. 254-63.

[19] Edward J. Stapleton, ed., *Some Official Correspondence of George Canning* (2 vols., London, 1887), II, pp. 71-116.

[20] Beaglehole, *Cook Journals*, part 1, p. 371.

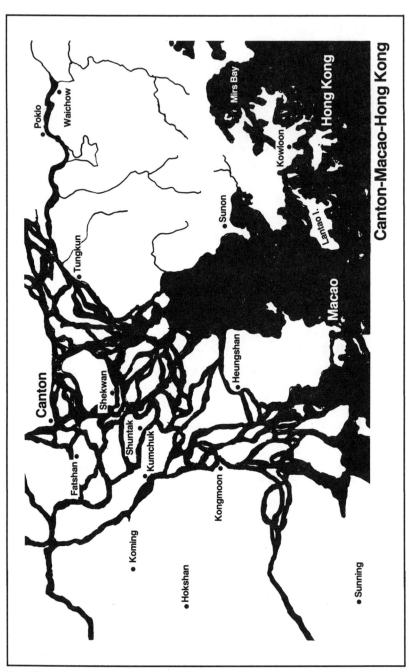

Canton-Macao-Hong Kong

Timothy J. Runyan and Andrew Dyczkiewycz

"I Don't Think Much of a Life on the Ocean Wave:"
Homeward Bound from China, 1855

Hugh F. Bell

On February 4, 1855 the ship *Alfred* was some 1200 miles east of Japan on the homeward voyage from Hong Kong to San Francisco. On board was the part owner and nominal captain, Edward Erastus Upham of Portland, Maine, who was completing his first and only China voyage and heartily sick of it. On that day, he commenced a rambling letter to his nephew, Charles Woodman Kittredge, a fellow citizen of Portland, a letter he finally completed on February 22nd when the *Alfred* was still 1500 miles from the Golden Gate.[1]

This letter can hardly be unique but it does bring into focus many of the elements of the world as it was in 1855, all filtered through the loneliness that a long voyage brought to men at that age. It was America in motion and in microcosm. It has additional appeal because it is not just an item in a collection of papers. There is no foundation and no sequel — it stands alone. Like the archeologist who hypothesizes a civilization from a potsherd, the curious historian will attempt to reconstruct the historical context around such an artifact.

The letter is a long one but by ignoring the host of personal allusions and rambling musings, the factual outline provides a starting point. The date, position, and the ship bearing the verbose correspondent are explicit. The letter also recites that the voyage to Hong Kong and Canton had been a "spec," or speculation, for Upham and that he was part owner of both the *Alfred* and a companion vessel, the *Leonore*. On board the *Alfred* he had, besides 600 tons of general freight, 500 piculs of sugar on his own account and 250 Chinese passengers, in special deck houses, a cargo item of more than passing interest. He was generally pessimistic as to the financial outcome of his venture.

But amid the general recital of gloom and doom, Upham's letter shows flashes of excitement and pride. The voyage had clearly been the "great adventure" in an otherwise humdrum life. "I have," he wrote, "experienced more blood stirring sensations in these last five months than I would have squeezed out of life in Portland in ten years." He had seen a Chinese army in battle array; he had fought the river pirates alongside Commander George Preble of the U.S. Navy; he had seen Houqua, the great tea merchant, and Han Sing, the silk dealer, and finally, he had eaten "Birds' Nest Soup" and discovered that voluntary chastity among Chinese women was "unknown."

So much for the bare outline of the letter, but breathes there a historian with soul so dead as to let the matter drop there. All kinds of questions, both factual and of broader significance come to mind. What happened to Upham; to the *Alfred*; to the *Leonore*; to the Chinese passengers? What was the Navy doing fighting pirates on the Pearl River? On another level, one should ask how this "spec" by a nondescript Portland merchant fit into the broad pattern of world events.

Many questions remain unanswered but a desultory investigation has filled in many of the gaps and the process gives an inkling of the connecting links between such seemingly diverse events as the

California gold rush, the Taiping Rebellion, the shipping depression of the 1850's, and the "Yankee exodus" to the American West.

The second United States census of 1800 reached as far as the tiny hamlet of Montgomery in the northernmost part of Vermont. This settlement consisted of only four families, one of them being that of James Upham who lived there with his wife Elizabeth, four children, and probably a hired man.[2] James had originally come from Brookfield, Massachusetts, married a Deerfield girl, Elizabeth Barnard, lived for a time in Mayville, New Brunswick, moved back to Brookfield, and finally to northern Vermont. The children kept coming, twelve in all, and in 1808, the eleventh, Edward Erastus, was born.[3] When Edward was nineteen, his father died and the youth left the family farm to seek his fortune in Portland where his older sister, Sarah Eliza, had preceded him. In 1824, Sarah had married a footloose young man, Joseph Woodman Kittredge, originally from Canterbury, New Hampshire, who was trying to make his way in the burgeoning Portland commercial community as a partner of Daniel Chamberlain dealing in "West India Goods."[4]

But Kittredge was soon on the move, first to Salisbury, New Hampshire, then on to Sutton, Vermont, and finally westward to Illinois. His peregrinations and exoduses were like those of a circling pigeon deciding on its ultimate course. The Kittredge's first child, Charles, the recipient of Upham's letter, had gone as far as Illinois with the family but had returned east after his father's death and gravitated to Portland where he, too, sought to make his fortune.[5]

Edward Upham, though not quite so mobile as the Kittredges, had his problems settling down. In 1830, the *Portland Directory* listed him as a partner with Edward Waite in the mercantile business. In 1834, he had joined a Mr. Bartels at "the head of Long Wharf" dealing in West India goods.[6] He then moved to Bangor where he continued his mercantile activities, but in December 1838, he came back to Portland to marry Julia Richardson, a Portland merchant's daughter. In 1839, their son, Edward Richardson Upham was born, and three years later, Julia was dead, probably a victim of that killer of the age, childbirth.[7] In 1850, Upham was back in Portland as a merchant in partnership with Frederick Davis on the Atlantic Wharf and evidently part of the game of musical chairs that marked the middle level of the

Portland mercantile community.[8] Such men as John Brown and John Wood (mentioned somewhat enviously, in Upham's letter) occupied the apex of this beehive of activity, but beneath this exalted level, the merchant partnerships were born and dissolved with bewildering rapidity.[9]

The early fifties were boom times in Portland with four or five hundred vessels clearing the port every year.[10] Prosperity was in the air and the discovery of gold in California had sparked an explosion in the New England shipping industry. Every vessel that would float was eagerly snapped up and dragooned into the San Francisco run. It is here that the *Alfred* and Upham's other ship, the *Leonore*, entered the picture.

Historians of this incredible era recount in glowing terms the meteoric rise and fall of the American clipper climaxed by the eighty-nine day run of Donald McKay's *Flying Cloud* from New York to San Francisco. Usually ignored is the less glamorous armada of aging packets, converted whalers, and even coasting schooners, that were loaded with knocked-down houses, pianos, shovels, and thousands of New England's young men — all bound for Eldorado.[11]

A common pattern was the formation of a local company, the sale of shares, the purchase of a vessel and cargo, and the urgent leave taking. Such was the New England Mining and Trading Company formed in the fall of 1848 by about 100 Boston men headed by Captain Herman H. Greene and Samuel Whitmarsh. The $1000 shares gave the venture a sound capital base and permitted the purchase of the *Leonore* for $30,000.[12] If ships could smile, the *Leonore* would have sported a grin from cathead to cathead for she had cost her original owner $8,429.25 fourteen years earlier when she slid down the ways at John Currier, Jr.'s yard at Newburyport.[13] In the intervening years, this 370 ton ship (with square stern and female figurehead according to her registration) was employed first as a Black Ball packet on the Liverpool run, and then moved to Boston as part of the New Orleans cotton fleet.[14]

On February 3, 1849, the *Leonore* cleared Boston and after a relatively fast and easy passage of 149 days arrived at San Francisco, where the eager gold seekers and would-be profiteers found neither gold nor profits. The company voted to hold the cargo for higher prices but with a glutted market the prices kept sinking and the *Leonore* joined the scores of abandoned vessels cluttering the harbor.[15] Eventually, she became an anchored store ship and quietly awaited Edward Upham's "spec."

The story of the *Alfred* was much the same if not so well documented. Captain George W. Bourne of Kennebunk launched her in 1833 and somehow eased her 453 tons down the river to start her career.[16] The *Alfred*, like the *Leonore*, began as a Liverpool packet and then shifted to the New Orleans trade about 1843. She apparently rounded the Horn and arrived in San Francisco in 1850, soon joining the *Leonore* as an anchored store ship.[17]

This forest of masts of abandoned vessels represented bargains to daring, or foolish, entrepreneurs, but where was one to find crews or profitiable freights? Upham apparently thought he had the answer, though when, or how, he made his move, remains a mystery. In the 1852-1853 *Directory*, he was still listed as maintaining an office on the Railroad Wharf and boarding at the United States Hotel, but the San Francisco ship registers reveal that on May 30, 1854, Upham became one-quarter owner and master of the *Alfred*.[18] The Naval Office cleared her for Hong Kong the same day. Ten days later, the *Leonore* was registered with Upham listed as one-quarter owner and was cleared for Hong Kong with Charles Melville Scammon as master.[19] Some twenty years later, Scammon was to gain some fame as author of the superb book, *Marine Mammals of the Northwestern Coast of North America*, and left his name on the lagoon in Baja California where the objects of his research, the California gray whales, still gather to mate every spring.[20]

There seems to be no record of the westward voyage other than the routine report of the U.S. Consul in Hong Kong of the arrival of the *Alfred* on August 14, in ballast. A further report, dated September 24, noted that the *Leonore* was "in port still" after arriving with a cargo of spars and ballast. Assuming no stops en route, the expedition was indeed a "spec" with no outbound freight.[21]

Upham's stay in Chinese waters is best traced in the diary of Commander George Henry Preble, U.S.N., an old Portland friend of

San Francisco Bay, 1850's (*National Archives*)

Upham's who, as executive officer of the *Macedonian*, was just completing an important role in the Perry expedition for the opening of "the Japanese Oyster," as Preble put it.[22] After leaving Japan, the *Macedonian* stopped at the Philippines and dropped anchor off Hong Kong on August 27. Preble noted that among the first visitors aboard was "Mr. E.E. Upham of Portland as large as life and twice as natural with his rosy cheeks and 'shining morning' face." Upham, wrote Preble, was at Hong Kong "as the nominal captain of a ship which he purchased in California," but that "he has an old salt for a mate to wet nurse him."[23]

From then until the *Alfred's* departure for San Francisco in January 1855, Preble and Upham saw each other on many occasions. The day after Preble's arrival at Hong Kong, he was sent up river to Canton to take command of the armed paddle wheel steamer, *Queen*, which Commodore Perry had chartered from the British to satisfy the demands of American merchants at Canton for protection. It was an odd command, but Preble was pleased on several counts. His pay was increased by $25 a month, he was called "captain," and he had considerable freedom to enjoy either his immense cabin or the social whirl of the international settlement at Canton.[24] The same whirl also attracted Upham who left his ships at Hong Kong and stayed with Wetmore & Co., American merchants who occupied the "Imperial Hong" on the Canton waterfront.[25]

Apparently one of the first things Upham learned was that if he had arrived two months earlier, he could have sold his ships at a fat profit, but while nursing this grievance, he had to dicker for a return cargo to make his "spec" pay off.[26] This presented problems for Canton and all of southern China was in the throes of the Taiping Rebellion, a bloody attempt to overthrow the Manchu dynasty that during its course resulted in over 20,000,000 deaths.[27] During Upham's stay, the rebel forces were besieging both Canton and Shanghai and Preble noted that not a chest of tea was coming down river for export.[28] The unsettled conditions did create an alternate opportunity, however, for many Chinese seeking both to avoid the war and to participate in the California gold rush were willing and able to pay good money for passage. It was probably through Wetmore & Co. that Upham arranged the charter of both his vessels. By October 29, he informed Preble that he had paying charters, the *Alfred* for $15,000 and the *Leonore* for $9,000. He was also expending time and money buying the usual gifts for friends at home, silk dresses and shawls.[29]

On 2 and 3 November, Upham had the big thrill of his voyage, his battle with the pirates. He was on board the *Queen* as a guest passenger for an errand run from Hong Kong to Macao and, as the *Queen* passed Tyho Bay on the south shore of Lantao Island, they were fired upon by a "Piratical Fleet of ten junks mounting heavy guns." Finding himself outgunned Preble secured the cooperation of British fleet units and returned to do battle a second day. Despite a reinforced pirate fleet, cannon fire and a landing party led by Preble destroyed the pirate village and most of the junks. Preble reported that during the battle, Upham "took off his coat — as we laughingly said — to save it."[30]

Upham's version as contained in his letter was ecstatic. "I have fought the pirates took seven deliberate shots at them with a musket loaded with ball & 3 buckshott — We finally conquered, and burnt their ships & the best part of their town. The little *Storm Queen* Comd Preble (Mr Cox's son in law) with whom I was guest and passenger, fought, six of their craft lashed together . . . We finally got help, and licked them. Preble is a brick, and it is an honor . . . to have fought these damned miscreants under so able & honorable a commander."[31]

At last, the homeward bound cargoes were complete. The Hong Kong consular despatches indicate that the *Alfred* with "passengers, rice, granite [?], etc" cleared for San Francisco and had to "put back" in December, an incident referred to by Upham as putting back for repairs after a gale that "blew half the hair off my head."[32]

On top of the prospect of a long and stormy voyage to California, Upham had an additional worry concerning his Chinese passengers. The "Chinese Problem" in California, and elsewhere, is beyond the boundaries of this account, but some background is necessary for the understanding of Upham's concern.[33] The massive emigration of "Celestials" from China took two forms during this period. First, there was the infamous coolie trade under which thousands of impoverished Chinese were enticed or "shanghied" as contract laborers either in the deadly guano pits of the Chincha Isles or the tropical plantation

Chinese painting of the *Queen* by Sungua (*Courtesy of the Massachusetts Historical Society. Photo by George M. Cushing.*)

systems of the colonial world.[34] At the very time of Upham's China venture, attention was being focused on this substitute for black slavery that was on the decline everywhere outside of the American south. The second branch of Chinese emigration was made up largely of middle-class Chinese farmers and urban workers who paid their fare to lands of greater opportunity, principally California. Upham's passengers were of the latter variety, but he was running against the grain of two movements. First, was the growing public awareness of the plight of all immigrants who were crammed like cargo beneath the hatches of miserably equipped ships bound for America across the oceans of the world. Secondly, there was the increasing resentment against the strange pagans who poured through the Golden Gate and into the gold fields and growing towns of California. The Chinese, by their seemingly unlimited capacity for hard work and frugality, were natural targets for envy and nativist bitterness.[35]

In 1847, Congress had passed "An Act to Regulate the Carriage of Passengers in Merchant Vessels" which prescribed fines and forfeiture for vessels not providing 14 square feet per passenger below decks, or carrying more than 2 passengers per 5 tons of register.[36] Officials tended to wink at violations of such regulations and Upham complained, "we have not infringed the law as practiced heretofore." But now he had 250 deckhouse passengers aboard a vessel of only 453 tons, a clear violation. Only weeks after the departure of the *Alfred* and the *Leonore* for Hong Kong in June 1854, a series of events had changed the "practice." On July 19, 1854, the bark *Libertad* arrived at San Francisco from Hong Kong reporting that 100 of her 500 passengers had died en route from scurvy or "ship fever." While being held in quarantine 45 more died. The captain was charged with violations of the state immigration laws and the ship was libelled under the Federal Act. Then, the *Exchange* arrived with similar sad results, and on August 21, the bark *Louisa Jacoba Johanna* was also libelled.[37]

It is obvious that this news followed Upham to Hong Kong for his letter reported that his charterer's bond would not be large enough to clear the ship if libelled. California's zeal in law enforcement was fleeting, however, for neither the *Alfred* nor the *Leonore* encountered difficulties on their arrival.[38]

Upham's attitude towards his charges was curious. At the end of his letter, he remarked "that you might feel some little insecurity from being shut up with 250 pagans whose *Chatterings* seem more the language of the Devil than anything human, but I have made them *like me tho*. They come around whenever I show myself — like — like flies."

The views Upham held of China and the Chinese were essentially those of a wide-eyed tourist. "This China is a great pagan long tailed Empire, full of wealth, Civil War and population . . . The men have as many wives as they can pay for, & all the females will *screw*, if they can get a chance . . . The women have no position, are mere slaves to the native lords and husbands, of course they will yield themselves to Europeans, who treat them like human beings."[39] After expressing concern for their souls, this credulous Yankee admitted that "their industry & numerical strength overcomes everything."

As he approached San Francisco, "Captain" Upham had started planning ahead. He had told Preble that he would return to Portland via Panama, but in his letter to Kittredge, he talked of selling his share in the *Leonore* and buying out the "sick owners" of the *Alfred* in order to send her to the Chincha Isles for guano, that valuable and generous deposit of natural nitrate fertilizer left by generations of sea birds.[40] But, business in San Francisco was too fluid to permit the execution of firm plans.

On March 14, 1855, the *Alta California* reported the arrival of the ship *Alfred*, 63 days out of Hong Kong, carrying merchandise and passengers for Bolton, Barron & Co. Three days later, consignees were requested to pay freight charges and deposits to cover average and to pick up their goods. On March 24, Captain Scammon brought in the *Leonore* with 172 Chinese passengers. Commercial notices in the newspapers indicate that cargo items such as 4000 gallons of Tea Oil [Tung oil?] and 986 sacks of Liverpool salt were sold on declining markets but there was no report as to the disposition of Upham's own venture in sugar.[41]

The picture now becomes murky. On April 11, the *Alta California* revealed that Messrs. Tubbs & Co. were fitting out the *Leonore* for a whaling voyage "at less cost than she could be from New Bedford, and get men on the same lay."[42] The next day, it was announced that the

Alfred was loading for Sydney and would accept cabin passengers ("with splendid accommodations") for $150. Her cargo was made up of Chilean barley and potatoes. The name of the master was left blank. The ship registrations are bewildering, but after rapid and successive shifts, Upham emerged as owner of 13/24 of the *Alfred* with Henry Havens as master and 1/8 owner. Thus owned and captained she cleared for Sydney on May 4.[43] Homesickness had won Upham away from the sea, apparently, for there is no evidence he was on board. The *Alfred* was next (and last) heard from in Tahiti. She arrived on June 22 where she was "sold" on July 29 and disappears from view.[44]

The *Leonore*, true to announcement, left on her whaling voyage under Captain Scammon on April 21 (but with Upham still listed as 1/4 owner). She continued as a whaler under Scammon's command until October 1856 when she was sold, her home port changed to Port Townsend, and her occupation to the carrying of timber.[45]

What of Edward Upham? He next surfaced in his home town of Portland in the 1856-1857 *Directory* as a partner in Butler & Co. and residing once again at the United States Hotel. The loneliness that had overcome him on the voyage to San Francisco soon caused him to forget, or ignore, the advice he had given his nephew about women — "In the dimnition distance you will see a petticoat fluttering in the breese and a leetle further on, you will see a ship in distress, with Colors at half mast, and I say, if you are wise you will keep your eye on the moral which reads as plain as the nose on your face, let em alone." On 9 September 1856, Upham married Miss Georgianna Deering, the daughter of another Portland merchant who three years later presented him with a second son, George, and disappeared so far as Portland records are concerned.[46]

Upham's mercantile career continued in its unstable ways. In 1856, he was a flour dealer and in 1864, his son Edward R. Upham joined him in the firm of Edward E. Upham & Son, flour millers. Upham then drifted out of this partnership into the "Real Estate and Insurance" business. By 1883 he had lost his health and moved back to his birthplace in Vermont where he died in September 1890. Oddly enough, his funeral was in Portland at the home of the widow of an old business associate.[47]

Charles Kittredge, the recipient of Upham's letter, followed his family west to Ottumwa, Iowa, where he was caught up in the Civil War, first as a captain with the 7th Iowa at Shiloh and later as colonel of the 36th Iowa Volunteer Infantry. His mother, Upham's sister, also moved to Ottumwa and is buried there, far from the Vermont hills of her childhood.[48]

George Henry Preble, confirming Upham's judgment, continued his distinguished naval career, finally retiring with the rank of rear admiral in 1878 to take up his next career as a historian.[49]

Edward Erastus Upham began his life with nothing and ended it where he began with not much more. His life would have been gray and featureless were it not for his "spec." But he had seen China, he had bought silks in Canton, he had fought the pirates, and he had seen what "would pale the cheeks" of his merchant friends in Portland "and bring their knees together like a pair of nut-crackers." He had found his great experience and perhaps that made it all worthwhile. There are many who are not even that lucky.

Notes

[1] The Upham letter is in the possession of Charles Kittredge's granddaughter, Charlotte Bannister, by whose permission it is here transcribed. She and her husband, Burn Bannister, have been most helpful in supplying information about the Kittredge family.

[2] *U.S. Census Office, Census Schedules*, 1800, Vermont.

[3] F.K. Upham, *Upham Genealogy — The Descendants of John Upham of Massachusetts* (Albany, 1872), p. 127.

[4] Mabel T. Kittredge, *The Kittredge Family in America*, (Rutland, VT, 1936); *The Portland Directory* (Portland: A.W. Thayer, 1823).

[5] A.A. Stuart, *Iowa Colonels and Regiments* (Des Moines, 1865), pp. 513-520.

[6] *The Portland Directory — 1830* (Portland: S. Coleman, 1830). *The Portland Directory — 1834*, (Portland: Arthur Shirley, 1834).

[7] *The Bangor Directory, 1843, 1846, 1848* (Bangor: Samuel Smith, 1848). Upham, *op. cit.*; John Vinton, *Richardson Memorial* (Portland, 1876), Item 6319.

[8] *The Portland Reference Book, and City Directory, for 1850-1851* (Portland: S. Becket, 1851). The continual shifting of merchants from firm to firm and from wharf to wharf during this period would be an interesting study in itself.

[9] John Brown and John Wood paid taxes in 1855 of $2696.14 and $4233.80, respectively, among the highest in the city. *Portland Reference Book, and City Directory for 1856-1857* (Portland: S. Becket, 1856).

[10] During the four year period, 1851-1854, 1768 vessels cleared Portland, but 1854 was marked by a severe drop, falling from 505 in 1853 to 309. This drop is roughly paralleled by Maine shipbuilding figures which soared from 77,000 tons in 1851 to 216,000 tons in 1855, and then collapsed to 41,000 tons in 1859. W.H. Rowe, *The Maritime History of Maine* (Freeport, 1966).

[11] See generally C. W. Haskins, *The Argonauts of California* (New York, 1890), and Rowe, *Maritime History of Maine*.

[12] Haskins, *op. cit.*, p. 495.

[13] Arthur H. Clark, *The Clipper Ship Era* (New York, 1910), p. 54; John J. Currier, *Historical Sketch of Shipbuilding on the Merrimac River* (Newburyport, 1877), and typescript addendum listing "Vessels Built by John Currier, Jr. Since 1831" (Ship No. 6), Essex Institute, Salem, MA.

[14] Carl C. Cutler, *Queens of the Western Ocean* (Annapolis, 1961), p. 448; *Registers and Enrollments*, Ship Records, National Archives, (Newburyport, 1835), R17; New York, 1838, R433; Boston, 1846, R312. The encyclopedic knowledge and assistance of Mr. Kenneth Hall of the National Archives is gratefully acknowledged.

[15] Oscar Lewis, *Sea Routes to the Gold Fields*, (New York, 1949), pp. 276-279.

[16] S.E. Bryant, *List of Vessels Built in the District of Kennebunkport, 1800-1874* (Kennebunkport, 1874).

[17] Cutler, *Queens*, pp. 504, 510, 511; *Registers and Enrollments*, New York, 1850, R125.

[18] *Ibid.*, San Francisco, 1854, R118.

[19] *Ibid.*, San Francisco, 1854, Permanent Register 40; Naval Office, San Francisco, *Clearances*, and Customs House, San Francisco, *Return of Seamen*, both at the National Archives.

[20] Charles Melville Scammon was born in 1825 in Whitefield, Maine, the son of Eliakim and Joanna (Young) Scammon. After leaving the *Leonore*, he entered the Revenue Service and in that capacity participated in the Russian-

American Telegraph Exploring Expedition of 1860, and as commanding officer of the Revenue cutter *Shubrick* welcomed the Russian fleet at San Francisco in 1863. His classic on marine mammals was published in San Francisco in 1874.

[21] *Despatches from U.S. Consuls in Hong Kong, 1844-1906*, Vol. 3, Consular Return of American Vessels arriving and departing Hong Kong, National Archives, (Microfilm M108, 10-7-1).

[22] Balislov Szczesniak, ed., *The Opening of Japan - A Diary of Discovery in the Far East, 1853-1856* (Norman, OK, 1962). See also G.H. Preble, *Genealogical Sketch of the First Three Generations of Prebles in America* (Boston, 1868).

[23] Szczesniak, *Opening of Japan*, p. 238.

[24] *Ibid.*, p. 239 *et seq.*

[25] *Ibid.*, pp. 258-259.

[26] *Ibid.*, p. 259.

[27] See generally S.Y. Teng, *The Taiping Rebellion and the Western Powers* (Oxford, 1971); John K. Fairbank, *Trade and Diplomacy on the China Coast* (Cambridge, MA, 1953); Eldon Griffin, *Clippers and Consuls: American Consular and Commercial Relations with Eastern Asia, 1845-1860* (Ann Arbor, 1938).

[28] Szczeniak, *Opening of Japan*, p. 249.

[29] *Ibid.*, pp. 261-262.

[30] *Ibid.*, pp. 263-265.

[31] Preble's vessel was sometimes referred to as the *Storm Queen*. His father-in-law, "Mr Cox" was John Cox, a fellow merchant of Upham's regularly listed in the Portland directories after 1823.

[32] *Despatches*, December 12, 1854.

[33] Griffin, *op. cit.*, pp. 194-199; Mary R. Coolidge, *Chinese Immigration*, (N.Y., 1909).

[34] *Encyclopaedia Britannica*, 11th ed., (London, 1910), Vol. 7, pp. 77-78.

[35] Rodman W. Paul, "The Origin of the Chinese Issue in California," *Mississippi Valley Historical Review*, 25 (1938-1939), pp. 181-96.

[36] *U.S. Statutes at Large*, 29th Congress, 2nd Session, Chap. XVI.

[37] Frank Soule, John H. Gihon, and James Nisbit, *The Annals of San Francisco, together with the Continuation, through 1855*, compiled by Dorothy H. Huggins (Palo Alto, 1966), pp. 4-14, (Continuation). See also p. 530 for vicious comment on Chinese immigrants in general.

[38] The flurry of immigrant deaths and resulting libels in admiralty apparently subsided. No further court proceedings were noted in the newspapers before Upham's arrival.

[39] Most historians of China assert that Chinese society as a whole was as straight-laced as any in the world. Upham must have been generalizing from his limited view in the foreign sectors of Canton, Hong Kong, and Macao.

[40] The guano pits on the Chincha Isles off Peru were booming in contrast to the depressed level of shipping world wide. The *Alta California* carried an advertisement on April 9, 1855 seeking "Guano Charters" at "the highest current rate." *Hunt's Merchant's Magazine* (Vol. 36, pp. 430-432), of 1857 carried an analytical article on guano arguing its trade value.

[41] Except for passenger traffic and gold shipments, San Francisco's trade had entered the doldrums. The *Annals* recited that beginning in 1853, goods were being shipped back to New York and that rents had fallen 30% (p. 516 *et seq*). The 1,902 ship arrivals of 1853 had declined to 1,606 in 1855 and customs duties collected declined by about 50% from 1853 to 1854 (p. 33 — Continuation). The shipment of "Liverpool Salt" on the *Leonore* must be some indication of cargoes circling the world seeking a market. The request for deposits to "cover average" concern the admiralty law practice of "general average." When, as in this case, a storm damages some of the cargo on a vessel, the loss is assessed against all the cargo so that each shipper bears his proportionate share.

[42] The future of San Francisco as a major whaling port was the subject of several news articles during this period. "Fitting out" labor was beginning to be available, as well as seamen. The obvious saving in distance to the prime sperm whale grounds was also a factor, *Annals*, p. 40 (Continuation).

[43] *Alta California*, April 11, 12 and 13, 1855; *Registers and Enrollments*, San Francisco, 1855, R42.

[44] *Despatches*, U.S. Consul in Tahiti, June 22 and June 30, 1855.

[45] *Alta California*, April 21 and 22, 1855; *Registers and Enrollments*, San Francisco, 1855, R40 and 1856, E270.

[46] *Portland Argus*, September 9, 1856.

[47] *Portland Reference Book, and City Directory, 1856-1857*, and *1858-1859*; "Portland Necrology," Vol. 1, Obituary Files of the Maine Historical Society, Portland.

[48] Stuart, *Iowa Colonels*, pp. 513-520.

[49] Szczeniak, *Opening of Japan*, xviii-xxi.

Transcript of Letter Written by
Edward Erastus Upham to Charles W. Kittredge

On board Ship Alfred at Sea
E. Long. 156 10′ N L 30.05
Feb 4 11 o'clock [1855]

Dear Charles

I have just finished a letter to Suzy which I enclose for you to forward. I should have written to you long ago, but I knew Mrs. Little read whatever I should write her to you, and from it you would be correctly posted in regards to my movements of every kind as I wrote more freely to her than to any one, and after seeing my letters to her, mine to you, would look to you like repeating myself, and as I have just finished four sheets to her, of all sorts of trash, to which I refer you, with an *order*, for her to stand & deliver so that I shall be concise in this and to the strong points of the case closely confine myself.[1] In the first place, the China voyage as a *Spec*, is somewhat wide of the mark, nothing will be made by either ship, to speak of. If I get out with only the loss of *time* I shall be well pleased, but of this you need not speak, my wages are large & will help up, and if the Govt don't bother the ship, I shall in the end do well enough, of course, I am all [ety]. I have the Charterers Bond, to hold the ship harmless against Gov't, but I fear it is insufficient to clear the ship, if she should be libelled for carrying Chinese passengers upon Deck, in houses built for that purpose. it will be a great injustice if they do, as we have not infringed the law as practiced heretofore, but Californians are opposed to Chinamen, and will raise the devil if they can, in fact. I was chartered long before the question was mooted about Deck passengers. I have 250, besides six or seven hundred tons of goods, have had to put back for repairs after a gale that blew half the hair off my head, the Cargo pays part of this expense, whether the ship is insured or not, on the principle of general average. I may not have time to write very soon after I get in, but shall always write Abba, so you will hear how I get on.[2] I have an adventure of 500 peculs of Sugar & some Rice aboard, and hope to make something if Sugar holds up in Frisco, shall do.

Well, my present intention is to sell my part of the Leonore & buy out the *sick owners*, in the Alfred, & send her to the Chincha Isles for Guana, can't of course tell, but as I am in for it shall put her through, you may depend. *I don't think much of a life on the Ocean wave tho*. I have seen enough to pay my admittance fee cheerfully, if I can get rid of my ships, or employ them profitably. it was a tall scheme & would have paid well, but we were 2 months too late. I should have cleared 20,000 $ easy if I had been in time, but I hope to live to tell you all about it yet. In the meantime I see you are in my old shoes, hope they fit easy, if your partner is right, you can't fail of doing well, only be *patient*, no particular virtue to my mind (generally, I mean) considering the uncertainty & shortness of life, but in your case it is everything - I have suffered some, sprinkled in, the grey hairs pretty thick, but no matter. I have seen *China*, bought silk & shawls in Canton, eat *Birds nest Soup*, seen a Chinese Army in battle array — *fought the Pirates took seven deliberate shots at them with a musket loaded with ball & 3 buck shott* — We finally conquered, and burnt their ships & the best part of *their Town*. The little Storm Queen, Comd Preble (Mr. Cox's son in law) with whom I was a guest & passenger, fought, six of their craft lashed together, forming a battery across the mouth of their Harbor. Three seperate times, our guns were too small for them, & we finally got help, and licked them, as before stated. Preble is a brick, and it is an *honor* and tell Mr. Cox, that I consider it so, to have fought these damned miscreants under so able & honorable a commander and my China trip would not be a total loss if I had done nothing else. I have learned much of the details of *Navigation* & things connected therewith & shall if I live turn my information to some account. I have experienced more *blood stirring sensations* in these last five months than could have squeezed out of life in Portland in ten years. — but you will say the *main point*, is not gained, no increase *in dollars* — it is a fact & I cave in, and yield the Palm of honor to your John B. Browns & your John M. Woods — and I see the people cry, as might be expected, hosanna — but I have seen in this little cruise what would pale their cheeks & bring their knees together like a pair of nut-crackers. This China is a great pagan long tailed Empire, full of wealth, Civil War and population, Some of the best informed estimate China to contain *five hundred millions* of people, some punkins, hey. — They are a funny set, as ever you saw. The men have as many wives as they can pay for, & all the females will *screw*, if they can get a chance, chastity, voluntary chastity, I believe to be unknown — its no object to them. They, the women, have no position, are mere slaves to the native lords and husbands, of course they yield themselves to Europeans who treat them like human beings. They are, as a people, of much higher intellect than I expected to find them. Some of the Chinese merchants are splendid men. Houqua, the great tea merchant and Han Sing the silk dealer, are big fish, and handle millions annually. In religion they are Idolaters — worship wooden Gods. Many of their forms of worship are after the style of the Roman Catholics, yet they are heathen and Pagan And I defy all Christendom to make anything else of them without the direct interposition of God. They obstinately adhere to their old customs, they use the old auger, and a plough, such as Adam, if he had not been confined to the limits of a Garden, would have scorned. And yet their industry & numerical strength overcomes everything. They possess ingenuity — excel in many of the finest specimens of manufacture. But what is the use, I did not propose to give you the history of China, so I will stop and cool off & finish at another sitting.

Saturday Feby 10, 1855

Since writing you the foregoing, we have *enjoyed* a constant gale of wind, as folks sometimes say — these marms enjoy very *poor* health, it has subsided a little, and the sun *is out*, whether the maternal is aware of it or not, and I confess it affords me a great relief as harbinger of a more *quiet* state of things ere long. The sea is still in a fearful mess and ready and willing to knock everything into a cockd hat that floats on its agitated bosom. The ship labours fearfully and I own to having entertained many doubts of her being able to hold together, if it continues, but here we are in the Middle of the Pacific. the gale so much abated as to enable us to run under double reef'd topsails The wind is fair and we have been making 200 miles on our Course pr day, which will in time take us to Cal'a, provided nothing *breaks* - a ships are not always as safe as the walls of Gibralter or Jerico, and ships may be a very good *institution*, dare say they are, but I must say personally, as a place of abode, they do not present many attractions, I hope we shall get in safe & that you will derive the benefit of these my thoughts on the subject, but it is awfully dusty travelling in these parts My advice to you is to trust nothing to the female gender. Never buy a vicious mare when you can obtain a noble horse and never do your *business* in the *great deep*. Ships resemble the women in more ways than one and especially as you can get no control over their motions except you are constantly at work at their *sterns*. Never trust either, at least while you can derive consolation from religion on shore. I have had a leetle experience, and can speak feelingly — *I* — am a disappointed man & if you ask me how, Echo will answer *there, whar I pint* — and in the dimnition distance you will see a petticoat fluttering in the breese and a leetle further on, you will se a ship in distress with Colors at half mast, and *I* say, if you are wise you will keep your eye on the *moral* which reads as plain as the nose on your face, *let em alone* — no harm comes on them if you don't *touch* em, good advice is often thrown away & it may be in this case, but I give it as the husbandman doth his seed to the ground hoping it may spring up and bear fruit. I find it much easier to preach on these subjects while imprisoned here, than I should to practice, if once let loose on the smiling world again. I am not well of my bruises yet but write in my berth and do the best I can to shorten the time as well as the distance of the Voyage. Remember me Kindly to Mr Davis & and any other friend who may enquire for me.[3] Stick to business and keep up the reputation of the old stand, as there is no knowing what may turn up yet. My head is dissy, The motion is so constant and violent I can write only by propping myself up in my bunk & and hold my paper on a book. I will add a post script when I get in sight of Land. until then : Adieu

22 Feby/55

This is Washington's birthday — and I am Fifteen hundred miles from my Port and a head wind, & I confess I find it hard work to get up much Patriotic ferver, yet I never before felt a stronger attachment for my *Country* than now. I fancy this feeling is strengthened in us by *visiting* other Countries. The contrast is striking. Yankeedom, with all its faults, is without doubt the greatest — *dom*, except the Kingdom of Heaven, that exists, and I long to reach her shores once again. I feel that I have lost that individual interest of a citizen. I have wandered too long — the freshing is gone, and much of that hope which was a prominent feature in my character has flown with it, the winds of the Autumn of Life have blown away, the beautiful foliage and left only the limbs and bare branches, to gase at. While the birds sang so sweetly, sheltered by the leaves of that beautiful Tree, why should one think of their ever falling, but everything has a dreary aspect, a December look and I must gather my worn garments about me, and shiver on to the end — My voyage to this part of the world has taken me to the culminating point of existance, and I dare not look forward, indeed I am too *blue* to write. What is life? one eternal grind, round and round eternally, the stone imperceptably wasting away each turn, and leaving nothing that pays. — try it, you are young — the result may vary a little, but yo ask the man who seems the most fortunate & then question the hard working laborer, who just squeeses enought out of the world around him to keep soul and body together. They will both tell you that they are neither happy or contented but perhaps may add, that they expect to be *tomorrow*, but they will *find* that tomorrow even as this day — only a leetle more so — The thing before us is a *damd* Phantom, and if overtaken by some fast runners is found to be a mass of fungus, & surrounding them with a dim sickly light that only exhibits their faults & imperfections more clearly to the pursuing crew around them — labor, be diligent, keep your blood in circulation, this the best part of the race & the clearer & calmer the atmosphere I grant therefor it is hardly worth your while to stop to pick up any one by the wayside — let your head not your *heart* direct you if you wish or hope to win. So on — on — Tan tiva Tan tiva.[4]

Now dont think because I have been writing under the influence of his Satanic Majesty's Army of *blue Devils* — that I am about to drown or give up the Ship. I shall try to make the best of everything around me, but it will be from a sense of duty — without a ray of hope for myself — Such a life is like bread made without yeast or Saleratus — dead & sour and the knowledge of it is good only as an example to thou who are bound the same road, it is for your good — You know something of my life & also something of your Uncle Chamberlin's — two opposites — both rather *mark'd* — look the surrounding circumstances in the face and go for the result, get you just such a wife as he did & be ruled by her & you will be *just* as well off as your uncle Chamberlin when you die & have *just* as *much fun* while you *live*, but I am afraid the conversation is taking rather a personal turn, so how is the weather do.[5] Ten days more of fair wind would take us to San Francisco, where if I arrive safe I propose to cut the web feathers out of my feet and try to keep the *dirt* under them in future. The "sea, the open Sea" has lost some of its poetic beauty this last voyage. The fact is I am tired of *hard* bread, *salt Beef* dirty stewards — vulgar sailors — as fellow prisoners — for a prison it is of the worst kind, while it lasts, wanting that very beautiful & satisfactory feeling of security which the prison affords, for to confess the truth in the last gale I did feel as though I might be put in pickel at any moment. And it is just possible that you might feel some little insecurity from being shut up with 250 pagans whose Chatterings seem more the language of the Devil than anything human, but I have made them *like me tho*. They come around me whenever I show myself — like — like flies a "rose by any other name would smell as sweet" — higho — Adieu, let the precious moral seed just sown by me find a proper soil & neglect not its careful culture

Your E.E.U.

Footnotes to E. E. Upham Letter

[1] "Suzy" may have been a nickname for Charles Kittredge's sister, Mary Elizabeth, who married a distant kin of Upham's, Henry B. Upham. Mabel T. Kittredge, *The Kittredge Family in America* (Rutland, Vt., 1936). "Mrs. Little" is obviously a friend, but impossible to identify with any certainty.

[2] "Abba" is possibly Abba Blanchard, wife of a Portland shipowner.

[3] "Mr. Davis" is Frederick Davis who was Upham's partner 1850-1853. *The Portland Reference Book, and City Directory* (Portland: S. Becket, 1851-53).

[4] "Tan tiva Tan tiva" derived from tantivy, or "full speed ahead."

[5] "Uncle Chamberlain" probably refers to Daniel Chamberlain who was a partner of Charles Kittredge's father in the 1820's. *The Portland Directory* (Portland, 1823).

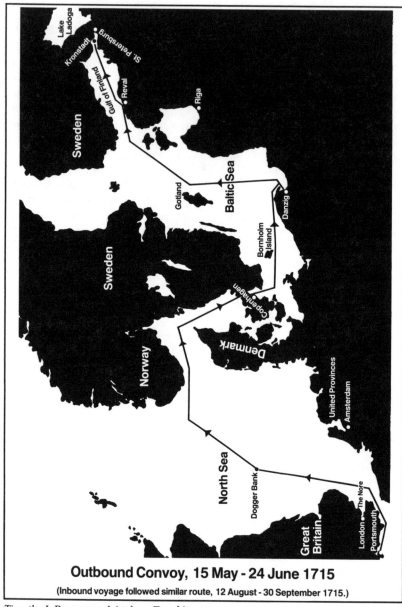

Outbound Convoy, 15 May - 24 June 1715

(Inbound voyage followed similar route, 12 August - 30 September 1715.)

Timothy J. Runyan and Andrew Dyczkiewycz

Naval Stores and Anglo-Russian
Encounters in the Baltic:
The English Expedition of 1715

Mary Emily Miller

The quest for naval stores to man the ships of England's maritime empire demanded access to the natural resources of the Baltic region. England triumphed in the contest of fleets in the late seventeenth century; France and Spain reduced their navies, the Dutch had only forty capital ships by 1711 and interest in naval affairs or careers was no longer the focus of young men even though the Dutch flute (*fluyt*) remained the principal trader of northern countries in the West. [1] But access to Baltic naval resources remained a principal feature of English diplomacy despite the contests with neighboring powers. Access to masts, planking, pitch, tar, and other materials was not assured because of the independent policies of Sweden and the emergence of Russia as a new contender for control of the Baltic.

The rise of the Russian navy is found in the familiar story of Peter the Great's fascination with boats and deserves brief recitation here. When he was fifteen (1687/88), Peter found an old boat on one of the estates outside Moscow. This craft was supposed to have been given to Ivan IV by Elizabeth I of England, but it was in dire need of repairs. Karsten Brant, a Dutch shipwright brought to Russia to serve Tsar Alexis, repaired the boat, and he put a mast and sail on it. Franz Timmermann, a Dutch sailor, taught Peter how to sail to windward, and he also taught him the craft and lore of the sea. Peter later called this sloop "The Little Grandsire of the Russian Fleet," and it is now kept in the superintendent's house in the Peter and Paul Fortress in Leningrad.[2] Brant and an English shipwright, Kent, built two or three other boats for Peter in 1688. But political matters now interfered. By 1689, Peter, obviously a threat to Sophia, heard news on 27 August that he was about to be seized. He fled, gathered his support from the troops, and ousted Sophia, who was forced into a nunnery. Ivan VI was no threat to Peter, and he remained co-tsar until his death in 1696.

From 1689 to 1694, Peter continued his own diversions while his mother and her relatives governed the country. He maintained contacts with foreigners: the German, Dutch, and English merchants, the Swiss, Francis Lefort, and the Scotsman, Patrick Gordon. From them he could hear about the activities of the West, especially the military and naval actions of the war in Europe. By 1692, he had a flotilla of small ships built by shipwrights from Holland. He travelled north to Archangel in 1693, where he saw and sailed on the sea for the first time. A second trip was made to Archangel in 1694, and it was about that time that Lefort wrote of the Tsar's intention of having a fleet of ships in the Baltic.

In 1695, war between Moscow and Turkey was resumed with Peter at the head of a force striking at Azov, the Turkish fortress which had cut off the Don Cossacks from the sea. The Russians lacked ships-of-war and engineers. They were unable to keep the Turks from resupplying Azov, and as a result, they had to withdraw from the campaign. Peter planned a new campaign, hired Prussian and Austrain engineers, and began a ship building program at Voronezh on

Dutch fluyt carrying timber from Norway stranded north of Kamperduin, Holland, February 6, 1713. (*Maritime History in Pictures*, no. 23. Danish Maritime Museum.)

the upper Don River. Using the nearby timber resources and Greeks and Italians from the south, a war galley fleet was soon developed. With Peter as a galley captain and senior officer of the van division, Azov was besieged. This time the Turks were unable to resupply the fortress, and Azov fell. Nearby on the open sea at Taganrog, construction of Russia's first naval station was begun. A ship building plan for the Volga River using Dutch shipwrights was also begun, but this construction had to be abandoned.

Now it was time to observe developments in Western shipbuilding and navigation at first hand, to check on the latest in naval, engineering, and gunnery skills, and hopefully to acquire loans and allies against Turkey. Thus, in 1697, the first Russians left to go abroad to study military and naval matters. The main group of about two hundred and fifty, including Peter, was headed by Lefort. But the Peace of Ryswick, 1697, ended European hostilities, and Peter could not get support for a war against Turkey. Instead, he concentrated on military and naval matters — recruiting shipwrights, seamen, engineers, artificers, doctors, and other specialists, and purchasing naval and military materials. Peter went from Russia to Riga, then East Prussia, then by land across north Germany to Holland. He stayed in a small house in Zaandam for a week, then moved to Amsterdam, where he worked in the East India Company yards. After five months in Holland, where he worked right alongside the other yard personnel, Peter sailed for England on the *Transport Royal*, the newest in royal yachts. The ship was a gift from King William III, whom he had met in Holland. Attracted by English naval power and the military activities of William III, Peter arrived in England in January, 1698. He lived first in Muscovy House, one of the row of Navy Board houses on Seething Lane, sometimes called Crutched Friars, where the Muscovy Company had originated. He later leased John Evelyn's house at Deptford, where "He spent most of his time in what related to war and shipping, and upon the water." [3] He was especially interested in the ability to draft a ship's plan before the actual building started.

Early in May, 1698, he was forced to return to Russia when some of the old special regiments, the *streltsy*, revolted. However, this eighteen month trip was extremely important to Peter. It confirmed his ideas of Westernization along technical and practical lines; it forced

Tsar Peter the Great Learning Shipbuilding at Deptford. Reproduction of an oil painting presented by Mrs. E. Beddington Behrens (née Princess Obolensky) to the Deptford Borough Council. (M. Mitchell, *The Maritime History of Russia, 848-1948,* opp. p. 184.)

him to contrast Russian cities with the more wealthy cities of the West; and it opened up to him the realities of European diplomacy and the value of theory and design in shipbuilding. The English had shown him the value of the latter, and after his trip, he preferred English shipwrights for his naval building program. He recruited somewhere in the neighborhood of 750 men to work in Russia: Dutchmen, Germans, Slavs, Italians, Greeks from the Adriatic, English, Scots, and Scandinavians. [4]

The shipbuilding program on the Don was expanding. It now included ships-of-the-line, frigates, galleys, and transports. In May, 1699, Count Feodore Alexeievitz Golovin was made High Admiral of the Azov fleet. The policy of "companies" financed by large landowners, the church, and merchants to pay for naval construction was ended by the use of appropriated state funds for shipbuilding. Extra conscription helped generate the labor force and extra taxes provided some of the money. Peter even acquired about 300 guns from Sweden. Although much of the timber used in the building was unseasoned, construction continued. A Ministry of the Admiralty was set up. Cornelius Cruys had been appointed a Vice-Admiral, and he was instrumental in getting some of the Dutch and Danes to come to Archangel and Voronezh. Joseph Ney, Richard Losens, John Deane (son of a Harwich master shipwright), master-builders Davenport, Hadley, Johnston, Gardiner, and Webb, builder's-assistant Baggs, and masters in block-making and sail-making were all involved in Peter's efforts, and these men were all English. [5] Some thirty ships, ranging from 80 to 40 guns, frigates, galleys, and transports were built for the move against Turkey. The *Predestination*, 60 guns, was designed by Peter and built by Russians. It was considered a fine ship. [6] By the summer of 1699, Peter had his southern fleet, and he actually sent his envoy to Constantinople in a forty-six gun frigate. He was now ready to turn his attention to the North and Sweden, little realizing the outcome.

Sweden and Russia had been enemies since the thirteenth century, and by 1700, Moscow was still cut off from the West except by the northern route at Archangel, ice-bound for at least half of the year. When Peter concluded his treaty with the Turks he declared war on Sweden. However, Denmark had just capitulated, and Sweden, under Charles XII, had the support of the fleets of the Dutch and the

English. It was a bad time to go to war, and Peter's new army was routed at Narva on 30 November. Gunnery works for artillery pieces were developed under Vinnius, a Russian-born Dutchman. New ironworks, powder-mills, cloth-mills, and sail-works were to supply some of the needed munitions and supplies since imports were now restricted to Archangel.

Between 1701 and 1704, Peter began the reconquest of Ingria. The decisive year was 1703. The Russians used *lotkeys*, small river craft, against the Swedes. Working from Lake Ladoga and down the Neva River, Swedish outposts were attacked. The Russians defeated a group of Swedes from Kotlina Island in May, 1703. A fort, Kronslot, was built to command the only passage to St. Petersburg on Kotlina Island, and opposite the castle two batteries were erected on shore. [7]

St. Petersburg began its rise as the new capital of Russia, while ship construction centered around Lake Ladoga. By 1705 and 1706, Peter had some frigates, although none carried more than thirty guns. He also had some snows, long, swift boats used by the Flemings, carrying up to twenty-five men each, and adapted by the Russians for their shallow water actions, and some vessels to carry cargo on the Neva River between Lake Ladoga and St. Petersburg. When Kronslot was finished, the Russian frigates and snows would assemble each year under the protection of the batteries to prevent any Swedish fleet from taking the island or moving on St. Petersburg. [8]

In 1709, Peter's efforts resulted in the victory over the Swedes at Poltava. Swedish prisoners were used to continue the building of the capital, to build and man Peter's fleet, and to work in cartography and navigation. The ships built at St. Petersburg participated in the successful siege of Viborg in 1710.

Peter's navy now included two 52 gun ships, the *Viborg* and the *Riga*. There were also many Russian galleys, well suited to the shallow water and islands off Finland. Russia now controlled the Gulf of Finland west to Reval and had moved into the Baltic to incorporate Riga. But Turkey declared war again, and by 1711, Peter had lost his Azov fleet. The sails and cordage had been transported by sled to Archangel, but the ships were lost or laid up. With the Turks in control in the south, Archangel and St. Petersburg became the principal shipbuilding centers.

The pattern for northern sea war was set. The ice at St. Petersburg broke up between 5 and 15 April. Eight to ten days later, the ice was out of Lake Ladoga, and by the end of April, the river was free. The Gulf of Finland was seldom clear for ships until 10 May, sometimes even a few days later. Since the campaigns usually did not begin until the end of May, operations continued over the summer months, and by the end of September the ships had to be settled in for the winter at Riga, Reval, St. Petersburg, or Archangel.

During this period, Peter added to his Baltic fleet. In 1712, the *Samson*, a 40 gun frigate bought in Holland, was given to the Tsar by Menshikov. She was rebuilt into a 32 gun frigate by using the first of the oak cut for Peter's shipbuilding which had taken three years to arrive in the north from Kazan. The *Katherine*, 60 guns, was launched in the spring, along with the *Poltava*, 54 guns, which " . . . was much too lean abaft and could never endure to ride in a great sea." [9]

In 1713, the campaign against the Swedes continued. This is usually considered the first serious engagement of the Russian fleet with an enemy at sea. Peter's treaty with Turkey that year had left him free for his northern war.

At Kronslot in May 1714, the Russian fleet assembled. By 11 June, it was at Reval. Ships coming from England and Holland, as well as from Archangel, had had some trouble with the Swedes. By the end of June, word arrived that the Russian galleys were tied up by the Swedes at Hangö Head. The battle in July saw another defeat for the Swedes. Some of the fleet wintered at Reval and others at St. Petersburg. Two ships with 60 guns each were launched in the autumn; one was the *Narva*. Despite the summer victory, the Russians were still having trouble with Swedish privateers. The ships of the Russian fleet assembled at Kronslot in the Spring of 1715. This would prove to be another important year in the Northern War for Peter.

Yet Britain was certainly keeping an eye on affairs in the Baltic. It was still the vital source of naval stores upon which she depended. [10] In 1700, Britain aided Sweden in her battle against Denmark, Poland, and Russia. Despite this, the Swedish monopolists in the tar industry

Battle near Greingame, Holland, 1721. Note use of galleys by the Russians. (*Grafika, 18th-20th century in the Russian State Museum*, no. 2, p. 61. Artist: A.F. Zubov (1682-1744). Photo by Fogg Photographic Dept., Cambridge, MA.)

had refused to ship anything except in Swedish ships, at high prices, and in quantities restrictive to British naval needs. The key to British policy in the Baltic lay with the concern over fleet needs. The British had passed the Act of 1704 to encourage the North American colonies to produce naval stores and to relieve Britain of her reliance on the Baltic. Some advantages to both sides resulted, but the Baltic remained an area vital to England. After Sweden's defeat at Poltava in 1709, she called upon England to help her in compliance with the Treaty of Altona. However, England was tied up in the struggle with France at that time, and she was unable to send any assistance. Sweden, caught up in the war with Russia, adopted measures which alienated British friendship and stopped all trade in the Baltic, which cut off British supplies of naval stores. Sweden continued this attitude after the War of the Spanish Succession had ended (1713) by issuing such ordinances as one forbidding all neutral trade in the Baltic. British supplies were very low in the Summer of 1714, and there was great concern about fitting out the fleet the next year. English politics were focused on the transition from Queen Anne to George of Hanover, who landed in England on 19 September. The Whigs were now in control, and the actions by Sweden had freed the British fleet to take action. Between 1715 and 1727, Britain sent ten fleets into the Baltic to assist allies and maintain the flow of supplies the British Navy depended upon.

The first of these fleets was sent in 1715 to protect British trade against Swedish privateers. It was joined enroute by a fleet of Dutch merchantmen with escorts also headed for the Baltic. The English commander was Admiral of the Blue, Sir John Norris, admiral since 1709, and "Commander in Chief of His Majesty's Ships employed and to be employed in the Channel." [11] His instructions of 10 May outline the general action of the fleet, leaving Norris room for using his own judgment on the scene after consultation with his other officers. Sir Thomas Hardy, Rear Admiral of the Blue, in the *Norfolk*, was part of the escort. Norris' flagship was the *Cumberland*. Both were listed as 3rd rate ships of approximately 60 guns in accordance with the Admiralty's classification of ships-of-the-line for battle order. There were two other 3rd rates, twelve 4th rates, a sloop, and one 5th rate, the *Mermaid*, Captain William Collier, 36 guns. Norris had already requested copies of the treaties between England and Denmark and

Sweden, along with sailing instructions for the merchantmen. [12] Two ships had been sent to collect the merchants from the ports between Yarmouth and the Firth of Forth in Scotland and to sail to Norway to wait for the rest of the fleet. Norris arrived at the Nore in the *Cumberland* on 1 May to supervise the provisioning of the squadron and to collect the 45 waiting merchantmen. Ten of these vessels were to acquire hemp for the Navy. The *Mermaid* was delayed and did not leave until 21 May. [13]

On her way to meet the fleet off Norway, *Mermaid* spotted the Dutch fleet with twelve men-of-war and some 200 merchant ships. She caught up with the English fleet on 25 May. Norris reported 106 English sails with eighteen naval vessels. After some delay, the fleet sailed for Elsinore, Denmark, arriving on 30 May. The Dutch fleet was in the harbor, and Norris met with the Dutch Rear Admiral. Flag officers discussed procedures to protect the various merchantships and to allow time for lading of cargo. On 1 June the fleets left Elsinore sailing past Falsterbo, headed toward Bornholm Island, reaching Danzig on 12 June. The *Mermaid* sailed on 20 June with the merchant ships, the British warships *Assistance* and *Weymouth*, and two Dutch ships of war. The Russian fleet was observed at Reval Bay. Norris sent the British Admiralty a report of the Tsar's line of battle fleet list with complement of men and guns for each ship, and a list of commanders. [14] All of the warships returned to Reval except the *Mermaid*, which proceeded with the merchantmen toward St. Petersburg. The combined British and Dutch war fleets were to control any Swedish naval or privateering actions.

On 21 June, seven ships of the merchant convoy headed for Viborg, while the rest continued on to St. Petersburg. The *Mermaid* picked up a mate from one of the merchantmen to serve as pilot since the Gulf of Finland was "a place little known or frequented by English before this time and was a very difficult passage." [15] On 22 June, the merchants, with the *Mermaid*, arrived at Kronslot, where they saw the Tsar's fleet, some twenty vessels ranging from 30 to 64 guns. Admiral Apraxin, in *Le Firme*, and Peter, as Vice Admiral of the Blue, were saluted with fifteen guns. The Russians returned the salute with fifteen guns. Peter came on board the *Mermaid* with some of the Russian nobility and gentry. Fifteen guns were fired for the Tsar on his arrival and

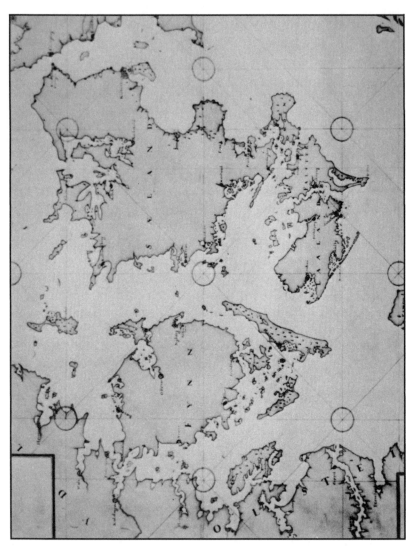

The Danish sounds and straits, drawn in 1715 by Jens Sorensen, Hydrographer Royal, as the result of many years of systematic charting of Danish waters. For tactical reasons these charts, excellent for their time, were not published. (*Maritime History in Pictures*, no. 10. Danish Maritime Museum.)

when he left. Prince Menshikov came aboard and was saluted with eleven guns. The Empress and other princes came aboard and were also saluted with eleven guns.

However, Peter was very interested in examining the *Mermaid*. He relied upon galleys in his victory over the Swedes in 1714, and wanted to add sailing ships to his fleet. The *Mermaid* had originally been built in 1651 at Limehouse. She had been rebuilt in 1689 at Woolwich by Joseph Lawrence, a 5th rate of two decks, a little longer and wider, small draft, and 343 tons. In 1707, she had again been rebuilt, this time at Chatham by Benjamin Rosewell. She was still a two deck 5th rate, but now had 108 feet on the gun deck, a 90 foot keel, 29.8 feet in width, a 12 foot draft, and 421 tons. [16] She was the only military vessel accompanying the 47 merchantmen. She carried 135 men, her middle complement, and 36 guns, her high listing. The guns were distributed as follows: 8 demi-culverins on the gun deck, 22 6-pounders on the upper deck, and six 4-pounders on the quarter deck. Their length ranged from 7 to 8 feet. The efficiency of the English gun crews had been well demonstrated in the recent war with France. The value of this frigate would not be lost on Peter.

The merchants and the *Mermaid* proceeded toward St. Petersburg on 24 June after saluting the Tsar's flag ship and that of Menshikov. The smaller merchants were able to sail right into the Neva River; the larger ones stayed off the bar and had to depend on lighters to unload their salt and load the hemp. They also ran into bad weather, with heavy rain and lightning, which delayed the work. The evening of 26 June the Tsar's ship, *Narva*, 64 guns, was struck by lightning and blew up. Of her 450 man crew, only 114 were saved. The captain, an Englishman named Vaughan, died in the explosion. Except for this incident, there was not much to note. The weather was lousy and the merchant ships were running behind schedule. The captain made a couple of trips into St. Petersburg, once to visit the Tsar to arrange the promised aid in lightering service for the fleet of merchants. The merchants did not get their salt unloaded until 5 July. The Tsar sailed from Kronslot with his fleet for Reval on 6 July.

Admiral Norris, who was operating out of Danzig, was keeping an eye out for the Swedish fleet. Cruising along the Finnish coast, he met a Russian squadron of seven sails on 22 July and the next day passed the Russian fleet of nineteen men-of-war, including the Tsar, near Reval. The British anchored at Reval, and the Russian fleet did the same. The next two weeks were spent in exchanging visits; the Admiral entertained the Tsar, the Tsarina, and the court on 2 August. The Tsar continued to show great interest in British ships and toured the *Cumberland*. Norris commented on the improvement of the Russian fleet occasioned by the help of English builders. He sent orders for the *Mermaid* to sail on 10 August. Five merchantships from Viborg were anchored at Kronslot waiting for the rest of the St. Petersburg merchants. It was not until 13 August that the merchant fleet was able to sail from Kronslot to rendezvous with Admiral Norris at Reval.

Later the *Mermaid* met the *Assistance*, the *Weymouth*, and a Dutch man-of-war off Holland to help fifty-seven merchantships to Reval. A gale struck the fleet. The only vessel reported lost was a Dutch man-of-war, the *Hayse T. Wermeld*, commanded by Captain de Groot. Of her 200 men, only 79 were saved. The combined fleets sailed from Reval 16 August. The reports were that the Russian fleet would soon be laid up for the winter as soon as the weather permitted them to return to St. Petersburg from Reval.

On 20 August, the fleet anchored in Danzig. There were already a great many ships in the anchorage. The merchants from Riga and the men-of-war sent to guard them were anchored ahead of the Admiral. On 25 August, the combined fleets sailed. But they had to spend some time anchored off Bornholm Island. The *Mermaid* was sent to Copenhagen for the Admiral's mail on 2 September. Eight of the English ships were detached to help the Danes in their fight with the Swedes. The merchantships sailed on up to Elsinore. The *Mermaid* anchored at Elsinore with the merchantships on 4 September. On 11 September, the Queen of Denmark was saluted with 13 guns. While still at Elsinore, the *Mermaid* fired a salute of 13 guns to commemorate the landing of George I in England the year before on 19 September. Bad weather prevented the convoy from leaving until 29 September. But the *Mermaid* stayed to pick up Captain Finbo, who had gone to Copenhagen for supplies, so that she did not leave until 1 October. She met up with the fleet, but again bad weather hit the convoy and scattered some of the fleet.

Most of the fleet had regrouped by 3 October, and it proceeded south from Norway. On 7 October, the three Dutch men-of-war and the Dutch merchantships left the convoy for Holland. By 10 October, the captain of the *Mermaid* felt that they had reached the Dogger Bank, and on the same day a Dutch pilot boat gave them the position of Texel. The *Mermaid* was sent to confirm their position. The northern English and Scottish merchantmen left the convoy on 11 October for their home ports, and the rest of the group continued to the Nore. On the 17th, Rear Admiral Hardy's ship *Norfolk*, ran aground while on the way to the anchorage of the Nore, but was refloated without damage. The remainder of the convoy moored on 18 October. On the 20th, ships were dressed, and 13 guns were fired to celebrate the anniversary of the coronation of George I. Admiral Norris struck his flag on the 21st, and Rear Admiral Hardy on the 22nd. After provisioning and picking up a pilot, the *Mermaid* headed for Spithead, where she anchored on 30 October and fired 15 guns to celebrate the Prince of Wales' birthday. The next day they moored at Portsmouth and began unrigging.

Thus ended a very successful convoy. The British succeeded in replenishing their naval stores of timber, hemp, salt, tar, and other essential commodities which were in very short supply. They observed the Tsar's fleet, and he theirs. A British presence in the Baltic would be maintained. The frigate, *Mermaid*, had performed her tasks well. She had indeed been the eyes and ears of the fleet, and she had successfully carried out her assignment without loss of life or the ships in her charge. She had entertained the Tsar, Tsarina, Menshikov, and the Russian court, certainly not the usual dull convoy duty. This would be the first of the ten convoys into the Baltic to protect British supplies of naval stores and to maintain neutral trade in that region between 1715 and 1727.

Notes

[1] See material in C.R. Boxer, *The Dutch Seaborne Empire, 1600-1800,* (London, 1965) and Peter Padfield, *Tide of Empires, Decisive Naval Campaigns in the Rise of the West, 1654- 1700,* (London, 1982), vol. 2.

[2] I was able to observe the boat on trips to Russia in 1962 and 1976. For more details see Robert K. Massie, *Peter the Great, His Life and World,* (New York, 1980).

[3] B.H. Sumner, *Peter the Great and the Emergence of Russia*, 9th ed. (London, 1976), p. 39.

[4] *Ibid.*, pp. 35-42. These included Farquharson, a mathematician from Aberdeeen, to establish a navigation school; John Parry, a naval engineer, to work on a canal project linking the Don and the Volga Rivers; and Cornelius Cruys, a Norwegian who had been in the Dutch merchant marine service and who was to become a Russian admiral.

[5] C.A.G. Bridge, ed., *The Russian Fleet Under Peter the Great: By A Contemporary Englishman (1724)*, Navy Records Society (London, 1899), pp. 4-6 and the List of Officers in the Russian Navy in the Baltic on pp. 128-130.

[6] Sumner, *op. cit.*, p. 48.

[7] Not called Kronstadt until 1721.

[8] Bridge, *op. cit.*, p. 11.

[9] *Ibid.*, p. 20.

[10] For details of the timber aspects of this trade see R.G. Albion, *Forests and Sea Power, The Timber Problem of the Royal Navy, 1652-1862,* (Hamden, CT, reprint, 1965, originally pub. 1926), chi, IV, pp. 138-199.

[11] Public Record Office, Kew, England, ADM 2/48 Orders and Instructions, 16 Oct. 1714 to 18 July 1716.

[12] Public Record Office, Kew, England, ADM 1/2 Admiralty and Secretariat Papers, 1660-1942, In-Letters, Baltic 1711 to 1718, Admiral Sir John Norris, 29 April 1715.

[13] Public Record Office, Kew, England, ADM 52/236 Masters' Logs, 1672-1840, Part 8, *Mermaid*, G. Rosbee, 20 Sept. 1714-20 Sept. 1715. ADM 51/4260 Captains' Logs, 1669-1842, Part 9, *Mermaid*, Captain William Collier, 18 May 1715 to 29 Nov. 1715. ADM 1/1596 Captains' Letters, Captain William Collier, 1713-1716. National Maritime Museum, Greenwich, England, ADM/L/M/171 Logs, *Mermaid*, 1710-1715, Captain William Collier.

[14] Public Record Office, Kew, England, ADM 1/2 In-Letters, Baltic, 1711-1718, Norris, 20 June 1715. See also Bridge, *op. cit.*, p. 42.

[15] Public Record Office, Kew, England, ADM 52/236 Masters' Logs, *Mermaid*, G. Rosbee, 21 June 1715.

[16] Admiralty Library, Dimensions Book B, 1660-1764, p. 21. Public Record Office, Kew, England, ADM 7/550 List of Ships and Captains, 1651-1737, *Mermaid*.

Part III

**Community
and
the Sea**

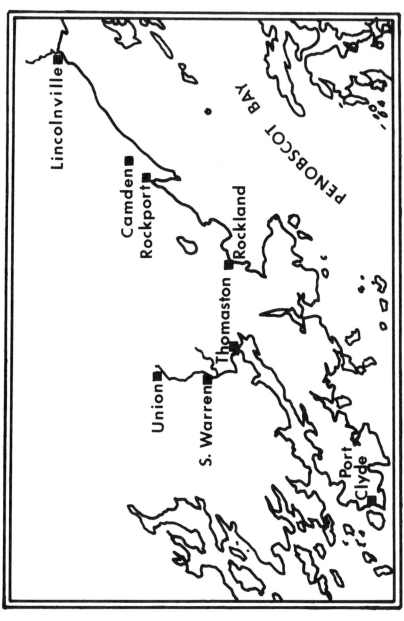

The Lime Coast of Maine

The Lime Coast:
A Maritime Nexus of Community

Lawrence Carroll Allin

Reaching Downeast and inland for thirty miles, Maine's historic "Lime Coast" runs from Union and Warren through Thomaston, Rockland and Rockport to Camden and Lincolnville. The headlands and bays of this coast offer examples of the natural conditions and forces, which, when acted upon by human ingenuity, can come together to form a maritime community, a maritime nexus.[1]

The forces of nature, ingenuity of man, technological progress, and urban development are all components of a process which occurred at this Downeast nexus. This nexus, its development and its processional change is exemplified by a key industry, that industry's evolution and its maritime ramifications. That industry is the Maine lime trade.[2]

Great physical changes moved in evolutionary procession across the Downeast shore and affected its three great resources: rock, wood and water. Three hundred million years ago this area was inundated. Inland streams debouched a fine, dark mud over its bottom. Uncounted diatoms inhabited the waters above the mud. During their life-cycles the diatoms deposited innumerable skeletons over the mud. The skeletons sank, accumulated and became limestone. The skeletons' weight and the weight of the water hardened the mud into Isleboro slate.

Pressures from inside the Earth's mantle worked under this accumulation. Tectonic forces pushed masses of hot lava through these strata. Enormous fingers of granite-making lava pushed and warped the limestone and slate, folding the coastal crust and giving it new contours. A half-million years ago, the Earth's temperature cooled. A mile-thick sheet of ice formed and pressed down on the coast. The ponderous weight of the ice further compacted the mud, lime and lava.

So great was this weight and so suppliant the Earth's crust that the Lime Coast was again "drowned" — submerged — under 250 feet of water. Successive glaciers came and went. With each melting, the glacial streams deposited fingers of fine earth, clay, across the littoral. In places the clay became fifty feet deep. Other marine organisms were born, grew, and died; and their skeletons became entwined in the great process.[3] As the coast emerged in the modern epoch, great deposits of limestone were brought into a particular relationship with the surface of the Earth and the shore of the sea. The limestone was close to the surface, easily mined and less than three miles from the sea. The rock was conveniently situated for mining and for transportation.[4]

Within the general evolution of the Earth, the North American coast became grown over with new vegetations. Great new forests of tall trees grew and spread inland from the shore for a thousand miles. These trees, and especially Spruce, covered the Downeast coast. They provided the energy and part of the raw material base for the development of the Lime Coast and the lime trade. The Spruce would be used to burn the stone and make casks for its packaging. Other arboreal species would go into vessels built to carry the powder.[5]

Conjoining the wood and rock were streams of freshwater and embayed arms of the world ocean. The Kennebec, St. George, Oyster and Penobscot Rivers, and hundreds of lesser streams, served as avenues over which wood could be brought to the rock. The ocean highway, indenting the land from Warren to Lincolnville, served both as a wood route and a road to market for the burned lime.[6]

The geological and oceanographic process which created the Lime Coast illustrates the importance of place and physical process. But, it was men who dug the rock, cut the wood, hauled them across land and water, and burned the lime. It is human needs and perceptions which create a community. The human touch affected the geography of local industry, its technology, the vessels which carried its products, its energy sources, its employment patterns, its business organization, and, finally, the changes which wrote *finis* to the process and to the community.

When wrenched and wrought by the hand of man, the results of the geological processes would yield granite for foundations, brick for walls, and slate for roofs. These would leave the Maine shore as materials for homes, factories and office buildings in the ever-growing and ever-changing cities of the new America. Limestone too, burned to a white powder in fires of local Spruce, would leave that coast as mortar to bind the bricks or to lime interior walls as an insulating and aesthetically pleasing surface. Eighty-percent carbonates of calcium and magnesia, the limestone gives off its carbon dioxide when calcinated — when burned. So fired, the quicklime becomes the city-building mortar and plaster and the *raison d'etre* of the community.[7]

The "human touch" came to the Lime Coast in 1734 when Samuel Waldo brought Robert McIntyre, an Irishman, to the New World. The "father of lime burners in these parts," McIntyre, (and Waldo), opened a quarry, built four kilns to heat the stone, a wharf from which to ship it, and two small schooners in which to carry it away. They established a pattern which continued long after McIntyre's death in 1750. They shipped their lime to the metropolitan market in Boston.[8]

After McIntyre's death, Mason Wheaton came to the coast in 1753 on business and formed a company, Wheaton, Briggs, and Whip-

Looking across the toll bridge from Brown's Hill in Thomaston the lime industry's domination of the coast is apparent. Three of the Burgess-O'Brien kilns and their sheds are the prominent features of the area. The schooner *Morea* lays alongside the wharf. She will depart for the open sea through the toll bridge. (Thomaston Bicentennial Committee, *Tall Ships, White House and Elms*, I, p. 7)

ple, to burn the rock. Wheaton, Briggs, and Whipple served the land patent-holders of the area and dominated the local industry until the American Revolution.[9]

Title to the land on much of the Lime Coast changed hands after the Revolution. General Henry Knox, a hero of the Republic and friend of George Washington, bought, or married, much of Waldo's land in the Thomaston area. Knox also turned his hand to burning lime and built three schooners to take it to market.[10]

These early, successful efforts attracted others into the business. One of them was George Ulmer who burned the first lime in what is now Rockland. Ulmer's career illustrates the lack of specialization which characterized the early years of the trade. He not only burned the lime but built and captained the vessels which transported it. David Gay followed Ulmer into the process. Gay is important in the history of the lime trade of Maine as he established its primary pattern. He began shipping the burned rock to New York City. For numerous reasons, that metropolis would become the Lime Coast's greatest customer.[11]

Lincolnville would also develop a special market relationship. Its quarries sat four miles inland and, in 1889, supplied one patent and eight "old fashioned" kilns. The product of the Lincolville kilns went almost exclusively to New Bedford, Massachusetts.[12]

By 1794 there were 35 kilns on the Lime Coast. They were burned three to five times a year. Consuming 25 cords of wood a firing, they yielded 200 fifty-gallon casks of lime with each burning.[13]

In 1795 the Reverend Paul Coffin, D.D., came to the Lime Coast on a preaching tour. He was impressed with what he saw. Coffin remarked on the iron-tired wagons which carried the stone, the substantial kilns and the active cooperages which all seemed to be new, fresh, and busy. What he saw was a young and firmly established economic community with almost unlimited natural resources available to it and with excellent transportation facilities literally at its doorsteps.[14]

The importance to Maine of what Coffin saw was stated by another writer: "Like the ice, the granite and the slate industries, the income to the State is almost absolutely a net income. The raw material is all here, and is inexhaustible. The labor employed is Maine labor. The earnings of that labor go directly to feed Maine families, and to build Maine homes . . . ."[15] Technological and business changes would come and go but, that observation would hold true for almost 200 years.

The development of the kilns; the search for fuel to fire them; the perfection of the powder's packaging; the creation of vessels to carry it and changing business organizations to market the lime are all a part of the community's story. Its details are interesting.

The earliest kilns, "field" or "flare" kilns, were simply piles of limestone laid over wood. Flare kilns often sat in the field of a farmer or of a professional man who was only a part-time limeburner. Such a man could enlarge his arable land by cutting and burning his own wood and digging his own rock. He fired his kiln, tore it down by hand, separated the impurities from his lime, and barreled it, often in barrels of his own making.[16]

By 1800 substantial, rectangular "primitive" kilns were replacing the field kilns. The primitive kilns were usually built against the side of a hill so that wood and rock could be brought up the hill and over a bridge to the kiln's top. Then alternating layers of wood and rock would be stacked in the kiln. When full, a metal top was placed on the kiln and its fuel lit off. For a week or ten days a man stood by night and day feeding wood to the burning kiln. Then its owner hired a crew for a day or two to draw the lime. The drawing crew received lunch and rum as well as pay for their effort.[17]

The rum figured in the story almost from its beginning. The Lime Coast's early trade was with the West Indies. Maine men cut wood to send to the Islands with the fish they salted: deals, planks, shingles, laths to plaster, and shooks for boxes and barrels went south. Once there, the barrel shooks were assembled, filled with "W.I. Goods" — rum, or sugar, or molasses, — and returned to Maine. These barrels or "hogsets," when duly emptied, became the first lime casks. More efficient methods and standards soon replaced this pleasant but haphazard method of securing packaging.[18]

With increasing demands for lime, casks, and timber for the West Indies, small saw mills appeared on every local stream. The hinterland, the country in back of the coast, became the scene of layered and complex human activities. Cooperages filled the area and men such as Robert Linnekin Weymouth made between 15 and 20 casks a day or three thousand barrels a year. By 1836 the services of 219 full-time coopers were required to supply the kegs for the trade. This number more than doubled by 1880.[19]

As the trade grew, it left patterns on the land. The towns themselves were the focus. The kilns and quarries made a second band of activity, the cooperages a third, and the hoop pole stands a fourth. The poles were supple young trees: cut, sized, quartered, and notched to become the hoops which held the barrels together. The hoops were generally cut in the spring by farmers who lived inland and who appreciated the extra income the effort brought.[20]

As the trade matured and the need for casks grew, so did the necessity for uniformity and quality control. As the technology of the trade progressed, regulations regarding cask size and the lime's quality became law. As early as 1808 there were fourteen lime inspectors on the coast insuring that the buyer would receive a uniform product.[21]

By 1828 there were 160 kilns on the Lime Coast filling the cooper's kegs. Eighty-nine sailing vessels carried the goods to market from thirty wharves. The trade flourished. And, the local forest retreated from the shore in front of the woodsman's ax.[22]

As local timber became scarce, the limeburners sent to North Haven and Vinalhaven Islands in Penobscot Bay for wood. Eventually they reached as far away as Eastport, Maine and the Canadian Maritime Provinces for their fuel. When the wood arrived at the wharves, it had to be unloaded and stacked in carts for carriage to the kilns at the quarries. It became apparent that the kilns should be built on the wharves, the rock hauled to them and the wood stacked on the wharves. This would save two handlings of the bulky wood and increase profits. As a result, most of the area's kilns moved to the waterfront during the 1830s.[23]

The ruins of some waterfront lime-wharves are still discernable and present an unusual picture. The tableau was made by the limeburners cutting and grading away half a shoreside hill so that a kiln could be built on foundation rock in the cut. Then a roadway was laid

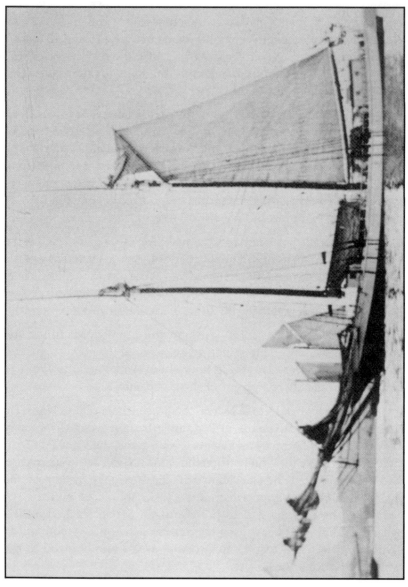

The "limedrougher" *John J. Perry* of the Perry Brothers fleet prepares to clear the bar outward bound. (Roger Grindle, *Quarry and Kiln* (Rockland, Me., 1971) and Rockland *Courier- Gazette*.)

Linwood and kilnsheds lined Rockport's shorefront. "Kilnwooders" ride their anchors awaiting the discharging of their cargoes while and unidentified limebrougher makes for the sea. (Roger Grindle, *Quarry and Kiln* (Rockport, Me., 1971) and Rockport *Courier-Gazette.*)

from the shore up the back of the hill and across a bridge to the kiln. The rock and wood came to the kiln over the road and bridge.

Piles, often cedar, to make a bulkhead or quay-wall, were placed in the onshore water in front of the kiln. Rock, rubble, and dirt were then dumped between the bulkhead and shore to even and complete the rough wharf. A kilnshed would then be built. It would enclose the kiln and an area in which to store wood and freshly-barreled lime. Some kilns had but a minimum of working and storage area between the water's edge bulkhead and the shed, others had a great open area from the water to the shed on which much cord-wood fuel could be stored.

The wharf-side move of the kilns helped the teamster, wagonwright, and farmer find employment. To carry the stone from the quarries to the furnaces, Rockland used 204 ox-wagons and rock-carts and 226 yoke of oxen. More teamsters were required to goad the animals, more rock-carts were needed, and additional food had to be grown to feed the men and teams. The change in kiln location brought additional prosperity to the Lime Coast. By 1890 over 3,000 men found work either directly or indirectly in the lime trade.[24]

The growing number and size of kilns gave employment to both kilntenders and to quarrymen. Work in the quarries could be both cold and dangerous. Work in the kilnsheds was hot and relatively safe. But, an unusual tidal conditon sometimes gave the kiln tenders a bit of a surprise.

The Lime Coast, and especially Rockland Harbor in Owl's Head Bay, is subject to high spring tides and strong on-shore winds. A combination of higher than usual tides and a blowing gale could slosh salt water into the kilnsheds. Stored there were the wood, flammable empty casks and full barrels of lime. When the barreled lime became wet it could heat, swell, burst its keg, and set the wooden aggregate ablaze. More often, the hot kilns would heat and burn the wooden yokes which held their roofs in place. These minor fires occurred almost weekly. Kilnwork was warm and safe, but, one had to be ready to run.[25]

However, one could not always run in the quarries. "Giants," great black powder charges, were used to pry the rock from nature's ribs. Too often the giants exploded prematurely, blinding the workers or ripping off their arms or legs. So close to one another were the quarries that a blast in one often toppled rock from the rim of another onto unsuspecting workers crushing them.

As an example, one can cite the case of poor Alfred Moore. In 1845 he lost his sight because of a premature explosion. But, he kept working in the pit. Later, he was struck on the head by a rock which was dislodged by a blast in another quarry. He was twenty-seven years old. And, he died.

No accident insurance nor workmen's compensation existed for the victims of the giants. There was some proviso for those luckier than Moore and who clung to life after their injuries. The city fathers auctioned them off. They were auctioned as paupers to the lowest bidding of local boarding-house owners.[26]

In the latter days of the trade, mechanics and stonecutters worked 250 days a year because the quarries shut down during the coldest weeks of the winter. For their efforts, they received $2.00 a day. Less skilled quarrymen had more dangerous employment and also received $2.00 a day for the 280 days they worked. Their average yearly wage amounted to $660.10.[27]

By 1845, 2,000 kegs of blasting powder were shot in the quarries each year. Forty-three thousand cords of wood came over the water annually to burn the stone. In Rockland alone, fifty teamsters, 100 quarrymen and 150 kilntenders received employment.[28]

The quarries and quarrymen benefited from technological advances made over time. Dynamite, safer than black powder, wire rope, pneumatic drills, and stronger cranes came on. Steam and electricity replaced muscle, lifted the lime, pumped the ever-accumulating water, lit the pits, and eased the work. But, it was not until 1895 that electricity came to any quarry. Then it came to Francis Cobb's "Engine Quarry."[29]

Technological advances could not overcome local civil strife. Thomaston was one large city but two distinct communities: Thomaston and the Shore Village, now Rockland. Thomaston went to sea through the St. George's River. The Shore Village went to sea through

The schooner *A.D. Henderson,* laying alongside some of the J.A. Creighton
Company's kilns in Thomaston, demonstrates by her size one aspect of technology's
impact on the Lime Coast. It brought larger sailing vessels. Dominating the skyline
is "Montpelier," home of the Revolutionary War hero General Henry Knox.
(Thomaston Bicentennial Committee, *Tall Ships, White House and Elms.*)

open Owl's Head Bay. The industries and habitations of the two communities were separated by headlands and a great meadow.

In 1848 Rockland and South Thomaston split off from Thomaston and a division of labor occurred. Rockland tended to engross the lime trade while Thomaston tended to build ships. Both sustained each trade but, by 1860, there were only three lime burners in Thomaston. Camden and Rockport repeated the mitosis in 1891. The first to build ships and to forge ship-iron, the latter to burn lime.[30]

Shipbuilding was a distinct function on the Lime Coast and its stock-in-trade and sustaining business was in the hulls it furnished to the rockburners. The "limers," "kilnwooders," and "lumber coasters" were the ordinary stock-in-trade of shipwrights who built and repaired the smaller vessels. Some were hulls of fishing schooners built by I.L. Snow of Rockland which changed trades and became "lime droughers." Most were schooners built for the lime trade itself. Thomaston built 144 "fore-and-afters" and Rockland built 189.[31]

Many of the local businessmen both burned lime and built their own vessels in their own shipyards. Francis Cobb of Rockland and Edward O'Brien of Thomaston built great Downeasters for the deep-sea trades and burned lime. John Pascal and his son built large, deep-water vessels for Carleton and Norwood of Rockport who also owned many smaller lime droughers.[32]

So needful of bottoms was the lime trade that, by 1850, Rockland had 120 kilnwooders bringing sticks for her fires and 120 limers carrying the powder away. On occasion, the great Maine-built cotton freighters and Downeasters carried lime to the southern states as ballast. It is held by one author that the humble workboats made Rockland the nation's third busiest port in her heyday. Statistics do not exist to sustain the claim but, in 1900 a total of 4,175 coastal sailing vessels entered and left Rockland Harbor and 1,250 of the craft had used it as a harbor of refuge during storms.[33]

Lincolnville had no such harbor, only an open roadstead, and burned her kilns only half-time to make 82,000 barrels of lime a year. Still, she had her own fleet of 23 lime schooners. Other vessels brought her wood.

Like Lincolnville's, Rockland's lime fleet is interesting. A summary of its efforts shows that in 1861, 137 lime-carriers entered New York Harbor. One hailed from Gloucester, Massachusetts and three from Rockport. The other 133 hailed from Rockland. By 1865, 145 vessels carried lime to New York City. One each came from Camden, Thomaston and Portland, Maine. All the rest hailed from Rockland.[34]

Any old hulk which could still float and make headway was suitable for carrying wood. But superior vessels were needed to carry the lime. These limers were generally moderate-sized schooners, sometimes ex-fishermen. They had to be tight vessels, craft which would admit little water. This was because of lime's proclivity to heat, swell, and burn when it became wet. The limers had sharp floors over which platfoms were built to raise the kegged lime above the water in their bilges.[35] Usually the limers had a half deck or platform built above their weather decks. Additional barrels of lime rode there. Although dunnaged up and tarpaulin-covered, these barrels were for emergency use. If the below-deck lime became wet and hot, the crew broke open the on-deck casks, made plaster and began to seal cabin doors, ports and deck seams with fresh-made mortar. Hopefully, this would starve the lime of oxygen and curtail its reaction.[36]

Wood to burn the lime came to the coast on various craft. Among them were small sloops from Little Deer Isle or Belfast, carrying only two to ten cords and bringing driftwood from the Penobscot River. This was scrap or wood which had broken loose from the booms and scores of sawmills up that mighty river. Fuel also came down "Bangor River" — the Penobscot — in old coasters, from Canada in "Johnny Woodboats," or from Nova Scotia in schooners which carried 200 cords.[37]

The Canadian Johnny Woodboats demonstrate the advantage of international commerce to any community, the ship as a tool, and some of the basic principles of shipbuilding. Built of inexpensive and abundant Spruce, sometimes in deep forests and hauled overland for launching, these St. John River vessels began coming south with wood in 1848. But, their heyday was in the 1870's and 1880's. In 1876 only six arrived on the Lime Coast. Five hundred and sixty-eight entered there in 1888 keeping Rockland in its place as a leading port.[38]

Great variety in size and workmanship existed in these vessels. They were carvel-planked and had bluff bows with pronounced tumblehome which made them substantial cargo carriers. In size, they ranged from 11 to 97 tons. The *Lyda Gretta* is typical of the type. She measured 60 tons, was 71 feet long, 25 feet at her beam, and drew 6 feet 6 inches of water.[39]

Peculiarities abounded on these Canadian kilnwooders. They carried brick fireplaces after cast-iron stoves had become universal aboard other vessels. Their rudders hung "out-of-doors."Clumsy wooden davits were slung over their sterns to carry their tending boats. And, they were probably the least expensive vessels built on this side of the Atlantic.[40]

Without a bowsprit, the St. John River vessels would poke into every creek and inlet on the long stretch of coast from home to the kilns. Their masters would pay a dollar and a half a cord at the creek and sometimes unload the wood in Rockland for five dollars a cord. Stacked like the hay they carried at home, the wood sometimes reached their booms. This pile of fuel obscured the helmsman's vision and a hand had to be stationed at the bow to maintain a lookout and help pilot by shouting course changes and warnings astern.

It has been said that the Johnny Woodboats were often crudely constructed and kept afloat only by the buoyancy of their cargoes. They frequently came into port with their decks awash. Some considered them more as hazards to navigation than legitimate sailing vessels.[41]

Whatever their quality, these vessels floated because of the need for lime in the construction industry. Building booms in New York City in 1825 and 1836 brought prosperity to the limeburners and their employees. By 1836 seven-eighths of Maine's lime went out-of-state. In 1843 Thomaston sent out a hundred cargoes of inspected, hence high-quality, lime to the metropolis. She sent out more than two hundred cargoes of the burned rock the following year and even more in 1845.[42]

The trade reflected national economic prosperity and the need for buildings of all kinds. During the tragic Depression of 1857, the volume of the trade fell off and unemployment became wide-spread on the Lime Coast. Only forty-one schooners carried the goods that year. Seamen, officers, shipbuilders, sailmakers, longshoremen, and chandlers who catered to the needs of the trade and its vessels were put on the economic beach with their shoreside compatriots by the hard times.[43]

By 1857 Rockland had become the economic as well as political shiretown of the Lime Coast and dominated the business. When prices and cargoes fell — she hurt. The Civil War also wreaked havoc with her economically as well as costing her many vessels which were transferred to foreign registry. In 1866 Rockland and her sister kiln towns sent out only fifty-five cargoes of lime. But by 1871 post-war prosperity was growing and 429 cargoes of lime left the harbors. Only one of those cargoes went to sea in a vessel not hailing from a Maine port.[44]

Tragic occurrences of 1872 greatly boosted the Maine lime and lumber economies. These occurrences were the great fires in Boston and Chicago. An 1873 fire in Belfast helped sustain the need for lime and lumber as well.

The Depression of 1873 allowed competition from inland kilns at Glen Falls, New York to threaten the Lime Coast's prosperity. Glen Falls lime sold at the same prices as that from Maine. But, the business stayed Downeast. Some say that the quality of Maine's inspected lime was superior to that of Glen Falls'. A more plausible reason that the trade stayed with Maine was that the wholesale buyers were located on New York's waterfront and had their storage facilities and transportation network centered there. The Glen Falls product had to come by rail and the rails did not run to the wholesalers' yards.[45]

Not content to fire the kilns, draw the lime and build, own and sail the vessels that carried it, the limeburners also dominated the sale of their product. Originally, individual captains sold their employers' cargoes. But soon, the kiln owners consigned their product to commission agents in New York. These were usually retired captains or individuals otherwise associated with Maine and its Lime Coast. A handsome living could be made by such an agent, as J.R. Brown's business records show. He was the dominant agent in New York in the 1870's. During that time he handled 1,166 of 1,730 cargoes sent out of Rockland.[46]

The lime trade within Maine was relatively unimportant. But the burners did send their goods to Bangor and to Portland. By 1870, when Bangor was approaching its greatest year as the timber port of the world, Rockland sent eleven schooners there. Only one left Bangor carrying a cargo of goods other than wood. The C.A.B. Morse Company handled lime for Portland. Vessels it owned or chartered made 199 round trips with lime to the city on Casco Bay in the early 1870's. These vessels took wood to the kilns and returned, almost always, with lime.[47]

Technological change came to the kilns as well as to the quarries. By the 1830's "pot" kilns came on to change production. These were fifteen feet high and wide, constructed of rock and cut granite, lined with clay and mortared on their exteriors. They could produce 300 casks a burning.[48]

As the demand for more efficient production grew, the kilns grew, and larger furnaces appeared on the waterfronts. Measuring forty feet in height and twenty-five feet on the side, their circular interiors had a fifteen-foot diameter lined with fire brick. The walls were often six-feet thick. Their cylindrical interiors held their diameter for three-quarters of their lengths. Then they tapered conically to a two-foot opening which was closed by giant shears. From the opening controlled by these shears, the lime was drawn for packing.

Twelve feet above the conical drawpit were the arches or fireboxes, one to a side. These could hold half a cord of four-foot logs. Above the arches was a metal cone lined with firebrick and then granite. These enabled the kilns to be loaded from bridges running to their tops as well as from their arches.[49]

Building these kilns called for some knowledge and local men specialized in that task. The effort called for considerable capital. Such large kilns demanded engineered wharves, considerable bridging and rails to move the rock to the loading apparatus and even larger sheds for the storage of wood and holding of the filled barrels.

The nation's surge of technological advances after the Civil War saw "patent" kilns being perfected. The combination of increasing wood prices and potentials of the new technologies permitted the growing family lime businesses to experiment with coal, gas, and, finally, electricity to fire the kilns. Some contend that Granville E. Carleton's 1889 patent of a soft-coal firing process brought on Rockport's era of greatness. That may have been, but, the first patent kiln was built in 1854 and there were 117 on the Coast by 1895.[50]

In addition to rising wood prices and advancing technology, international competition from New Brunswick, in Canada, demanded more efficient production. That efficiency came about when the Downeasters realized that their schooners could bring coal home from their trips to market. The coal could help supplant wood as a source of energy.[51]

The patent kilns did have advantages. They saved on fuel and on time in burning. The first serious experiments in coal-firing came in 1888 and those in oil-firing proved their practicality in 1892. While coal, oil, gas, and eventually electricity were economical fuels, there were those who contended that the best lime was still drawn from Spruce-fired kilns.[52]

However efficient, or romantic, the Spruce, the patent kilns and the results of the fuel experiments demonstrate one of the truly revolutionary changes in American history, the change from a wood to a coal-burning society. Simply stated, but with startling ramifications, coal supplanted wood in the kilns and on the coasting lanes. The small Johnny Woodboats and the kilnwooders disappeared from the Lime Coast as larger and larger schooners were needed to bring in the coal. A way of seafaring life gradually disappeared as well. No longer did the coasters haphazardly pick up wood where they could. The coal came from predictably stationary scuttles in huge quantities and with monotonous, but steady, regularity.[53]

Statistics for the coasting trade are difficult to obtain but, figures available from the Army's Corps of Engineers show how coal tonnage supplanted wood at Rockland in the latter days of the trade.

Change also came to the cooper's and hoop-cutter's crafts. Mill-sawn shook components, iron bands, and nails replaced some of their mysteries. Additionally, Camden's C.M. Barstow Company began using heading machines. The value of a skilled hand and keen eye was replaced by the predictable uniformity of dumb machines.[55]

Year	Lime	Coal	Wood and Cooperage
1898	122,400	68,400	145,400
1899	159,000	65,000	50,000
1900	135,000	70,000	55,000
1901	150,000	75,000	50,000
1902	209,900	70,000	45,000
1903	205,000	70,000	45,000
1904	225,000	80,000	50,000
1905	205,000	75,000	45,000
1906	250,000	110,000	50,000
1907	250,000	110,000	50,000
1908	250,000	115,000	not given
1909	235,000	110,000	17,500
1910	313,000	147,000	16,500
1911	285,000	153,105	21,251
1912	100,000	150,000	107,500 [54]

The teamsters, stockbreeders and wagonwrights also saw startling changes come to the transportation of the rock. In Lincolnville, they had taken lime to the waterfront over an ox-powered wooden-railed plank railroad. Rockland had used a plank road as a thoroughfare for the rock carts. It was beaten apart within two years. Then the roadway was paved. It proved less than satisfactory. Finally, ingenuity provided a better method of moving the rock.

The better method was the Limerock Railroad. Incorporated in 1864, its construction begun only in 1888, it was not completed until 1891. It was simply 12.5 miles of track and a train hauling rock two miles from a dozen quarries to 39 kilns on the waterfront. The railroad ran to the kiln tops on great trestles made of yellow pine brought from Georgia. Its rolling stock consisted of four engines, four flatcars, a caboose, and 401 small dumping cars which carried the rock. The dump cars were made to the same dimensions of the old iron-tired, horse-drawn rock-carts to preserve uniformity in measuring and handling

Cheap transportation was the key to the Lime Coast's success. Early on part of this success depended on the iron-wheeled rock carts such as this which drug the stone from the quarries to the wharf-side kilns. (Roger Grindle, *Quarry and Kiln* (Rockport, Me., 1971) and Rockport *Courier-Gazette*.)

The Lime Rock Rail Road was built in Rockland to carry the stone to the kilns. Its Engine Number Two is shown here atop the trestle at the Bird Kiln. (Roger Grindle, *Quarry and Kiln* (Rockport, Me., 1971) and Rockport *Courier-Gazette*.)

the stone. A narrow gauge railway was also built to carry the stone the short distances from Simonton's Corners to Rockport's kilns. This was the Rockport Limerock Railroad.[56]

These technological advances meant jobs for engineers, firemen, conductors, brakemen, section crews, crossing guards, and office workers. These were new and interesting jobs. But, they were not the jobs which built the community and its traditions.[57]

New technologies did change the lime trade and the trade reflected changes in the larger American society, especially changes in its methods of business organization. Waldo had been McIntyre's patron. Mason Whipple had been the primary agent for a group of landowners whose first aim in burning lime had been to enhance the value of their properties. General Knox burned lime in this same speculative way. Ulmer, Day, and their ilk were individual entrepreneurs on the make, looking for the Main Chance.[58]

By 1821 such organization faced a need for change. Economic maturity and full production had come to the Lime Coast. Much lime was burned. Competition was fierce and prices dropped disastrously. The burners made an agreement not to have more than one kiln for sale at a time and not to undersell one another. It was a loose, protective business arrangement. These stipulations proved difficult to enforce and the agreement eventually broke down. So did another attempt to control supply in the Forties.[59]

Another increment of changing business methods came to the Coast in 1869. That year Francis Cobb and twenty-four other manufacturers set up a lime exchange. Its purpose was to control the sudden price fluctuations in materials which made the business hazardous and profitless. The Lime Exchange was a loose community of interest. It did not function well.[60]

In 1871 Cobb again attempted to rationalize the business. He merged his family firm, F. Cobb and Company, with seven other concerns. They owned the majority of the quarries, and the new organization, the Cobb Lime Company, controlled one aspect of the trade. The Cobb Company sold the rock to area burners on a set-price-per-cask basis. Two business trends are represented by this merger. One is the family firm reorganizing to dominate an incorporation of interests. The other is the development of a monopoly, the control of one segment of an industry. In 1872 the new Cobb Lime Company was preeminent in reactivating the Lime Exchange. A board of seven directors controlled the Exchange, three were from the Cobb Company, and the Exchange was then styled the Knox County Lime Association. It was a trust of sorts, authorized to purchase lime from individual manufacturers and to sell it for the joint benefit of association members.[61]

The Association did not become effective until the 1880's. It was then able to make effective price-supporting agreements. The price of lime rose to the satisfactory range of $1.50 to $1.75 a barrel.[62] The lime-burners sold 1,478,000 casks in 1884 and 1,800,000 in 1888. They burned 85,000 cords of wood the latter year, 52,173 of the cords imported from the Maritimes.[63]

On January 3, 1900, Cobb's son, William, took the Lime Coast into the world of the integrated monopoly. He merged the Cobb Lime Company, A.F. Crockett Company of Rockland and the H.L. Shepard Company of Rockport into the Rockland Rockport Lime Company. Small in comparison with the great monopolies formed at the time, "The Lime Company" did control much of the Atlantic Coast lime trade. Capitalized at two million dollars, the quarries, many sheds and kilns, the Limerock Railroad, half the Rockport Limerock Railroad, and the Rockland Transportation Company were the firm's integrated subsidiaries.[64]

The story of the lime community could end with the Rockland Transportation Company but, it will not. The sentimental link with wooden hulls and white sails did end with the coming of the Lime Company and its subsidiary. The Company acquired six self-discharging steel barges. They had several advantages over the schooners. They could be towed by steady, steam-powered tugs and escape being becalmed. They had their own booms for discharging cargo. They could more easily bear the charges of waiting days at a New York wharf to be unloaded. And, finally, they could carry the lime in paper or cloth bags, the products of other Maine industries.[65]

With the coming of the "Lime Company," an era, a community, and a nexus ended. The *Addie Cushing* took the last sail-carried lime to

Thomaston, where these kilns of the J.A. Creighton Company were located did not build a railroad to its kilns. Here a horse and wood cart may be seen on a kiln bridge. An empty cart prepares to enter a woodshed for another load of the sticks to fire the kilns. (Roger Grindle, *Quarry and Kiln* (Rockport, Me., 1971) and Rockport *Courier-Gazette*.)

While many farmer-coopers brought their kegs to the sheds in hay-ricks, some Lime Coast coopers built wagons expressly to carry their barrels to the shore. Here one such wagon is seen on its way to the coast. (Roger Grindle, *Quarry and Kiln* (Rockport, Me., 1971) and Rockport *Courier-Gazette*.)

sea in 1914. The A.J. Bird and A.J. Creighton interests insisted on burning wood until 1918, and the obdurate Creightons insisted on burning — and selling — lime until 1931.[66]

The Lime Company went through many vicissitudes and changes. During World War II the trestles of its raiload were dismantled and its metal sold for scrap for the war effort. Other than water-filled quarries and the granite ghosts of dilapidated and unused kilns, there is little physical evidence of its existence today. But, at this writing, the "Lime Company" still exists, owns land, and carries on a consulting business.[67]

There are no discrete and final endings in this story of man that is called history. There is, instead, the on-going process of continuity and change. For that reason — and out of sentiment — it is suggested that the Lime Coast ceased to exist as a vibrant entity on March 3, 1907. On that day the lime-burning, shipbuilding town of Rockport was consumed in kilnfire flames. Today Rockport is a quaint summer resort where yachts and pleasure schooners call and where the uninformed ask as to the nature of those impressive stone ruins which line its waterfront.[68]

Notes

[1] J.P. Cilley to LTCOL George Thom, USA, December 4, 1878 in the *Annual Report of the Chief of Engineers for 1878* (Washington, D.C.: Government Printing Office, 1878), pp. 277-278. Hereafter, ARCE and the year. A.C. Both to Mjr. R.W. Roessler, of December 22, 1899, *Examination of Camden Harbor, Maine*, House Document 85, 56th Cong., 1st Sess., p. 263; *Third Annual Report of the Bureau of Industrial and Labor Statistics for the State of Maine, 1889* (Augusta: Burleigh and Flynt, 1890), p. 59. Hereafter *Labor Statistics* and the year. Michael McGuire, "Rockport and Lime Once Synonymous," *Bangor Daily News*, December 25, 1978, p. 23. It was a pleasure to have had Mr. McGuire as an undergraduate student in my course "Maine and the Sea."

[2] Cyrus W. Eaton, *History of Thomaston, Rockland and South Thomaston* (Hallowell, Maine: Masters, Smith and Co., 1867), *passim*. Eaton's is the classic on the early lime trade. See too, "The Lime Trade" in B.R. Harden, *Shore Village Story: An Informal History of Rockland, Maine* (Rockland: Courier Gazette, 1976); L.C. Allin, "The Ocean Construct," *The Social Studies* (July/August 1977); and L.C. Allin, "Hot Lime, Cold Water and Tall Trees: The Lime Coast As a Teaching Vehicle," *Proceedings of a Conference on Maritime Education* (Orono, Maine: University of Maine Press, 1978), present the factual and philosophical foundations of this study.

[3] *Sixteenth Annual Report of the Bureau of Industrial and Labor Statistics of the State of Maine, 1902* (Augusta: Kennebec Journal Printers, 1903), p. 62; E.S. Bastin, "The Lime Industry of Knox County, Maine," in *Contributions to Economic Geology, 1905* (n.p., n.d.) and Alexander Monroe, *New Brunswick* (Halifax: R. Nugent, 1855), p. 108.

[4] R.H. Oberg and G.V. Guidett, "The Geology of the Camden-Rockland Area" in P.H. Oberg, (ed.), *Guidebook for Field Trips in East Central and North Central Maine* (n.p.: Orono, 1974), pp. 48-60 and *Labor Statistics, 1889*, p. 59.

[5] *Thirteenth Annual Report of the Bureau of Industrial and Labor Statistics of the State of Maine, 1899* (Augusta: Kennebec Journal Printers, 1900), p. 59; Louise Dickinson Rich, *The Coast of Maine* (New York: Thomas Crowell & Co., 1970), pp. 4-12; Ernest Maxey, "Evolution of Coal Limeburning Kiln," *Rockland Courier Gazette*, March 20, 1976, p. 3 and J.F. McCamant "Thomaston Lime Then and Now," paper delivered to Thomaston Historical Society November 6, 1976. McCamant was operations manager for Martin-Marietta Company which once produced cement from the old quarry grounds.

[6] *Ninth Annual Report of the Bureau of Industrial and Labor Statistics of the State of Maine, 1895* (Augusta: Burleigh and Flynt, Printers to the State, 1896), p. 25; and William Hutchinson Rowe, *The Maritime History of Maine* (Freeport, Maine: Bond Wheelwright, n.d.) Chapter 1, "The Maine Coast."

[7] Grindle, *Quarry and Kiln*, pp. 13-14 and A.L. Packard, *A Town That Went to Sea* (Portland: Maine's House of Falmouth, 1950), p. 89.

[8] F.E. Lynch, "Chapters in the Social and Economic History of Thomaston, Maine," (Unpub. M.A. Thesis, University of Maine, 1956), *passim*; Albert J. Smalley, *St. George, Maine* (Tenant's Harbor, Maine: Pierson Press, 1976), *passim*; Joseph Williamson, *Samuel Waldo, 1696 and 1759*, Collections of the Maine Historical Society, Volume 9; *Labor Statistics, 1889*, p. 59 and *Labor Statistics, 1899*, p. 25.

[9] Cyrus W. Eaton, *Annals of the Town of Warren* (Hollowell, Maine: Masters and Livermore, 1877) tells of the landowners, the Muscogongus Patentees. See: Lynch, "Social and Economic History of Thomaston," p. 9.

[10] Irene Cousins, "General Henry Knox, the Country Gentleman," (Unpub. M.A. Thesis, University of Maine, 1941) and Grindle, *Quarry and Kiln*, pp. 4-5.

[11] J.J. Stahl, *History of Old Broadbay and Waldoboro* (Portland: Bond Wheelwright, 1965) tells of the Ulmer family's early history and is a fine example of what town history can be. Grindle, *Quarry and Kiln*, p. 4 and *Labor Statistics, 1903*, p. 62. It is reported in *Labor Statistics, 1889*, p. 63 that Samuel Rankin sent the first lime to New York City aboard the schooner *Leo* in 1823.

[12] *Labor Statistics,1889*, p. 63.

[13] Lynch, "Social and Econmic History of Thomaston," p. 10.

[14] Packard, *Town That Went to Sea*, p. 90.

[15] *Labor Statistics, 1895*, p. 133.

[16] Lewis Bates Clark, "A Brief Economic History of the City of Rockland, Maine," (Unpub. M.A. Thesis, University of Maine, 1925), pp. 77-80 and *passim* and Grindle, *Quarry and Kiln*, p. 20.

[17] Ruel Robinson, *History of Camden and Rockport, Maine* (Rockland: Huston's Book Store, 1907), p. 607; N.V. Knibbs, *Lime and Magnesia* (London: Ernest, Ernest and Benn, 1924), *passim*; Lynch, "Social and Economic History of Thomaston," pp. 13, 24 and *Labor Statistics, 1899*, p. 31.

[18] Packard, *Town That Went to Sea*, pp. 88-89.

[19] B.W. White, "The Disappearing Art of Coopering," *Downeast* (November, 1967), p.32; Grindle, *Quarry and Kiln*, p. 6 and Packard, *Town That*

Went to Sea, pp. 93-94. Grindle states that the Lime Coast used 554,600 casks in 1836. By the 1880's over 1,200,000 casks were used each year.

[20] *Labor Statistics, 1899*, pp. 27-28.

[21] G.S. Wasson, *Sailing Days on the Penobscot* (Salem: Marine Research Society, 1932), p. 195; Robert Greenhalgh Albion, fwd., *The Journals of Hezekiah Prince, Junior, 1822-1828* (New York: Crown Publishers, 1965), *passim*; Grindle, *Quarry and Kiln*, pp. 5-7; Packard, *Town That Went to Sea*, p. 94, Lynch, "Social and Economic History of Thomaston," p. 11 and White, "The Disappearing Art of Coopering," p. 33. Lynch notes that cask sizes varied through the years and were set at 200 then 100 then 50 gallon capacities.

[22] Lynch, "Social and Economic History of Thomaston," p. 14.

[23] A.W. Wall, "Lime Kilns of Rockport," *Downeast* (May, 1969), pp. 34-35; Grindle, *Quarry and Kiln*, p. 5 and Packard, *Town That Went to Sea*, pp. 91-92. On pages 5 and 105 Grindle points out that kilnwood was the greatest expense of the limeburners and that as early as 1848, they had to import it from Canada.

[24] E.W. Maxey, "End of the Lime Era in Rockland," *Rockland Courier Gazette*, March 20, 1976, p.4; *Bangor Whig and Courier*, May 4, 1844, p. 3; *Portland Advertiser*, March 30, 1853, p. 3; *Labor Statistics, 1889*, pp. 62, 64 and Wasson, *Sailing Days on the Penobscot*, p. 194.

[25] A.C. Both to LTCOL A.M. Damrell, of December 4, 1895, *Survey of Rockland Harbor, Maine*, House Document 85, 54th Cong., 1st Sess., pp. 3-6; *Labor Statistics, 1895*, p. 134; *Bangor Whig and Courier*, April 26, 1884, p. 3; Packard, *Town That Went to Sea*, p. 89 and Wasson, *Sailing Days on the Penobscot*, pp. 199-200.

[26] *Labor Statistics, 1895*, p. 135; Grindle, *Quarry and Kiln*, p. 32 and Packard, *Town That Went to Sea*, pp. 94-95. Packard claims that the inhabitants of the Lime Coast believed the smoke from the kilns warded off diptheria and cholera. Local and national newspapers such as the *Rockland Free Press, Rockland Gazette, Rockland Opinion, Bangor Whig and Courier, Portland Eastern Argus, New York Daily Tribune*, and the *New York Times* carried many terse stories of accidents in the trade. Town records could be explored to ascertain which boarding-house owners made a business from the quarry paupers.

[27] *Seventh Annual Report of the Bureau of Labor and Industrial Statistics for the State of Maine, 1893* (Augusta: Burleigh and Flynt, 1893), p. 174.

[28] Packard, *Town That Went to Sea*, p. 92.

[29] *Labor Statistics, 1889*, p. 60.

[30] *Bangor Whig and Courier,* December 11, 1846, p. 3 and Lynch, "Social and Economic History of Thomaston," pp. 19-22.

[31] William Armstrong Fairburn, *Merchant Sail,* Vol. V (Center Lovell, Maine: Fairburn Educational Foundation, 1945-1954), pp. 3383-3448 explains a great deal about Lime Coast shipbuilding but fails to mention the lime trade or any of the limers. Barbara F. Dyer's *"Grog Ho!" The History of Wooden Vessel Building in Camden, Maine* (Rockland: Barbara Dyer, 1984), is an amateur's work of love, but contains a great deal of information on the Coast and its vessel construction.

[32] *Labor Statistics, 1899,* p. 29; Harden, *Shore Village,* p. 133; and Wasson, *Sailing Days on the Penobscot,* pp. 145-199. The best available biographies of the Lime Coast shipbuilders are scattered through the late John Lyman's *Log Chips.*

[33] Packard, makes the assertion in her *Town That Went to Sea,* pp. 89 and 92-93; Mjr. R.W. Roessler to Brig. Gen. G.M. Gillespie of July 12, 1901, *ARCE,* 1901, p. 1002; Wasson, *Sailing Days on the Penobscot,* p. 196. Lynch claims in his "Social and Economic History of Thomaston," that the town built its first vessel in 1787. It had built vessels before that date. The Lime Coast was second only to Bath and the Kennebec region in Maine shipbuilding. Its building activites cry for a chronicle such as W.A. Baker's *A Maritime History of Bath and the Kennebec Region* (Bath: Marine Research Society, 1973). In addition to Baker's book, the Marine Research Society [of Bath] spawned the Maine Maritime Museum.

[34] *Labor Statistics, 1902,* p. 63.

[35] Packard, *Town That Went to Sea,* pp. 96-97 and Wasson, *Sailing Days on the Penobscot,* pp. 199-202.

[36] John Leavitt, "The Lime Droughers," in his *Wake of the Coasters* (Middletown, Conn.: Wesleyan University Press, 1970), has an excellent description of the limers. Packard, *Town That Went to Sea,* p. 95 and Wasson, *Sailing Days on the Penobscot,* pp. 200-205.

[37] George MacBeath, "Johnny Woodboat," *American Neptune XVII* (January, 1957), p. 14; *Labor Statistics,1889,* p: 63; Wall, "Lime Kilns of Rockport," pp. 34-35 and Wasson, *Sailing Days on the Penobscot,* p. 195.

[38] Grindle, *Quarry and Kiln,* p. 108 and Wasson, *Sailing Days on the Penobscot,* p. 196.

[39] MacBeath, "Johnny Wooodboat," p. 7.

[40] Wasson, *Sailing Days on the Penobscot,* pp. 196-197.

[41] Packard, *Town That Went to Sea,* p. 93.

⁴² MacBeath, "Johnny Woodboat," p. 7 and Wasson *Sailing Days on the Penobscot*, p. 197.

⁴³ Grindle, *Quarry and Kiln*, p. 7.

⁴⁴ J.F. McCamant, "Development of the Thomaston Lime Industry," pp. 6-9; Grindle, *Quarry and Kiln*, pp. 7-9 and Harden, *Shore Village*, p. 100.

⁴⁵ G.F. Bacon, *Rockland, Belfast and Vicinity* (Newark: Glenwood Publishing Company, 1892), pp. 9, 78, 123 and 137 and Grindle, *Quarry and Kiln*, pp.11-12.

⁴⁶ *Bangor Whig and Courier*, December 30, 1873, p. 3 and Harden, *Shore Village*, p. 112.

⁴⁷ Grindle, *Quarry and Kiln*, pp. 6, 11 and 14.

⁴⁸ Grindle, *Quarry and Kiln*, pp. 6, 13 and 14. The *Bangor Whig and Courier* of the era carries many stories of Bangor's trade in wood to the kilns.

⁴⁹ Grindle, *Quarry and Kiln*, pp. 20-21 and Lynch, "Social and Economic History of Thomaston," p. 24.

⁵⁰ Lynch, "Social and Economic History of Thomaston," p. 24 and Wall, "Lime Kilns of Rockport," pp. 33-34.

⁵¹ *Belfast Republican Journal*, August 3, 1876, p. 1 and *Labor Statistics, 1889*, p. 64.

⁵² Clark, "Economic History of Rockland," p. 79.

⁵³ Grindle, *Quarry and Kiln*, p. 3; Harden, *Shore Village*, pp. 101-104; Packard, *Town That Went to Sea*, p. 97; Lynch, "Social and Economic History of Thomaston," p. 22-24; Maxey, "Evolution of Coal Burning Lime Kilns," p. 7; McCamant, "Development of the Thomaston Lime Industry" pp. 4-7; Wall, "Lime Kilns of Rockport," p. 34; and "Telling You Some Things You Don't Know About Lime," *Lewiston Evening Journal*, March 15, 1922, p. 22; all have something to say about kiln technology. In 1895 there were 112 patent kilns in Knox County located: seventy in Rockland, twenty in Thomaston, sixteen in Rockport, six in Warren and two in Camden. Grindle also shows in his *Quarry and Kiln*, pp. 105, 126 and *passim* how the limeburners manipulated tariffs to beat Canadian competition. Nonetheless, by 1893 the Canadians were able to compete in the Boston market.

⁵⁴ These figures are taken from the *Annual Report of the Chief of Engineers* for the years given. The figures are not totally reliable as they have been "rounded off." Still, they give the best approximations available.

[55] *Labor Statistics, 1889*, p. 63; *Labor Statistics, 1899*, pp. 27-28 and White, "Disappearing Art of Coopering," pp. 33-34.

[56] L.W. Moody, "The Rockport Railroad," in *All Aboard for Yesterday* (Camden: Downeast, n.d.), pp. 48-51; LTCOL George Thom, USA to Brig. Gen. A.A. Humphrey of December 16, 1979, ARCE, 1879, pp. 275-276 and *Labor Statistics, 1889*, p. 61.

[57] Lew Dietz, "Goose River Portrait," *Downeast* (October, 1963), pp. 16-23; *Labor Statistics, 1889*, p. 61; *Labor Statistics, 1899*, p. 27; *Labor Statistics, 1902*, p. 65; Wall, "Lime Kilns of Rockport," p. 18; *Bangor Daily Commercial*, June 5, 1889, p. 3; Harden, *Shore Village*, pp. 104-116 and Robinson, *History of Camden and Rockport*, p. 610.

[58] Shirlee Connors Carlson, *Rockport, Camden and Lincolnville, 1776-1976* (n.p.: Camden Town Crier, 1975), p. 75 gives an example of the contention.

[59] Lynch, "Social and Economic History of Thomaston," p. 17.

[60] Harden, *Shore Village*, p. 111.

[61] Harden, *Shore Villge*, p. 111 and McCamant, "Thomaston Lime: Then and Now, pp. 8-11."

[62] *Statistics of Industries and Finances of Maine for 1884* (Augusta: Sprague and Son, 1884), p. 100; *Labor Statistics, 1889*, pp. 62-63; *Bangor Daily Commercial*, July 6, 1885, p. 4; *Bangor Whig and Courier*, June 19, 1885, p. 3 and July 14, 1885, p. 3; Harden, *Shore Village*, p. 112, and McCamant, "Development of the Thomaston Lime Industry," p. 4.

[63] Emmett Meara, "Rockland Has Potential as Oil Mini-port," *Bangor Daily News*, July 17, 1974 and *Labor Statistics, 1899*, pp. 62-3.

[64] *Labor Statistics, 1902*, p. 66-7.

[65] *Ibid.*

[66] J.W. Thomas, *Rockland, Maine* (Rockland: Rockland Board of Trade, 1910), n.p., and *Rockland, Maine* (Rockland: City of Rockland, 1977), p. 9.

[67] Thomas, *Rockland, Maine* (1977), pp. 9-10.

[68] *Lincolnville Early Days*, (Lincolnville: Lincolnville Historical Society, 1976), Vol. I, p. 29. and Lew Dietz, "Goose River Portrait," pp. 20-21.

Doxies at Dockside: Prostitution and American Maritime Society, 1800-1900

Linda M. Maloney

"In Amsterdam there lived a maid . . . and she was mistress of her trade." The song is evocative of the sailor's shipboard dream: a port, new clothes, plenty to drink, and a woman. Of one thing we may be sure: the doxy who awaited the sailor at dockside was not the rosy-cheeked lass that fancy painted in the long night watch. But who she really was and why she was there, are questions not heretofore asked, nor answered.

I propose to ask a lot of questions to which I do not yet have the answers. A lifetime of research in maritime matters has yielded me very little knowledge about the women who were part of maritime so-

ciety, but I suspect I have been looking in the wrong places, and that
the answers to some of my questions do exist.

Who were the women who became prostitutes in maritime
America before, let us say, World War I? The received wisdom on the
subject is that city prostitutes were mainly country girls bewitched by
the metropolis, or, in the industrial era, immigrants from abroad. This
is questionable. An investigator who interviewed 1,106 prostitutes in
New York City in 1912 (a sample of some 15,000 then in the city) found
that 762 were American born, and a majority of those were natives of
New York City. A study of 746 women committed to Bedford State
Reformatory in that same year found that 491 were American-born,
404 of them born in cities.

The important factor, it appeared, was not place of birth, but social class: 21.3% of these women had fathers who were unskilled
laborers; 22.4% had working mothers who were, in most cases, the
sole family support and were also doing day labor as maids, laun-
dresses, etc. Many of the prostitutes had tried such work and found it
did not yield a living wage; even a fifty-cent brothel was better than
drudge work at $1 to $3 per week.[1]

In the pre-industrial period immigrant women formed a larger
proportion of the prostitutes in American cities. William Sanger, ques-
tioning 2,000 New York City prostitutes in 1858, found 1,238
foreign-born among them, the larger numbers being, predictably,
from those countries which sent the most immigrants: Ireland, England and Germany. But of the three-eighths of his sample who were
American-born, disproportionate numbers came from the maritime
Northeast: 42 from Connecticut, "the land of steady habits," 24 from
Maine, 71 from Massachusetts, 69 from New Jersey, 77 from Pennsylvania, 18 from Rhode Island (one for every 8,000 inhabitants) and 394
from New York.

Sanger attributed much of this to the rigors of New England factory life, from which he believed these native American women were
fleeing (although only 37 gave their previous occupation as factory employment), but he also remarks on the influence of maritime society:
"Beyond the effect of manufactures, . . . the immense maritime business of New York City, . . . must be taken into consideration. This

constantly fills some localities with sailors, men proverbial for having 'in every port a wife,' and many of them are notorious frequenters of houses of prostitution. This circumstance proves that this infernal traffic is governed by the same rules which regulate commercial transactions, namely, that the supply is in proportion to the demand. If, by any miracle all the seamen and strangers visiting New York could be transformed into moral men, at least from one half to two-thirds of the houses of ill fame would be absolutely bankrupt." [2] Sanger also thought that immigrant girls were frequently seduced on their passage, either by sailors or fellow-passengers.

None of this is news. What may, I believe, shed a new light on the sailor's doxy is to look at her as the seaman's dependent. She was so, obviously, insofar as her customers and therefore her means of livelihood were sailors. The chronically depressed state of seamen's wages kept the price of her services low. Kneeland's survey of New York bawdy houses as late as 1912 showed the "dollar house" as most common and fifty cent brothels widespread. These were the houses frequented by sailors. It is important, I think, as the new social history concerns itself with the low estate of seamen, to remember that the woman who served their sexual needs was also kept in chronic poverty by the penny-pinching wage scales of the Navy and the merchant-owners.

But beyond this, I wish to suggest that a significant number of prostitutes were "in the life" because at some previous time they had been sailors' dependents in the more conventional sense. Christopher McKee has pointed out that in the late eighteenth and early nineteenth century, when an able seaman in the Navy drew $204 per year (before purser's deductions) his wife, if he left a half-pay ticket for her, was entitled to draw $102 per year, and that the letters these women wrote to the Accountant of the Navy reveal "that $102 a year emphatically did not support a family and that the wife had to work as a domestic servant, laundress, or some similar occupation simply to make ends meet."[3] What a rich fund of information on the lives of poor women these letters provide! But we may safely surmise that if the wife took up an occupation not very similar to domestic service or washing, she did not confide in the Accountant of the Navy. That she, or more likely her daughters, might be driven to such an expedient was not, however, far from the minds of husbands, fathers, and even unattached males in maritime society. Isaac Hull commented angrily on his feelings about the rejection by Congress in 1808 and 1810 (while he was still a bachelor) of the Navy officers' petition for a pension plan similar to that accorded the Army: "They even went so far as to say that the daughters of officers killed fighting for their country, could when *fifteen* get a living for themselves, meaning, I suppose, that they could take in washing or *something still worse.*" [4]

These were by no means idle fears. William Sanger's survey of prostitution in 1858 found thirty-one women who listed their father's occupation as "naval officer." Thirty-five were the daughters of sailors, though these outnumbered officers at least twenty to one. (Seafarers and boatmen were estimated at 2/17 of employed men.) Many more were the wives or widows of seafaring men. Sanger found 490 married women and 294 widows in his sample of 2,000. Thirty-nine of the married women reported that their husbands had gone to sea. Most of these married or widowed women were mothers of two or more children.

Sanger reported a number of heart-rending cases of women brought low by seafaring men: there was a Southern girl, daughter of a merchant, who while on a voyage in one of her father's vessels was seduced by the captain, became pregnant, and was then deserted by the wretch after they reached port. (Naturally, her parents would not take her back, and she was reduced to prostitution.) Or consider the testimony of C.H., a wife and mother:

> I was married when I was seventeen years old, and have had three children. The two boys are living now; the girl is dead. My oldest boy is nearly five years old, and the other one is eighteen months. My husband is a sailor. We lived very comfortably till my last child was born, and then he began to drink very hard, and did not support me, and I have not seen him or heard any thing about him for six months. After he left me I tried to keep my children by washing or going out to day's work, but I could not earn enough. I never could earn more than two or three dollars a week when I had work, which was not always. My father and mother died when I was a child. I had nobody to help me, and could not support my children, so

> I came to this place. My boys are now living in the city, and I
> support them with what I earn by prostitution. It was only to
> keep them that I came here. [5]

Clearly, this set of circumstances frequently presented itself to the sailor's wife even when he did not maliciously desert her, but simply enlisted for a China voyage or a two-year hitch in the Navy. How often was the sequel the same?

Sanger pursued his researches to the red-light districts of New York, and he gives a lively description of the different ethnic neighborhoods and types of accommodations. He ranked the houses in four classes: the first, or "parlor houses," and the second class, were mainly inhabited by native American women, the third by Germans, and the fourth, which catered to sailors, by Irish. The landlord of a sailors' house was usually himself a seafarer, "for no one else would be deemed fit to keep a house where sailors resort." [6]

This degradation of the sailor's doxy is further suggested by the fact that moral reformers considered her beyond redemption. When the New York Female Moral Reform Society (later the American Female Guardian Society) was formed in 1834 its stated aim was to convert the prostitutes of New York City (then estimated at 10,000) and to close the brothels. But, while the Society did make gestures to the uplift and reform of prostitutes, it directed its major efforts at the "parlor house" where, it was hoped, the "respectable" male patrons could be shamed into repentance. [7]

These instances by no means constitute a systematic survey of the question of the relationship of prostitutes to American maritime society. They are merely suggestive, and I hope serve to open the subject for further inquiry. We desperately need more "history from the bottom up" in this area, to recover the viewpoint of the woman herself. A fine, pioneering study for England has been done by Judith R. and Daniel K. Walkowitz, "'We Are Not Beasts of the Field': Prostitution and the Poor in Plymouth and Southampton under the Contagious Diseases Acts," [8] but it is not matched by similar research on America, where a lively debate over legalized prostitution and medical inspection raged through the late nineteenth and early twentieth century. The debate, conducted by high-minded and well-to-do citizens, has been amply documented, [9] but the attitude of those most intimately concerned has not been sought.

With regard to the Navy, we know that women were found on board the ships, even in wartime, from a very early date, although the only period for which we have a quantity of documentation so far is the Barbary Wars. The difficulty is that the American Navy, unlike its British counterpart, gave no official notice to the presence of women on board, except when granting permission for officers' wives to accompany them. But private journals, logs and letters show women in the 'tween decks, bearing a hand occasionally in battle, and even giving birth to little "sons of guns" like Melancthon Woolsey Low, born and christened in *Chesapeake* in the spring of 1803, as Midshipman Henry Wadsworth detailed in his journal:

> On the 22d Febry. it being the day after we left Algiers: Mrs. Low (wife to James Low Captain of the Forecastle) bore a Son, in the Boatswain's Store Room: on the 31st (March) the babe was baptiz'd in the Midshipmen's apartment: The Contriver of this business, was Melancthon Taylor Woolsey a Mid: who stood Godfather on the occasion & provided a handsome collation of Wine & Fruit: Mrs. Low being unwell Mrs. Hays the Gunner's Lady officiated: Divine Service by Rev. Alex McFarlan. The Childs name Melancthon Woolsey Low: All was conducted with due decorum & decency no doubt to the great satisfaction of the parents, as Mr. Woolsey's attention to them must in some measure have ameliorated the unhappy situation of the Lady who was so unfortunate as to conceive & bare, on the Salt Sea. NB. The other Ladies of the Bay* (*The Forward Most part of the Birth Deck) — viz. Mrs. Watson: the Boatswain's Wife, Mrs Myres the Carpenter's Lady — with Mrs. Crosby the corporal's Lady: got drunk in their own Quarters out of pure spite — not being invited to celebrate the Christening of Melancthon Woolsey Low. [10]

These women, however, so far as evidence survives, were the respectable "ladies" of the ship's warrant and petty officers: boatswain, gunner, carpenter, corporal, captain of the forecastle and a few others. I have not yet seen evidence that American officers permitted prostitutes on board their ships — while at sea, that is. The disciplinary reasons are clear.

In port, of course, it was another matter. In "civilized" ports most Navy commanders tried — without notable success — to keep "visitors" out of the ship. But when a Navy ship went voyaging to Polynesia or other strange and scented isles, attitudes changed, and what was vice in America became necessary recreation. One of the most famous incidents of this sort was the visit of the schooner *Dolphin* to Oahu in 1826.

Dolphin had been five months at sea when she anchored at Honolulu, and her crew were expecting a pleasant interlude after their long cruise. Their feelings were fully shared by their sympathetic commander, Lieutenant John "Mad Jack" Percival, and the other officers. What was their chagrin, therefore, to learn that a taboo on women visiting ships in the harbor had been imposed only weeks before their arrival, through the influence of the American missionaries at Honolulu. The officers were able to establish comfortable quarters on shore, complete with "wives," but it was bad luck for the sailors on board *Dolphin* and the trading and whaling ships. They protested to Percival, and he in turn had "words" with the missionaries and with the dowager queen Kaahumanu, the effective ruler of the islands. The eventual result, on Sunday, 26 February 1826, was a riot in which several houses were damaged and a few heads cracked. Percival, again confronting Hiram Bingham, the leading missionary, warned him that "you are going on too fast." Percival was, I think, one of the earliest pioneers in using the concept of national honor in a dubious cause: he contended that a denial of women to his sailors would be dishonor to the United States, because women had been permitted the men of H.M.S. *Blonde* the previous year. One way or another, he won his point, and the taboo was lifted for the duration of *Dolphin's* stay.

When I wrote an account of this incident a few years ago [11] I took the sailors' point of view; now I would rather like to go back and do it again, from the other side. What were the customs of Oahu in sexual matters before the whites came? What were Kaahumanu's motives in seeking to end this traffic? Were they wholly Calvinist, due to her recent conversion, or were they political or even proto-feminist? Gwenfread E. Allen points out that after the death of Kamehameha I, in 1819, a year before the missionaries came, Kaahumanu joined with Keopuolani, his highest ranking widow, in persuading the new king to eat publicly with women, thereby breaking one of the most stringent taboos, and that she was generally dissatisfied with the religious taboos which bore heavily upon women.[12]

What about the feelings of the ordinary women of Oahu? Did they share Kaahumanu's convictions? In February or March Lieutenant Percival's "wife" ran away from him and was forcibly returned: obviously she was not entirely satisfied with the concubinal arrangements. Was there in fact a system of prostitution in early Oahu, or was it merely seasonal recreation — or business?

I hope I have demonstrated that a great deal of research remains to be done on the subject of prostitution and maritime society. And yet, to me this is the least interesting aspect of the greater subject: women in maritime America. The least interesting because it views women in the traditional way, as objects. I am eager to move on to inquiry about women as active participants in the growth of maritime culture, and I hope many of you will want to sign on for the cruise.

Notes

[1] George J. Kneeland, *Commercialized Prostitution in New York City* (Appleton-Century, c1913; reprint Patterson Smith, 1969).

[2] William W. Sanger, *The History of Prostitution* (New York: Harper, 1858), pp. 458-459.

[3] Christopher McKee, "Fantasies of Mutiny and Murder: a Suggested Psycho-History of the Seaman in the United States Navy, 1798-1815," *Armed Forces and Society*, IV. no. 2 (Feb. 1978), p. 297.

[4] New-York Historical Society, Isaac Hull LB: Hull to David Daggett, 18 Nov. 1814. Second emphasis supplied.

[5] Sanger, pp. 497, 508-509.

[6] Sanger, p. 563.

[7] Cf. Carroll Smith-Rosenberg, "Beauty, the Beast and the Militant Woman," *American Quarterly* XXIII (Oct. 1971), pp. 562-584.

[8] In *Clio's Consciousness Raised*, ed. Lois Banner and Mary Hartman (New York: Harper, 1974), pp. 192-225.

[9] David J. Pivar, *Purity Crusade: Sexual Morality and Social Control, 1868-1900* (Westport, Conn.: Greenwood Press, 1973).

[10] *Naval Documents Related to the United States Wars with the Barbary Powers*, II, p. 387: Henry Wadsworth Journal, 2 April 1803.

[11] Linda McKee, "'Mad Jack' and the Missionaries," *American Heritage* XXII, no. 3 (April 1971), pp. 30-37, 85-87.

[12] In Edward T. James, Janet W. James and Paul S. Boyer, eds., *Notable American Women* (Cambridge: Belknap Press, 1971), vol. II, p. 302.

A flogging at sea before an unappreciative crew. (J. Ross Browne, *Browne's Whaling Cruise and the History of the Whale Industry* [n. pl., n. pub., 1846].)

"All Hands Drunk and Rioting:"
Disobedience in the
Old Merchant Marine

Allan A. Arnold

Richard Henry Dana, in his narration of the flogging incident in *Two Years Before the Mast* explains why the crew did not intervene in this cruel treatment of their shipmate by the tyrannical captain: "What is there for sailors to do? If they resist, it is mutiny, and if they succeed, and take the vessel, it is piracy." Indeed, the one sailor who dared to ask the captain why he was flogging this man was himself flogged.[1]

Yet, it is also Dana who tells us how, later in the same voyage, the crew dealt with the loss of their Sunday off by staging a subtle work slow-down that induced the officers to compromise.[2]

A captain like Dana's Frank Thompson was not often openly disobeyed, and nineteenth century merchant seamen in general did work under strict discipline and often lived in constant fear of their officers. Yet there are numerous cases of seamen disobeying orders and receiving little or no punishment. Often they were made to obey in the end, but sometimes they even got their way.

This paper is not concerned with attempts to depose the captain and seize the ship; a much more common, and more prudent form of maritime disobedience was a refusal to work.

A concerted work stoppage by the crew was, of course, more effective than a single man's refusal to work. This might occur at sea, where a quick resolution of the issue was imperative, or in port, where the crew were not endangering their own safety by striking. Whether or not the crew won the objectives of their strike depended upon the physical circumstances, the wisdom and determination of both sides.

Richard Cleveland was sailing along the China coast in 1799 with a crew of deserters and escaped convicts. After three weeks of very hard work and exposure for the crew, ten of them, led by the bosun, announced that they would not work unless the captain agreed to their demands. These amounted to an abdication of his authority over the crew, and Cleveland responded by locking the harness-casks: no work, no food. The eleven loyal men stood on the quarterdeck, each armed with a musket and a brace of pistols, and two four-pound cannon were loaded with grapeshot and pointed forward. The mutineers had only handspikes and hatchets; they did not attack. Cleveland then offered to put the mutineers ashore on Quemoy Island where the ship had anchored for shelter. The men agreed, confident that the ship could not sail without them. After three days Cleveland had coaxed four of the men back aboard without making any concessions, refused to take the two ringleaders back and sailed away, leaving six men behind. These men would be badly missed on the rest of the long voyage, but the captain had not compromised his authority.[3]

In 1850, Captain Charles Barry could not find a crew in Savannah, and went up to Charleston, where he signed up a crew of tough characters and paid them advance wages. Of course, they did not show up in Savannah on the agreed day, and Barry sent the sheriff to round them up. He managed to bring 13 of the 14 men on board after two more days, at a cost of $140, but when it was time to sail the next morning, eight of them refused to work.

The captain never seems to have considered putting them ashore. Not only had money been invested in this crew, there was also no prospect of replacing them. He put the mutineers in irons, separated as much as possible from each other. There were just enough loyal men to raise the anchor, after which Captain Barry planned to drift out to sea, where he would use a work or starve ultimatum to get the crew to raise the sails. All this he wrote in a letter to his wife that was given to the pilot to mail.

We do not know if the crew worked or starved, because the ship was never heard from again. It is possible that this impasse between labor and management was fatal to both.[4]

Captain Wallace of the *Cutty Sark* also tried to put to sea with a rebellious crew. The captain was ordinarily well-liked by his crew, but he made a serious error in judgment by helping the mate, who was hated by the crew, escape to another ship in the Singapore Straits. The entire foc's'le crew refused to work until the mate was returned so they could prosecute him. Wallace decided to raise the anchor and set sail using six boys, the cook, the steward, the carpenter and the sailmaker. When the sailors tried to interfere, he put the four ringleaders in irons. But his determination did not succeed in getting the crew back to work, and after four days at sea he jumped overboard to his death.[5]

The reactions of Captain Cleveland and Captain Barry to mass disobedience by their crews was courageous, not entirely successful, and not at all typical. Captain Benjamin Neal of Salem commanded the whaling bark *Reaper* off Madagascar in 1839. His log entries speak for themselves:

> *February 25th:* This morning the whole of my crew came aft to know when I intended to go into port, saying that if I did not go in soone, they would not work the Ship . . . I shall try to git into Fort Dauphin as soon as the weather wil permit.

> *March 7th:* I have bin in this Port 9 dayes . . . If I can git the Barque oute it will be after this when I come here again in a

Whale Ship . . . A Whale Ship ought if possible to avoid all ports in which rum can be obtained.

March 8th: The crew are worse than the devel could wish them to be. They sent aft to night to know if I wold sleep onshore to let the women come on board. This of corce I refused. If I am obliged to detain the Ship in this port by the bad conduct of the Crew I shall have to send to the Isle of France for help . . . Last night there was complete hell on board.

March 11th: Last night slept on shore and let the girls come on board for the purpose of keeping the crew quiet. This is hard but I am forced to do it . . . The crew wish to have the girls . . . to night. I have told them it cannot be done. I have tried to reason the case with them but it is of no use. They have combined togeather tonight that thay will do no more duty.

March 12th: Blowing hard from NE. The men have acted up to the agreement wich thay made last night [That is, not to work.] . . . The Governor sent a man on board to request me to go to sea if it is practable saying if the weather should be worse he is afraid the ship will go on shore. To comply with his request is impossible.[6]

Another captain who decided to indulge a difficult crew was Captain Marshall of the steamer *California* during the 1849 gold rush. A man who stowed away in Panama was being sheltered by the firemen, and the captain freed the stowaway to keep the firemen working.[7]

Charles Abbey, who sailed before the mast on several ships in the 1850's, remarked casually in his journal in reference to no particular incident: "Crews often (nowadays) knock off duty and refuse to work until some shipmate who has been put in irons is freed." [8] Apparently Dana was being too rigid in allowing no middle ground between unquestioning obedience and mutiny.

Crewmen going ashore without leave was a very common problem. Captains shook their heads, entered the offense in the log, and then, as far as the records show, did nothing about it.

The log of the brig *Matilda* in 1797 records "Curtis Comstock absent thirty hours with out libety" and the next day "Curtis Comstock came on Board." There is no further comment.[9]

If a master did not give his crew shore leave on a holiday, they might go anyway. A British seaman in Shanghai did not hesitate to record in his diary that on December 25th, 1857, he and a friend "went on shore without leave or licence." [10]

While the brig *Camilla* was unloading in Antwerp for two weeks in December of 1834, men went ashore without liberty on the 24th. On the 25th the captain suspended all work, but when he tried to resume unloading on the 26th, all the crew were ashore without liberty. [11]

Some unauthorized leaves turned into sagas. The clipper ship *Granger* spent over a month in port at London in 1877. On 20 June, the ship's carpenter reported aboard with his tools and clothes, in an intoxicated state. The mate's entry in the log for 21 June reads: "5:30 A.M. Carpenter left ship without permission and at 4:30 P.M. he returned quite intoxicated. 6 P.M. went off again and was called to but he would not listen." The carpenter did not reappear for the next four days, and there was apparently no attempt made to find him. The 26 June entry says: "Carpenter on board but not on duty. Feels quite unwell from Drink." He did not work again until 28 June, a week after his binge began. [12]

Captain John Clark kept his brig *Betsey* in Wilmington for a month in 1796, and probably wished that he hadn't. On 2 December, Joshua Vallit went ashore overnight without leave. On 3 December the cook ran away with all his clothes, meaning that he intended to desert. This time the mate went after him and brought him back in two hours. On 4 December Isaac Williams ran away with his clothes and was not pursued.

This may have been a signal to the crew, for on 6 December they all went ashore without leave. One of them returned at midnight badly wounded, and an officer dressed his wounds. The next day it was learned that the crew had joined those of other ships at a whorehouse on the hill, where a fight between Americans and Frenchmen had left one man killed, several wounded, and six Frenchmen in jail.

When the crew found that they could go ashore without leave and get away with it, they must have lost respect for the captain completely. On 12 December, "Captain Clark told John Plazur to Gow in the boat After Lomber And he Told Capt Clark that he wod Not Gow

And he Did Not Gow." There is no mention of punishment for any of these offenses. When the *Betsey* left Wilmington on 16 December, the log noted: "All hans Drunk & Riting." [13]

Charles Abbey was a sober seaman from a good family who hoped to become an officer. He admits in his journal that he fell asleep on watch, when he was the lookout for the bell. The third mate, Mr. Conway, woke him when he failed to ring four bells and ordered him to keep another two hours' lookout at the weather gangway during his own watch. It was a fine moonlit night and Abbey refused the order to stand a lookout that he considered unnecessary.

> 'You wont do it' says he, 'No I wont' says I. A fracas then ensued in which he got worsted. He then asked me again if I would do it. 'No sir I wont' he then walked aft told the mate. He wouldnt make me & Conway couldnt so he concluded to let me alone. [14]

Apparently Abbey's opinion that the order was unjustified harassment was shared by the first mate, who did not insist on blind obedience of every order by an officer.

Captain Depeyster of the Black Ball packet *Columbus* also declined to punish seamen who were provoked into a fight by his two mates. The captain came on deck to find his officers knocked down and bleeding, surrounded by sailors with handspikes and belaying-pins. Fearing a real mutiny, Captain DePeyster issued pistols to the mates and some passengers, then approached the seamen who had barricaded themselves forward. When the mates urged the captain to shoot the men, he ordered them below. The seamen cheered the captain and put down their makeshift weapons. The captain said, "Now, men; what's all this? . . . Turn to and let's hear no more of it." The men replied, "If this thing is to be called square we're satisfied, always providing that you let them gents understand that they're no going to kill any one on this passage if we can help it." The captain's answer was, "Well, so be it, my men, and now turn to and do your duty like men," and that was the end of the incident. [15]

Each of the last two incidents involved a physical fight between officers and men. Though a physical attack on an officer, or even a threat or verbal abuse by a crewman was supposed to be a very serious offense, there are many cases where punishment was very light or was not given at all, once order was restored. Sometimes this was a policy of wisdom, rather than of weakness.

Captain Charles Forbes, the regular commander of the Pacific coastwise steamer *California* in 1849, made this brief entry in the log:

> At 5 1/2 A.M. the cook threatened to run a sword through me. I knocked him down & lashed him to an eye Bolt.
>
> At noon he concluded to behave himself & I let him go without flogging him. Last part of this day calm and very, very hot.[16]

Isaac Hibberd, mate of the *Cyrus Wakefield*, was supervising the crew who were hauling the braces, when a sailor lunged at him with a knife without any warning, tearing his shirt but missing his body. Hibberd told the man to throw the knife overboard, which he did after some delay. The mate then told the man to go back to work and not to have any more foolishness, and the matter was ended. Hibberd shrugs off the incident as the result of confining 30 men in a small space for four months.[17]

The captain of the whaler *Frances* wrote that David Young:

> . . . was saucy & provoking[.] I struck him and he returned it [.] Mr. Spencer & I took him aft & there he kept his Jaw a going[.] We had a clinch[.] The Crew Came aft & Myer & Conklin clencht Me by the throat[.] We put Young in Irons[;] sent the people forward[.] Yong got the Irons off and run forward & hove them over board[.] Called him & put on another pair & put him down the run . . . Morning let Young out of Irons[;] he promist to behave him self.[18]

This incident took place in 1845. Neither Young nor his two friends who dared to grab their captain by the throat was flogged, though flogging was allowed in the American Navy and on merchant vessels until 1850, and on whalers until 1853. Though flogging was routine in the old navy, it does not seem to have been widely used in the merchant marine. If Dana's notorious Captain Frank Thompson is representative of floggers, then that punishment was used the most by those who had the least justification.

The commonest punishment in the old merchant marine was irons: that is, shackling the offender hand and foot. It is hard for us to judge today how much of a deterrent this was in a sailor's mind, but it certainly kept him out of mischief for a while.

The whaling bark *Charles Morgan* kept a special log of punishments during 1906. Ten men refused to go into the boats after whales. This, of course, was intolerable disobedience and they were threatened with irons and went. Men who refused commands were put in irons for periods from two hours to 5 1/2 hours. When they were released they were made to promise to obey in the future. One man was sent to stand at the masthead, which was another common punishment, but he came right down and refused to return. He was then put in irons for 16 hours.

The *Morgan's* mate apparently did not believe in the adage about "sticks and stones." The carpenter, who tried to hit him with an ax, was only put in irons until 2:30 p.m., but Charles King, who told the mate where to go and what to do to himself in very explicit terms, was given 2 1/2 days in irons.[19]

The problem with using irons as punishment was the loss of labor and merchant ships did not carry spare crewmen. If several men were punished at the same time, the problem was compounded. Captain Cressy of the clipper ship *Flying Cloud* once released men from irons because he needed their services.[20]

About a third of the incidents used in this study come from accounts by men before the mast. Those sailors who kept journals or who wrote autobiographies later in life were obviously not maniacs or hopeless derelicts, and they had some respect for authority in general. They, and many of their well-behaved but less literate shipmates, disobeyed their superiors when they felt strong moral justification in doing so, and when they felt that the crew was united against a cruel or incompetent officer.

Dana's shipmates knew that a ship had to be navigated seven days a week, but were genuinely outraged to be put to work on a quiet

Sunday in port. Since the safe countermove of a slowdown was available, they used it, but only on that occasion.[21] The men on the *Cutty Sark* as well as those on the packet ship *Columbus* respected their captains as long as they did not back up the tyrannical mates.[22]

Every captain presumably begins a voyage with a certain amount of respect granted to him by virtue of his office. He can then reinforce or diminish that respect according to his conduct. There are, of course, infinite variations of leadership qualities among different commanders, and much depends on the nature of those whom he must lead. But there have been a few captains whose conduct was so grossly improper that they completely forfeited the respect of their crews, and invited open defiance.

One such captain was L.B. Griswold, who sailed the ship *Governor Clinton* around the Horn in 1828. Since the captain compelled the mate to make false entries in the log, the mate kept a secret log of his own. Captain Griswold had many faults: He stole silverware from the owners of the ship, until caught by the supercargo; he tried to turn the crew against the mates; like so many captains, he did not stock adequate provisions, and he excused some healthy men from duty when the ship was undermanned.

But the captain's most glaring fault was drunkenness. The first hint of this vice is a humorous one. The captain had to be lowered over the side up to his neck in the water to inspect a leak, and, says the mate, "never failed to come below after It most Proberly to Wet his Insides as well as out." This suspicion was voiced on 8 July. On 19 July, the captain was using poor seamanship because he was under the influence. Over the next few days, the log records him as "2/3 drunk," "3/4 drunk," "bellowing," and "occasionally taking a dram at 6 A.M."

Captain Griswold was totally drunk during storms, once for 35 hours, and another time when the ship was leaking and listing. He insisted on setting sails during squalls on several occasions. His irrational orders wore out the crew and damaged the ship.

The captain fraternized with the sailors, and the mate noted the effect: "The Little Discipline we Formily had on board is lost and The People take advantage of his Freedom & show him No Respect."

During the first 34 days of the homeward passage from Peru to New York, that is, during a winter passage of Cape Horn, Griswold singlehandedly finished a demijohn (5 gallons) plus 6 bottles of cognac brandy. After a few sober days, he found a 12-gallon whiskey barrel and set to work on it. All this is by way of creating the background for disobedience by the first and second mates.

When the captain verbally abused the first mate before the crew, the mate dared him to remove him from duty, and he did, the mate going below. Griswold soon followed and invited him to return to duty, but when he refused, the captain ordered him to "Go & live Forward for Damm me If you Stay In my Cabin." "Damm me if I dont stop Where I am And Dare any one to touch my Property." The mate tells us that "for a few moments It Was hot Work & *As I was on the right side* (italics mine) I returned to him Words as Good & Bad as he Sent & felt Perfectly Independant[.] he then requested & Entreated me to resume my Duty again which I Consented to."

The second mate was less political-minded but very practical. On the 43rd day of the passage he entered the cabin where the captain was sleeping off his latest binge, and pulled the cork of the 12-gallon whiskey barrel. The smell woke Captain Griswold, but too late to save any. It seems significant that, just as the first mate spoke up to the captain when he felt himself to be in the right, the captain never complained about the loss of his whiskey, because he knew he was wrong.[23]

This is not to argue that disobedience only took place under outrageously bad officers, but to offer a possible explanation for some disobedience by otherwise respectable merchant mariners.

One is led to speculate that the examples given here are but the tip of the iceberg. Those crew members who were most disobedient were least likely to write their autobiographies, and it must have been embarrassing for a captain to admit in his ship's log that one or more of his men had successfully defied him. One can only imagine how many such incidents were omitted from the record.

Notes

[1] Richard Henry Dana, *Two Years Before the Mast* (London, 1912), p. 84.

[2] *Ibid.*, pp. 60-61.

[3] Richard J. Cleveland, *Voyages of a Merchant Navigator* (New York, 1886), pp. 44-47.

[4] Norman E. Borden, Jr., *Dear Sarah* (Freeport, Maine, 1966), pp. 177-181.

[5] Basil Lubbock, *The Log of the Cutty Sark* (Glasgow, 1945), pp. 154-156.

[6] Norman R. Bennett and George E. Brooks, Jr., eds., *New England Merchants in Africa* (Boston, 1965), pp. 186-187.

[7] John E. Pomfret, ed., *California Gold Rush Voyages, 1848-1849* (San Marino, California, 1954), p. 228.

[8] Charles Abbey, *Before the Mast in the Clippers* (New York, 1937), p. 221.

[9] Log of the Brig *Matilda*, May 17, 1797, MR 19, G.W. Blunt White Library, Mystic Seaport Museum, Mystic, CT.

[10] Alexander Whitehead, "China and Back," *Diaries from the Days of Sail*, ed. R.C. Bell (London, 1974), p. 96.

[11] Log of the Brig *Camilla*, Dec. 24-30, 1834, New York Historical Society.

[12] Albert Joseph George, *The Cap'n's Wife* (Syracuse, 1946), pp. 109-111.

[13] Log of Brig *Betsey*, Dec. 3-12, 1796, MR 19, Mystic.

[14] Abbey, *Before the Mast*, p. 106.

[15] Richard C. McKay, *South Street* (New York, 1934), pp. 211-213.

[16] Pomfret, *California Voyages*, p. 240.

[17] Isaac Norris Hibberd, *Sixteen Times Round Cape Horn* (Mystic, 1980), pp. 26-27.

[18] Log of Whaler Ship *Frances*, Oct. 15, 1845, Log 377, Mystic.

[19] Discipline Log of Whaler Bark *Charles W. Morgan*, pp. 43-51, Log 154, Mystic.

[20] Frank O. Braynard, *Famous American Ships* (New York, 1978), p. 89.

[21] Dana, *Before the Mast*, pp. 60-61.

[22] McKay, *South Street*, pp. 211-213; Lubbock, *Log of Cutty Sark*, pp. 154-156.

[23] Log of Ship *Governor Clinton*, pp. 4-23 (1828), New York Historical Society.

America's first floating school, the *Ontario*, 1857 (Courtesy of the Peale Museum, Baltimore, Md.)

America's First Floating School

Fred Hopkins

Although American merchant sail reached its high point in the mid-nineteenth century, not all of the owners and merchants were happy with the situation as it existed. At the 3 April 1854, meeting of the Baltimore Board of Trade, a resolution was passed that before the next meeting of the Board a memorial should be drafted to the Congress of the United States requesting that all United States merchant vessels be required to carry a predetermined number of apprentices.[1] A month later, at the 1 May 1854 meeting, the memorial was read into the minutes. The main thrust of this document was to point out the lack of trained American seamen. Vessels had been detained for months, not only in Baltimore but also in all other major ports, while owners and officers attempted to hire adequate crews. When seamen finally were hired, they turned out to be mostly foreigners, many of whom were of questionable character and training. As a result of this circumstance, the Baltimore Board of Trade urged Congress to pass a law requiring that each vessel under United States registry be required to carry a certain percentage of apprentices relative to the vessel's tonnage. Over a period of time this program would alleviate the shortage of trained seamen.[2]

The Board of Trade's plea to the lawmakers in Washington, D.C., had little or no effect. The minutes of the 5 October 1854, Board meeting indicate that no response had ever been received from Congress. Not to be deterred, the Baltimore Board of Trade, under the leadership of Captain Robert Leslie, decided to take matters into its own hands.[3]

Robert Leslie had been born in Scotland in 1793 and shortly thereafter was brought to Baltimore by his parents who opened a watch-making and instrument repair shop in Fells Point. Young Robert, however, chose to follow the sea and by his mid-thirties was both owner and captain of his own vessel. In all Leslie would own and sail four different ships out of Baltimore. By his late forties, Robert Leslie had retired from the sea and became a successful Baltimore merchant.[4] He became very active in civic affairs and was one of the founders of the Maryland Historical Society in 1844.[5] In 1859 he was appointed as one of the initial trustees of the Maryland Inebriate Society,[6] and in 1860 he was appointed by Mayor Swann of Baltimore to the committee which was to select the site and purchase the property for the city's first public park — Druid Hill.[7]

Captain Leslie's proposal to the Board of Trade was that Baltimore itself establish a "floating school" to teach not only the basic "three R's" but also seamanship and navigation. Leslie based his idea on observations of similar schools in Great Britain and Scandinavia during his years as a sea-captain. Leslie's proposal was passed on to the Board of School Commissioners who appointed a six man committee to confer with the Board of Trade for the purpose of establishing a floating school.[8]

The idea of a floating school to teach seamanship gained momentum after the news of the *Arctic* — *Vesta* collision of 27 September, 1854, reached Baltimore.[9] Minutes of the 20 February, 1855, meeting of the Board of Trade contain rather pointed comments relating the loss of life on *Arctic* to the poor seamanship and lack of discipline of the crew. During this same February meeting, the Baltimore Board of Trade agreed to join with the Boards of Trade from other major East Coast ports for a meeting, to be held in Washington, D.C., which hopefully would convince Congress to act in the area of marine safety and seamanship. One recommendation to Congress called for the federal government to subsidize a system of floating schools in all the major ports of the United States.[10] It appears that the pleas of the Boards of Trade went unheeded in Washington, for on 5 November 1855, the Baltimore Board of Trade appointed a standing committee to confer with the Commissioners of the Public Schools of Baltimore City in order to mount a joint effort in the establishment of a locally controlled school for apprentice seamen.[11] On 23 December 1856, a city ordinance was passed which permitted the school commissioners to operate a school of seamanship aboard a vessel provided by the Board of Trade. The ordinance stipulated that the vessel would be owned by the City of Baltimore; but should the vessel be sold, the proceeds would be divided between the city and the Board of Trade. A joint committee would supervise the affairs of the school.[12]

The vessel purchased by the Board of Trade was U.S.S. *Ontario*, which had been serving as a receiving ship in Baltimore harbor. Having anticipated the legislation creating the floating school, the Board of Trade had purchased *Ontario* at auction on 15 July 1856, for $8,017.00. *Ontario* was then insured against fire for $6,000.00.[13]

Baltimore and *Ontario* were not strangers to one another. Due to President Thomas Jefferson's policy of a gunboat navy, the United States was lacking in ocean-going ships of war in 1812. In order to remedy this situation, Congress, in January of 1813, authorized the construction of three frigates and six eighteen-gun sloops of war. On 8 February, 1813, William Doughty was appointed chief constructor at the Washington Navy Yard. One of his initial tasks was to draw plans for the ships Congress had approved a month before. Doughty eventually produced one frigate and two sloop-of-war designs. The sloop-of-war designs differed greatly in hull design. Three sloops-of-war, *Argus*, *Erie*, and *Ontario*, were built to a hull design resembling a Baltimore Clipper. Thomas Kemp completed both *Erie* and *Ontario* at his Fells Point yard; but *Argus* was burned by the British in the Washington Navy Yard. *Ontario* had measurements of 117 feet, eleven inches between perpendiculars, a beam of 31 feet, six inches, and burthen of 14 feet, six inches. She was capable of carrying armament of twenty thirty-two pounder carronades and two long eighteen-pounders. Kemp launched *Ontario* on 25 October 1813, at a cost of $25,461.05. The British blockade of the Chesapeake prevented both *Ontario* and *Erie* from leaving Baltimore.[14] Crewmen from both vessels were enlisted into Joshua Barney's Chesapeake Flotilla, over the objections of the sloops' officers.[15]

Ontario's lack of action came to an end in May of 1815 when under the command of Jesse D. Elliott she sailed from New York with *Guerrière; Macedonian, Constellation, Épervier, Firefly, Flambeau, Spark, Spitfire,* and *Torch* as part of Commodore Stephen Decatur's squadron ordered to suppress the piratical activities of the Dey of Algiers. On 17 June 1815, Decatur's squadron sighted the Algerian flagship *Mashuda,* 46, Admiral Rais Hammida, off Cape de Gat. After a forty-five minute exchange of broadsides with *Constellation, Guerrière, Épervier,* and *Ontario, Mashuda* lowered her flag. The defeat of his flagship forced the Dey into negotiations with the United States. Although a treaty was ratified in April of 1816, *Ontario* remained on patrol in the Mediterranean until early 1817 when she returned to New York.[16]

After refitting, *Ontario,* under the command of Captain James Biddle, departed New York on 4 October 1817, for the announced purpose of protecting American shipping interests off the coasts of Brazil and Argentina. Biddle's true purpose, however, was to take formal possession of the Oregon Territory which had been returned to the United States under the terms of the Treaty of Ghent. Sailing with Captain Biddle was Mr. J.B. Prevost whose mission was to assist with any possible diplomatic complications. By January of 1818, *Ontario* was off Valparaiso, Chile, aiding American merchantmen caught in the Spanish blockade of the harbor. From the time of their arrival until May of 1818 Biddle and Prevost conducted negotiations with both the Spanish and Chilean leaders for the release of American seamen which they held captive. While Prevost remained in Valparaiso, Biddle sailed in *Ontario* to Callao to negotiate with the viceroy.[17] After successful negotiations, Biddle returned to Valparaiso carrying $10,000 in Spanish gold for the relief of Spanish prisoners in Chile.[18]

Since an uneasy truce now existed between the Spanish and Chilean forces, Biddle decided to sail for the Oregon Territory while Prevost remained in Chile. On 19 August, 1818 Biddle and *Ontario* anchored off Cape Disappointment near the Columbia River bar and took possession of the Oregon Territory for the United States. Later he sailed twenty miles up the river showing the flag at Indian villages. Returning to Valparaiso by way of Monterey, California, and Callao, Peru, Biddle arrived on 27 December 1818, just in time to cross paths with Admiral Lord Thomas Cochrane and the Chilean fleet.[19] Cochrane was later to claim that he was forced to chase Biddle, who outsailed him, because Biddle was smuggling money and people out of Lima and Callao to Rio de Janeiro.[20] J.B. Prevost, in the meantime, had departed Valparaiso aboard H.B.M. *Blossom* to receive the official surrender of the territory. Biddle sailed for home without Prevost, arriving off the Virginia Capes on 23 April, 1819.[21]

Ontario was ordered to the New York Navy Yard where she spent the next two years in ordinary. In early 1821 *Ontario* was ordered to the Mediterranean where she would do three tours of duty lasting until May of 1832.

After a refit in Norfolk, *Ontario* was assigned to the South American station until June of 1836. From 1836 until 1844 *Ontario* spent much of her time in ordinary in Pensacola, Florida, with several two-year cruises to the West Indies and the coast of Mexico. On 22 May 1844, *Ontario* returned home to Baltimore for the first time since the spring of 1815. From 1844 until 30 April 1852, *Ontario* served as a receiving ship in Baltimore harbor. Her long naval career ended in July of 1856 when she was purchased by the Board of Trade.[22]

After her purchase by the Board of Trade, *Ontario* was anchored at the lower end of Bond Street in Fells Point, Baltimore. Classes began on 14 September 1857, and seven days later *Ontario* was moved to her permanent berth at the mouth of the Jones Fall.[23] The Floating School's first staff consisted of Robert Kerr, principal; Captain P.S. Marshall, nautical instructor; and George W. Smithson, janitor and first officer. On 27 December 1857, Robert Kerr and Captain Marshall made their initial reports to the joint committee. Principal Kerr reported that enrollment had increased from eight pupils on opening day to a total of forty-nine by December. Captain Philip Marshall commended the pupils by pointing out that five days after classes had begun the boys had learned to ascend to the loftiest part of the ship and had bent the mizzen to sail. Additional details presented by Robert Kerr included a survey of the occupations of the parents of the forty-nine students. Nine of the students came from homes where the father was a sea captain; in second place were the sons of laborers with seven; while the sons of widows and merchants each accounted for five students respectively. Kerr's major academic problem appears to have been the arrangement of classes equal to the varied level of achievement. The report complains that some students were deficient in reading while others appeared not even to recognize the alphabet. At the conclusion of the first academic year, Principal Kerr filed a financial report stating that the total cost of maintaining the Floating School during the period was $3,063.99; the principal's salary was $900.00.[24]

From 1858 until 1863, the Floating School enjoyed continued success. The enrollment increased to 139 students in 1858 and by 1860 reached a high of 243. The 1858 academic year also saw the introduction of navigation courses using instructional aids donated by Lt. Matthew F. Maury. One indication of the success of the school appeared in the 1860 principal's report when thirty-three students were listed as having withdrawn from classes because their newly learned skills made them so employable.[25]

In 1861, the school's principal, Robert Kerr, died and was replaced by George Hale. In his first report in 1861, Hale noted that although initial enrollments remained high, the number of students withdrawing in order to support their families was on the rise. By 1863 the end of the Floating School appeared to be at hand. The standing rigging had deteriorated to such a degree that students were not permitted aloft. Although the school commissioners were unwilling to fund repalcement of the rigging, the Board of Trade donated the necessary funds to keep the school in operation. In addition to the rigging problems, Principal Hale also noted in his 1863 report that interest in the school was declining. He attributed this situation to the lack of lower level feeder schools which would send interested, prepared students to his institution. This same year also marked the addition of a course in martial music to the curriculum for the purpose of instilling proper patriotic fervor among the pupils.[26]

In 1864 William Thomas Markland became the Floating School's third and last principal. In his report for the year 1864, Mr. Markland noted the steady decline in attendance. It was his feeling that the lack of room and board facilities were the causes of declining interest. By 1865, however, the end of the Floating School was in sight.[27] Since the total enrollment had dropped to twenty-six students with a daily average attendance of only five students, the Board of School Commissioners on 28 September 1865 sent a note to the Board of Trade stating that in two days the school would close its doors. In addition to lack of enrollment, the yearly maintenance costs had risen to $1,500. The Board of Trade, however, was not willing to give up the idea of a maritime school in Baltimore. Since the school was a going venture, the Board of Trade forced the school commissioners to keep the Floating School open for the 1865 academic year.[28] Enrollments continued to decline and by the end of the spring semester even the Board of Trade was convinced the school was attracting little attention. One last effort to keep the school open was made when the Board of Trade attempted to interest the State of Maryland in sponsoring the institution. The state ignored the request.[29] On 16 May 1867 the City of Baltimore, the Board of Trade, and the Board of School Commissioners agreed to dispose of *Ontario* and divide the proceeds between the city and the Board of Trade. After fifty-four years of service, *Ontario's* career ended on 5 June 1867 when she was auctioned off at $2,900 for scrap. The Board of Trade claimed $1,964.54 as its share.[30]

Although the short ten year history of Baltimore's Floating School would seem to indicate that this joint venture by the Board of Trade and the School Commissioners was a failure, a brief review of the political and economic forces at work during this period may provide some hints as to why the school eventually failed. The main purpose of the school was to prepare young men for a career in the American merchant fleet. In 1861 the United States deep-sea fleet totaled 2,496,894 tons; by 1868 the deep-sea tonnage had dropped to less than a million and a half tons.[31] Although coastal shipping tonnage increased under the protection of the Navigation Act of 1817, the type of vessel developed for this trade kept crew size at a minimum. The demand for trained seamen gradually declined.[32] The Floating School was, however, conceived for the young men of Baltimore, Maryland, and it was the political and economic fortunes of the city that affected the success of the school most directly. Prior to the Civil War, Baltimore was primarily a commercial city with trade patterns closely associated with the South. The war disrupted these patterns and Baltimore became an occupied city. For the first few years of the conflict a recession occurred until wartime opportunities increased economic activity.[33] The reports of the second principal, George Hale, in 1861 and 1862 note that although initial enrollments at the Floating School were increasing, the number of students required to withdraw to support their families was also on the rise. There would appear to be a possible correlation between the recession and the withdrawal rate at the school.

During the post-Civil War period, as attendance at the Floating School continued to decline, Baltimore changed from a commercial to an industrial city. Now the potential student at the Floating School was not forced to work to help support his family, but why should he seek a career at sea when by looking around his own city he could discover better financial opportunities? The average wage of an ordinary seaman during this period was $12.50 per month. Living conditions in the forecastles were barbaric. A captain was paid $100 per month while first mates averaged $50.[34] At the same time a cutter in the shoe industry averaged $1.50 per day or $36 per month. An overseer in a textile mill averaged $65.04 per month.[35]

The demise of the Floating School in Baltimore, therefore, appears not to be a result of poor management or bad planning, but the result of local and national economic factors that indicated few advantages in a maritime career.

Notes

[1] Minutes of the Meeting of the Baltimore Board of Trade, 3 April 1854, Maryland Historical Society, Manuscript Collection File No. 177.

[2] *Ibid.*, 1 May 1854.

[3] *Ibid.*, 5 October 1854.

[4] Hayward File, Maryland Historical Society, Baltimore, Maryland.

[5] J. Thomas Scharf, *Chronicles of Baltimore* (Baltimore: Turnbull Bros., 1874), p. 510.

[6] J. Thomas Scharf, *History of Baltimore and County* (Baltimore: Regional Publishing Co., 1971), p. 600.

[7] *Ibid.*, p. 273.

[8] Board of Trade Minutes, *loc. cit.*

[9] James M. Morris, *Our Maritime Heritage* (Washington, D.C.: University Press of America, Inc., 1979), p. 194.

[10] Board of Trade Minutes, *op. cit.*, 20 February 1855.

[11] *Ibid.*, 5 November 1855.

[12] *Ibid.*, 23 December 1856.

[13] *Ibid.*, 7 September 1857.

[14] Howard I. Chapelle, *The History of the American Sailing Navy* (New York: Bonanza Books, 1949), pp. 256-58.

[15] Letter, Secretary of Navy to Joshua Barney, microcopy 149, roll 11, letter 373 (Washington, D.C.: Navy and Old Army Branch, Military Archives Division, National Archives and Records Service).

[16] J.R. Spears, *The History of Our Navy* (New York: Charles Scribner's Sons, 1897), III, pp. 343-57.

[17] D.W. Knox, *A History of the United States Navy* (New York: G.P. Putnam's Sons, 1936), pp. 138-43.

[18] *Niles' Weekly Register* (7 November 1818), pp. 166-67.

[19] Knox, *loc. cit.*

[20] *Niles' Weekly Register* (15 May 1819), p. 208.

[21] Knox, *loc. cit.*

[22] Logs of U.S.S. *Ontario*, November 1820-September 1856 (Washington, D.C.: Navy and Old Army Branch, Military Archives Division, National Archives and Records Service).

[23] *Baltimore American and Daily Commercial Advertiser*, 12 September 1857.

[24] "Reports of the Principal of the Floating School," *Reports of the Commissioners of Public Schools, 1857-1867* (Baltimore, Maryland: Public Relations Dept., Baltimore City Public Schools System Central Office).

[25] *Ibid.*

[26] *Ibid.*

[27] *Ibid.*

[28] Board of Trade Minutes, *op. cit.*, 7 October 1865.

[29] *Ibid.*, 25 October 1866.

[30] *Ibid.*, 5 June 1867.

[31] Samuel W. Bryant, *The Sea and the States* (New York: Thomas Y. Crowell Co., 1967), p. 334.

[32] *Ibid.*, p. 335.

[33] Eleanor Bruchey, "The Industrialization of Maryland," *Maryland, A History, 1632-1974*, ed. Richard Walsh and William Fox (Baltimore: Maryland Historical Society, 1974), p. 406.

[34] Bryant, *Sea and the States*, p. 333.

[35] Bruchey, *op. cit.*, p. 437.

Part IV
**Seafaring
in the
Americas**

Characteristics of Privateers
Operating from the British Isles
Against America, 1777-1783

Walter E. Minchinton and David J. Starkey

Much of the discussion of privateering has concentrated on the romantic aspect of the activity, narrating the derring-do of individual privateers.[1] Such accounts present a distorted view of an occupation which was a significant business in many British ports in time of war.[2] The purpose of this study is to present an analysis not of the adventures of individual privateers but of the characteristics of British-based vessels which operated against American commerce during the American Revolution. The discussion, limited to ships registered in the British Isles, obviously understates the true extent of British privateering activity against the rebels for many ships were commissioned by and operated from loyal colonies in the western hemisphere, notably from the British West Indies.[3] It must also be borne in mind that many of the privateers under review did not cruise exclusively against American trade but could operate against French, Spanish and Dutch vessels also. Thus, the present account deals with a small aspect of a complex global struggle involving the naval, mercantile and privateering fleets of the major European maritime powers as well as those of Britain and the rebel colonists.

I
The Privateers

In the eighteenth century, economic warfare was at the heart of the sea strategy of all the maritime powers in time of war. Privateering played an important role in this attempt to destroy the enemy's commerce and thereby sap his fighting strength. Essentially, privateers were privately-owned vessels commissioned by their respective governments to make prizes of enemy vessels and property encountered at sea. The American Revolutionary War was no exception and during the course of the conflict all the belligerent powers fitted out private men-of-war to cruise against enemy commerce. From 23 August 1776 the rebel colonists began to fit out commerce raiders at Philadelphia and other ports and soon these swarmed around the British West India islands and the North American seaboard.[4] The losses incurred by British merchants as a result of this privateering activity are fully chronicled in the British mercantile press.[5] However, it was not until April 1777 that the British government decided that the efforts of the Royal Navy needed to be supplemented and accordingly sanctioned cruising against the vessels of the American rebels. Before this date the Admiralty was reluctant to issue letters of marque in the hope that the colonies would be reconciled.[6] Furthermore, American sea-borne commerce was relatively small and distant and thus there was little mercantile pressure for the granting of commissions. Indeed, the complaints of neutrals, particularly the Dutch and Danish, suggest that much of British privateering activity in 1777 and 1778 was against foreign ships carrying American produce rather than against colonial ships.[7] The escalation of the war with the entry of France in July 1778, Spain in April 1779 and Holland in December 1780 further stimulated privateering activity from the British Isles.

II
The Letter of Marque Declarations

The authorization granted to commanders of British privateers was known as a letter of marque, a term which dates back to 1293 at least.[8] Until the eighteenth century these commissions were issued under Orders in Council, but from 1739 the issuance of letters of marque had to be authorized by Parliament at the beginning of each war by the passage of an act of parliament. They were valid for the duration of hostilities unless there was a change in the vessel's name, its master or its principal owners when a new letter of marque was needed. In the American Revolutionary War a separate Commission was required to legitimatize privateering activity against each of the hostile powers and, thus, it was not unusual for a vessel to receive as many as four letters of marque on the same day. The fact that letters of marque needed to be renewed occasionally and were issued against each enemy means that many commissions were duplicated and, accordingly, the number issued exceeds the actual number of vessels engaged in privateering.

From the late seventeenth century the issue of letters of marque was standardized and a captain had to go through a formal procedure before receiving his commission. He, or somebody acting on his behalf, was required to appear at the High Court of Admiralty in Doctors' Commons, situated to the south of St. Paul's Cathedral in London.[9] There, he was required to offer a surety which he would forfeit if he, his officers or crew contravened the instructions given to privateers at the commencement of hostilities. The amount of surety depended upon the size of the crew: if more than 150 men were on board the bond was £3000, if less than 150 men, it was £1500. The commander was also obliged to produce a "warrant . . . from the Lord High Admiral of England and Ireland for the granting of a letter of marque" and make, before the Admiralty judge or his surrogate, a declaration containing a "particular true and exact account of the ship or vessel" in question.

These declarations made by commanders of British privateers form the basic source for this study. Although the details demanded of declarants varied slightly from war to war, in the vast majority of cases they were obliged to state the name of the vessel concerned, its tonnage, crew size, armament and ammunition, the length of time for which it was victualled, the tackle carried and the names of its master, officers and principal owners.[10] After 1759 commanders were also required to declare the port to which the vessel belonged, to describe the stern and to state the number of masts and type of figurehead of their vessels. In all, nearly 22,000 declarations made during the wars of the period 1689-1815 have survived and these are bound in the 104 volumes which comprise the Public Record Office classification HCA 26.[11] Eleven of these volumes (HCA 26/60-70) concern the privateering war against the American colonies, 1777-83. These declarations were the most detailed made by privateer masters during the entire period. As well as the standard information presented in all the declarations, those made against the rebel colonists contain details of the cargo carried and the intended destination of the commissioned vessel.[12] This additional information was required to ensure that the commissioned vessels were not trading with the rebel colonies in contravention of the Prohibition of Trade Act 1775 (16 George III c5) and that none were carrying unlicensed arms or ammunition.

III
Characteristics of the Privateering Fleet Operating from the British Isles, 1777-83

a) Size of fleet

During the American Revolutionary War 7,356 letters of marque were issued under the jurisdiction of the High Court of Admiralty. This considerable total of over 1,225 a year compares with 1,570 (about 157 a year) during the War of the Austrian Succession 1739-48, 2,104 (about 300 a year) during the Seven Years' War 1756-63 and 4,613 (513 a year) during the French Revolutionary War 1793-1801. In terms of the number of letters of marque issued, therefore, the American war represents a peak in British privateering activity during the eighteenth century. This was due partly to the fact that commissions were issued separately against each of the hostile powers thus obliging a captain to take out four letters of marque to authorize cruising against all enemy trade.[13] Of the 7,356 commissions issued between 1777 and 1783, some 2,285 (31 per cent) were against the American colonies. They were distributed throughout the conflict as follows:

Table 1
Letters of Marque Against America by Month of Issuance

	Jan	Feb	Mar	Apr	May	Jun	Jul	Aug	Sep	Oct	Nov	Dec	Annual Total
1777				97	40	23	35	43	40	51	37	27	393
1778	23	38	44	32	14	18	23	66	76	100	67	51	552
1779	42	61	78	52	36	40	34	34	28	28	40	34	507
1780	22	28	26	41	37	12	25	11	11	18	14	61	306
1781	160	40	27	16	18	7	14	11	13	23	15	11	355
1782	7	5	31	10	18	12	12	12	19	18	11	11	166
1783	6												6
Total													2285

Source: PRO HCA 26/60-70

This table indicates that the first three years of the privateering war against America were the most active, with 1782 the least active year. The monthly breakdown closely follows the course of the war. The first letter of marque against the rebels was issued on 3 April 1777 to Archibald Greig, master of the *Ceres*, a 240-ton London vessel.[14] A further 96 commissions were issued in April, the peak month of 1777. The table clearly reflects the entry of France into the war in August 1778. In that month there were 66 letters of marque issued, a substantial increase on the earlier months of the year. The increase continued into September and October when 100 commissions were taken out against the American colonists. The entry of Spain in June 1779 does not appear to have precipitated any marked increase in activity, the rate of issue subsiding gradually during 1779. The Dutch intervention in December 1780 clearly stimulated privateering activity with 221 letters of marque issued against the rebels between 26 December 1780 and the end of January 1781. Thus, the peaks of privateering activity against the colonists were at the commencement of the private war at sea and at the entry of the various European powers into the conflict, notably France and the United Provinces. It should be noted, however, that a second influence was also of significance, the seasonal clearances of vessels from England in the oceanic trades.

The fact that the issue of commissions against America peaked on the entry of the other belligerents was no coincidence. The intervention of a new adversary generally induced more privateers into the conflict and normally these would be commissioned against all Britain's enemies. Furthermore, previously commissioned vessels might renew their letters of marque on the entry of a new enemy. The *Enterprize* of Liverpool affords an example of this procedure. She was commissioned nine times during the war: on 31 October 1778 her commander, Thomas Pearce, took out letters of marque against the American colonies and France; a new captain, James Haslam, took out three commissions, against the American colonies, France and Spain, on 2 September 1779; and a third master, William Robertson, commissioned the *Enterprize* against the American colonies, France, Spain and the United Provinces on 5 March 1782. Thus nine commissions were issued for one vessel, three each against America and France, two against Spain, and one against the United Provinces.

The *Enterprize* is, perhaps, an extreme example of the duplication of letters of marque for a single ship. But it is clear that the number of commissions issued overstates the actual number of vessels engaged in privateering activity. Not only did vessels have to carry letters of marque against each adversary but commissions had to be renewed when a new commander took over a privateer or there was a significant change in its ownership. To reduce the total number of letters of marque to the actual "stock" of vessels is a task rendered difficult by the occurrence of discrepancies between declarations made for what is, ostensibly, the same vessel. Careful comparison of the declarations is necessary to isolate actual vessels from recommissions, using a set of criteria which includes the name of the ship, the name(s) of owner(s), master's name, tonnage, crew size and armament, and the description of the vessel's stern, masts and figurehead. Such a detailed examination reveals that the total of 7,356 letters of marque granted during the war as a whole were issued to the commanders of 2,641 separate vessels, the other 4,715 being recommissions.

Though the letter of marque declarations provide a wealth of information on the characteristics of British privateers, they do not allow a distinction to be made between the two types of privateer. First, there were the private men-of-war which cruised in search of enemy merchantmen, carrying no cargo and flying their own ensign. These vessels were usually converted merchantmen. Thus the *Caesar* of Bristol was in the Jamaica trade until May 1779 when she was fitted out as a privateer. Sometimes vessels were built specifically as privateers, as was the *Hero Snow* of Bristol fitted out in Messrs. Noble's dry dock in October 1778.[15] A few were former naval vessels purchased by merchants and fitted out as privateers: the *Enterprize* of London was formerly the *Aquilon* frigate. The *Morning Chronicle and London Advertiser* of 1 September 1778 relates that "when in the King's service the *Enterprize* mounted 28 guns with 200 men, but now has 32 guns and 220 men." Generally, the private ships-of-war were heavily armed and carried large crews to man the extra guns and provide crews for any prizes taken. The second group of privateers were the armed traders or "letter of marque" ships. These were ordinary merchant vessels which carried letters of marque in order that they might be able to capture lawfully vessels of enemy countries which they might encounter in the course of their normal trading operations. They were usually less well-armed and manned than the private men-of-war, although extra men and arms were often carried to provide protection against enemy privateers or ships-of-war. Despite the difference in the intentions of the private men-of-war and the armed traders, the letter of marque declarations do not distinguish the two types and, thus, it is not possible to state, with any accuracy, the number of vessels engaged in each kind of privateering activity.

b) Port of Registration

Altogether, 1793 vessels from 80 ports in the British Isles were commissioned against the American colonies, 1777-83. Table 2, below, presents a regional breakdown of the issue of letters of marque, the numbers in brackets indicating those ports from which merchants or ship owners took out ten or more commissions.

Table 2
Vessels Commissioned Against America, 1777-83, by Port Group[16]

Group		Number of commissions	Actual vessels
London		696	509
Bristol		215	171
Liverpool		473	359
Channel Islands	Alderney (16), Guernsey (70) Jersey (68) 3 ports	214	154
West Scotland	Clyde, Glasgow (97), Greenock, Irvine, Ayr 5 ports	200	177
East Scotland	Aberdeen, Perth, Kinghorn, Kincardine, Carron, Bo'ness, Dunbar 7 ports	26	23
East coast (to London)	Berwick, North Shields, Newcastle (11), South Shields, Stockton, Whitby, Scarborough, Hull, Lynn, Wells, Yarmouth (15),Harwich 12 ports	77	75
South coast (London-Southampton)	Chatham, Margate, Ramsgate, Dover (13), Folkestone (49), Hastings, Brighton, Chichester, Portsea, Portsmouth, Cowes, Southampton 12 ports	88	80
South-west coast	Poole (16), West Lulworth, Weymouth, Bridport, Lyme, Exmouth, Topsham, Exeter (12), Teignmouth, Brixham, Dartmouth (43), Plymouth (10), Looe, St Austell, Penryn, Falmouth, Penzance, Scilly Isles, St. Ives, Ilfracombe 20 ports	144	123
West coast	Workington, Whitehaven 26, Douglas, Lancaster (24), Chester, Milford, Haverfordwest 7 ports	70	65
Ireland	Belfast, Strangford, Down Patrick Newry, Drogheda, Rush, Dublin (23), Waterford, Cork (15) Kinsale, Londonderry 11 ports	63	57
		2266	1793

Source: PRO HCA 26/60-70

As Table 2 shows, London, by far the largest shipowning port,[17] was, as in previous wars, the most important privateering port. In relative terms, however, the American Revolutionary War witnessed a decline in London's pre-eminent position. Although 30.5 percent of the commissions issued were for London vessels, the capital's share in earlier conflicts had been as high as 53.5 per cent in the War of Austrian Succession and 38.5 per cent in the Seven Years' War. In the subsequent Revolutionary and Napoleonic Wars, London's share again rose to 43.8 per cent in the 1793-1801 war and to 37.8 per cent in the 1803-15 war. The reason for this marked trough in London's share of the national issue during the American War, 1777-83, lies in the unique conditions of the war. The dislocation of the Atlantic staple trades due to the closure of the North American market and the activities of American raiders in the Caribbean and British waters resulted in the large-scale unemployment of ships, men [18] and resources in ports such as Liverpool, Glasgow, Bristol, and Lancaster. Liverpool's slave trade was severely disrupted, the number of ships leaving the port for the African coast declining from 105 in 1773, to 11 in 1779.[19] Glasgow, the premier tobacco port of the Empire, suffered greatly during the American war with the import of tobacco falling rapidly from 46 million pounds in 1775, to 210,000 pounds in 1777.[20] Faced with this trade depression, the merchants and shipowners of Liverpool, Glasgow and other ports with major Atlantic interests employed their idle vessels in privateering, one of the few viable alternatives open to them.[21] This was particularly true of Glasgow and the other Clyde ports in the American war, for in previous wars their interest in privateering had been negligible.

Thus, the contribution of the ports dependent on the Atlantic trades to the British privateering effort was greater in the American War than it had been in earlier conflicts. In addition to the major privateering bases — London, Bristol, Liverpool, Glasgow and the Channel Islands — a number of other ports fitted out a sizeable number of privateers. Of those responsible for more than 20, Folkestone sent out 49, Dartmouth 43, Whitehaven 26, Lancaster 24 and Dublin 23. But since privateering, like the East India trade and the slave trade, required capital, 33 ports fitted out only a single privateer during the whole of the American Revolution. In such a way, small ports such as Chatham,

Margate, Exmouth and Irvine were able to participate in the private war at sea.

c) Tonnage

The tonnage of the privateers varied considerably. The smallest vessel commissioned against America was the *Hunter*, a Jersey private man-of-war of 12 tons, with a crew of 18 men and 6 guns; on the other hand, the largest declared tonnage was that of the *Locke*, a London vessel, burthen 1100 tons, with 99 men on board and 26 guns. The average tonnage of all the vessels carrying letters of marque against America amounted to 221 tons, although only those from London and the ports of the south coast were of above average tonnage, as Table 3 shows. Those from other British ports tended to be smaller than average, with the smallest setting out from the Channel Islands.

Table 3
Average Tonnage of Privateers, 1777-83, by Port Group

Port group	Average tonnage
London	328
Liverpool	197
Bristol	175
Channel Islands	106
Scotland	172
East coast	179
South coast	238
South-west coast	185
West coast	198
Ireland	173
National average	**221**

Source: PRO HCA 26/60-70

As the wide range of tonnage suggests, many different types of vessel — cutters, packets, sloops, snows, brigs, schooners, galleys and ships — carried letters of marque. Although they do not enable the private men-of-war to be distinguished from the letter-of-marque merchantmen, the declarations do identify certain vessels engaged in specialist occupations. Ships hired by the East India Company, for instance, were declared as such. During the American Revolutionary War, 84 vessels in the employ of the East India Company, all registered in the port of London, received commissions. In general, the East Indiamen were the largest, most costly and most heavily-armed British merchant ships of the eighteenth century, though not always the most seaworthy and certainly not the fastest. The size of the Indiamen commissioned during the war varied from 606-ton *Blandford* to the 1100-ton *Locke* with the burthen of the majority about 750 tons. Most carried 26 carriage guns, were navigated by 99 men and were victualled for between 12 and 24 months. The other great trading company of the day, the Hudson's Bay Company, took out commissions for four of its vessels during the American war. These were much smaller than the Indiamen, ranging from the 177-ton *Sea Horse* to the 290-ton *King George*.

The declarations made against the Americans also identify those vessels hired for government service. The movement of troops, provisions and equipment was an essential part of the war effort and to facilitate it the state frequently hired merchant vessels, some for specific voyages, others for longer terms.[22] The port of London provided 106 commissioned ships for government service during the war; 33 were hired by the Ordnance Board, 33 by the Lords of the Treasury, 25 by the Navy Board, two by the Victualling Board, whilst a further 13 were "retained in His Majesty's service." The majority were bound for north America or the West Indies with provisions, naval stores or ordnance the usual cargo.

d) Crew size and composition

In time of war the size of crews manning all types of British vessel tended to increase for defensive as well as offensive purposes. The requirements of the navy, privateers and armed traders created labour shortages as the reservoir of trained seamen proved to be too small for wartime needs. Problems arose in manning the British navy for, quite naturally, some seamen preferred work on the private men-of-war where the potential rewards were higher and the discipline less demanding. Impressment, therefore, was used to obtain men for the navy. According to reputation, as the following recruiting quatrain for a Bristol privateer suggests, press gangs were more active in London than elsewhere:

> Here is our chief encouragement, our ship belongs to Bristol
> Poor Londoners when coming home they surely will be press'd all,
> We've no such fear when home we steer, with prizes under convoy
> We'll frolick round all Bristol town, sweet liberty we enjoy.

During the American War the press gangs were particularly active in Liverpool and there were frequent clashes between naval crews and privateer crews as the latter resisted the press.

The size of crews on board British privateers varied, naturally, with the tonnage of the vessel and the intended purpose of its voyage. Generally, private men-of-war carried more men than did armed merchantmen of the same size — indeed, the large crew was the main distinguishing feature of the private ship-of-war. Vessels such as the 80-ton *Cato* of Bristol, with 100 men on board, and the 300-ton *New Eclipse* of Folkestone, whose complement was 145 men strong, were clearly carrying more men than was necessary to operate them. The extra men were undoubtedly enlisted for offensive purposes and to provide prize crews to navigate captured vessels back to a friendly port. Other ships are less easy to categorize although it seems probable that vessels such as the *Mary* of Newcastle, burthen 400 tons with a crew of 18 men, and the *Count of Scarborough*, a London vessel of 300 tons and 25 men, were "letter of marque" ships, primarily interested in trading, armed with a commission as a precautionary measure. The smaller vessels tended to carry more men per ton for, even in wartime, economies of scale were apparent. Thus, privateers of less than 100 tons would frequently have relatively larger crews than their counterparts of over 500 tons or so. For instance, the typical Channel Island corsair of about 50 tons might carry 50 men whereas an average East Indiaman of 750 tons or so usually had the standard Company complement of 99 men.

The letter of marque declarations provide details of the composition of crews manning British privateers. Naval terminology was used and privateers carried lieutenants instead of mates and midshipmen instead of apprentices. The crew also included a gunner and a surgeon, indicating the belligerent and dangerous nature of privateering cruises, as well as a boatswain, carpenter and cook. The remuneration received by the crew depended upon the type of privateer. On board a private man-of-war a seaman normally received a share in any prizes taken but nothing else apart from his keep and a small "signing-on" wage. On armed merchant vessels the crew was paid regular wages but if any prizes were taken each seaman shared in the prize-money. The spoils were divided according to an agreement drawn up between the owners, captain and crew before the start of a voyage. Normally, two-thirds of the proceeds went to the owners and fitters-out of the successful vessel with the remaining third being divided amongst the captain and crew members. The amount each received depended upon his rank; in the case of the *Enterprize* of Liverpool, for example, it was agreed that the captain should receive sixteen shares in any prize condemned, the first lieutenant eight shares, the surgeon and the carpenter six shares each, whilst an ordinary seaman was entitled to two shares, a landsman one share and the cabin boys half a share each.[23] Thus, serving on board a privateer might prove very lucrative for the crew if a rich prize was seized. However, spectacular captures were rare and it seems probable that only a limited number of crews benefited from privateering.

e) Arms and Ammunition

In making his declaration before the High Court of the Admiralty, a commander was required to state the number and type of weapons and ammunition on board his ship. The standard armament carried by British privateers in the American War was the carriage gun. The calibre of these carriage guns varied from 2 lbs to 24 lbs, most privateers being equipped with either 6 or 9 pounders. The number carried depended, to a great extent, on the size of the vessel concerned, although few, if any, carried more than the East Indiamen, normally equipped with 26 guns. The carriage gun was frequently supplemented by the lighter swivel gun, a small cannon mounted on the upper decks of a vessel and used mainly at close quarters. These swivel guns were more common on the smaller commissioned vessels, although, in general, the evidence from the declarations suggests that fewer were fitted in the American War compared to earlier conflicts.

Three other types of gun — cohorns, howitzers and carronades — were also in use on board British privateers during the American War. Only a few cohorns and howitzers were fitted to British privateers during the war. These were small pieces of ordnance for high angle firing at lower velocities than a carriage gun. Like swivel guns, they usually supplemented the main armament; the *Eagle* of Liverpool, for instance, carried 4 howitzers to back up her 14 carriage guns. The carronade was the result of technological advance in the 1770's. Manufactured by the Carron Company in Scotland, it was lighter and more maneuverable than the standard carriage gun.[24] Initially it was tested, with great success, on the Company's own merchant vessels, the first external sale, in November 1778, being to a Liverpool firm, Zuill & Co., fitting out the *Spitfire* private man-of-war. She was equipped with sixteen 18-pound carronades and apparently acquitted herself favorably against heavier odds, a good advertisement for the Carron ordnance. Orders for the weapon increased and by the end of the war a number of British privateers were equipped with them. The carronade, or "smasher" as Nelson was later to dub it, fired an out-sized ball at low velocity and was thus very destructive at short range.

The declarations also detail the number of cutlasses and small arms carried on the ship. The better-equipped privateers carried a cutlass and a small arm for each member of the crew, for use when taking a prize or repelling boarders. Captains were also obliged to declare the ammunition on board their vessels: this included barrels of powder, rounds of great shot and hundredweight of small shot, the amount varying with the armament of the ship and the length of the voyage.

f) Length of Cruises, Destinations, and Cargoes

The intended length of voyages undertaken by British vessels granted letters of marque during the American War can be gauged from the declaration. The declared victualling periods, which range from 1 month to 36 months, were clearly inflated by the presence of the armed traders in the list. Small Channel Island privateers intent on harassing the French coastal trade would only carry victuals to last a month or two, whereas the larger ocean-going vessels might embark on a voyage planned to last two or even three years. In the latter category fall the East India Company's vessels. The *Royal Charlotte*, for instance, commissioned on 17 November 1779 and bound for St. Helena, Bombay and China, was victualled for 36 months. West Indiamen generally carried sufficient supplies for voyages of 6 to 12 months duration: thus, the *Holdernesse*, bound for Jamaica from London, was victualled for nine months whilst the *Lord Germaine*, a London slaver destined for the West Indies via the African coast, carried victuals for a 12-month voyage. Table 4 below, presents the average declared victualling periods by port group. Although there was not a great deal of variation between ports, those privateers which confined themselves to the shorter cruises came from the Channel Islands and the south coast of England while the longest cruises were made by vessels from London and Liverpool.[25]

Table 4
Average Declared Victualling Periods by Port Group (months)

London	8
Liverpool	8
Bristol	7
Channel Islands	5
Scotland	7
East coast	7
South coast	5
South-west coast	5
West coast	7
Ireland	6

Source: PRO HCA 26/60-70

The declarations made against America contain additional information as to the destination and cargo of the commissioned vessels. Detailed studies of this data for the ports of London and Liverpool suggest that a large percentage of the vessels taking out letters of marque against the colonies were bound for North America and the West Indies. As Table 5 shows, 217 of the 509 London vessels and 147 of the 234 Liverpool vessels[26] whose destinations were declared, were bound for the West Indies. A further 102 London vessels and 32 Liverpool vessels were bound for various ports of North America, the only other destinations of note being Lisbon and Africa. The analysis suggests that most of the vessels which carried letters of marque against America were bound for American or Caribbean waters.

The cargoes carried by Britain's commissioned vessels naturally depended upon their destinations; linens and an assortment of manufactured goods were carried to Africa to purchase slaves; bricks, coals and salt were transported to Newfoundland, New York and Halifax; salt went to Riga and Archangel; provisions and dry goods were generally carried to the West Indies; and bullion, ordnance and naval stores to the East Indies.

Table 5
Destination of London and Liverpool Letter of Marque Vessels, 1777-83

Where bound	London vessels	Liverpool vessels
West Indies	203	106
Africa and West Indies	14	41
Africa	12	20
New York	39	9
Halifax, Nova Scotia	13	10
Newfoundland	18	6
South Carolina, Georgia, Florida	19	4
Quebec	13	3
Lisbon	54	20
Mediterranean	21	0
East Indies	66	4
Others	37	11
	509	234

Source: PRO HCA 26/60-70

g) Ownership

The declarations list the "principal owners and setters out" of each commissioned vessel. As such they do not include the names of all those who invested in privateering, only those with the major shareholdings. Sufficient information is contained, however, to gain an accurate impression of the types of people investing in privateering. In the first place, very few women appear to have taken shares in privateers. A few widows are recorded as having a share in a vessel but only one woman, Elizabeth Tyler, appears to have had any major interest, investing in nine London vessels during the American War. Secondly, most of the privateer owners were recorded as being "merchants." This general term covered a wide range of occupations, the typical merchant having interests in many different areas of enterprise. Thomas Staniforth, of Liverpool, personifies the successful general merchant of the day. He was principally engaged in the Greenland whale fishing trade but also had an interest in a ropery, supplying much of the cordage to Liverpool's privateers during the American War. He was also a partner in a wine, rum and brandy firm and, along with other Liverpool merchants, he had shares in slaving vessels.[27] During the war, with other trades disrupted or curtailed altogether, Staniforth invested in four privateers. Many privateer owners were general merchants like Staniforth, indulging in a wide range of commercial ventures, largely to offset the high risks involved in eighteenth-century trade. The declarations, however, are sometimes more specific when describing owners' occupations. Thus, bankers, insurance brokers, ships' chandlers, shipbuilders, biscuit bakers, bakers, gentlemen, grocers and ship's captains were among those who had shares in privateers.

Thirdly, the owners recorded in the declarations generally resided in the port where the vessel was registered. Privateering capital tended to come from local resources although there are a number of examples of investment from elsewhere. London merchants, for instance, had shares in 44 vessels registered in outports such as Jersey, Cork and Leith. A number of Liverpool and Scottish privateers were partly owned by agents resident in the West Indies.

Thus, the typical privateer owner was a general merchant usually involved in a number of maritime-based trades. Privateering was one of the alternatives open to him in wartime and frequently he would resort to it if his other, less speculative, interests were adversely affected by the state of war. In this way privateering was an important business in time of war, utilizing capital, labor, and resources which might otherwise have lain idle with the disruption of normal trade. This was particularly true of the west coast ports during the American War when the major Atlantic trades were largely brought to a standstill by the closure of the American market and the activities of enemy privateers and naval vessels. The fitting out of privateers also sustained the maritime-based industries of the British ports which were inevitably depressed when ships were laid up.

Conclusions

The letter of marque declarations provide a wealth of information about the characteristics of British-based privateers cruising against the American colonies, 1777-83. During the course of the war some 1,793 vessels sailed from British ports with authority from the High Court of Admiralty to attack American property on the high seas. This sizeable fleet formed part of the force intent on the destruction of American commerce along with the Royal Navy and privateers fitted out in British bases overseas, notably in the Caribbean. Indeed, its aim was not confined to the demolition of colonial trade for many of the commissioned vessels were also licensed to seize the property of the other hostile powers. The fleet comprised private men-of-war cruising in search of American ships or produce carried by neutral vessels, merchantmen carrying letters of marque for precautionary purposes and specialist trading vessels, such as those belonging to the East India Company or hired by the government. The privateers displayed a wide variety of tonnage, crew size and armament ranging from the small Channel predators intent on harassing the French coastal trade to the large ocean-going vessels cruising in the Atlantic and the Caribbean in search of prizes and, sometimes, trade.

Privateering activity, as reflected in the issue of commissions, was at its peak in the early months of the privateering war and was further stimulated by the successive entry of the continental powers — France in 1778, Spain in 1779 and the United Provinces in 1780. London was the most active privateering port, as in previous wars, but the capital's relative position was eroded by the emergence of the western outports, notably Liverpool and the Clyde ports, as major privateering bases. The unique circumstances of the war, with the collapse of the Atlantic staple trades, were responsible for this development. Merchants dealing in such commodities as sugar, slaves and tobacco found their trade curtailed by the closure of markets and by enemy privateering activity and thus employed their idle ships and capital in retaliatory action, privateering offering one of the few alternatives to trade. Many of the smaller British ports also sent out privateers to prey on American, French, Spanish and Dutch trade, further adding to London's relative decline.

The majority of British privateers were owned by merchants who generally had many different interests. Privateering represented a speculative wartime investment and, as such, large profits were sometimes earned. In addition, privateering stimulated the shore-based industries of British ports — ropemaking, chandlery, etc. — at a time when trade was depressed. Thus, as well as supplementing naval forces, privateering helped stimulate the economies of British ports during the American War.

In sum, privateering activity from Great Britain during the American Revolution was greater than in previous wars, west coast ports were involved to a greater extent than in earlier conflicts and the combats were more ferociously contested than hitherto with heavier armament being employed.[28]

Appendix

Example of a Letter of Marque Declaration

Appeared personally Godfrey Thornton of Austin Fryers, London, on behalf of Captain John Powell now at Liverpool and produced a warrant from the Right Honourable the Lords Commissioners for executing the office of Lord High Admiral of Great Britain and Ireland for the granting of a commission to him the said John Powell's ship is called the ACTIVE, is square-sterned, has one mast, that the said ship is employed in trade and her cargo consists of porter, earthenware, wine, cheese, beer, sugar, rum, pickles in cases and salt, that the said ship is of the burthen of 100 tons, that the said John Powell goeth commander of her, that she carries twelve carriage guns carrying shot of four pounds weight two cohorns carrying shot of four pounds weight and six swivel guns, twenty-four men, fifty small arms, twenty cutlasses, thirteen barrels of powder, forty rounds of great shot and about five hundredweight of small shot, has two suits of sails, three anchors, two cables and about five hundredweight of spare cordage, that Lochlan McGuair goes mate or lieutenant, Peter Hadley gunner, Samuel Cowley boatswain, Thomas Powell carpenter, John Thomas cook and Thomas John surgeon of the said ship, that the said ship is belonging to the port of Liverpool and that the said ship is bound on a voyage from the port of Liverpool to New York and to return to Liverpool and that Nicholas Ashton of Liverpool, merchant, is the sole owner and setter out of the said ship.

On the same day   Signed Godfrey Thornton
This declaration was made
before me, signed, Colle Ducaret
                 Surrogate

Source: PRO HCA 26/61

Notes

[1] For a full bibliography of privateering, see the *National Maritime Museum Catalogue of the Library, volume IV. Piracy and Privateering* (HMSO, 1972). General accounts such as those by W. Branch Johnson, *Wolves of the Channel, 1681-1856* (London: Wishart, 1931), Charles W. Kendall, *Private Men-of-War* (London: Philip Allen, 1931) and Edward Statham, *Privateers and Privateering* (London: Hutchinson, 1910) dwell on the romance of the topic. Scholarly work on privateering from the British Isles during the eighteenth century is largely absent although earlier periods have been covered by Kenneth R. Andrews in *Elizabethan Privateering During the Spanish War, 1585-1603* (Cambridge, 1964), George N. Clark in "English and Dutch Privateers under William III," *Mariner's Mirror*, VII (1921), pp. 162-7, 209-17, and by John S. Bromley in "Channel Island Privateers in the War of the Spanish Succession," *Société Guernesiaise Reports and Transactions*, XIV (1949), 444-62; but see Walter E. Minchinton, "Piracy and Privateering in the Atlantic, 1713-76" in *Course et piraterie* (Paris: Institut de Recherche et d'Histoire des Textes, 1975), I, pp. 299-330.

[2] Bromley, "Channel Island Privateers," p. 448, discusses the importance of privateering to the economy of the Channel Islands. In the Seven Years' War and the American War privateering helped revive Liverpool's economy which was severely disrupted by war: see Cyril Northcote Parkinson, *The Rise of the Port of Liverpool* (Liverpool, 1952), pp. 112-13, 137-8, and Gomer Williams, *History of the Liverpool Privateers and Letters of Marque, with an Account of the Liverpool Slave Trade* (New York: Heinneman, 1897), pp. 182-5. Patrick Crowhurst's study of Bayonne indicates the counter-cyclical value of privateering. "Bayonne Privateering, 1744-1763," in *Course et piraterie* I, pp. 452-86.

[3] For the activities of West Indian privateers in earlier wars, see Howard M. Chapin, *Bermuda Privateers, 1739-1748* (Hamilton, Bermuda, 1923); Richard Pares, *War and Trade in the West Indies, 1739-1763* (Oxford: Clarendon Press, 1936; reprinted Cass, 1963) and Violet F. Barbour, "Privateers and Pirates of the West Indies," *American Historical Review*, XVI (1911), pp. 529-66.

[4] For American privateering, see the general studies by Ralph M. Eastman, *Some Famous Privateers of New England*, (Boston 1928) and Edgar S. Maclay, *A History of American Privateers* (New York: Sampson Low, 1900). For the American Revolution, see William Bell Clark, *Ben Franklin's Privateers: A Naval Epic of the American Revolution*, (New York: Greenwood, 1956) and William J. Morgan, ed. *Naval documents of the American Revolution* (Washington DC, 1964-).

[5] For instance, the *Liverpool General Advertiser* of 29 September 1775 reported that "our once extensive trade to Africa is at a stand; all commerce with America is at an end."

[6] However, sea officers were unanimous in considering that privateering detracted from the resources available to the Royal Navy. We owe this point to Nicholas Rodger.

[7] See Isabel de Madariaga, *Britain, Russia and the Armed Neutrality of 1780* (London: Hollis & Carter, 1962), p. 14.

[8] For the derivation of the term, see Francis R. Stark, *The Abolition of Privateering and the Declaration of Paris* (New York: Columbia University Press, 1897) pp. 49-78.

[9] The cost of obtaining a letter of marque for the *Hawke* of Liverpool which sailed from that port on 3 June 1779 is given as £34 7s by Francis E. Hyde, Bradbury B. Parkinson and Sheila Marriner in "The Nature and Profitability of the Liverpool Slave Trade," *Economic History Review*, 2nd series, V (1953), p. 375.

[10] Declarations could be made in the outports before local officials and posted to Doctors' Commons. In general, these lacked the detail of those made in London, although the standard information is to be found in them.

[11] Those made between 1808 and 1815 are to be found with the letter of marque bonds, HCA 25.

[12] For an example of such a declaration, see Appendix .

[13] The letter of marque declarations against the other belligerents are classified as follows: French, HCA 26/33-44; Spanish, HCA 26/45-52: Dutch, HCA 26/53-9.

[14] HCA 26/60.

[15] These examples are taken from John W. Damer Powell, *Bristol Privateers and Ships of War* (Bristol: Arrowsmith, 1930), pp. 254, 265.

[16] In addition, there were 5 commissions for 5 vessels which cannot be allocated to a port and 14 commissions for 14 vessels which were obtained in London for vessels owned in Quebec, New York, Antigua, Barbados, Bermuda, Jamaica, Gibraltar and Bombay.

[17] See Walter Minchinton, *The Growth of English Overseas Trade in the Seventeenth and Eighteenth Centuries* (London: Methuen, 1969), especially p. 35.

[18] In the early phase of the war seamen were unemployed due to the disruption of the Atlantic trades. This caused rioting in Liverpool in 1775; see

Williams, *Liverpool Privateers*, pp. 555-60. As the war escalated, however, the demands of the navy and privateers created a labor shortage.

[19] Liverpool Record Office, Holt & Gregson MSS, 942 HOL 10, p. 363.

[20] Thomas M. Devine, *The Tobacco Lords: A Study of the Tobacco Merchants of Glasgow and their Trading Activities, c1740-90* (Edinburgh: John Donald, 1975) pp. 161-2.

[21] There were a number of different ways that a shipowner could employ his vessel during a war. He could carry on as usual and run the risk of capture; he could operate under convoy; he could convert his ship into a privateer; or he could rent his ship to the government, with or without a privateer's commission, to serve as a transport, victualler, etc. The navy also hired armed cutters, crews and all, to be used as warships. About 25 of these vessels were deployed in the Downs after the French came into the war. At any given time during the American War the government had hundreds of rented ships in service. The thirty-three ships with commissions in the service of the Navy Board were just a small fraction of the hired shipping used by the agency. We owe this comment to David Syrett.

[22] The logistical problems posed by the scale of the American war were great. See David Syrett, *Shipping and the American War, 1775-1783: A Study of British Transport Organisation* (London: Athlone Press, 1974).

[23] Liverpool Record Office, Holt & Gregson MSS.

[24] Roy H. Campbell, *Carron Company* (Edinburgh: Oliver & Boyd, 1961), pp. 87-103.

[25] The victualling period for the private man-of-war was likely to be from 1 to 4 months and at the most 6 months, while the armed merchantmen, whose voyages were often longer, required supplies for up to two or even three years.

[26] Although the information relating to the destinations and cargoes of London vessels is complete, that for Liverpool is lacking for 125 vessels whose captains made their declarations in Liverpool as explained in note 10.

[27] John R.T. Hughes, *Liverpool Banks and Bankers* (Liverpool: Young & Sons, 1906), pp. 127-43.

[28] In preparing this paper we have benefited from comments from Professors John Bromley and David Syrett, Dr. Stephen Fisher, and Dr. Nicholas Rodger.

John Paul Jones: New Perspectives
Revealed By His Papers

James C. Bradford

John Paul Jones, America's foremost naval hero, has been the subject of many biographies and even more works of fiction. Perhaps only writers of fiction can hope to come to terms in their own way with so complex and controversial a figure as Jones. Certainly enough novelists have tried, so many in fact that their works have become the subject of study.[1] Jones has not lacked biographers by any means. Biographical sketches abound and full-length biographies number in the twenties. Half of the biographies were done in the nineteenth century and, as Mrs. Reginald de Kovan, Jones' first modern biographer, said, none "may properly be called adequate, as none of them was prepared with a comprehensive knowledge of the existing material, with exhaustive research for unpublished documents, or with full attention to contemporary memoirs or historical publications."[2] Mrs. Reginald de Kovan attempted to fill the void and, in 1913, produced a "life-and-letters" biography which reprints approximately 120 Jones' documents with what Samuel Eliot Morison calls "fair accuracy." Jones has been the subject of several later biographies, of which the best is Admiral Morison's 1959 Pulitizer Prize-winning *John Paul Jones: A Sailor's Biography*. Admiral Morison, himself an experienced sailor, comes closest to capturing the character of Jones, but even his biography is not a complete one. In his preface, the admiral noted that he was writing "a sailor's biography, which will give a lucid description of Jones' complex and fascinating character, as it develops, as well as a clear narrative of his war cruises and battles."[3] Morison's emphasis is clearly on the latter, and he devotes over 80% of his work to Jones' decade of naval service.[4]

This division varies little from that of other biographies and is partly due to the nature of previous known collections of Jones papers. The events of his childhood and early career as a merchant captain in the West Indies are clouded, and many of the events of his years in Europe following the American Revolution are difficult to follow because there is no accurate or complete set of his papers.

Unlike most other early American naval figures, Jones conducted a voluminous correspondence with a variety of individuals. He was also careful to preserve his papers, but it appears that someone, perhaps Jones himself, "weeded" embarrassing letters from the others. If he did so it was probably done just prior to his departure from America in 1783 to become American agent for prize money in Europe. At that time Jones definitely sorted through his papers. Some, including certain logbooks and account books were left with John Ross, a Philadelphia merchant, who served as his financial agent in America. Jones took part of his papers to Europe, and those in his possession at the time of his death passed by the terms of his will to his family in Scotland.

In 1797, his eldest sister, Mrs. William (Jane Paul) Taylor, sent a part of the papers to Robert Hyslop, a New York attorney, in the hope that he could use them to press claims Jones had made to Congress for money. Hyslop was unsuccessful but held onto the papers until his death, when they passed to his cousin, John Hyslop, a baker, at whose death they were sold as a part of his bake shop. The new owner began selling parts of the papers. A Captain Boyd of Greenock, Scotland purchased the logbooks of *Ranger* and *Bonhomme Richard*, which passed through several hands until 1830 when the ninth Lord Napier presented both to Lady Isabella Helen Douglas, daughter of the fifth Earl of Selkirk. She then placed them in the family estate on St. Marys Isle where they were destroyed when the housed burned in 1940.

One day, George A. Ward, of New York City, passed by the bakeshop, sighted some of the papers on display in the window and purchased all that remained. These he made available to John Henry Sherburne, Register of the Navy, who used them, and papers supplied by Thomas Jefferson and the Marquis de Lafayette, to produce a life-and-letters study of Jones which remains of value because it contained the only extant copies of several important Jones papers.[5] Most of the papers purchased by Ward were later acquired by Peter Force and sold to the Library of Congress in 1867.

The papers which remained in Scotland came into the hands of Jones' niece, Miss Janette Taylor, and formed the basis for two studies of Jones published during the 1830's. The first work was *Memoirs of Rear Admiral Paul Jones*. Its compiler, probably Sir John Malcolm, claimed in the preface to have "been furnished with the letters written by Paul Jones to his relations in Scotland, from the time he was a ship-boy at Whitehaven until he died an Admiral in the Russian services," but devoted only twenty pages to Jones' life before the revolution.[6] The rest of the first volume deals with Jones' service during the Revolutionary War. The work's second volume deals almost entirely with Jones' two years of Russian service and includes a transcription of the journal Jones prepared for his employer, Empress Catherine the Great.

Following the completion of the Edinburgh book, Janette Taylor came to the United States bringing with her the papers remaining in his possession. She planned to revive the claims of Jones' heirs for money due them from the United States government. Upon her arrival, she lent the Jones papers she had brought with her to Robert C.

Sands, who hurriedly prepared his *Life and Correspondence of John Paul Jones, including his narrative of the Campaign of the Liman*. Although frought with errors of both transcription and fact, Sands' work did provide the publicity Miss Taylor undoubtedly hoped for. Joined by the heirs of several men who had served with Jones, Taylor petitioned Congress in 1836 for the money owed their ancestors.[7] Sands biography remains important, because most of the materials he used have since disappeared.

Many Jones items undoubtedly found their way into the hands of autograph collectors. One of the foremost of these was the historian Jared Sparks, who collected a number of Jones manuscripts, now in the Harvard College Library Collection, with plans to write a biography. Sparks never completed his projected study of Jones but lent the papers he had collected to Alexander Slidell Mackenzie, a naval officer, who for some unexplained reason does not appear to have made use of them — he failed to quote from them — in his 1841 *The Life of John Paul Jones*. Many other collections followed routes similar to the papers collected by Sparks and likewise came to rest in the libraries of colleges and historical societies.

Following the Spanish-American War there was a great revival of interest in the navy in general and in John Paul Jones in particular. Groups holding his papers began publishing excerpts from them, and two works of seminal importance to Jones scholars appeared. The first of these was Charles H. Lincoln's *Calendar of John Paul Jones Manuscripts in the Library of Congress* (1903) which catalogues and described the papers collected by Force. The second work was Mrs. de Koven's aforementioned biography, which made available in print a number of previously unknown Jones items. Four small collections of Jones' correspondence were published in 1905, the year his body was returned to the United States from France.[8]

In 1911, the Naval History Society began publishing various items from its holdings, several of which concerned Jones. The first volume in this series contained the logs of *Serapis*, *Alliance*, *Ariel*, and portion of the log of *Bonhomme Richard*, Jones' ships during 1779 and 1780. It was edited by the Society's president, Captain John S. Barnes, who followed it a year later with an annotated edition of Nathaniel

Fanning's memoirs. Fanning served for a time as Jones' secretary and his repeated harsh descriptions of Jones nicely complement those of Dr. Ezra Green whose diary had been published a number of years before.[9]

Numerous other individuals, including Franklin Delano Roosevelt, gathered materials for Jones biographies, but the only completed products worthy of note to appear after Mrs. de Koven's are those of Lincoln Lorenz and Admiral Morison.[10] Lorenz worked from previously-known documents, but Morison went to original manuscripts whenever possible and conducted a search for new materials in the United States, Great Britian, and France. The focus of Admiral Morison's work on Jones' service at sea has already been discussed, but it is worth noting that he, in his words, "never attempted to penetrate the Russian archives" for Jones materials.[11] Morison's biography does contain excerpts from transcriptions made by the Admiral in a series of notebooks which he used to organize his research materials. These notebooks are today in the possession of the Admiral's grandson, Mr. Samuel L. Morison.

There are three other large collections of Jones materials. The National Archives has numerous Jones letters and documents scattered through its collections: many are in Record Groups 45 and 217, the "Naval Records Collection of the Office of Naval Records and Library" and the "Records of the U.S. General Accounting Office." Two groups of papers have been culled from the second collection and other Treasury records. The first group of documents, referred to as "The Pre-Federal Records," brings together all of the financial papers found in the Civil Archives Division of the National Archives for the period before the establishment of the government under the Constitution. This includes such items as the "Blotters of the Register of the Treasurer, 1782-1789," the "Ledger of Ferdinand Grand." Grand was the Parisian banker who handled many of the Continental Congress' affairs in France, and from these records an interesting picture emerges of Jones' finances. The second culled group of records comprises the three-box "Manning File" of papers pulled from several groups of Treasury records by Frederick Manning, the Chief Clerk of the General Accounting Office during the 1930's and 1940's. Another record group, number 360, "The Papers of the Continental and Confederation Congresses and the Constitutional Convention" contains a great number of Jones items. The entire collection was microfilmed in 1959, a guide was issued in 1971, and a computerized index recently has been completed and is now available in a letterpress edition.

The United States Naval Academy Museum's collection of Jones materials ranks third in size after those of the Library of Congress and the National Archives. Its most important item, the only extant Jones letterbook, covers the period 5 March 1778 to 30 July 1779.

There is a major collection of copies of Jones papers in the Office of Naval History, which is currently conducting the most ambitious papers collection and publication project underway in America. Begun in 1957, under the leadership of William Bell Clark, Admiral Ernest M. Eller and William James Morgan, the project has conducted an exhaustive search of both American and European repositories, collecting copies of literally hundreds of thousands of naval documents from the period 1774-1783. Seven massive volumes of transcriptions have been published from this collection to date and the eighth is on its way. These volumes are by necessity highly selective and can include only a portion of Jones' papers, but copies of many others have been collected for the war years.

Such were the vicissitudes of John Paul Jones' papers prior to 1977, when a project was begun to collect copies of all Jones documents for publication in a complete, scholarly microform edition. Sponsored by the United States Naval Academy and the National Historical Publications and Records Commission, the project is still in the early stages of collecting. Still, it has resulted in a number of interesting discoveries and gives promise of facilitating some new avenues of research in naval history.

Probably the foremost hope of everyone who edits an individual's papers is that the user will, by reading the finished product, gain a more complete understanding of the subject's life and of his personality. Indeed, some editors believe that their editions will, in effect, become biographies of their subjects.

John Paul Jones' life can be divided into four basic eras: Early Years, 1747-1774; Years of the Revolution, 1775-1783; Diplomatic Service in Europe, 1784-1788; and Russian Service and Retirement,

1788-1792. The second and fourth of these eras have been the subject of extensive study. The vast majority of works on Jones focus on his service in the Continental Navy, and there are two monographs which deal exclusively with his Russian service.[12]

The greatest mystery shrouds Jones' early life. When the current project was undertaken, it was hoped that new documents might be discovered that would shed light on his thirteen years in Scotland and his fourteen years of merchant marine service. Unfortunately, nothing has turned up, to date, to add significantly to our knowledge of those years. A couple of letters and cargo receipts have been uncovered, but none add much to what is already known. A letter of 8 May 1773 from Jones to John Leacock is typical. Jones opened by repeating in abbreviated form the explanation he had sent on 15 April for his failure to arrive in Madeira as expected. Such repetition was common during the age of sail, when one could never tell which of two letters mailed a fortnight apart would reach a common destination first. Jones then went on to explain that he had tried to forward his cargo by another ship but that "the Custom H°. Gentry . . . would not permit it." Jones also noted that he had written to Leacock from Plymouth on 18 February, thus disproving Admiral Morison's supposition that Jones had sailed from England in January.[13]

The second period of Jones' life has been so thoroughly researched that few new papers were expected to come to light. For that period, the era of the Revolution, the project's main contribution will be the gathering into one place copies of all Jones items.

It is for the half decade between the American Revolution and the time that Jones entered Russian service that the greatest number of previously unknown papers have come to hand thus far. The major importance of these discoveries is not that they alter greatly our view of Jones but that they flesh out what we know about his day-to-day activities. None of the papers found is of particular interest alone, but taken together the papers clearly reinforce Joshua Barney's description of Jones as being "not entirely free from moroseness" during the period and Admiral Morison's conclusion that this feeling was brought on by Jones' frustration at the many disappointments he had suffered.[14] Most of the newly-discovered items concern Jones' finan-

Letter of John Paul Jones to Messrs. De Neufville & Sons in Amsterdam introducing Capt. John Barry. (*Courtesy of U.S. Naval Historical Center* and U.S. Naval Academy Museum.)

cial dealings and his attempt to obtain the prize and other monies due him from the war. Together there are certainly enough records to support a more detailed examination of Jones' financial affairs than has yet appeared.

Historical editing projects take as their main goals the collection of known papers and the preparation of them for publication, but every editor hopes, perhaps secretly, to find papers not previously known to historians. The thrill of the hunt, of stalking the elusive ALS (autographed letter signed), provides a part of the attraction of such work. When the Jones project was begun it appeared that the most fertile hunting grounds would be the civil records of the National Archives in Washington and the many repositories in Russia. This belief has been borne out with regard to the financial records of the United States, but to date Russian sources have been less fruitful.

Jones papers in Russia were first sought by Mrs. de Koven for use in her biography. F.A. Golder printed a number of Jones' items, including almost all of his letters to Prince Potemkin, in 1927, but his transcriptions were found to contain a number of important errors when they were checked against photostats obtained by Mr. John L. Senior in 1931. A decade later, Senior presented his collection of Jones materials to the Naval Academy Museum where they were used by Lincoln Lorenz and Samuel Eliot Morison.[15]

The most recent assault upon Russian repositories has been undertaken as a part of the Soviet-American cultural agreement of 1973, which included plans for a joint publication, *The Development of Russian-American Relations, 1765-1815*, in 1980. In preparation, fifty American and ten Soviet repositories were searched for documents from the era reflecting Russian-American contacts in areas from California to the Black Sea. It has been tentatively decided that the final volume will include only six "documents relating to Jones' service with the Russian navy." Many other documents were copied but the joint selection board concluded "that Jones had very little that was memorable to say about his stay in Russia, at least from the board's point of view."[16] Copies of all Jones items found were supplied to the Jones project, they were compared to the photostat collection of John L. Senior, and it was discovered that the new search had uncovered only two letters which had eluded Senior.[17] Still, the Russian-American project is ongoing, and the hope remains that some new items will be turned up.

In summary, then, little has been discovered which will force substantial revision of current views of particular periods of Jones' life. What does emerge from the papers, however, and what they will make possible is a more subtle understanding of Jones — the man.

His level of education is one area where a new edition of his papers makes possible a fuller understanding. Most biographers assume that he must have attended the parish school kept by the Reverend James Hogg, but there is no solid, documentary evidence to support this. Most of Jones' biographers also speak of him as a self-educated man, but, again, without solid evidence to substantiate this judgment.[18] What does emerge from reading Jones papers as he wrote them is a feeling for the level of his education. "As he wrote them" is a key phrase and reflects one of the important differences between the manner in which his papers have been published in the past and how they will appear in the edition now underway.

Editors of the pre-modern school, *i.e.,* generally those who worked before the middle of the twentieth century, viewed any misspellings or grammatical errors to be "corruptions" and took the correction of such errors to be a part of their function as editors. The result is the presentation of a series of letters which gives a less than accurate picture of the Jones' education.

An examination of the original papers shows that Jones was basically a phonetic speller, thus rendering Tarpaulin Cove on Martha's Vineyard as Tarpowling Cove, but not a consistent one — within a month he used both "Corke" and "Cork" for the Irish port of that name.[19]

Jones' diction was generally sound, but editors of his papers have usually corrected any slip which might have occurred as, for example, in the case of a letter he wrote saying, "by the time my water and wood began to run short which induced me to head to the Northward for some Port of Nova Scotia or Cape Briton." Mrs. de Koven rendered those phrases: "By the time my wood and water began to run short, which induced me to run to the northward, for some port of

Nova Scotia or Cape Breton." The changes are not great, but within these few words she does correct Jones' spelling of Cape Breton, reverse the words "water" and "wood," change his capitalization on three words (By, Northward, and Port), insert two commas, and change the phrase "to head to the "Northward" to make it read "to run to the northward."[20] Changes of this nature may appear unimportant, but, when constantly repeated, they result in the reader gaining a slanted view of Jones.

Jones' grammar was usually quite good, with the exception of verb tense usage, which he never seemed to master. This is evident in a letter Jones wrote to Thomas Jefferson. He opened by saying, "I received the kind note you wrote to me this morning . . . . " Several editors corrected the passage to read "I have received the kind note you wrote to me this morning . . . . "[21] Modern editors view corrections or alterations of the text of any sort to be corruptions of the document, rather than the grammatical and spelling errors made by the original writer.

A more subtle understanding of Jones is possible if his papers are read in facsimile form. This is important because the contents of his papers clearly indicate that he had acquired a certain level of knowledge and a degree of sophistication that is perhaps most apparent in his poetry. His poem "Lines Addressed to a Lady," for example describes the reception Juno gave to Jove upon his return from Mount Ida. The work is obviously allegorical, and it is interesting to note that Jones composed alternate versions of two lines in the fourth stanza so that it could be sent to ladies on both sides of the Atlantic.[22]

Both Jones' weakness with regard to grammar and his knowledge of classical mythology is reflected in a single letter written to Hector McNeill:

> I am on the point of sailing — I have just wrote to you — pray be so good as to put the Inclosed into the hands of the Celebrated Phillis the African Favorite of the Nine and of Appollo —[23]

The two errors in verb usage nicely balance his reference to the Muses. Together they reveal a man who probably lacked a lower school education (regardless of suppositions that he attended the Reverend Mr. Hogg's school for a number of years), but one who by self-education and reading in the classics was able to obtain at least a veneer of sophistication.

Since it was known that many of Jones' papers were used by his heirs in efforts to gain their portions of the money they felt was due Jones, it was decided that all aspects of the heirs' actions should be investigated in the hope that some Jones letters might have been enclosed by petitioners to bolster their cases. This search resulted first in the gathering of the most complete collection of papers dealing with particular prize cases yet assembled; papers which will easily support a much expanded study of Jones' finances, and of the efforts by his heirs to obtain money from the American government.

Three important letters dealing with Jones' 1788 prize-money mission to Copenhagen were discovered in "Record Group 76: Boundary and Claims Commissions and Arbitrations," where they had been filed after being used by the State Department in the 1840's to try and obtain payment for three prizes Jones had sent into Bergen back in 1779. The Danes refused to pay any money, but the documents are of value to diplomatic historians of the Confederation era and to those interested in early Danish-American relations. These papers, when used with other documents collected over the last half century make possible a much fuller account of Jones service as American Prize Agent in Europe than those currently available.[24]

The hundreds of pages of documents collected in the Manning file will be of similar value to historians studying the petitioning process and congressional politics during the middle part of the nineteenth century. The papers collected include not only the formal petitions of the heirs of those who served with Jones, but also letters of support from various political leaders of the day, extracts from official records, many of which are now lost, used to prove the service of individuals with Jones, and the various financial records showing exactly to whom, how much, and why the money was paid.[25]

Perhaps the most exciting discovery was a bundle of papers relating to Jones' estate that turned up in the Virginia State Library in Richmond. These came from an 1837 case in which the Husting Court of Norfolk upheld the claim of Janette Taylor to three-tenths of her uncle's estate.[26] Following her success, several other family members filed similar suits and submitted depositions describing the ancestry and descendants of Jones in support of their claim.

Research will be facilitated in two other areas besides those previously mentioned. A complete set of Jones' papers for the post-American Revolution period will make possible a thorough examination of his ideas about naval strategy and the roles of navies in society. His proposals for wartime operations, his observations on America's need for a peacetime navy, his writings on naval education, and his comments on his brief service with the French navy, have often been dismissed by writers as simply attempts to further his own career. Doubtless there was some of that involved, but his writings also reveal the careful consideration that he gave to such topics.

These writings, his poetry, his "A Plan for the Regulation and Equipment of the Navy Drawn Up at the Request of the Honorable, The President of Congress," the memoire, which he prepared for Louis XVI, his "Journal of the Campaign of 1788," and the *pièces justificatives* which he prepared to defend his conduct in Russia constitute his only formal writing intended for a wide audience. Thus, they should be Jones' best works and reflect the highest development of his philosophical, analytical, and literary powers. Beyond this, the writings reflect the state of naval and military thinking of the era and are of value as the only systematic statement of such subjects by an American during the eighteenth century.[28]

Lastly, the collection of Jones papers should facilitate research in at least one field of admiralty law, that of courts-martial, because Jones had the misfortune to be involved in half a dozen trials. He gave depositions in the Congressional Inquiry which looked into Esek Hopkins' handling of his fleet in its engagement with H.M.S. *Glasgow* and in the court-martial of Pierre Landais and James Degge, arising out of the strange happenings aboard the Continental frigate *Alliance*. Jones sat as a member of the boards which tried Captain Abraham Whipple and Captain John Hazard and was the presiding officer in the court-martial of James Bryant, gunner on the brigantine *Hamden*.[29] In addition to the cases he was personally involved in, Jones commented in his writings on other trials and on court-martial procedures in general. Of particular note is his letter of 4 September 1776 to Robert Morris in which he comments on precedents in British naval history.[30] Jones' interest in such affairs may have been personal as well as professional, because he must have known that his commander, Esek Hopkins, once wrote to John Hancock, Chairman of the Congressional Marine Committee saying:

> I have had so many complaints against Captn Jones that I should be glad of your directions whether it will be best to call a Court Martial upon him or not . . . .[31]

These comments are suggestive of what materials are currently available and of the types of inquiry they can support. The collection of naval documents of the Revolution is still underway at the Naval History Center under the direction of William James Morgan, and the joint Russian-American documentary history project continues at the State Department under David Trask.

The Jones project at the Naval Academy is still in the initial stages of collecting and will continue to draw on these and many other sources. Danish archives, for example, are currently being searched for Jones documents. In short, source materials are not only abundant at present, but there is promise that their number will be even greater in the future.

Notes

[1] Professor Charles J. Nolan, Jr., of the U.S. Naval Academy is currently exploring the ways in which the life of John Paul Jones has been treated in American literature and the cultural implications of the varying views presented by authors.

[2] Mrs. Reginald de Koven, *The Life and Letters of John Paul Jones*, 2 vols. (New York, 1930) I, p. viii.

[3] Samuel Eliot Morison, *John Paul Jones: A Sailor's Biography* (Boston, 1959), p. xii. All intervening biographies are eulogistic in tone, and only Lincoln Lorenz's *John Paul Jones, Fighter for Freedom and Glory* (Annapolis, 1943) is worthy of notice by serious historians.

[4] *Ibid.* By page count, approximately 8% of the biography deals with Jones' life to 1775, 77% with his service in the Continental Navy, 5% with the years 1783-1788, 8% with his service in the Russian Navy (1788-1789), and 3% with his final years in retirement and the return of his body to America.

[5] In his preface, Sherburne describes the route by which the papers he used reached him. John Henry Sherburne, *Life and Character of the Chevalier John Paul Jones* (Washington, 1825).

[6] *Memoirs of Rear-Admiral Paul Jones . . . compiled from his original journals and correspondence: including an account of services under Prince Potemkin, prepared for publication by Himself*, 2 vols. (Edinburgh and London, 1830), I, p. xi.

[7] *Memorial of Janette Taylor, et al.*, 12 December 1836, 24th Congress, 2nd session. House of Representatives Document Number 19.

[8] Letters to John Brown, Secretary to the Board of Admiralty and later a member of the Navy Board of the Eastern Department were printed in *Letters of John Paul Jones Printed from the Unpublished Originals in Mr. W. K. Bixby's Collection* (Boston, 1905). Letters from Jones to his patron were printed in "Letters from John Paul Jones to Joseph Hewes," *The Virginia Magazine of History and Biography*, XIII (1905). During the same decade other Jones' papers were printed in "Letters of John Paul Jones, 1780," *The Pennsylvania Magazine of History and Biography*, XXIV (1905), pp. 334-38, and Charles W. Stewart, comp., *John Paul Jones: Commemoration at Annapolis, April 24, 1906*, (Washington, 1907), pp. 115-64.

[9] Fanning was far more critical of Jones than was Green. John S. Barnes, ed., *The Logs of the Serapis — Alliance — Ariel Under the Command of John Paul Jones (1779-1780)* (New York, 1911); John S. Barnes, ed. and annotator, *Fanning's Narrative, Being the Memoirs of Nathaniel Fanning an Officer of the*

Revolutionary Navy, 1778-1783 (New York, 1912 [1806]); Ezra Green, *Diary of Ezra Green, M.D., Surgeon on Board the Continental Ship-of-War* Ranger, *Under John Paul Jones* (Boston 1875). The Naval History Society also published some letters addressed to Jones in Charles Oscar Paullin, ed., *Out-Letters of the Continental Marine Committee and Board of Admiralty*, 2 vols. (New York, 1914), I, pp. 65-70, 89, 133, 143-145.

[10] Lincoln Lorenz, *John Paul Jones, Fighter for Freedom and Glory* (Annapolis, 1943).

[11] Samuel Eliot Morison to Curtis Carroll Davis, 11 March 1959, quoted in Curtis Carroll Davis to James C. Bradford, 12 December 1978. Mr. Davis states that he "corrected the galleys of Admiral Morison's biography of Jones, at his request."

[12] F.A. Golder, *John Paul Jones in Russia* (New York, 1927) and Lincoln Lorenz, *The Admiral and The Empress: John Paul Jones and Catherine the Great* (New York, 1954).

[13] John Paul Jones to John Leacock, 8 May 1773, original owned by Dr. Paul R. Patterson, Albany, New York. Morison, *Jones*, p. 23. Cf. Phillip Russell, *John Paul Jones: A Man of Action* (New York, 1927), p. 29.

[14] Barney quoted in Morison, *Jones*, p. 337.

[15] John L. Senior, President of the Cowham Engineering Company of Chicago, made arrangements through Mr. P.A. Bogdanov of the Amtog Trading Corporation of New York City and Moscow to have the Russian archives searched. Evidence in the collection indicates that the photostats were made by a Russian archivist, A. Yanson, in Moscow in July of 1931.

[16] Dane Hartgrove (American editorial staff member) to James C. Bradford, 6 March 1979.

[17] Jones to Catherine II, 8 March 1791, and Jones to Baron Grimm, 9 July 1791.

[18] Mrs. de Koven believed that Jones attained his education during a prolonged visit to the home of Willie Jones by reading in Jones' library and mixing with educated neighbors. Jones "gathered an education unusual in those times from the very air about him," she says. De Koven, *Jones*, p. 64. Cf. Morison, *Jones*, p. 9.

[19] Jones to Esek Hopkins, 2 November 1776, "Papers of the Continental Congress," National Archives. An extract of the letter in William James Morgan, *Naval Documents of the American Revolution*, VII, 16, maintains Jones' original spelling. For the varied spellings of Cork, see 15 April and 8 May 1773, Naval Academy Museum, Collection of Dr. Paul R. Patterson.

[20] Jones to the Marine Committee, 30 September 1776, original in the Papers of the Continental Congress, reprinted in de Koven, *Jones*, I, p. 113.

[21] Jones to Thomas Jefferson, 28 February 1786. The original is in the Colorado College Library. Julian P. Boyd, ed., *The Papers of Thomas Jefferson* (Princeton, 1950-), IX, p. 305, reprints one of the versions with corrected grammar and discusses the letter's provenance.

[22] De Koven, *Jones*, II, pp. 162-163 reprints the entire poem. Jones changes:

> "Thus when thy Warrior, though no God,
>   Brings Freedom's standard o'er the main,
> Long absent from thy blest abode,
>   Casts anchor in dear France again;"

to read:

> "Thus when thy Warrior, though no God,
>   Brings Freedom's standard from o'er the main,
> Long absent from thy blest abode,
>   In fair Columbia moors again,"

[23] Jones to Hector McNeill, c.1 November 1777, the Pierpont Morgan Library, New York.

[24] The most complete account is C.O. Paullin, "The Diplomatic Activities of John Paul Jones, 1778-1792," in his *Diplomatic Negotiations of American Naval Officers, 1778-1883* (Baltimore, 1912). Cf. Morison, *Jones*, pp. 337-40, 350-59; de Koven, *Jones* II, pp. 242-69.

[25] Two of Jones' three main biographers (de Koven and Lorenz) do not discuss the prize money. Admiral Morison gives it a paragraph saying that "in 1837 his niece . . . revived [the claims] and, as a result of persistent pressure . . . Congress in 1848 generously assumed that the three prizes of 1779 had been worth fifty thousand pounds . . . and voted $165,598.37 to be distributed among officers and men of *Bonhomme Richard* and *Alliance*, or to their heirs." (Morison, *Jones*, p 358.) This essentially ignores the act passed by Congress on 3 March 1837, the payments recorded in *An Account of the Receipts and Expenditures of the United States for the Year [1838-1846]* (Washington, 1839-1847), and the supportive documentation in "Record Group 217: Records of the General Accounting Office."

[26] The shares consisted of her portion and those of her deceased mother and brother.

[27] George D. Thompson to James W. Cheevers, 13 January 1977.

[28] Several authors rely heavily on the writings for their work, but none of them have been published in full. Morison writes of them briefly (*Jones*, pp. 334-35) as does de Koven (*Jones, passim.*) but neither analyzes his ideas.

[29] Portions of the records of the Hopkins inquiry have been printed in various works, the National Archives has issued many of the records of the Landais and Degge trials on microfilm ("Correspondence of Capt. Paul Jones, and Letters and Papers Relative to the Trials of Captain Landais and Lieutenant Degge, 1778-81," on roll 200 of *The Papers of the Continental Congress*), and the records of the Bryant trial in which Jones served as president of the court are in "The Correspondence of Esek Hopkins" in Record Group 45: Naval Records Collection of the Office of Naval Records and Library.

[30] Morgan, *Naval Documents*, VI, pp. 685-87.

[31] Quoted in Morison, *Jones*, p. 96.

American
Maritime Prisoners of War,
1812-1815

Ira Dye

The maritime prisoner of war situation in the War of 1812 was different by an order of magnitude from that in any other American war. Even in World War II, America's largest and longest-lasting maritime war, only a minute fraction of U.S. naval and merchant manpower fell into enemy hands — about 0.2%.[1] In the War of 1812 about 14% of American naval and private seamen were held as prisoners for at least part of the war — about 14,000 out of the roughly 100,000 men in the seafaring manpower pool.[2] Much of the basic data relating to the entire experience have fortunately survived. The letters and memoranda of the policy makers — British and American, although scattered, are available. A large volume of detailed administrative information also survives. Detailed personal information on the prisoners themselves is available, probably the richest single source of information on American seafarers of the time, meticulously recorded on standardized forms by British civil servants.[3] Similar data, although not as complete, were taken on the seafarers captured under the British flag by Americans and taken into the United States.[4]

Taken together, these data allow the consideration of three different categories of questions:

Questions on the POW system and process:

How the POW system worked, the flow of prisoners, the policies and how they were followed.

Questions on our merchant, letter of marque and privateer vessels:

Crew sizes and composition, age distributions of crews, where and when they were captured and by what enemy ships. For this last, no other source seems to exist for merchant vessel captures and only limited sources on privateers and letter of marque vessels.

Questions relating to the maritime work force and to the men themselves:

Growth rates of young sailors, career lengths, racial mix, age distributions of the work force, personal descriptions of individual seafarers including height, body build, wounds, scars and tattoos. Also, the relationships between these factors and rank/rating and ship type.

This paper is limited to the first area — the prisoner of war system and process. Full treatment of the second and third areas depends on the computer processing of the data from the *General Entry Books for American Prisoners of War*, housed in the Public Record Office, London, which is not expected to be completed until the end of 1986.

This paper will examine briefly three aspects of the prisoner of war system and process:

1. The policies pursued by the British and American governments with regard to prisoner of war issues.

2. The administrative framework used by the British to implement their POW policies, and the American reaction.

3. The impact of these policies and reactions on prisoners.

The principal focus of the paper will concern the policies followed by the British government toward American POW's, and because of interactions with these policies, the British policies with regard to British maritime prisoners held by the United States. British policy was more clear and consistent than American policy toward either American or British POW's.

On the British side the real architects of prisoner policy were the Lords Commissioners of the Admiralty. A few decisions were referred to a higher level — to the Prince Regent's staff through Lord Bathurst, the Secretary of War. At a level below, day-to-day policy decisions were made by a separate organization under the Admiralty consisting of the Commissioners of the Transport Board and its administrative arm, the Transport Office. This organization also had the functions of managing troop transport and handling the Navy's medical problems.

While the Admiralty never formally articulated in one document an overall policy toward American POW's, it is clear from the orders given and statements made, and from the administrative pattern that emerged, that the following objectives were emphasized. These are in order of the priority that the British government seems to have placed on them:

1. To deny to the United States the use of as many American seafarers as possible for as long as possible.

2. To encourage the entry of as many American POW's as possible into British service, primarily the Royal Navy, but also the merchant service and the Army.[5]

3. To recover as many British maritime prisoners held in the United States as possible, as rapidly as possible, and to use these returned POW's as a direct manpower source for British fleet units operating in American waters.[6]

4. To restrict entry of British maritime POW's into American service.[7]

5. To minimize the costs of caring for POW's, consistent with presenting a public posture of humane treatment.[8]

American policy toward both American and British POW's seems to have been made by the Secretary of State, James Monroe, until mid-1813 when General John Mason was appointed as the Commissary General for Prisoners of War, under the Secretary of War.[9] American policy seems to have had the following objectives:

1. To obtain the return of American prisoners held by the British in Canada and the West Indies by exchange for them of the limited number of British POW's in American custody.[10]

2. To obtain the return of American POW's held in England when British POW's were available for exchange in excess of those required for Canadian/West Indian exchanges.

3. To ameliorate the living conditions of American POW's, particularily those held in England, but within very tight cost restraints.[11]

4. To encourage the entry of British maritime POW's into the U.S. Navy, privateer fleet and merchant service.

To describe American policy in such specific terms leaves the impression that it was more constant and highly developed than it probably was: During most of the war the British held the greater number of prisoners, and were therefore in a dominant position and American policy tended to be ad hoc and reactive.

Figure 1 diagrams in simple form the policy relationships that existed within the two governments and between them. The functions of the two men shown as the British and American agents for prisoners of war, both of them interesting personalities, will be discussed in the following section concerning administration.

The British had been dealing with French prisoners of war since 1793 and by 1812 had a thoroughly developed and tested system. This system included a wide-spread network of prison ships, prisons or "depots," some of them built specifically as POW detention centers (*e.g.*, Dartmoor, Norman Cross and Perth[12]), plus a full-blown administrative structure with printed regulations, forms to be filled out and an experienced bureaucracy. To give some idea of the scope of the operation, the system is estimated to have processed about 122,000

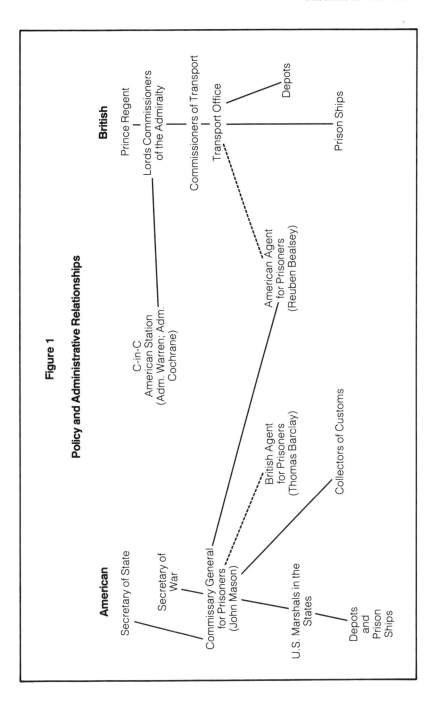

Figure 1

Policy and Administrative Relationships

POW's between 1803 and 1814, most of them, of course, French.[13] The number of Americans handled was somewhere around 10,000. There are some figures available in the records that show the exact number actually on board at a certain depot at a specific time. However, information on how many were actually captured and processed, and how the number in the system fluctuated over time is not expected to be available until later in this project, when the most of the records have been computerized. The reason that it is difficult to make reasonably accurate estimates of the number of prisoners is that each time that a POW was moved within the system, to another depot or even to an external hospital and back, another record on him was generated. The total number of records is in excess of 40,000.

Figure 2 shows the locations of prison ships and depots for which records survive showing that American prisoners were confined there. This is probably a complete listing of the locations where American prisoners were kept, although a few individual Americans may have been confined with French, Dutch or Danish POW's and listed in the *General Entry Books* for those nationalities. Nowhere in the records so far examined is there any mention of Americans being transferred to or confined at other locations.

Each depot or prison ship was supervised by an agent of the Transport Office who was an officer of the Royal Navy. At Dartmoor, a large depot, this was a captain. Individual prison ships were normally supervised by lieutenants.

The agents were governed by a set of detailed printed instructions for the management of prisoners of war that had been established by an Order in Council in 1808.[14] These were very humane regulations, although very strict on the prisoners, and very rigid when it came to detailed methods of economizing on expenditures. The regulations held the agents and the contractors supplying food and materials to very tight standards, including prohibition of conflicts of interest on the part of the agent with regard to supplies for the depot he supervised.

The regulations describe the form of the data to be taken on each prisoner, and how to record the information in the *General Entry Books*. They define who was entitled to parole and how prisoners in the depots and ships were to be mustered. They provide for barbers from among the prisoners and specify their rate of pay. They describe the ration allowance for prisoners, how the prisoner messes were to be organized, and provided for a prisoner committee to inspect the food delivered by the contractors. They provide for a daily market in which prisoners could buy extra food and clothing and sell the products of their manufacturing activities.

Figure 2
Detention Locations of American Prisoners of War, 1812-1815

England
    Ashburton---Parole Location
    Chatham--Prison Ships
    Dartmoor---Depot
    Odiham---Parole Location
    Plymouth---Prison Ships
    Portsmouth--Prison Ships
    Reading--Parole Location
    Stapleton---Depot

North America
    Halifax---Depot & Prison Ships
    Newfoundland---Prison Ships
    Quebec---Prison Ships

Atlantic Islands
    Bermuda--Prison Ships
    New Providence---unknown

West Indies
    Barbados---Prison Ships
    Jamaica---Prison Ships

Mediterranean
    Gibraltar---unknown
    Malta--unknown

Africa
    Cape of Good Hope--Prison Ships

At locations outside of England, officers entitled to
parole were paroled ashore in the same area as
the prison ships.

The evidence from both official records and prisoner journals indicates that the regulations were followed, and that under them the POW's were treated fairly, although strictly, and often with considerable forbearance — as is borne out in the descriptions in prisoner journals of the Fourth of July celebrations in 1813 and 1814. The toughest jobs in the whole system of POW administration fell to the two men who were for the U.S. and Britain the agents for prisoner affairs in the enemy's country. These were two very interesting, minor historical characters. They each had the task of trying to press their country's policy objectives for prisoners in the face of the almost diametrically opposed policies of the enemy host country. It was particularily difficult for Reuben G. Beasley, the American agent for prisoners in England. As noted earlier, the British had strong and definite policies on POW issues, and they held nearly all of the powerful cards. They were completely intransigent on most of the matters that the U.S. Government wanted Beasley to negotiate.

Reuben Beasley was a good deal more than simply our agent for prisoners. The recall of our Minister in 1811, and the departure of the Chargé d'Affaires in 1812 left Beasley, then the American Consul in London, to administer American affairs in England.

A large volume of Beasley's correspondence for this period survives in the National Archives and the Public Record Office. From this and from the contemporary journals of prisoners, he can be seen fairly clearly. What emerges is the outline of a man who was flawed and complex, human in the privacy of his letters, yet austere and unable to bend in personal contacts.

About one-half of Beasley's time was spent on prisoner affairs, judging from the volume of his correspondence in this area. The other half was divided between reporting to Secretary of State Monroe on political affairs and handling American commercial matters such as prize court cases. Beasley apparently presented a cold exterior in most personal relationships. He disliked meeting with the prisoners and in his exchanges of letters with the Transport Office, he apparently only twice requested to visit the prison ships and depots (in February and September, 1813). In the prisoner journals, his only two recorded visits to them were at Chatham and Dartmoor, in 1813. He met only with a small group of prisoner delegates, and then briefly. He apparently expressed distaste not only for the conditions at the prisons, but for the men themselves. His few letters to the prisoners were brief and cold.

The prisoners expected much from him in terms of improved clothing, more rapid exchange or release and a money allowance, partly because they had been led by the British staff at the prisons to believe that the amelioration of their misery depended on him as the American agent. When Beasley was unable to meet their expectations, they were at first frustrated and confused, but quickly began to hate him, and in spite of much improvement in their condition, continued to focus their resentment upon him even more than on their British jailors. The prisoners were particularily angered by his apparent neglect in not responding to their letters. However, after the war Beasley wrote Monroe that he had sent large numbers of letters to prisoners and to impressed Americans in the Royal Navy, but that most of them had been held up by the British and not delivered.[16]

There were few effective actions that Beasley could have taken to deal with the prisoner grievances, caught as he was between the intransigence of the British and the reluctance of the American government to spend money on prisoner support.

The British policy positions on three issues put the United States at a great disadvantage in the matter of prisoner exchanges, particularily for POW's held in England. First, the British insisted that American seafarers who happened to be present in British ports at the outbreak of the war either as merchant crews or as casual mariners "on the beach," were to be treated differently from other private American citizens and commercial travelers in England, and were not to be released without exchange. This was justified on the curious ground that inasmuch as British vessels had been excluded from United States ports in the pre-war period, that the United States had no counterpart concession to make in the release of British mariners.[18]

Second, the British announced that prisoner exchanges would only be recognized when made through the designated official POW agents and that exchanges made by commanders at sea, or more importantly, prisoners sent in for exchange by capturing ships, would not be credited toward future exchanges (even though the British recognized such exchanges with the French).[19] The main and most effective American activities at sea were the cruising operations of the privateers, letter of marque vessels and a few Navy brigs and sloops of war. These were small ships, usually far from a home port, to whom prisoners on board were a heavy encumbrance. Being unable to get credit for prisoners sent into English ports, and it being very inconvenient and expensive in food to carry them home for the bounty and for exchange, these vessels often simply released their prisoners, to the disadvantage of the U.S. prisoner account balance.[20]

The third issue on which the United States was disadvantaged in prisoner exchanges was with regard to Americans transferred from the Royal Navy to POW status at their own request, to avoid having to fight against their own country. These were men who had been, in most cases, illegally impressed. The British decreed that these men were not eligible for exchange or release until the end of the war except in a very few cases. From the start of the war until about mid-1813, men in this status comprised the largest single category of American prisoners.[22] Even in October 1814, after a great number of captures at sea had been made by the British, these "surrendered" men made up about 15% of the total of American POW's.[23] Thus, one large group of men was completely excluded from the possibility of exchange.

Further, both Britain and the United States treated the POW situation in the western hemisphere for all practical purposes as a separate system. Exchanges were made routinely of Americans held at British depots in America for British prisoners held in the United States. Only infrequently, usually when it was convenient to bring their to-be-released prisoners home to England, or when British prisoners taken by American ships were landed in France and exchanged to England from there, were exchanges of Americans made from the prison depots in England.[24] As a final difficulty on exchanges, the British in August, 1813, stopped all releases of American prisoners from depots in England until the account of British and American POW releases was brought into balance.[25]

All this, of course, frustrated the hopes of American POW's in England. Notwithstanding these problems, and others to be discussed below, Beasley should probably have realized that if he had gone to the prisoners in the depots and on the prison ships, and explained to them why he was unable to help them, given them sympathy and listened patiently to their complaints, he would almost certainly have had their goodwill. Instead, he put his efforts into continually and un-successfully pressing the British for more releases and exchanges of prisoners, and for more favorable terms of exchange, neglecting the day-to-day affairs of the prisoners.

The problems of clothing, rations and cash allowances for the American prisoners in England were made very difficult by a set of basic, possibly deliberate, misunderstandings between the two nations as to who was to pay for what for the prisoners being held by both sides.

This leads to the introduction of a second interesting character. On the first of December, 1812, the British government appointed Colonel Thomas Barclay as British agent in the United States for prisoners of war. Barclay, 59, was an American, born in New York. He had been an active loyalist during the Revolution, and went to Nova Scotia after the British defeat. He was sent to New York as British Consul General in 1799 and served as such until the start of the War of 1812. He lived on an estate that he owned in then-rural Harlem and by 1812, although a loyal British subject, with a son an officer in the Royal Navy, New York was his home in all respects, and he had many friends and financial interests there. He had hardly arrived in England in August, 1812 when he volunteered in November to go back to the United States as agent for prisoners. He also offered to provide His Majesty's Ministers, and the British naval and military officers in America with "early information." [26]

He apparently had his own agenda, separate from British government objectives: After his appointment to the post of Agent for the Relief of British Prisoners of War in the United States, but before leaving England, he wrote to the Transport Office requesting the release of a particular American POW held in England. His request was refused. He obtained permission from both the Transport Office and the U.S. Government to locate himself at Harlem so that he could be in his own house and among friends, even though it was 200 miles from the U.S. officials in Washington with whom he dealt most closely, and over 100 miles from the nearest American depot for British prisoners of war.

Barclay received extremely detailed instructions from the Transport Office, and particularily was told what the terms of an overall "cartel" (*i.e.*, agreement) with the United States on prisoner treatment and exchange should be.[27] A month later he was sent a copy of a provisional cartel agreement made between British and American officials at Halifax and told what the Transport Board liked and disliked about it.[28] He either didn't thoroughly read, or disregarded these instructions and proceeded to negotiate with General John Mason, the U.S. Commissary General for Prisoners of War, a cartel on prisoner affairs that was very favorable to the United States. Signed by Barclay and Mason at Washington on May 12, 1813, it agreed to valuations for exchange of the various military ranks that favored the U.S. and differed significantly from the valuations used by the British in exchanges with the French. It agreed to a slightly larger ration with more variety than the American POW's in England were receiving — larger than given to French prisoners, etc.[29] Barclay sent the cartel to the Transport Office for ratification.[30] They took a look at it and sent it to the Lords Commissioners of the Admiralty. It was apparently controversial enough to need higher consideration — perhaps Barclay had enough influence that they were reluctant to take him on directly — so they sent it to Lord Bathurst to get the Prince Regent's opinion. There was no reply for several months and then Barclay was sent a set of specific directions for changes in the cartel and flatly told to get them accepted by the United States.[31]

Thus until at least early 1814, perhaps for the whole war as I have seen no evidence that a cartel on prisoner treatment was ever officially agreed upon by the two governments, the British treated the American POW's as though their proposed cartel terms were in force. The United States acted as though the Mason-Barclay cartel agreement of May 12, 1813 was in effect, and Mason told Beasley to insist on its terms with respect to treatment of American POW's in England (there is no evidence that he did so, probably recognizing the fruitlessness of such an effort).[32] Mason told Beasley in January, 1814 that as of the May 12, 1813 date of that cartel, he was responsible for providing clothing as needed to American prisoners in England.[33] The effect of all this on the American prisoners in England was that they were not furnished with clothing by the U.S. until May, 1814, while the British were very reluctant to continue to clothe them. The prisoners blamed all this on the stiff-necked, but unfortunate, Mr. Beasley.

At a later time, May 1814, Mason finally became convinced that the British had reduced the ration given to American POW's in the British prison depots and ships at Halifax, Barbados and Jamaica, below the level agreed to in the May 12, 1813 cartel, and regretfully ordered a similar reduction to the British prisoners in American depots. At that time he also told Barclay that he planned to send extra beef and pork via cartel vessels to American POW's in those three locations.[34] Apparently no attempt was made to supplement the ration of the American POW's in England, who had always received the lower ration specified in the British "Instructions for Agents." This was a reasonable course to follow, given the logistical effort that would have been involved, and the fact that the differences between the two rations, while significant, were not life-threatening.

In January 1814, Mason gave Beasley the authority to pay a small money allowance to the prisoners for soap, tobacco, sugar, etc., of 1 1/2 English pence per day, later raised to 2 1/2 pence.[35] This money, called by the prisoners "tobacco money," was issued every thirty-two days in the form of two one pound notes to each mess of six men, to be divided among them as they saw fit.[36] A little later U.S. Navy men began receiving half pay and some ex-Royal Navy men received long overdue pay and prize money from the Admiralty. At this time there was probably a flow of cash from these sources in the Dartmoor depot of roughly 2,500 pounds per month. With money in some quantity circulating among the prisoners, they were able to set themselves up in the market, some buying out departing French entrepreneurs at the time of release of the French in late spring, 1814. Extra food and clothing could be bought or bartered for prisoner manufactures, and life became more bearable.

In late 1813, the Admiralty had ordered that transports expected to be returning home empty from Quebec in the spring of 1814 were to bring American POW's from Halifax to England.[37] Then after the peace with France in April, 1814, when the French prisoners in England were released and sent home, a decision was made to concentrate the American POW's at one depot and Stapleton, near Bristol, was tentatively chosen. This was a good choice from the perspective of the prisoners: It was a healthy location, close to a major city (making for a more diverse market), and was liked by the prisoners there. Some American prisoners sent from the Plymouth prison ships had been there since early 1813. However, before this decision could be more than partially implemented, it was changed and new orders given to concentrate all Americans at Dartmoor.[38]

Dartmoor had been built in 1806 specifically as a POW depot. It was (and is) as grim a location as can be found in England. Its weather is cold, rainy and foggy, often when good weather prevails only a few miles away. Politics had been a large factor in the selection of this location for a prison depot: The Prince Regent, then the Prince of Wales, and some of his friends, owned land in the area and stood to profit from the activity at the prison.[39] In 1814 the same political reasons, this time aimed at maintaining the prosperity of the the Prince Regent's friends, probably led to the decision to concentrate the Americans at Dartmoor rather than Stapleton. It was a decision that was hard on the prisoners. They hated and dreaded Dartmoor and there were probably a number of unnecessary deaths from weather-related diseases as a result of the move. However, the conditions there aided British policy, as a significantly higher number of Americans from Dartmoor volunteered for the Royal Navy than from other depots, due partly to the bad conditions there.

Before it was all over, one other major policy and administrative disagreement between the two governments had a major adverse impact on the American prisoners in England.

H.M. sloop *Favourite*, which in January, 1815 brought the Treaty of Ghent to the United States to be ratified, also brought a British representative, Sir Anthony St. John Baker, authorized to negotiate on administrative matters related to the ending of the war. Baker and Mason discussed means and terms for repatriation of both American and British prisoners. As happened often before in U.S.-British discussions, there was not only disagreement but also misunderstanding.

The position of the United States was that each nation should charter and pay for shipping for the repatriation to the other country of the prisoners that it held. Put another way, the U.S. should ship home British prisoners in America and the British ship home the American prisoners in England, with any imbalances in costs to be adjusted later. The British view, expressed by Baker, was that each nation should charter shipping to bring home its own men. Mason sent Beasley copies of his exchange of correspondence with Baker, and instructed him to approach the Transport Board with the American proposal, in the hope of overturning Baker's position.[40]

These opposing views were self-serving and stemmed in large part from the circumstance that the United States held about 3,500 British prisoners at the war's end (many of them Canadian or West Indian), while the British held about 8,000 Americans, the majority of them in England. The result of this deadlock, and the implementation in England of the British position, was a delay in the obtaining of shipping to bring the Americans there home. Meanwhile, the American prisoners at Dartmoor became more and more restive. They had known of the peace treaty since Christmas week of 1814, and could not understand why the U.S. Government was not getting them released and brought home.

Actually, in mid-January, Beasley had asked the Transport Board to release as many Americans as he could get ships for, subject to exchange if the treaty was not ratified.[41] The Transport Board agreed, but the Admiralty turned him down.[42] Again in late January he asked for the release of the Americans in prison depots who had been sent in from British ships of war, release that previously had been promised to take place at the end of the war.[43] He received no reply. On March 15th, two days after H.M.S. *Favourite* returned to England with the ratified treaty, he asked the Transport Board that all American prisoners be released to him.[44] Two more weeks elapsed before he was notified by them that they were ready to release the prisoners when he provided ships for their transportation home.[45] He immediately chartered four vessels and started looking for more. This was difficult: He was unable to find other vessels and the four he had arranged for were slow in arriving at Plymouth. Part of the problem was that with the war over, shipowners were expecting a large demand for vessels in a postwar rush to re-establish trade, and most of them were looking for cargoes more profitable than a government charter to carry prisoners. The situation was further complicated by the disagreement over which nation was to pay, and by the weak credit rating of the American government. In any event, Beasley was unable to find more ships and the delay in release of the prisoners continued.

Tensions were further increased by the arrival at Dartmoor of a notice to the prisoners from Beasley stating that he would be unable to pay them their two-and-one-half pence per day now that the war was over, as his authority for payment was limited to wartime and he would have to get additional instructions from home. As their pay was due about March 20th, anticipation was running high and this word from the already-hated Beasley infuriated them.

Finally, on the 6th of April, 1815, three-and-one-half months after the end of the war and three weeks after the ratified treaty had reached England, the pent-up frustrations of the prisoners at Dartmoor broke loose and a major confrontation between them and their captors took place. When it was over, seven Americans were dead and sixty more wounded, in the infamous "Dartmoor Massacre," when the garrison of British soldiers at the depot fired into the mass of prisoners crowded in the prison yard.

The British public was shocked, and the public shock was transmitted to the government. As a result, within two weeks the Admiralty told the Transport Board to get ships together to take the Americans home, and to settle the bills later as part of the overall settlement of the war.[47] It was quickly done and by early July most of the American prisoners were on their way. However, some were not liberated until early August. Some were not sent directly home but provided crews for American ships laid-up in Russia and Sweden. Also, the U.S. frigate *Congress*, sailing to Europe at about this time was to stop in England and fill out her crew from among the prisoners.[48]

Even after their release, the prisoners' hatred of Beasley did not diminish. A group of the more articulate of the ex-POW's memorialized the government and talked to influential people. While factors other than the prisoners' views entered the decision, Beasley, who had been expecting to receive the plum of appointment as the postwar Consul in London, was offered Gibraltar instead. He turned it down and came home. His last letters to the State Department show that he was unable to comprehend why all of this had happened to him.[49]

This brief paper has covered only one facet of the captivity of the American seafarers in 1812-1815. A statistical study of the prisoners, both as POW's and as seafarers of the period, is expected to be ready for publication in late 1986. However, these studies do not incorporate most of the anecdotal material and many of the important incidents relating to the prisoners of 1812. A mass of this material, plus detailed chronological accounts of the life of the POW's can be found in the several journals and reminiscences written by the prisoners themselves or dictated to others. Appendix II gives a listing, discussion of authorship and brief critique of the journals and diaries that the present writer has been able to locate up to this time.

Notes

Research for this paper was conducted with the support of a grant from the Penrose Fund of the American Philosophical Society.

[1] The number of maritime POW's in World War II was reported after the war as 6,232 (5,622 Navy and Marines, plus 610 Merchant Marine). The peak number of men in the Navy was 3,4000,000, in the Merchant Marine about 250,000.

[2] Adam Seybert, *Statistical Annals of the United States* (Philadelphia: Thomas Dobson and Son, 1818), pp. 308-309, gives the tonnage in trade as 1,302,925 tons and the tonnage in fishing as 69,294 tons. On page 315 he states that American vessels in trade averaged 6 men per 100 tons and those in fishing 8 men per 100 tons. The total Navy estimates for 1815 are given as 15,200 men. Sea-letter vessels comprised another 12,200 tons (page 314). Thus the total manpower to man all classes of vessels was about 100,000. An independent rough estimate can be made from the total number of men registered under the 1796 *Act for the Relief and Protection of American Seamen*. Between 1796 and 1812, about 107,000 men were registered. The total number of American prisoners of war was about 14,000 to 15,000, of which a few hundred were U.S. Army men.

[3] *General Entry Books for American Prisoners of War*, Public Record Office, London. Admiralty 103 (Hereafter cited as ADM 103).

[4] *Kalendars of Maritime Prisoners of War*, National Archives, RG 94. (Records relating to War of 1812 prisoners).

[5] Beasley to Monroe, January 22, 1813, *Consular Letters from London, 1812-1816*, Records of the Department of State, National Archives, Mircrofilm T-168, Roll 10.

[6] Transport Office to Barclay, December 1, 1812. Public Record Office, London. *Letterbook of the Transport Office*, Admiralty 98/292. (Hereafter cited as ADM 98).

[7] Among the many references to this problem are: Transport Office to Barclay, January 5, 1813, ADM 98/292, and Barclay to Transport Office, June 5, 1813, in G.L. Rives, editor, *Selections from the Correspondence of Thomas Barclay, Former British Consul-General at New York* (New York: Harper and Brothers, 1894), p. 333. (Hereafter cited as Rives, *Selections*).

[8] Anonymous, *Instructions for Agents under the Commissioners for conducting His Majesty's Transport Service, for taking care of Sick and Wounded Seamen, and*

for the Care and Custody of Prisoners of War, respecting the Management of Prisoners of War at Home; as proposed by the Commissioners appointed for Revising the Civil Affairs of His Majesty's Navy, and Established by His Majesty's Order in Council, Dated the 14th of September 1808 (London: Printed by the Philanthropic Society, St. George's Field, 1809), *passim*. (Hereafter referred to as *Instructions for Agents*).

[9] John Mason, a younger son of George Mason of Virginia, who was 46 years old in 1812. His son J.M. Mason became famous in the Mason-Sidell incident in 1861.

[10] Mason to Beasley, January 25, 1814. National Archives, *Office of the Commissary General of Prisoners: Letter Books*, Volume 1, RG 47, Microfilm NNFL 68, Roll 198. (Hereafter referred to as OCGP).

[11] Mason to Barclay, January 6, 1814, OCGP Vol. 1.

[12] Ewart C. Freeston, *Prisoners-of-War Ship Models, 1775-1825* (Annapolis, 1973), p. 7.

[13] *Ibid.*, p. 2.

[14] *Instructions for Agents*.

[15] Anonymous (Benjamin Waterhouse, M.D.), *A Journal of a Young Man of Massachusetts, Late a Surgeon on Board an American Privateer, etc.* (Boston, 1816; reprinted New York, 1911 as Extra No. 18 of the *Magazine of History)*, pp. 135-40; Charles Andrews, *The Prisoners' Memoirs, or, Dartmoor Prison; Containing a Complete and Impartial History of the Entire Captivity of the Americans in England* (New York: Printed for the author, 1815), pp. 33-35, 97.

[16] Beasley to Monroe, November 16, 1816, *Consular Letters*.

[17] Beasley to Transport Office, December 15, 1812 and December 31, 1812, and Transport Office to Beasley, December 29, 1812, *Consular Letters*.

[18] Transport Office to Beasley, November 24, 1812, ADM 98/291.

[19] Beasley to Monroe, November 30, 1812, *Consular Letters*.

[20] Anonymous (Josiah Cobb), *A Green Hand's First Cruise, Roughed Out from the Log-book of Memory, of Twenty-Five Years Standing: Together with a Residence of Five Months in Dartmoor, by a Younker* (2 vols.; Baltimore, 1841), vol. 2, p. 199, describes an example of this.

[21] Irving to Gallatin, June 3, 1814, *Consular Letters*.

[22] Andrews, *Prisoner's Memoirs*, p. 17.

[23] Commissioners of Transport to J.W. Croker, Secretary of the Admiralty, November 2, 1814, Public Record Office, London. Admiralty In-Letters, ADM 1/3767. (Hereafter cited to as ADM 1).

[24] Transport Office to Beasley, April 23, 1813, *Consular Letters;* Beasley to Monroe, July 28, 1813, *Consular Letters;* Beasley to Monroe, August 6, 1813, *Consular Letters.*

[25] Beasley to Monroe, August 21, 1813, *Consular Letters.*

[26] Barclay to W. Hamilton, November 21, 1812, Rives, *Selections*, pp. 318-19.

[27] Transport Office to Barclay, December 1, 1812, ADM 98/292.

[28] Transport Office to Barclay, January 8, 1813, ADM 98/292.

[29] The standard ration served by the British to POW's in England is described in the *Instructions for Agents*, Appendix No. 13. The ration agreed to in the Mason-Barclay cartel of May 12, 1813 is given in Barclay's lettter to the Transport Office dated May 20, 1813, and in Mason's letter to Barclay of April 2, 1814. Translated into modern nutritional equivalents, after assumptions for the loss of water in drying meat, the two rations compare with each other and with the ration served to sailors in the Royal Navy as follows:

May 12 cartel rations: 2520 calories per day; 23% protein, 20% fat, 57% carbohydrate, by weight.

Standard POW ration: 2410 calories per day; 23% protein, 13% fat, 64% carbohydrate.

R.N. ration in 1812: 3900 calories per day; 24% protein, 16% fat, 60% carbohydrate, without including spirits or beer.

The National Academy of Sciences Food and Nutrition Board in 1968 recommended that an American male 69″ tall, 147-154 lb., 18-35 years old (roughly the average size and age of 1812 sailors) should have 2,800 calories per day, including 60-65 grams of protein. The proportions of protein, fat and carbohydrate in both POW rations are roughly the same as those recommended as dietary goals for the United States in 1977 by the Senate Select Committee on Nutrition and Human Needs. It should also be noted that American POW's in England had access to additional food (for cash) in the prisoner market.

See *Appendix I* to this paper for a more detailed comparison of the various rations.

[30] Barclay to Transport Office, May 20, 1813, ADM 98/292.

[31] Transport Office to Barclay, August 18, 1813, and November 6, 1813, ADM 98/292.

[32] Mason to Beasley, January 7, 1814, OCGP Vol. I. Beasley informed Monroe in August 1813 that the Mason-Barclay cartel would not be ratified by the British. Beasley to Monroe, August 21, 1813, *Consular Letters*.

[33] Mason to Beasley, January 6, 1814, OCGP Vol. I.

[34] Mason to Barclay, May 2, 1814, OCGP Vol. II.

[35] Mason to Beasley, January 7, 1814, OCGP Vol. I.

[36] Cobb, *Green Hand's Cruise*, pp. 172, 186.

[37] Transport Office to Barclay, December 3, 1813, ADM 98/292.

[38] Basil Thomson, *The Story of Dartmoor Prison* (London, 1907), p. 122.

[39] Justin Atholl, *Prison on the Moor* (London, 1953), p 15.

[40] Mason to Beasley, March 6, 1815, OCGP Vol. I.

[41] Transport Board to Admiralty, January 19, 1815, ADM 98/123.

[42] Beasley to Monroe, February 15, 1815, *Consular Letters*.

[43] *Ibid*.

[44] Transport Board to Admiralty, March 15, 1815, ADM 98/123.

[45] Transport Board to Admiralty, March 31, 1815, ADM 98/123.

[46] Cobb, *Green Hand's Cruise*, pp. 187-191.

[47] Transport Office to Beasley, April 19, 1815, ADM 98/291.

[48] Mason to Beasley, April 24 and 25, 1815, OCGP Vol. II.

[49] Beasley to Monroe, November 16, 1816, *Consular Letters*.

Appendix I

Food Content and Nutritional Value of Rations Provided to American Prisoners of War, 1812-1815

(Figures are weight of ration item in pounds per week per person, unless noted.)

Ration Item	I POW Ration provided in England [1]	II POW Ration agreed to in May 12, 1813 Cartel [2]	III POW Ration provided at Halifax [3]	IV POW Ration provided at Bermuda [4]	V Ration provided to American POWs on British Cartel Vessels [5]	VI Ration provided to Ex-POWs on American Cartel Vessels [6]	VII Ration provided to British POWs on British Cartel Vessels [7]	VIII Royal Navy Fleet Ration [8]	IX US Navy Fleet Ration [9]	X Modern Recommended Diet [10]
Beef	2.5	7.0	7.0	3.5	7.0	7.0	7.0	3.5	3.5	
Salt		or		or		or	or		0.5	
Pork		5.25		3.5		7.0	7.0	1.76	3.0	
Cheese								0.66	0.38	
Salt fish	2.0									
Bread	10.5	7.0	7.0	10.5	7.0	7.0	7.0	6.13	6.13	
Biscuit					3.5	0.5 (Sun.)				
Potatoes	2.5	—		7.0						
Turnips	1.25 oz.	or								
Onions	5 oz.	—								
Barley										
Pease		1.75 pt. or 2.625	7 gills		7 gills	3 pints (Mon–Sat)		1.76 pt.	1 pint	
Oatmeal								2.64 pt.		
Rice		2.625							1.0	
Flour									1.0	
Vinegar										
Molasses							1 gal.		0.25 qt.	
Butter								0.44	0.13	
Beer								6.16 gal.		
Spirits							1.75 pt. rum		1.75 qt.	
Calories per day	2410	2520	(See note 11)	2460	(See note 11)	(See note 11)	(See note 11)	3900	2950	2800
Grams protein	126	121		99				140	144	65
% Protein (by weight)	23	23		17				24	23	12
% Fat (by weight)	13	20		12				16	19	30
% Carbohydrate (by weight)	64	57		71				60	58	58

Notes: 1. From *Instructions for Agents*, Appendix 13. 2. From Letter Mason to Barclay, April 2, 1814, OCGP Vol. 2. 3. From Waterhouse, p. 24. 4. From Palmer, p. 19. 5. From Palmer, p. 202. 6. From Letter, Beasley to Monroe, August 6, 1813, *Consular Letters*. 7. From ADM 98/292. 8. From C. Lloyd and J.L.S. Coulter, *Medicine and the Navy* (Edinburgh, 1961), Vol. III, p. 81; Reduced to reflect Purser's share. Without beer or spirits allowance. 9. From E.K. Eckert, *The Navy Department in the War of 1812* (Gainsville, Fla., 1973), p. 46; without spirits allowance. 10. Calories and grams of protein allowance from "SCOPE" Manual on Nutrition," (Upjohn Co., 1970); Protein, fat and carbohydrate percentages are on "percent of total calories basis," and are from "Dietary Goals for the United States," Select Committee on Nutrition and Human Needs, U.S. Senate, 1977. 11. Nutritional values in these columns are roughly the same as in column 2.

Appendix II

A Descriptive List of Prisoner of War Journals

1. Charles Andrews, *The Prisoners' Memoirs, or, Dartmoor Prison, contain-ing a complete and impartial history of the entire captivity of the Americans in England, from the commencement of the late war between the United States and Great Britain, until all prisoners were released by the Treaty of Ghent* (New York, printed for the author, 1815), 283 pages.

Charles Andrews was the second mate of the mechant vessel *Virginia Planter*. Born in Newport, R.I., he was 36 years old at the time of the capture of his ship off Nantes, France, by H.M.S. *Pyramus*. Although he asserts in his journal that he was one of the first prisoners captured, the *General Entry Book* of the prison ship *Hector* shows him to have been captured on March 18, 1813. Along with other POW's from the *Hector*, he was sent to Dartmoor on July 1, 1813 (he says April 3, 1813 in his journal). He states in his journal, and the Dartmoor *General Entry Book* agrees, that he was discharged from Dartmoor on April 20, 1815.

Andrews' journal has a stronger anti-British tone than any of the other journals located so far. It also has more day-to-day detail than any of the other journals. It agrees with the other journals and with the official records on most important details, except for dates in the early part of the journal. Perhaps he started it after he had been in Dartmoor for some time, and was relying on memory for the earlier dates. It is apparently the only journal that was kept with the purpose of providing a log of the prisoner experience, as contrasted with a personal diary. He gives a list of American deaths at Dartmoor. There is a copy in the Library of Congress.

2. Anonymous (Benjamin Waterhouse, M.D.), *A Journal of a Young Man of Massachusetts, Late a Surgeon on Board an American Privateer* (Boston: Rowe and Hooper, 1816; reprinted, New York: William Abbatt, 1911, as Extra Num-ber 18 of the *Magazine of History*). There are 272 pages in the 1911 edition.

Sabin credits the authorship of JYMM to Dr. Waterhouse, who was 59 in 1813, and who is not recorded as serving at sea during the war. Accepting him as the author leaves the question of who underwent the experiences described and told them to Dr. Waterhouse after the war.

From the details given in the journal, the ship that the "young man" was captured in, on May 24, 1813 off Martha's Vineyard, was the privateer *Enter-prize*. The crew was taken to Halifax. The "young man" was apparently not the surgeon of the vessel, although the journal identifies him as such: The surgeon was one Amos Babcock, who was released without exchange in less than a month. The "young man" could have been the surgeon's mate. Although no such rating is listed among the *Enterprize* crew, seamen often served in that capacity.

Following out the details of subsequent transfers, to England, first to Portsmouth, then the Chatham prison ships and finally Dartmoor, only one member of the *Enterprize* crew in the official records fits the narrative in the journal. He was Henry Torey, a 21 year old seaman from Massachusetts.

Assuming that the "young man" was Henry Torey, how did he make the connection with Dr. Waterhouse after the war? There is no direct evidence but a possible answer is this: Also listed as a prisoner at Chatham and later at Dartmoor during the same period as Torey, was a Moses Waterhouse, 23, of Massachusetts. The two men arrived at Chatham aboard the same transport, and their prisoner numbers were close together, indicating that they stood near each other in the line when being processed at Chatham and may have been acquainted. Perhaps Moses Waterhouse was a relative of Dr. Benjamin Waterhouse, and the two young men went to see him after their return home and jointly narrated their adventures — the Doctor choosing to use Torey's context for the part of the journal giving the adventures up to the arrival at Chatham.

JYMM is particularily useful for the description of life aboard the prison ships at Chatham. The description of events and details is much more vivid and usually more complete than in Andrews' journal, but of course it is all second hand, apparently having been narrated to Dr. Waterhouse who wrote it down, but who was not present at the events. However, the descriptions are rich in detail, and the journal checks out with other contemporary information, both in journals and in official records. There is a copy of the 1911 edition in the Library of Congress.

   3. E.G. Valpey, editor, *Journal of Joseph Valpey, Jr., of Salem, November 1813-April 1815, with other papers relating to his experience in Dartmoor Prison* (Michigan Society of Colonial Wars, 1922), 71 pages.

Joseph Valpey, 22, was captured in the privateer *Herald* on August 15, 1814. He was received in Dartmoor on October 28, 1814, and was released on April 20, 1815, having bought another man's turn to be released, a common practise. He therefore spent about six months in Dartmoor.

His descriptions of prison life convey a sense of the interminableness and boredom that must have been a major feature of the existence of the POW's. He describes the contacts between shipmates and Salem town-mates which served to fill the time. He was also a prolific poet, and the poems give additional insights into the life of the POW's and their attitudes. The first ten pages give a vivid description of the privateering life. There is a copy in the Library of Congress.

4. Benjamin Franklin Palmer, *The Diary of Benjamin F. Palmer, Privateersman*, (Printed for the Acorn Club by the Tuttle, Morehouse and Taylor Press, 1914), 274 pages.

Benjamin Palmer, 21, was captured in the *Rolla* privateer by H.M.S. *Loire* on December 10, 1813. He was taken to Bermuda and put in a prison ship until August 1814, then transferred to England, arriving at Dartmoor on October 5, 1814. He was released on April 27, 1815, having bought the name of another man.

This journal is especially valuable for its description of the daily life of the American prisoners at Bermuda, and is the best of two surviving accounts of this. For the seven months that Palmer spent in Dartmoor, his diary is consistent both with official records and the other journals.

Palmer also describes in detail the trip home in a hired ship after the war, with the taking over of the ship by the ex-POW's in order to divert her into New York rather than the planned destination of Norfolk. There is a copy in the Library of Congress.

5. Anonymous (Josiah Cobb), *A Green Hand's First Cruise, roughed out from the log book of memory, of twenty-five years standing: Together with a residence of five months in Dartmoor. By a Younker.* (Baltimore: Cushing and Brother, 1841), Volume I, 247 pages; Volume II, 329 pages.

Neither the author's name nor that of the ship he served in are given in the text. However, the author gives a prisoner number that he says was his at Dartmoor — 6632. Also, the Library of Congress card catalogue gives the author as Josiah Cobb. A check of the information in the Dartmoor General Entry Book shows Josiah Cobb as a 19 year old seaman captured in the *Prince de Neufchatel* privateer on December 28, 1814 and received in Dartmoor on January 30, 1815. His number was 6234, and all details of his capture in the journal check with the official records. Prisoner number 6632 does not fit these details at all.

Both the title page and the preface state that this is a reminiscence, set down from memory twenty-five years after the events took place. Thus in historical value, it ranks behind the contemporaneously written journals. However, in descriptive details given, it is far more extensive than any of the other journals located so far. It reads like a Victorian novel, which to a certain extent it is, but gives much small detail that is not available from any other source. It is the basic source apparently used by most popular authors in describing life and events at Dartmoor. Cobb could have used the Andrews journal or JYMM to jog his memory, then filled in the wealth of detail from his own recollection.

He gives a detailed description of the voyage home after the war in a hired vessel, including the ex-prisoners seizing the ship and changing the destination from Charleston, South Carolina, to Boston. There is a copy in the Library of Congress.

6. Nathaniel Pierce, "Dartmoor Prison, December 28th, 1814, Plymouth near Devonshire, Nathaniel Pierce, His Book, dated at Dartmoor this 28th day of December in the year of our Lord one thousand eight hundred and fourteen 14. In No. 7 Prison S.E. end Middle Deck, England. Nathaniel Pierce of Newburyport, Mass." Typescript copy of a manuscript in the Widener Library, Harvard University, The double-spaced typescript has 48 pages.

In the Dartmoor *General Entry Book* his name is spelled "Pirss," however phonetic spellings are not uncommon in these records. The details in the official records jibe closely with the journal. He was captured from the *Halifax Packet*, a prize to the *Harpy* privateer, by H.M.S. *Bulwark*. He was received in Dartmoor on December 27, 1814 and released on July 3, 1815 — one of the later prisoners to be received and one of the last to be released.

I have found his journal to be the most useful of all from the point of view of a late twentieth century researcher trying to see these early nineteenth century men and events through their own eyes. The journal has lots of detail, unusual insights, and to me at least, it has a distinct "sailor-like" flavor. He ends the journal on July 2nd, 1815, "for want of paper," and says, "tomorrow I leave this cursed depot." The *General Entry Book* confirms that he did.

7. Francis G. Selman, "Extracts from the Journal of a Marblehead Privateersman Confined on Board British Prison Ships, 1813, 1814, 1815," contained in *The Marblehead Manual*, compiled by Samuel Roads, Jr., (Marblehead, Mass.: Statesman Publishing Co., 1883), pp. 28-96.

Francis G. Selman was the First Lieutenant of the privateer *Growler*, which was captured on July 7, 1813 near Newfoundland by H.M.S. *Electra*. The crew was taken first to St. Johns, Newfoundland, and put in a prison ship there. After about a month, he was taken to England, first to a prison ship at Portsmouth, then another at Chatham, and finally to Dartmoor, where he arrived October 8, 1814. He provides information on the deaths of prisoners of his acquaintance, and the journal includes a list of men who died in Dartmoor hospital and at Stapleton. He was released on April 27, 1815. There is a copy in the library of the Essex Institute, Salem, Mass.

8. Nathaniel Hawthorne, editor, "Papers of an Old Dartmoor Prisoner," published in the *U.S. Democratic Review*, New York, in seven parts, January to September, 1846.

This is the journal of Benjamin Brown, which was raised into literature by Nathaniel Hawthorne. Brown was a pharmacist in Salem who went to sea on the *Frolic* privateer as a Captain's Clerk. Captured in the West Indies by H.M.S. *Heron*, the *Frolic* crew was taken to Barbados, and after a brief stay, to England. Brown arrived at Dartmoor on September 30, 1814 and was released on May 1, 1815. He went home to Salem, where he remained for the rest of a long life. He wrote down the narrative of his experiences shortly after the war. He was a neighbor of Nathaniel Hawthorne, who edited the narrative and arranged for its publication.

Brown's narrative closely matches the official records, and is consistent with the other journals. It is good reading and in addition contains some details not found in the other journals. There is a copy in the Alderman Library at the University of Virginia.

9. James Fenimore Cooper, *Ned Myers; or, A Life Before the Mast* (New York: Stringer and Townsend, New Edition, 1852; first published 1843), 232 pages.

Ned Myers told the story of his experiences to Cooper in the early 1840's, and as with Ben Brown and Hawthorne, Cooper turned the yarn into literature. Myers escaped from the sinking in a squall on Lake Ontario of the U.S.S. *Scourge*. Transferred to the U.S.S. *Julia*, he was captured, still on Lake Ontario, by H.M.S. *Wolfe* and sent to the Melville Island POW depot at Halifax. He was sent to Bermuda and placed aboard a prison ship, then later returned to the depot at Halifax. He was released on March 8, 1815 and sent to Salem, Mass. Ned Myers' story has special interest because the U.S.S. *Scourge*, from which he escaped as it sank, survives underwater in excellent condition off Hamilton, Ontario, and together with the U.S.S. *Hamilton*, which was lost at the same time, is the focus of a current marine archaeological project. There is a copy in the Alderman Library at the University of Virginia.

10. George Little, *Life on the Ocean, or Twenty Years at Sea* (Baltimore: Armstrong and Berry, 1843).

Little was a prizemaster on a prize taken by the *Paul Jones* privateer when he was captured in January 1813. Taken to Plymouth, he spent about a month in a prison ship and was then sent to the depot at Stapleton. When Stapleton was closing, he was sent to Dartmoor.

This is one of the best journals for description of the prisoners and their appearance and habits. It is also excellent for its description of the privateering life, particularily its seamy side and the vicious actions of some of the people involved. There is a copy in the Maryland Room, University of Maryland Library.

11. Two letters: G. Bayly, to Lavinia Bayly, August 24, 1813, and John Baker, to his father, August 4, 1814. Manuscript letters, in MS 1846, Maryland State Historical Society.

Neither of these men can be traced in the official records because no information on their capture is given in either letter and their names are too common to be of help in identifying them. Bayly's letter is fifteen pages long in a double-spaced typescript copy, and gives a very useful description of POW life in a prison ship in Jamaica. Baker is writing home from Dartmoor asking for money to be sent to enable him to buy provisions and clothing. The letter is two pages of manuscript.

Black Seamen and the Federal Courts, 1789-1860

Gaddis Smith

Americans in the nineteenth century often compared the seaman's lot to black slavery. Recall the outburst of Captain Frank Thompson to his crew on the brig *Pilgrim* as recounted in *Two Years Before the Mast*. "You see your condition! . . . I'll make you toe the mark, every soul of you, or I'll flog you all, fore and aft, from the boy up! You've got a driver over you. Yes, a *slave-driver — a nigger-driver*! I'll see who'll tell me he isn't a *nigger* slave!" [1] Or listen to a seaman on a whaler in the 1850's complaining of brutal discipline: "And now I ask what slave at the south suffers more hardships or feels more keenly the bitterness of oppression than the poor care worne sailor." [2]

But if white seamen thought of themselves as slaves, what of the lot of real slaves at sea — black men hired out by their owners? Was the slave seaman's lot better or worse than his land based brother's? The evidence, ironically, is that the maritime life for the real slave meant relative freedom and often brought an opportunity for escape. And what of free black seamen? The sea for them was an important source of livelihood at wages equal to a white man's, of equal skill, but they encountered restrictions and risks not faced by white shipmates. The greatest special risk was being forced into slavery.

This paper is not a comprehensive discussion of black seamen.[3] Its purpose is to use one type of source, Federal admiralty court cases, to illuminate the special circumstances encountered by black seamen, both slave and free. This subject will tell us something about the lot of all seamen. It will also illustrate the conflict of races, geographical sections, economic interests, and systems of law in antebellum America.

Black seamen sailed in great numbers on American vessels and on foreign vessels visiting American ports. They were cabin boys, green hands, able seamen, cooks, stewards, firemen and engineers, enlisted men and petty officers in the Navy. They could be found on packets, tramps, whalers, privateers, pirate craft, and even slavers. They were prisoners of war and victims of impressment; they were heroes and cowards, criminals, and victims of crime. Some were masters and owners of coasting, river, and harbor craft. A very few commanded deepwater vessels. There are no firm estimates of their total number, but the vast majority of large American vessels from colonial times until the Civil War had at least one black hand. A few had white officers and all black crews. Preliminary evidence indicates that at least 10 per cent and possibly as many as 20 per cent of all American seamen in the period 1789 to 1860 were black.[4]

Surviving admiralty cases from the colonial period show many instances of black seamen in a variety of circumstances,[5] but only after the Revolution does the condition of black seamen begin to intersect larger issues of American society. With the abolition of slavery in the northern states, southern slave-owning states became increasingly fearful of the loss of slave property through waterborne escape. They became equally fearful of the introduction by sea of insurrectionary ideas carried by free blacks. Accordingly, southern states enacted statutory restrictions on the movement of blacks, both in and out. These restrictions came into conflict with the mobility of maritime enterprise.

The Virginia Assembly legislated fines against shipmasters on whose vessels runaways were found, established a system of special inspection for vessels proceeding beyond the Capes, and even called for the forfeiture of vessels in certain circumstances when runaways were found aboard. In 1796 Congress, in response to southern fears, began to debate legislation which would require "every master of a vessel to have a certificate of the number and situation of any negroes or mullatoes he may have on board." Southerners sought the legislation as a means of inhibiting the "mischievous practice . . . of carrying these people away . . . and selling them in other parts." Northern supporters saw the law as protecting free blacks who, because of their color, were often assumed to be slave. People "black or white, if free . . . ought to be protected in the enjoyment of their freedom," said a Pennsylvania congressman.[6]

These laws were frequently tested in court. In 1802 one Willis, owner of the small coasting sloop *Hope*, hired a slave named Anthony from his owner in Alexandria for eleven months at $10 a month. Anthony escaped in Philadelphia and in spite of the captain's best efforts was not recovered. The owner received Anthony's full wages and the court also ruled that Willis had violated the Virginia law requiring that he register the presence of a slave on his vessel with a magistrate.[7] In another case a slave stowed away on the sloop *Eve*, unknown to the captain. The slave escaped. Two judges in the three-man appeals court acquitted the captain of violating Virginia law. A third judge dissented and voted to convict. "The mischief intended to be remedied," he said, "was that seafaring men would secretly remove or countenance the escape of slaves." Since it would be impossible to prove that a captain knew a slave was on board, the offense should not depend on that point.[8]

Slaveowners frequently hired out their slaves for foreign voyages and went to court when the slaves did not return. In 1811, Arthur Emerson of Norfolk hired out his slave Ned as a seaman on the ship *Ann Alexander* for a voyage to Liverpool, thence to one or more European ports, and back to the United States. Ned's wages, payable to Emerson, were $22 a month. The ship reached Liverpool and then set off for Archangel, only to be captured by a Danish cutter and sent into Trondheim, Norway. The captain of the *Ann Alexander* discharged Ned and arranged in 1813 for him to return to the United States on a British safe conduct vessel as a passenger. When the British vessel reached New York, Ned was not found. His owner never saw him again. In 1814, the *Ann Alexander*, having been released, returned to the United States. How much did the owners of the ship owe the owner of Ned? In 1816 the case reached the Circuit Court of Appeals in Massachusetts.

The owners of the ship said that wages were due up to the day of discharge in Norway — the same wages as were paid other seamen who accepted a voluntary discharge. They argued that "in a distant region, where slavery is not allowed, the slave enjoys the same rights as any other citizen, and is able to dissolve a contract made by his owner, if it should be expedient for him to so to do." Emerson, Ned's owner, countered that the captain should have confined the slave. By not doing so, he deprived the owner not only of wages for the remaining portion of the voyage but also of the slave himself.

Justice Joseph Story denied that Emerson could receive damages for the loss of Ned. The owners of the ship had no responsibility to guaranty Ned's return. But the laws of Virginia should be heeded in the matter of wages and the discharge:

> In Virginia slavery is expressly recognized; and the rights founded upon it are incorporated into the whole system of the laws of that state. The slave . . . is incapable of making or discharging a contract; and the perpetual right to his services belongs exclusively to his owner.

Emerson thus was awarded Ned's wages to March 1813 when he was supposed to have returned to the United States on the safe conduct vessel and thereby been restored to Emerson's service.[9] In 1818 Jane Slacum went to court in a similar case. She had sent her slave at $25 a month for a voyage from Alexandria to Lisbon and return to the United States on the brig *Virginia*.

In Lisbon the slave was jailed for nine days for disorderly conduct. As soon as the brig reached New York and before the cargo was unloaded, the slave departed and was never seen again. The owner of the brig, in a tactic often applied against the rights of free seamen, claimed the slave had forfeited his wages by being jailed and away from the vessel for more than 48 hours in Lisbon and for deserting in New York. The court in the District of Columbia decided that Jane Slacum should receive her slave's wages for the entire voyage. Although a slave's wages were liable to forfeiture for any act which would lead to forfeiture of a free seaman's wages, neither the episode in Lisbon nor the leaving in New York before the cargo was unloaded were grounds for forfeiture.[10]

A Virginia law designed to control the entrance of blacks into the state came into play in an 1820 case decided by John Marshall, sitting on the Circuit Court. The Virginia law prohibited the importation of negroes or mullatoes. A complementary Federal law provided for the forfeiture of any vessel which imported negroes or mullatoes contrary to a state law. The brig *Wilson*, a Venezuelan privateer, ran afoul of these laws. In 1819, she put into Norfolk and was declared forfeit because some of her black crew members were granted discharge and went ashore. The master of the vessel, a man with the wonderful name of Ivory Huntress, testified that his crew had been reinforced at St. Thomas by some 18 seamen, "principally people of colour, all free." Marshall, always concerned to ensure the freest possible movement of commerce, declared that the Virginia law did not apply to crew members "employed in navigating such ship or vessel."[11]

Two years later a far more serious issue arose in South Carolina, an issue which was to place special burdens on free black seamen until the Civil War. In December 1822, the South Carolina legislature, in panicked reaction to the abortive slave uprising led by Denmark Vesey, enacted the first of the so-called Negro Seamen Acts with the purpose of insulating the state from free black agitators. The key section of the law provided:

That if any vessel shall come into any port or harbor of this state, from any other state or foreign port, having on board any free negroes or persons of color, as cooks, stewards, or mariners, or in any other employment on said vessel, such free negroes, or persons of color, shall be seized and confined in gaol until such vessel shall clear out and depart from this state; and that when said vessel is ready to sail the captain of said vessel shall be bound to carry away the said free negro or free person of color and to pay the expenses of his detention; and, in case of his neglect or refusal so to do, he shall be liable to be indicted, and on conviction thereof shall be fined in a sum not less than one thousand dollars, and imprisoned not less than two months; and such free negroes, or persons of color, shall be deemed and taken as absolute slaves, and sold. . . .[12]

The law was a great concern to both northern and British captains as well as a threat to their black crew members. The masters of 41 vessels lying at Charleston, all with black crew members, memorialized Congress in an effort to obtain relief.[13] The British Government lodged an official complaint with Secretary of State John Quincy Adams who, in turn, tried to persuade South Carolina to repeal the obnoxious legislation. Adams failed.[14] In 1823, therefore, one Henry Elkison, Jamaican-born black seaman from the British ship *Homer* of Liverpool, applied to Judge William Johnson, Associate Justice of the Supreme Court of the United States, then sitting in Circuit. Elkison was in jail under the law and wanted his freedom.

In a famous and widely publicized decision, Johnson reviewed the history of the law and the Federal Government's efforts to secure its repeal. Johnson observed that on one occasion the enforcement of the law had so stripped a British ship that there remained not "a single man on board the vessel to guard her in the captain's absence." Johnson then declared the law absolutely unconstitutional, as violating both the commerce clause and the supremacy of treaties. He speculated on the repercussions if the law remained:

. . . the state of Massachusetts might lately, and may perhaps now, expedite to this port a vessel with her officers black, and her crew composed of Nantucket Indians, known to be among the best seamen in our service. These might all become slaves under this act . . . retaliation would follow; and the commerce of this city, feeble and sickly comparatively, as it already is, might be fatally injured. Charleston seamen, Charleston owners, Charleston vessels, might, *eo nomine*, be excluded from their commercee or the United States involved in war and confusion.

The judge's comment on a possible Massachusetts vessel with black officers and Indian crew was an allusion to Captain Paul Cuffe, the only well-known black sea captain of the early nineteenth century. Judge Johnson's decision was denounced in South Carolina, and defied. An appeal from President James Monroe had no effect except to elicit from the Governor of South Carolina the blunt claim that his state "has the right to interdict the entrance of such persons into her ports, when peculiarly calculated to disturb the peace and tranquility of the State, in the same manner as she can prohibit those afflicted with infectious diseases to touch her shores."[16]

South Carolina's lead was followed by Georgia, North Carolina, Florida, Alabama, and Louisiana. Protests from shipping interests were repeated. Judge Johnson's opinion was echoed in other cases — most notably in the opinions of Judge Peleg Sprague of the Federal District Court of Massachusetts. In 1844 a Massachusetts master deducted the costs of imprisonment in New Orleans from the wages due a black seaman. The seaman engaged an attorney, none other than Richard Henry Dana, Jr., and won the full amount of his wages from Judge Sprague who declared:

> A State cannot thus interfere with the navigation of the United States, nor dictate to the owners of an American vessel the composition of her crew. The only ground of disability is color. If one color may be excluded, any other may; — if dark complexions may be subject to prohibition, white may be equally so; — or both whites and blacks may be excluded; or any other physical quality, or religious or political opinion, may be selected as the criterion of exclusion, or admission. If the parties may be subjected to imprisonment, expenses and bonds, any other penalties and punishments may be inflicted. Such legislation is not consistent with the regulations of commerce established by the laws of the United States, pursuant to authority expressly given by the constitution; and this statute is invalid.[17]

Sprague could declare, but the southern states persisted. Also, in 1844 the Massachusetts legislature sent Samuel Hoar, an eminent lawyer, on a special mission to South Carolina to seek relief. Hoar was met by a mob which threatened to burn the Charleston hotel in which he was staying. He departed under duress. When Hoar reached Washington on his way back, his friend Edward Everett Hale felt for the first time that war between north and south was inevitable.[18]

And only war did remove the Negro Seamen Acts. Until then Judge Sprague continued his attack at every opportunity. In 1855 he declared that New Orleans was not a port suitable for the discharge of black seamen. "They are not free to go where they please, and to find other voyages." The case involved some free black seamen who signed. for a voyage from Halifax to England and thence to a port of discharge in the United States at $24 a month. When the vessel reached New Orleans, the captain attempted to discharge them and sign them to another set of articles, at $15 a month, for a voyage to New York.[19] In an 1859 case involving a crew consisting entirely of black seamen, Sprague awarded each man wages and an indemnity because the captain had attempted to use the Louisiana law to cheat them. Sprague dismissed the argument that Congress had not expressly said that blacks could he seamen on American vessels. "It is sufficient that there is no prohibition, and that all persons, of every shade of color, stand upon the same ground of right to constitute a part of the crew."[20]

The rare black mariner who aspired to command also came under special legal restrictions as the nineteenth century progressed. Attorney General William Wirt in 1821 declared that free blacks in Virginia were not citizens of the United States within the meaning of the law requiring that those in command of American vessels in foreign and coasting trades be citizens. Wirt argued that blacks could not testify against whites, but that any shipmaster would need to testify under oath on many occasions. Ergo, no black could be a shipmaster.[21] Not until 1862 did another Attorney General reverse this ruling.

Free black seamen, thus, were less free than whites in any trade which took the vessel to southern ports. They were subject, of course, to the same perils of the sea and of the ship's work as any white seaman. They were just as prone to injury and death. Ironically, slave seamen, or rather, the owners of slave seamen, received greater compensation under the law then free seamen and their heirs for injury and death. To put it bluntly: a dead slave was more valuable than a dead white man. For example, a slave was hired out to a steamboat on the Mississippi. In violation of the contract, the steamboat went to New Orleans where the slave fell ill and died. The owner of the slave received $1,500.[22] Another slave drowned while carrying out orders. The widow or other heir of a free man would have received nothing. But in this case the court awarded damages to the owner and ruled that "Unlike white persons, the slave does not upon entering into the service of another voluntarily incur the risks and dangers incident to such service. He has no power to guard against them by refusing to incur the peril, or by leaving the service of his employer. He is but a passive instrument . . . "[23] The owners of a steamboat also had to pay the owners of a slave, hired out to them, who was killed because of the negligence of another slave in the crew. Had the dead man been free, there would have been no liability on the vessel to pay damages because of the reigning "fellow servant" doctrine whereby employers were not held responsible for the negligence of their employees toward one another.[24]

Salvage cases illustrate a further anomaly in the position of slave seamen. American courts, following the British lead, were generous in awards to salvors for the successful saving of ships and cargo. Where great risk and heroism were involved, awards of half the value of ship and cargo were common. The law provided no award for saving life, only for property. Slaves, however, were both life and property. Awards, therefore, were made for saving slaves. For example, in 1803 one Captain Bass, 180 miles offshore on his way to Charleston, came upon five runaway slaves in a canoe. They had been without food and water for four days and were near death. Bass carried them in. Judge Thomas Bee of the South Carolina Federal District Court agreed that the slaves could not have survived without rescue. This fulfilled the first prerequisite of a salvage award: property must be saved from certain or probable injury or destruction. But since Captain Bass had incurred no risk and almost no inconvenience in the operation, the award was low — $300, or one-tenth of the value of slaves and canoe.[25]

Judge Bee ruled in a more substantial case five years later. The brig *Norfolk* came upon the ship *Leander* 250 miles from Charleston. There were 56 slaves and no whites on board. The slaves indicated that the whites had simply died, but the judge found evidence that there had been an uprising and that the whites had been killed and thrown overboard. The fact that the *Leander* when found was in watertight condition and contained ample provisions created some difficulty for Judge Bee. But, he finally concluded, "there being no white persons on board and the slaves being regarded as cargo, I must consider the *Leander* as derelict." The salvors were awarded one-third of $16,000, the value of ship and slaves.[26]

In an ordinary salvage case the judge would divide up the award — so much for the owners of the ship doing the salvage so much for officers, so much for crew. But if a crew member participating in salvage was a slave, the slave's share went to his owner. As the author of the leading nineteenth century treatise on salvage, himself a southern judge, wrote, "The condition of a slave is different. He cannot, by any extra exertions or extraordinary services, entitle himself to the benefit of his earnings, nor own property independently of his master."[27] This rule is well illustrated in an 1804 case. The French ship *Blaireau*, Martinique to Bordeaux, was in a collision with a Spanish warship. The *Blaireau*, apparently about to sink, was abandoned. Passengers and crew continued to Europe on the Spanish vessel. The American ship *Firm*, Lisbon to Baltimore, came upon the *Blaireau* still afloat. Six crew went aboard and after great risk and exertion brought the *Blaireau* into port. The Supreme Court made a substantial award, including $1,134 for the efforts of "Negro Tom, a slave." This was about what an ordinary seaman could earn in five years. But Tom's share went to the Rev. John Ireland, his owner. The story had a happy ending. The Reverend Ireland kept eighty per cent of the award, and gave Tom the balance together with his freedom under the Maryland manumission law:[28]

A less dramatic case illustrates the common practice of operating small craft with a white captain and one slave hand. Amos Lyon was working his small fishing smack in the Gulf Stream with a single crew member, a slave. They came upon an abandoned ship, the *Cato*. The two men in the smack managed to tow the *Cato* toward shore and anchor her. But the anchor cable parted in a gale. The ship was subsequently salvaged by another vessel. The judge awarded Lyon a share, for bringing the *Cato* into safer waters.[29]

The edict that slaves should receive no award themselves was not always followed. Judge Peters of the Pennsylvania District Court decided two salvage cases in 1807 involving blacks. James Parker and Robert Sennett, white men, and negroes William, Joe, Europe, Lewis, Jerry, and Peter, slaves, all seamen, were all awarded equal shares ($23.87) for saving cargo from the dismasted schooner *Messenger*. The captain, mate, and eight crew were also saved; seven other crew members had perished. The judge directed that the slaves receive the money for their own use.[30]

In a more dramatic case, the Philadelphia ship *Harmony* was seized by a French corvette. A small number of *Harmony's* crew were left on board. They recaptured the ship from the French prize crew. Two of the Americans were free blacks — Steven Revel, cook, and James Bowen, steward. Judge Peters awarded Revel and Bowen full shares of $3,353.41. The judge commented that the award "should follow the spirit and beneficial exertions of one, whose station in life does not always produce persons of such courage and good conduct . . . these are not the only instances I have had judicially before me, of virtuous, patriotic, and spirited conduct of men of the African race."[31]

Black seamen figure in hundreds of other court cases in circumstances common to all seamen and not necessarily illustrative of race. In 1822 Captain Nathaniel Garland of the Boston ship *Tatler* subdued a mutiny after the mate had been killed. He would have failed but for the help of "Peter, the black boy, and his friend throughout" who brought Garland his gun.[32] The captain of the brig *Holkar* was less fortunate. He was killed on a voyage from Curaçao. All but one of the rebelling crew were black.[33] In 1842 the ship *William Brown*, Liverpool to Philadelphia, with passengers, struck an iceberg and went down. The crew in the overcrowded longboat threw fourteen passengers over in order to save themselves. The court noted that the black cook, participating in the crime, intervened to allow one passenger five minutes to say his prayers before being thrown over.[34] A black Haitian crew member murdered a shipmate, a black seaman from Baltimore, on a voyage from Apalachicola to Boston in 1845.[35] "A colored boat-steerer" was among the survivors of the wrecked whaler, *Harvest*, in 1848.[36] The captain and mate of a brig trading legitimately in 1851 on the West African Coast died of fever. The surviving crew consisted of five blacks and the second mate.[37]

Judges often ruled against as well as for black seamen in disputes with captains and owners, but there is no indication that blacks were treated any worse than whites in similar circumstances. Five blacks on an 1849 voyage from Apalachicola to Marseilles were deemed "at times perverse and offensive to the officers . . . deficient in ready subordination and alacrity in the performance of their duties." They received wages to Marseilles, but the court upheld their discharge in that port.[38] Also, in 1849 a judge refused to accept a claim of some black seamen that their vessel was unseaworthy and the food bad. "I am compelled," said the judge, "to regard the allegations . . . as gotten up by these black men to excuse their refusal to work the vessel. . . ."[39] Black seamen took sick and received the usual quality medical treatment of the age. For example, Ned, a slave employed on the steamer *Vanleer* in 1851 contracted cholera. "Much exertion was made to save him, by rubbing him with brandy, cayenne pepper, and by administering Dr. Cannon's anti-cholera preparation." He died.[40]

Court cases relating to black seamen demonstrate that the sea connects all things: slavery and freedom; the efforts of men to earn a living and the special barriers erected by society on the grounds of color; the racial fears of the South and the desire of the North for unfettered commerce; bravery and cowardice without regard to race. We could extend the list. But court cases do not tell a full story. They raise as many questions as they answer, but the raising of questions is the first step in the historian's search. Far more work is necessary. We know little, for example, of how blacks were treated by their shipmates — although fragmentary evidence points to friendly acceptance. What of black seamen ashore? Was their lot better or worse than that of white seamen? We do not know whether the numbers and proportion of black seamen were changing decade by decade. The number of slave seamen, except on coastal and river craft within slave states, seems to have declined after 1820. Did opportunities for free blacks also diminish? Probably not — until after the Civil War.[41] Court records are only a start on our search.

Let us return, in closing, to the comparison between American seamen and slaves. In 1865 the Thirteenth Amendment to the Constitution declared that "Neither slavery nor involuntary servitude, except as a punishment for a crime where-of the party shall have been duly convicted, shall exist within the United States, or any place subject to their jurisdiction." But Federal law still provided for the imprisonment and forced return to their vessels of deserting seamen. In 1896 four seamen — after refusing duty because of intolerable conditions on the American barkentine *Arago* in Astoria, Oregon — deserted, were caught like runaway slaves, jailed, forcibly returned to the vessel, and jailed again when they refused duty. They appealed their sentences to the Supreme Court. Does not the existing law of seamen, they asked, violate the Thirteenth Amendment? No, said the majority of the Court. The Thirteenth Amendment was never intended to apply to seamen's contracts. "From the earliest historical period the contract of the sailor has been treated as an exceptional one, and involving, to a certain extent, the surrender of his personal liberty during the life of the contract."

Associate Justice John Marshall Harlan delivered a magnificent dissent. The Thirteenth Amendment "established freedom for all," save only for convicted criminals. "A condition of enforced service, even for a limited period, in the private business of another, is a condition of involuntary servitude." The ancient laws, on which the majority relied, "were enacted at a time when no account was taken of man as man, when human life and human liberty were regarded as of little value." Under the view of the Constitution expressed in this decision, "we may now look for advertisements, not for runaway servants as in the days of slavery, but for runaway seamen."[42]

The answer to Harlan's concern and to the very real oppression under which seamen worked lay with Congress. In 1915 the LaFollette Seaman's Act repealed imprisonment as a penalty for desertion, while retaining the penalty of forfeited wages and the loss of personal property left on board the vessel. Fifty years after the abolition of slavery, seamen gained freedom before the law comparable to that enjoyed by workers on land.

Notes

[1] Richard Henry Dana, Jr., *Two Years Before the Mast*, (New York: Dodd, Mead, 1946) p. 85.

[2] Christopher Slocum, journal kept on board the ship *Obed Mitchell* quoted by Stuart G. Sherman, *The Voice of the Whaleman* (1965), p. 42.

[3] There is no comprehensive historical study of black seamen. Lester Rubin, William S. Swift, and Herbert R. Northrup, *Negro Employment in the Maritime Industries* (1974) concentrates on the present and is thin on history. Several articles examine the place of blacks in the Navy: L.P. Jackson, "Virginia Negro Soldiers and Seamen in the American Revolution," *Journal of Negro History*, 27 (1942), 247-287; Herbert Aptheker, "The Negro in the Union Navy," *ibid*, 32 (1947), 161-200; and Harold D. Langley, "The Negro in the Navy and Merchant Service, 1789-1860," *ibid*, 52 (1967), 273-286 — almost exclusively concerned with the Navy. Dennis D. Nelson, *The Integration of the Negro Into the United States Navy, 1776-1947* (1948) is not of scholarly quality. None of these authors have used court cases. Secondary works on blacks in American life often mention their participation in maritime affairs, but none go into any depth. See, for example, Ulrich B. Phillips, *American Negro Slavery* (1918); Carter G. Woodson and Charles H. Wesley, *The Negro in American History* (11th ed., 1966); H.E. Sterx, *The Free Negro in Ante-Bellum Louisiana* (1972); Leon F. Litwack, North of Slavery: The Negro in the Free States, 1790-1860 (1961). Very little exists on individual black seamen, but see Okon Edet Uya, *Robert Smalls, 1839-1915: From Slavery to Public Service* (1971); Sheldon H. Harris, *Paul Cuffe: Black America and the African Return* (1972); and Lorin Lee Cary and Francine C. Cary, "Absalom F. Boston, His Family, and Nantucket's Black Community," *Historic Nantucket*, 25 (Summer 1977), 15-23. In 1822 Boston commanded the whaleship *Industry* with an entirely black crew. John W. Blassingame, *Slave Testimony: Two Centuries of Letters, Speeches, Interviews and Autobiographies* (1977) contains some valuable material.

[4] Pre-Civil War census figures on occupation underestimate the number of mariners, because sailors at sea were not counted unless they were heads of families residing at an established address. Few seamen fitted that description. City directories were similarly biased in favor of landsmen with established addresses. Crew lists did not always indicate race and when they did include a column under "complexion", used ambiguous adjectives. "Black" and "colored" are clear enough, but what of "brown", "dark", and "swarthy"? And what percentage of black ancestry makes a man black? Nevertheless, there are some useful statistical fragments. The most valuable study

is Ira Dye, "Early American Merchant Seafarers," *Proceedings of the American Philosophical Society*, 120, No. 5, (October 1976), 331-360. Using protection certificates for the years 1812-1815 for seamen from Philadelphia and War of 1812 prisoner of war records, Dye finds that blacks comprised 17.6 per cent of merchant seamen. One-half were cooks and stewards, one-half seamen. His analysis of 25 crew lists of Philadelphia vessels in 1805 shows 21 per cent blacks. Martha S. Putney in her "Black Seamen of Newport, 1803-1865: A Case Study in Foreign Commerce," *Journal of Negro History*, 57, (1972), 156-68, reports that more than 90 per cent of all vessels in foreign commerce had at least one black crew member; more than 50 per cent of the crew in some vessels were black; occasionally a vessel sailed with an all-black crew. There were no black officers. A special census in Charleston, South Carolina, for 1848 notes 227 "pilots and sailors" resident in the city. One was a free black, 50 were slaves, 176 were white. Cited in Ulrich B. Phillips, *American Negro Slavery*, p. 403. In New Haven in 1850, 33 seamen had sufficiently permanent addresses so that they appeared in the *City Directory*. Nine of these were "colored." The 1850 Federal census for Connecticut reported 4,325 mariners of whom 316 were black. New York had 11,102 total, and 434 black. These figures were probably low. The keeper of the Colored Sailor's Home in New York reported that there were 2,000 black seamen sailing from the city in 1839. *Sailor's Magazine*, 21, (1849), p. 253. That figure seems high.

[5] The best published collection of colonial cases is Dorothy S. Towle, ed., *Records of the Vice Admiralty Court of Rhode Island, 1716-1752* (1936). In a 1743 salvage case we find a Newport captain leading a party of white and black seamen in an attack against Portuguese pirates on the coast of Sierra Leone (p. 226). In 1747 the vice admiralty judge overruled an objection and permitted testimony by James, a black mariner (p. 409). In the same decade the court heard dozens of prize cases, the result of vigorous work by Rhode Island privateers in the West Indies. Almost every French and Spanish vessel captured had black crew members. The court tried to decide if these men were slave or free, subject to be sold as prize property or released. Once a black on a French prize claimed he was free. The court gave the sailor three years to produce proof. In the meanwhile he was to serve in the custody of his captors. The record does not indicate whether the poor fellow ever proved his claim. The captain of a captured Spanish sloop testified that his black crew member was free but had "committed some heinous crime for which he was sent away." The court appears to have condemned the man to be sold. (p. 288). Sometimes the court declared vessel and cargo neutral and hence no prize. One Dutch sloop, released by the court, included a slave, eight free blacks of Curaçao, and five Spaniards in her crew (p. 422). Similar cases appeared in New York.

See Charles Merrill Hough, ed., *Reports of Cases in the Vice Admiralty Court of the Province of New York and in the Court of Admiralty of the State of New York, 1715-1788* (1925). Some fragments of Massachusetts vice admiralty reports appear in George Ticknor Curtis, *A Treatise on the Rights and Duties of Merchant Seamen* (1841), appendix I. One interesting case deals with the wreck on Scituate beach of the ship *Dragon*, Jamaica for Boston. George, the cook, was a slave. The owner was awarded George's wages out of proceeds from the sale of gear salvaged from the wreck (p. 379).

[6] P.M. Berman, ed., *The Negro in the Congressional Record* (1969-), II, p. 113.

[7] Park v. Willis, 18 Federal Cases 1109 (1813). This paper employs the standard form for legal citations. Reports for Federal District and Circuit Courts for cases before 1880 have been collected and published in alphabetical order in 30 huge volumes entitled *Federal Cases*. The first number following the name of the case is the volume in *Federal Cases*; the second number is the page on which the report begins; the date in parentheses is the year in which the decision was rendered, not, necessarily, the year in which the event under litigation occurred. Supreme Court cases are reported thus: 165 U.S. 275.

[8] McCall v. Eve, 15 Federal Cases 1232 (1804).

[9] Emerson v. Howland, 8 Federal Cases 634 (1816).

[10] Slacum v. Smith, 22 Federal Cases 317 (1810). In one 1808 case the owner of a Charleston schooner employed his own slave as a cook on a voyage to Africa. The cook deserted in Sierra Leone and gained his freedom. The owner deducted the value of the slave from the wages due the remainder of the crew, charging them with negligence in permitting the man to escape. The crew went to court and won. Judge Bee could not accept the owner's argument. "The discipline on board of this vessel appears to have been very relaxed; there seems to have been no watch appointed for the night when the negro made his escape; if there was, no persons are named as having been upon that watch, and it is possible that the negro himself may have been upon that duty. If so, how can blame attach to others?" Carey et al v. The *Kitty*, 5 Federal Cases 59 (1808).

[11] The *Wilson* v. United States, 30 Federal Cases 239 (1820).

[12] Elkison v. Deliesseline, 8 Federal Cases 493 (1823).

[13] *The Negro in the Congressional Record*, VIII, pp.144-6.

[14] The pioneering articles on this subject are by Philip M. Hamer, "Great Britain, the United States, and the Negro Seamen Acts, 1802-1848," *Journal of Southern History*, I, (1935), pp. 3-28, and "British Consuls and the Negro Seamen Acts, 1850-1860," *ibid.*, pp. 138-168.

[15] 8 Federal Cases 493.

[16] Quoted in Hamer, p. 5.

[17] The *Cynosure*, 1 Sprague 88 (1844).

[18] George F. Hoar, *Autobiography of Seventy Years* (2 vols., 1903), I, pp. 24-28.

[19] Stratton v. Babbage, 23 Federal Cases 225 (1855).

[20] The *William Jarvis*, 29 Federal Cases 1309 (1859).

[21] *Official Opinions of the Attorneys General of the United States* (1852), I, pp. 506-9.

[22] Helen Tunnicliff Catterall, ed., *Judicial Cases Concerning American Slavery and the Negro*, (5 vols., 1926-37), III, p. 358.

[23] *Ibid.*, p. 115.

[24] *Ibid.*, p. 16

[25] Bass v. Five Negroes, 2 Federal Cases 1007 (1803).

[26] Flinn v. The *Leander*, 9 Federal Cases 275 (1808).

[27] William Marvin, *A Treatise on the Law of Wreck and Salvage* (1858), p. 240.

[28] Mason v. The *Blaireau*, 6 U.S. 240 (1804).

[29] Ryan v. The *Cato*, 21 Federal Cases 107 (1807).

[30] Small v. The *Messenger*, 22 Federal Cases 366 (1807).

[31] Clayton v. The *Harmony*, 5 Federal Cases 994.

[32] U.S. v. Haskell, 26 Federal Cases 207 (1823).

[33] U.S. v. Jones, 26 Federal Cases 644 (1824).

[34] U.S. v. Holmes, 26 Federal Cases, 360 (1842).

[35] U.S. v. Mingo, 26 Federal Cases 1270 (1845).

[36] The *Harvest*, 11 Federal Cases 726 (1848).

[37] Robson v. The *Huntress*, 20 Federal Cases 1060 (1851).

[38] Tingle v. Tucker, 23 Federal Cases 1294 (1849).

[39] Bibbins v. Brookfield, 3 Federal Cases 331 (1849).

[40] *Judicial Cases Concerning American Slavery and the Negro*, III, pp. 609-10.

[41] With the withering away of the American merchant marine after the Civil War, opportunities for seamen, black or white, in foreign commerce

dried up. At the same time a new element of racial discrimination in employment in the north appears to have driven black seamen from coasting vessels.
This hypothesis, however, requires to be tested through more research than
anyone has yet undertaken. Court cases after the Civil War are of little use on
the subject since slavery and the southern black codes, which generated so
many disputes before 1861, no longer existed. Herbert Gutman has published
some suggestive documents on the post Civil War practice of Baltimore
boarding-house keepers to refuse to supply white seamen for any vessel with
a black crew member. "Documents on Negro Seamen during the Reconstruction Period," *Labor History*, 7 (1966), pp. 307-11. An overview of black maritime
employment can be found in Rubin, Swift, and Northrup — see footnote 3
above.

[42] Robertson v. Baldwin, 165 U.S. 275 (1897).

The United States Navy in the Adriatic in World War I

Paolo E. Coletta

Stating that Austria's attack on Serbia late in July 1914 violated the terms of the Triple Alliance, Italy remained neutral in the Great War until 26 April 1915.[1] She then joined the Triple Entente and in the Treaty of London received generous territorial, naval, and financial terms and the right to command in the Adriatic.[2]

The geography of the Adriatic so highly favored Austria that it overcame Italy's naval superiority. Except for Venice, Italy lacked good harbors along the Adriatic, and Taranto was poorly located for ships to operate in that sea. Austria, however, had the magnificent ports and naval bases of Trieste, Fiume, Pola, Zara, Sebenico, Spalato, and Cattaro and offshore islands from which Austrian forces could hit

Italy's ships or coast and retire to safety. Lacking natural resources, Italy depended on her allies for food, fuel, munitions, and shipping. About 80 percent of her trade went by sea, whereas what little maritime trade Austria had moved safely behind her Dalmatian island chain.

When Austria refused a fleet engagement, Italy's strategy was to have her navy support her army's drive from the frontier to Trieste and eschew offensive naval action in favor of a war of attrition in keeping with the principle of calculated risk except for trying to obtain some Dalmatian island or coastal territory. For the last, the army could never spare troops. Nevertheless, having seized Valona, Albania, in 1914, her navy could operate from both shores of the southern Adriatic. Most important, with a net and mine barrage at the Strait of Otranto she could put a cork in the Adriatic bottle. On the other side. Austria's strategy was to keep her heavy ships in port, leave the destruction of Italian ships to U-boats, have ships bombard Italian coastal cities and its littoral railroad, and engage in mine and aerial warfare.[3]

Because she concentrated against Austria and gave little thought to the Anglo-French Front, the British and French did not invite Italy to confer until February 1916. Although the British and French sent Italy some ships, Italian and French naval command relationships remained unresolved. Moreover, until Italy declared war on Germany, in August 1917, she could do nothing to counter German U-boats which were attacking Allied ships on the Mediterranean. In consequence, more thought was given to improving the mine barrage at Otranto. However, the extension of Austrian control southward along the Dalmatian coast, including the harbors of Cattaro and Durazzo, meant that Austrian attacks against the Otranto barrage and U-boat sorties could start from far to the south.

When the United States went to war on 6 April 1917, Germany's renewed unrestricted submarine campaign was two months old. The United States, therefore, concentrated upon downing the U-boat especially in the western approaches to the British Isles, and paid little attention to the Italian mission that visited Washington.[4] Not until July was President Woodrow Wilson convinced to change the 1916 naval building program, which favored capital ships, to build

The Adriatic Sea, 1914-1918

Timothy J. Runyan and Andrew Dyczkiewycz

antisubmarine (A/S) ships instead.[5] That Italy was peripheral to American thinking is shown by the fact that during the war no heavier ships and only thirty-six of the approximately 400 submarine chasers built were sent to the Mediterranean or Adriatic.

Upon becoming Britain's prime minister in December 1916, David Lloyd George demanded offensive as well as defensive operations. He sought a trustful cooperation between civil leaders and military experts and predicted that the stalemate both on land and sea could be broken only by a strategy that held enemy strength in France and hit enemy weaknesses in Austria, Bulgaria, and Turkey.[6] Not until urged to do so by visiting Admiral Henry T. Mayo, the commander in chief of the U.S. Atlantic Fleet, did the British First Sea Lord, Admiral Sir John R. Jellicoe, call for an interallied meeting, on 4 and 5 September 1917. The American representative therein was Rear Admiral William S. Sims, commanding U.S. naval forces in Europe. Although Sims had to discuss Italy's problems separately because the United States was not at war with Austria, the conference was a useful step toward fuller interallied cooperation.[7] Yet to be convinced that sea power would be the prime determining factor in winning the war, however, were the devotees of the "Western theory" — those who would continue the war of attrition in France and Flanders until enough of the enemy were killed and the Central Powers gave up. For about another year, therefore, generals like Douglas Haig lost hundreds of thousands of men in the mud of Flanders while British naval craft failed time after time to destroy the U-boat bases in Belgium.[8]

On 3 September 1917 Lloyd George told President Wilson that Allied policy for three years had been to concentrate, at great cost, against the strongest enemy, Germany. This was "because there has been no body in existence on the Allied side which could consider the military problem as a whole regardless of the traditions which have grown up in each army, and of the national prejudices and prepossessions of the several Allies in the use of their forces." He then demanded the creation of *"some kind of Allied Joint Council"* that would submit operation plans to the governments concerned and suggested that Wilson send a mission to study European problems at close hand.[9] Wilson created the Edward M. House mission for the purpose.

Among its members was Admiral William S. Benson, the Chief of Naval Operations. "All possible cooperation," Secretary of the Navy Josephus Daniels instructed Benson, "but we must be free." [10] When Jellicoe told Benson that he favored the creation of an Allied naval council, Benson agreed and obtained permission from Washington to appoint Sims as America's representative to it. But when Italians asked for aid, Benson told them to go through regular diplomatic channels because the United States was not at war with Austria. [11] In any event, the Allied Naval Council formed later in the year wrote its constitution and began preparing working papers for the first official session, which would be held on 22 January 1918. Sims said later that his most important work while abroad was performed in the Council. [12]

With the establishment of the interallied military council mentioned below and the naval council, Lloyd George thought that parochialism must give way to cooperation. His conclusion was severely tested by Italians. At an interallied conference held at Corfu between 28 April and 1 May 1917, the majority had overruled the minority, Italians among them, who advocated convoy instead of A/S patrols and increasing the effectiveness of the Otranto barrage. In turn, Italians objected to having either British or French admirals command all Allied ships in the Mediterranean. However, they accepted British help in building a fixed rather than mobile net barrage at Otranto Strait. [13]

While Italy did not expect the United States to participate actively in the Mediterranean as long as she was not at war with Austria, she hoped that since American warships were operating in British and French waters, these powers would send some of their ships to the middle sea. But this would not occur. Indeed, Italy had already stated that if the naval and merchant ships she needed were not provided she must close her factories and shipyards by March 1917 and soon thereafter cease military operations. Surprised when asked what kinds of operations should be conducted in the Adriatic, her spokesmen said that their situation was analogous to that in the North Sea, in which the British and German fleets were being used for political purposes. *Sotto voce* they added that her Allies were completely ignorant of the situation in the Adriatic. Her allies agreed that for the moment she could not undertake operations "in grand style" but that she should press minor operations vigorously. Admiral Mark Kerr, commanding British naval forces in the Aegean, noted that the Adriatic, being out of sight of the Western Front and shores of the North Sea, was out of mind at home and that only poor ships of little use at home were sent to the Straits of Otranto. The difficulties were increased by the divided commands that mirrored the parochial minds in the Mediterranean.[15] In any event, Italy's strategy was still to "hold" until she acquired additional forces and meanwhile "hit" Austria with light ships, submarines, mines, and aircraft. Since Austria retained her fleet, both opponents continued to wage a war of attrition and followed the principle of the calculated risk. American, British and French leaders therefore concluded that Italy's naval policy reflected less the requirements of war with the Central Powers than such political considerations as fulfilling the terms of the Treaty of London. In any case, until December 1917, when the United States declared war on Austria, the United States abstained from direct participation in the war on the Italian front and limited its aid to supplies which the Italians had to transport. In addition, Wilson told the Allies that he would not be bound by any treaties they had made. Until he went to war against Austria, then, he was protecting Austria against Italy while his Italian ally fought with him against Germany. However, on 1 September 1917 he said he would send Italy 500 aircraft pilots, open a $38 million credit with which Italy could fight against Germany, and arranged with Italy to have her build aircraft from American materials at her own expense.[16]

The thirty-six destroyers the United States sent to Queenstown, Ireland, were used exclusively in the Atlantic because, said the Italians, Sims was imbued with British ideas. Sims then cut the Italians to the quick by stating that the extended port time they gave their destroyers reduced their operating time on the Otranto barrage. Sims had new ships, Italy's were old and worn out, Italians rejoined. Italy's demands for American help remained unheard and the British, with hundreds of destroyers in their fleet, said they could spare none. Nevertheless, by direction of the Allied Naval Council, on 30 December 1917 a British admiral was given command of all convoy routing in the

Mediterranean. In this instance, Allied cooperation at sea produced a decrease in U-boat sinkings.[17]

However, debate flared over the subjects of attacking Austrian bases and defending the drifters on the Otranto barrage. At an Allied naval conference held in Paris on 24 July 1917 the Italian chief of the Naval Staff, Admiral Paolo Thaon di Revel, had commisserated about the small number of drifters allotted the barrage. He said that the Adriatic was the only sea in which an ally faced an enemy fleet and that his ships must always be ready to counter enemy forces. He stated further that the United States was providing him no help, and he had to support the Italian army in the north and divide his fleet in order to counter Austrian ships using both northern and southern bases along the eastern Adriatic coast.[18] Not until September did the delegates at a interallied naval conference held in London begin to concern themselves with downing the U-boat in the Adriatic. As for undertaking offensive operations in the Adriatic, Italy described the horrendous difficulties involved but said that plans for attacks were under study. Italy's need of resupply was so great that in late September Jellicoe sent her six destroyers and three suhmarines and in addition two sections of the fixed mine barrage for Otranto Strait. Nevertheless, it was widely suspected that Italy, intent upon her postwar status, intended to end the war with as many heavy ships as possible.

With British General Douglas Haig bogged down in Flanders and Russia knocked out of the war in the summer of 1917, Germany and Austria shifted some of their best divisions from the Eastern to the Western Front and decided to hit Italy in a surprise attack in October. Their defeat of General Luigi Cadorna's army left open Italy's northern plain; Venice was threatened. Were the Central Powers able to turn the southern end of the Allied front, they would shift the Mediterranean balance and perhaps win the war. Fortunately, Cadorna had established defenses to cover Venice, and his stand at the Piave saved the Italian navy from being forced to move about 500 miles south to the naval base at Brindisi and allowing the northern Adriatic to pass into Austrian hands.[19]

Upon hearing of Cadorna's defeat and retreat, General Ferdinand Foch, heretofore opposed to weakening the French Front to help Italy, told Cadorna that he would send six infantry divisions to him beginning 25 October. In addition, Lloyd George sent five. After more than three years of war, British and French troops finally arrived in Italy. Even more important, Caporetto forced the Western allies to abandon their tunnel vision and see the Western front as a strategic, tactical, and logistic unity stretching from Belgium to Venice. Lloyd George thereupon proceeded to Rapallo, near Genoa, where on 5 November a Supreme War Council was created. At subsequent interallied meetings, agenda topics were viewed with respect to the general strategic situation on both the sea and land fronts by political as well as military leaders.

As already noted, at an interallied conference held in Paris on 29 November 1917, Sims and others had called for the creation of an interallied naval council wherein all member nations must subordinate their particular objectives to the common good — a conclusion not relished by Italy. However, after 10 December, when she finally declared war on Austria, the United States assured Italy that she would provide her colliers, tankers, machine guns, merchant tonnage, patrol craft, guns, sheet steel, and American-built torpedo boats. Meanwhile, with Italian naval aid, Cadorna was able to save Venice.

A program to build more than 250 destroyers was adopted by the United States in May 1917. The first of some 400 submarine chasers were ready for sea in June, when plans were well under way for transporting the American Expeditionary Force, aircraft, and supplies to Europe. If the two million American soldiers provided the Allies the margin of superiority needed to defeat Germans on land, few soldiers and little naval aid reached Italy. Nor did President Wilson's Fourteen Points for ending the war, dated 8 January 1918, please Italy. By following the principle of self-determination, for example, Italy would not obtain fulfillment of the terms of the Treaty of London. Secretary of State Robert Lansing then deepened Italy's gloom by saying he favored Yugoslav over Italian claims to Dalmatia.[20]

Sims was pleased with the results of the first meeting of the Allied Naval Council, held on 24 January 1918, and determined to visit Italy in its behalf. In an estimate of the situation on the Adriatic front dated 30 January he demanded the adoption of an offensive attitude whenever possible, unity of command, and adherence to the principle of concentrating against enemy weakness rather than strength. Once the enemy was driven from the Adriatic, he concluded, Allied forces there could be transferred to "areas of critical importance." Since the Allies overwhelmingly commanded the surface of the Adriatic, he recommended concentrated air and surface attacks on U-boat bases, especially Cattaro, and improvement of the Otranto barrage.[21] At a meeting held in Rome on 8-9 February, he demanded that Italy undertake offensive operations in the Adriatic. Di Revel instead supported Italy's defensive policy. The discussion became acrimonious; Sims was furious with di Revel and di Revel obstinately refused his demand for aggressive action. By stating that "the Adriatic question is essentially an Italian question, and any action on the sea is to be carried out by the Royal Navy and an Italian admiral," di Revel disclosed that political considerations counted more than naval considerations.[22]

Sims' plans for offensive operations in the Adriatic were approved by the Allied naval and military councils and by Washington. Soon afterwards, at the third meeting of the Allied Naval Council, held in London on 12-14 March, Sims insisted that they be implemented. Among other things he would occupy and fortify specified islands and Dalmatian littoral areas and use them as bases from which to cut Austria's coastal railroad and to support an attack on enemy ships in Cattaro. In addition he would establish patrolled zones in the southern Adriatic to prevent the sortie of U-boats; keep Cattaro under persistent aerial attack; maintain a naval surface force at Corfu ready to enter the Adriatic to block the sortie of heavy enemy ships; and lay an extensive mine barrage north of the one at Otranto. For these purposes he would provide battleships and marines trained in amphibious operations, but he specified that an Allied admiral should command the entire operation. When di Revel disagreed, Lloyd George and France's Georges Clemenceau asked Premier Vittorio Orlando to put pressure on di Revel. Still disagreeing. Di Revel questioned that Sims could accomplish the objectives he mentioned with the ships and men he said he would provide and insisted that an Italian command the operations. Sims rebutted that the Adriatic was not exclusively Italian and that the enemy's bases along its shores affected all the Allies particularly with respect to U-boats. When he charged that di Revel had a unilateral vision of the war, others mollified the Italian, who then cited the naval convention of Paris of 1915 and the conference of London of February 1916 to prove that command in the Adriatic belonged to Italy. Sims therefore concluded that di Revel represented the desire of his navy of "getting through the war without loss of any of the Italian Naval power." Nevertheless, to strengthen the Otranto barrage he promised to send thirty submarine chasers to Corfu. With French help, Captain Charles Nelson built a base and sent his chasers out on A/S patrol.[23]

When Austrian Admiral Nicholas Horthy sent four battleships, four light cruisers, and eight destroyers to attack the Otranto barrage, on 10 June Lieutenant Luigi Rizzo was able to get his motor torpedo boat inside the destroyers flanking the battleship *Szent Istvan* and send her down with torpedoes. Vienna thereupon cancelled the operation. Austrian battleships remained in port for the rest of war and no more attacks would be made on the Otranto barrage. Moreover, U-boat sinkings in the Mediterranean dropped to a new low of 49,000 tons on August, and no attacks at all were made on British shipping therein at least between 16 October and 2 November. The only exception to di Revel's defensive policy was his sending of some cruisers and coastal motor torpedo boats to join British cruisers and destroyers escorted by a dozen American submarine chasers to bombard Durazzo, Albania, on 2 October in the last naval operation of any consequences in the Adriatic.[24]

It was General Henri Philippe Pétain who bolstered Lloyd George in the latter's battle against the devotees of the Western Theory by suggesting that a generalissimo was needed to decide where and when the Allies would attack or defend. Although his powers were circumscribed, Foch was selected to serve in an advisory capacity as commander in chief of the British and French armies on the Western Front but not of the American, Belgian, or Italian armies. However, the Western Front was defined so as to include "from the North Sea to the Adriatic." Though Foch's authority to coordinate now extended to the Italian Front, Italy still controlled her army. The tactical deployment of all Allied armies rested with their generals, who could appeal to their governments if they felt that Foch's directions placed their armies in danger.

After repulsing several strong German attacks on the Western Front in the spring and early summer of 1918, Foch ordered attacks that forced the Germans back in the Second Battle of the Marne. At the same time Italians foiled an Austrian attack on their front along the Piave and the Asiago plateau.

The first steps leading to the defeat of the Central Powers occurred not on the Western but on the Southeastern Fronts. The mostly French army from Salonika that attacked Bulgaria opened a road to Germany and Austria-Hungary; it also encouraged the subject nationalities of the Dual Monarchy to open revolt. General Sir Edmund Allenby's routing of the Turks at Megiddo portended Turkey's fall. On 3 October, when Germany's new chancellor, Prince Max von Baden, asked for an armistice on the basis of the Fourteen Points, Italian troops pressed forward in Albania, and on 24 October, Cadorna's relief, General Armando Diaz, began an advance that ended a few days later in the decisive victory at Vittorio Veneto and Austria's request for an armistice. Foch now planned to attack Germany via Bavaria, thus providing a triumph for Lloyd George's policy of action on the Southeastern as well as the French Front.

When the Supreme War Council drafted naval as well as military terms for an armistice, the members of the Allied Naval Council objected in part because they demanded stiffer terms than did the military men. While the British largely dictated the terms for Germany, di Revel proposed terms acceptable to Italy. The final draft of the armistice terms were completed by the Supreme War Council and sent on 5 November to Wilson, who forwarded them to Germany, whose representatives accepted them on the eleventh. Subsequently, while most of the German High Sea fleet and all U-boats were surrendered in British harbors, Austria's King Karl sought to avoid surrendering his fleet to Italy by transferring it on 28 October to the newly created Yugoslav state. On the thirtieth, General Diaz sent Austria armistice terms to which she must agree by midnight of 3 November. Stating that "The Navy must completely crush the enemy before an armistice is signed," di Revel approved a unique operation. Raffaele Rosetti and Raffaele Paolucci, two powerful swimmers taken to Trieste harbor, rode a navigable torpedo which pushed two mines fitted with time fuses and battery-powered electromagnetic clamps. Early the following morning the men attached a mine to the hull of the Austrian flagship, the *Viribus Unitis*, without seeing that the flag she flew was Yugoslav. In any event, the *Viribus* was destroyed. Italians then disregarded the Yugoslavs and sent forces to take over all important Austrian military and naval sites. Italy thus obtained most of what she had been promised in the Treaty of London.[25]

Italy's objectives in World War I included Austria's surrender of "unredeemed" territory inhabited by about 800,000 Italians, frontier rectifications to enhance her security, control over the Dalmatian shore that would make the Adriatic a closed sea, and additional territory from other defeated powers. These objectives were guaranteed her in the Treaty of London. With the United States seeing the Adriatic as a secondary theater, late in providing aid to Italy, and sending her very little help at that, Sims found it impossible to divert Italy from a strategy that supported her purely national interests and get her to engage in the coalition warfare needed to win the war.

Notes

[1] Among many other studies, see Hans Sokol and Teodor Braun, *Osterreich-Ungarns Seekrieg, 1914-1918*, 4 vols. trans. Raffaele de Courten and Silvio Salza, as *La Guerra Marittima dell'Austria-Ungheria 1914-1918*, 4 vols. (Roma: Instituto Poligrafico dello Stato, Libreria, 1931-1934), I, pp. 12, 57, Luigi Albertini, *Le Origini della Guerra del 1914*, 3 vols. (Milano: Fratelli Bocca, 1942-1943), I, pp. 565-70; Antonio Salandra, *Italy and the Great War: From Neutrality to Intervention*. Trans. by Zoe Zendrick Pyne (London: Edward Arnold, 1932, pp. 217-62; Z.A.B. Zeman, *The Break-up of the Habsburg Empire 1914-1918: A Study of National and Social Revolution* (London: Oxford University Press, 1961), pp. 1-48; W. S. Askew, "The Austro-Italian Antagonism, 1896-1914," in L. P. Wallace and W. C. Askew, eds., *Power, Public Opinion, and Diplomacy* (Durham: Duke University Press, 1959), pp. 172-211; and Leo Valiani, "Italian-Austro-Hungarian Negotiations 1914-1915," *Journal of Contemporary History* 1 (July 1966), pp. 113-36. While neutral, Italy helped France by releasing for action the 250,000 troops guarding the Franco-Italian frontier, and helped Russia by pinning down the Austrian troops on the Italo-Austrian frontier.

[2] Italy was to obtain not only the Trentino and Trieste, but Cisalpine Tyrol, Gorizia, and Gradisca, a large part of the Istrian Peninsula and southern Dalmatia, Valona and Saseno in Albania, and the Dodecanese Islands Italy had seized during her war with Turkey in 1911-1912, and compensation in Africa if Britain and France annexed German colonies or Turkish territory after the war. Britain also promised to float a 50 million pound loan and offered a proportionate share of postwar indemnities.

[3] Austria could not operate in the Mediterranean because her light ships lacked sufficient range and she had no intermediate ports south of Cattaro or in the Mediterranean. In consequence, Hungary's military chieftain, the Archduke Frederick, directed Admiral Anton A. H. Haus to cooperate with the Austrian army if Italian troops landed at Cattaro, stop contraband from reaching Serbia, and deny Serbia and Montenegro access to maritime traffic, the last by blockading the Montenegrin coast. For the rest, he was to limit his efforts to defending the Adriatic.

[4] Robert Lansing, *War Memoirs of Robert Lansing, Secretary of State* (New York: Bobbs-Merrill, 1935), pp. 73-80.

[5] Conf. Senior Member Present, General Board of the Navy to Secretary of the Navy, 5 Apr. 1917, GB No. 425, Serial 699; SMP, GB, to Secretary of the Navy, 28 Apr. 1917, GB No. 435, Serial No. 721; GB to Secretary of the Navy, 3

May 1917, GB No. 525, Serial 724, Washington: Naval History Center, Operational Archives Branch; Josephus Daniels, *Diary*, 14 May 1917, in Josephus Daniels Papers, Manuscript Division, Library of Congress.

[6] David Lloyd George, *War Memoirs of David Lloyd George*, 6 vols. (Boston: Little, Brown, 1933-1937), II, pp. 321-22, 432-33, 439; III, p. 586; IV, pp. 322-69; Arthur J. Marder, *From the Dreadnought to Scapa Flow: The Royal Navy in the Fisher Era*, 5 vols. (New York: Oxford University Press, 1961-1970), IV, *1917: Year of Crisis*, pp. 63-68; LCOL Charles a Court Repington, *The First World War, 1914-1918*, 2 vols. (Boston: Houghton Mifflin, 1920), I, pp. 371-74; Sir Frederic Maurice, *Lessons of Allied Cooperation: Naval, Military, and Air, 1914-1918* (New York: Oxford University Press 1942), pp. 74-75.

[7] Julian S. Corbett and Henry Newbolt, *History of the Great War, Based on Official Documents: Naval Operations*, 5 vols. (London: Longmans, Green, 1920-1931), V, pp. 120-34; Admiral of the Fleet [John R.] Jellicoe, *The Crisis of the Naval War* (London: Cassell, 1920), pp. 164-75, and *The Submarine Peril: The Admiralty Policy in 1917* (London: Cassell, 1934), pp. 1-18., Marder, *1917: Year of Crisis*, pp. 232-36.

[8] See among others: Robert Blake, ed., *The Private Papers of Douglas Haig, 1914-1919* (London: Eyre & Spottiswoode, 1952) and Admiral Reginald H. Bacon, *The Concise Story of the Dover Patrol* (London: Hutchinson, 1932).

[9] Lloyd George to Wilson, 3 September 1917, Woodrow Wilson Papers, Manuscript Division, Library of Congress. The letter is printed in Lloyd George, *Memoirs*, V, pp. 301-02.

[10] Daniels, *Diary*, 11, 12, 27, 28 September, 1917; Lloyd George, *Memoirs*, V, pp. 301-02.

[11] Daniels, *Diary*, 5, 6 Dec. 1917; Italia. Stato Maggiore Ufficio Storico della Marina Militare, *La Marina italiana nella grande guerra*, 8 vols. (Firenze: Vallechi Editore, 1935-1942), VI, pp. 360-80, 383 (hereafter cited as *MI*).

[12] Paolo E. Coletta, "The United States and Italy in the Allied Naval Council of World War I," in *Atti del Congresso Internazionale di Storia Americana. Italia a Stati Uniti Dall'Indipendenza Americana ad Oggi (1776-1976)* (Genova: Tilgher, 1978), p. 94.

[13] *MI*, IV, pp. 116-23; Mark Kerr, *Land, Sea, and Air: Reminiscences of Mark Kerr* (New York: Longmans, Green 1927), p. 213; Vice Admiral C. V. Usborne, *Smoke on the Horizon: Mediterranean Fighting 1914-1918* (London: Hodder and Stoughton, 1933), pp. 266-67; for excellent details on the U-boat and Allied antisubmarine war in the Mediterranean, see Courten and Salza, *La Guerra marittima dell'Austria-Ungheria*, II, pp. 10-30.

[14] Italia. Ministero della Marina. Stato Maggiore Ufficio Storico. Cart. 497-3. "Cooperazione interalleato durante la guerra marittima mondiale in Mediterranean," and Cart. 742. "Conferenza de Londra" (23-24 gennaio, 1918); *MI*, IV, pp. 253-71; Vice Admiral Henri Salaun, *La Marine française* (Paris: Les Editions de France, 1934), pp. 253-55.

[15] Kerr, *Reminiscences*, pp. 205-12.

[16] Italia. Ministero della Marina. Stato Maggiore Ufficio Storico. Cart. 707. Piloti Americani in Italia da montarsi aeroplani americani da montarsi in Italia., *MI*, VI, pp. 35, 54; Secretary of the Navy to Department, 21 Apr. 1917, War Department to Secretary of the Navy, Apr. 1, 1917, Washington, Naval Archives and Records Service, Record Group 80, Papers of the Secretary of the Navy, File C-20.

[17] *MI*, V, pp. 122, 249-52, VI, p. 165. Courten and Salza, *La Guerra marittima dell'Austria-Ungheria*, III, pp. 96-102; Richard Gibson and Maurice Prendergast, *The German Submarine War* (New York: Richard R. Smith, 1931), p. 259.

[18] Italia. Ministero della Marina. Stato Maggiore Ufficio Storico. Cart. 741-2. "Conferenza di Parigi" (24-25 giunio 1917); *MI*, V, pp. 302-12; Camillo Manfroni, *I Nostri alleati navale; ricordi della guerra Adriatica 1915 1918* (Milano: A. Mondadori, 1927), pp. 180-81; *MI*, IV, pp. 189-218.

[19] *MI*, VI, pp. 235-36; Manfroni, *I Nostri alleati navale*, pp. 200-01; Cyril Falls, *The Battle of Caporetto* (New York: J. B. Lippincott, 1966).

[20] Walter Hines Page to Woodrow Wilson. Feb. 5, 1918, Wilson Papers; Rene Albrecht-Carrié, *Italy at the Paris Peace Conference* (New York: Columbia University Press, 1938), pp. 38-40; Lawrence Gelfand, *The Inquiry: American Preparations for Peace, 1917-1919* (New Haven and London: Yale University Press, 1963), p. 222; Dragan R. Zivojinovic. "The Emergence of American Policy in the Adriatic: December 1917-April 1919," *East European Quarterly* 1 (Sept. 1967), pp. 176-78.

[21] Allied Naval Council Papers No. 48, "Estimate of the General Naval Situation by the Planning Section of My Staff," forwarded by Sims to Secretary of the Navy (Operations), 19 Mar. 1918, and Paper No. 49 "The Adriatic Problem," NARG 45, QC; U.S. Department of the Navy. Office of Naval Intelligence. *The American Naval Planning Section in London* (Washington: GPO, 1923), pp. 59-77. In the last see also pp. 137-38, 224, 248-49, and 252-54.

[22] Sims to Benson, 15 Feb. 1918, William S. Sims Papers, Manuscript Division, Library of Congress.

[23] Sims to Opnav, 14 Mar. 1918, ANC Letters, NARG 45, QC, "Report on Second Meeting of the ANC, Mar. 12-14, 1918, with enclosures." See especially Papers No. 48, "Estimate of the General Situation by the Planning Section of the Staff," and No. 49, "The Adriatic Problem," and also "Report of the Commission that Met in Rome to Discuss the Mediterranean Situation," NARG 45, QC; *MI*, VII, pp. 205-73.

[24] For Rizzo's exploit, see NARG 38, Naval Attaché Reports, "The Sinking of the *Szent Istvan*, June 9-10, 1918"; *MI* VII, pp. 545-73; LCDR E. E. Hazlett, "Davids of the Sea," U.S Naval Institute *Proceedings* 54 (Dec. 1928) pp. 1037-38. For details on U-boat operations in the Mediterranean and Adriatic, see Courten and Salza, *La Guerra marittima dell'Austria-Ungheria*, IV, pp. 43-78, 100-15.

[25] *MI*, VIII, pp. 509-19; Commandante Guido Po, *Il Grande ammiraglio Paolo Thaon di Revel* (Torino: S. Lattes & C., Editori, 1936), pp. 194-96, and Appendix 4, pp. 292-93, the latter of which contains a list of the territory occupied by Italy at or soon after the time of the armistice. For the Austrian viewpoint, see Courten and Salza, *La Guerra marittima dell'Austria-Ungheria*, IV, pp. 270-77. Italy's loss of Dalmatian territory in the Treaty of Versailles is beyond the scope of this paper.

Index